The use of fulfilment Quotations in the Gospel according to Matthew

Jonathan Samuel Nkhoma

Kachere Series
Zomba
2005

Kachere Series,
P.O. Box 1037, Zomba, Malawi
Email: *Kachere@globemw.net*
www.sdnp.org.mw/kachereseries/

This book is part of the Kachere series, a range of books on religion, culture and society in Malawi. Kachere Monographs published so far:

Andrew C. Ross, *Blantyre Mission and the making of Modern Malawi*

Harry Langworthy, *Africa for the African: The Life of Joseph Booth*

Kenneth R. Ross, *God, People and Power in Malawi*

Isabel Apawo Phiri, *Women, Presbyterianism and Patriarchy: Religious Experience of Chewa Women in Central Malawi*

Matthew Schoffeleers, *Religion and the Dramatization of Life: Spirit Beliefs and Rituals in southern Malawi*

Ernest Wendland, *Buku Loyera: an Introduction to the New Chichewa Bible Translation*

J.C. Chakanza, *voices of Preachers in Protest: The Ministry of two Malawian Prophets: Elliot Kamwana and Wilfred Gudu*

John McCraken, *Politics and Christianity in Malawi 1745-1940*

Klaus Fiedler, *Christianity and African Culture: Conservative German Protestant Missionaries in Tanzania 1900-1940*

Ernst R. Wendland, *Preaching that Grabs the Heart*

Martin Ott, *African Theology in Images*

George Shepperson and Thomas Price, *Independent African*

J.W.M. Van Breugel, *Chewa Traditional Religion*

This Kachere Series is the publications arm of the
Department of Theology and Religious Studies of the University of Malawi.

Series Editors: J.C. Chakanza, F.L. Chingota, Klaus Fiedler, P.A. Kalilombe, Fulata L. Moyo, Martin Ott, Shareef Mohammed

Contents

Preface

The central mission of the Christian Church is the proclamation of the Good News of Jesus Christ. This essentially consists of his Person and his redemptive work. This is what is called the *Kerygma* or Gospel. The New Testament gospel writers seek to explain this *Kerygma* by using Old Testament categories like Messiah, Son of God, Son of Man and others.

In the search for an understanding of the concept of Messiah in the Gospel according to Matthew, a study of the evangelist's fulfilment quotations offers one of the most significant alternative approaches. This approach is exactly what the present inquiry, in the following pages, seeks to apply in an attempt to determine how this particular evangelist understands Jesus as the Messiah.

The study of fulfilment quotations in the Gospel according to Matthew is not a new development. Throughout the past century, scholars have in many ways contributed to our understanding of these special Matthean quotations. The primary focus in these studies was, however, on the literary problems of these quotations. To my knowledge, none of these previous scholarly attempts focused on their theological significance in light of their Old Testament prophetic word.

The objective of the present research is to investigate how an understanding of these quotations, in view of their Old and New Testament contexts, would contribute to our understanding of the evangelist's theology, especially in terms of his views of Jesus as the Promised Messiah. It also aims at investigating the problem of origin, and character, of the fulfilment quotations under study. In the process, the research seeks to contribute to the on-going documentation of Matthean theology.

The research presents to us quite a significant challenge. It demands that we engage in a five-step hermeneutical procedure required in the investigation of any genre of Scripture. These are, according to Virkler, historical-cultural and contextual analysis; lexical-syntactical analysis; theoogical analysis; genre identification and analysis; and application. This analytical method is later referred to simply as an exegetical literary approach or as grammatical-historical method. As the reader will soon discover, these hermeneutical concepts are used as tools and instruments in the exegetical-theological process of the present inquiry.

These analytical tools are applied to the quotations in their double settings of Old Testament prophecy and Christian gospel.

The results of the research shed new light on the role of the prophetic word in the evangelist's Christological understanding of the Messiah. The results also have implications for the manner in which the evangelist wrote his gospel, and these are likely to stimulate further discussion, especially on Matthean authorship and the Synoptic Problem in general.

The study does not claim to be exhaustive, let alone conclusive, at all the crucial points. Despite this limitation, however, the research provides a new perspective on the role of prophecy in the Christological understanding of the New Testament writers, especially the evangelist Matthew. It also presents the evangelist as an independent Christian theologian with the ability, like his New Testament counterparts, to construct a Christology of his own, using the raw materials of gospel tradition (both oral and written) and Biblical prophecy, a role which Matthean critical scholarship has for long denied him. Previous Matthean critical scholarship, with a few exceptions, has generally seen the evangelist as a Marcan "disciple."

The original manuscript of the present study was successfully submitted to the Faculty of Humanities in the University of Malawi as a dissertation for the degree of Masters of Arts in Theology and Religious Studies in July, 2001.

I therefore, wish to express my gratitude to my supervisor, the late Associate Professor, Dr. H.B.P. Mijoga for his untiring and careful guidance and constructive criticism throughout the research; and to my co-supervisor, Rev. Dr. F.L. Chingota for his critical reading and invaluable comments in the early stages of my work and on my first draft of the manuscript.

Special thanks are also due to Dr. Klaus Fiedler for the moral, financial and technical support offered throughout the research. Further, I wish to thank the Association of German Protestant Churches and Missions (*Evangelisches Missionswerk*) in Hamburg, Germany, for the financial support offered throughout the research.

My deepest appreciation is offered to my wife, Edina, for her loving care and moral support throughout the long hours of research and writing, and to my children, Peter, Daniel and Limbikani for their understanding and refreshing cheerfulness. I dedicate this study to them.

List of Abbreviations

AB	Anchor Bible
AKJV	Authorized King James Version
ATJ	Africa Theological Journal
CBQ	Catholic Biblical Quarterly
DSPS	Duquesne Studies Philosophical Series
ET	English Translation
Heb	Hebrew
Gr	Greek
ICC	International Critical Commentary
ITC	International Theological Commentary
JBL	Journal of Biblical Literature
JSOT	Journal for the Study of the Old Testament
JSNT	Journal for the Study of the New Testament, Supplement Series
JTSA	Journal of Theology for Southern Africa
LBC	Layman's Bible Commentary
LXX	The Septuagint, Id est Vetus Testamentum Graece, i.e. The Greek Old Testament Bible
MSS	Manuscripts
MT	Massoretic text
NCBC	New Century Bible Commentary
NICOT	New International Commentary on the Old Testament
NIGTC	New International Greek Testament Commentary
NIV	New International Version
NKJV	New King James Version
OTL	Old Testament Library
RSV	Revised Standard Version
SBL	Society of Biblical Literature
SBT	Studies in Biblical Theology
SJT	Scottish Journal of Theology
SNTS	Society for New Testament Studies
TNTC	Tyndale New Testament Commentaries
TOTC	Tyndale Old Testament Commentaries

Dead Sea Scrolls

CD	The Damascus rule, a Cairo Genizah text of the Damascus Document
IQS	The Community Rule from Qumran Cave 1
IQM, 4QM	The War Rule from Qumran Caves 1 and 4
4QP Bless	The Blessings of Jacob from Qumran Cave 4
4Q161-4	Commentaries on Isaiah from Qumran Cave 4
4Q166-7	Commentaries on Hosea from Qumran Cave 4
IQ14	Commentary on Micah from Qumran cave 1
4Q169	Commentary on Nahum from Qumran Cave 4
IQP Hab.	Commentary on Habakkuk from Qumran Cave 1
4Q171, 4Q173	Commentaries on Psalms from Qumran Cave 4
4Q174	The *Florilegium*, A Midrash on the Last Days from Qumran Cave 4
IIQ Melch from	The Heavenly Prince Melchizedek, document Qumran Cave 11
4QMMT	*Miqsat ma'ase ha-torah*, a letter-like text from Qumran cave 4

Chapter 1

THE STATE OF THE QUESTION

Introduction

This chapter will introduce to the reader the main focus of the research, its aim, objectives, the method that guides it, the relationship the research has to other research, and its contribution to scholarship. The major focus of the chapter will be on pivotal secondary literature. The results of this investigation will clearly reveal to the reader that previous research on Matthean fulfillment quotations has not sufficiently addressed itself to the problem of the theological significance of these quotations in their gospel settling in light of their prophetic background. The results will also show that this failure is partly due to methodological considerations. In the subsequent chapters, the research will draw support from Jewish literature, patristic writings, and an original exegetical - theological investigation of the fulfilment quotations, to establish the thesis that the evangelist has used these quotations theologically in light of their prophetic setting.

The main focus of the present inquiry is the theological significance of the fulfilment quotations in the Gospel according to Matthew seen in the light of Old Testament prophecy. Previous research on Matthean fulfilment quotations mainly centred on their literal background and formulation. The problem of their theological significance, and the role of prophecy in that regard, remains an unfilled gap within Matthean fulfilment quotations research. The present inquiry is a contribution toward the filling of this gap in Matthean scholarship It is also a contribution toward the ongoing discussion on their origin and character. Therefore, the research problem of the thesis is that previous research on Matthean fulfilment quotations focused on literary techniques of the evangelist in his use of the Old Testament. Little effort has been made to link the evangelist's exegesis of the Old Testament and his theology in the light of the Old Testament context of his fulfilment quotations.

This study aims at addressing this shortfall by relating these quotations to their Old Testament context in an attempt to understand the theology of the evangelist. Hence, the thesis for my study is that the fulfilment quotations in the Gospel according to Matthew have a significant theological role, and that this theological significance is reflected in the way these Old Testament quotations are formulated and in the manner in which, they are used by the evangelist in his application to the Christ-event. The thesis further asserts that the evangelist is himself responsible for the formulation of these quotations and that they were designed to serve his theological purpose.

In view of the foregoing aim of the research, the study has three main objectives. First, it was intended to test my assumption that the fulfilment quotations have a significant function in defining the theology of the evangelist, and, if so, to document these theological implications as a contribution to the knowledge that is already available on Matthean theology.

Secondly, the research was intended to test my assumption that the fulfilment quotations come from the evangelist himself and, if so, examine the nature of that origin and its implications to the theology of the evangelist.

Thirdly, the research was intended to contribute to current debate on Matthean authorship, not by way of offering a detailed theory on the Synoptic Problem, but by way of offering critical observations that may stimulate further research on this problem. This third objective is to be met not directly through any systematic development of an argument on Matthean authorship, but indirectly by drawing some critical observations implicated by the main results of the research. These critical observations drawn from the main results of the research will further lead to a statement on a provisional theory of the Synoptic Problem as a possible area for further research.

The research methods that are used in this research fall into two categories. The first category involves an investigation of all relevant literary sources both primary and secondary. This means that the research is literary-based. Insights drawn from these literary sources in many ways contribute to the shape and content of the work. A selected list of these sources appears in the bibliography. The second category relates to the analytical method, which governs the conceptual framework of the whole research. The research is guided by the grammatical-historical method, also referred to as an exegetical-literary approach.

As the reader will see, there are several areas to which the research offers a remarkable contribution. The research provides further insights on the theological significance of the Matthean fulfilment quotations. The research also offers a new perspective on the role of prophecy in the evangelist's theological reconstruction. It sees the evangelist using these quotations theologically in the light of their prophetic context. The research also offers some valuable insights on the evangelist's freedom and independence as a writer as he brings to bear upon his theological reconstruction the raw materials of gospel tradition and prophecy. His remarkable success in this points to an early date for his gospel. This further suggests parallel development of the synoptic tradition whether Mark was written a little earlier or not.

The work is divided into four chapters. In this chapter, I have discussed the nature of the problem and indicated the scope of the study. I have also discussed in more detail the rationale for my choice of the grammatical-historical method as the analytical tool for this research. A philosophical rationale for the structure of the thesis is also stated. The thesis discusses the Person of the Messiah before it discusses his redemptive mission. This is in line with Christian philosophical understanding of the concept of *persona* over against ancient and modern philosophical traditions which see *persona* essentially as a project, or product, of individual and social construction. The main thrust of the present chapter is a discussion of the secondary literature whose bearing on the subject is pivotal. The results clearly reveal the hiatus that exists in Matthean fulfilment quotations research.

Chapter 2 is based on primary sources. the Mishnah, the Dead Sea Scrolls, early patristic writings and Old and New Testament apocryphal literature are investigated in more detail to see how they use quotations. The results establish the thesis that biblical quotations are used theologically in religious literature of ancient Judaism and early Christianity and these form a literary background to the work of the evangelist. It is then concluded that the evangelist used the fulfilment quotations in a similar way. The old age and the pre-Christian character of the Dead Sea Scrolls, and some of the traditions incorporated into the *Mishnah,* support an early date for the Matthean gospel.

Chapter 3 discusses the origin and character of the fulfilment quotations in the infancy narrative. It also offers an exegetical-theological analysis of these fulfilment quotations, taking into account their double settings of Old and New Testaments. The results show that they are formulated by the evangelist himself and that they provide him with a theological background understanding of the Person of Jesus Christ.

Chapter 4 offers an exegetical-theological analysis of the fulfilment quotations that are in the ministry and passion narratives. The results show that the fulfilment quotations in these sections of the gospel are also formulated by the evangelist and that they also offer him a theological background understanding of the redemptive mission of Jesus Messiah. The conclusion to the whole research in Chapter 5 brings together the main results of the research.

The research reaches quite stimulating, if not provocative, conclusions. It offers critical remarks on the role of prophecy in the evangelist's theology, and on his freedom and independence as a writer in the formation of fulfilment quotations and in the reconstruction of his theology. It also draws implications with regard to the questions of Matthean authorship and the Synoptic problem. Above all, the conclusions support the thesis that the evangelist applies his fulfilment quotations to the Christ-event theologically with full regard to their prophetic contexts

The Problem

There are fulfilment quotations in the Gospel of Matthew. These are a series of quotations drawn from the Old Testament prophets and the Psalter and introduced by a special formula, namely, "in order that it might be fulfilled which was spoken through the prophet saying" (*hina plērōthę to rēthen dia tou prophetou legontos)*[1]. These quotations are essentially a Matthean phenomenon. They are also technically known as "formula quotations". But for the purpose of this study I will refer to them

---

[1] There is some variety within the wording of the stereotype introductory phrase itself as it applies to the various Old Testament fulfilment quotations. The introductory phrase *hina plerothe to rethen* is found at 1:22; 2:15; 4:14; 12:17 and 21:4. The introductory phrase *hopos plerothe to rethen* is found at 2:23; 8:17 and 13:35. The one at 2:17 and 27:9 is necessitated by the context. The introductory phrases at 3:3 and 13:14 are quite different. 3:3 has *hotos gar estin ho retheis*, and 13:14 *kai anapleroutai*. These substantially depart from the rest and cannot be treated as proper introductory phrases to fulfilment quotations. The text in 26:56 is unreliable. Therefore, the quotations at 3:3; 13:14 and 26:56 fall outside the scope of the present inquiry.

as "fulfilment quotations" because this phrase focuses on their function while the former is merely suggestive of their stereotype introductory phrase.

Previous research on fulfilment quotations focused on literary techniques of the evangelist in his use of the Old Testament. Little attempt was made to link the evangelist's exegesis of the Old Testament and his theology in the light of the Old Testament context of his fulfilment quotations. This study is aimed at addressing this shortfall by relating these quotations to their Old Testament context in an attempt to understand the theology of the evangelist. It has also been suggested by some scholars that the evangelist drew these quotations from such sources as the Testimonia, the Gospel of Mark or the Source Q and that the changes he made to them were so insignificant to justify any theological role in his gospel. Others have attributed them to the evangelist's imaginative creation patterned on Old Testament phraseology as part of the evangelist's midrashic approach to Old Testament interpretation. These suggestions will be critically discussed later in the present chapter. In this study I will argue that these quotations come from the evangelist himself, that he either draws them directly from the Old Testament itself or he has sufficient knowledge of their Old Testament contexts to enable him to use these quotations theologically, and that he is responsible for their mixed text-form.[2]

Hence, the thesis for my study is that the fulfilment quotations in the Gospel according to Matthew have a significant theological role. It is my contention that this theological significance is reflected in the way these Old Testament quotations are formulated and in the manner in which the evangelist uses them. They are mixed in their formulation and tend to be integrated in their usage by the evangelist so that they serve their intended theological purpose. The widely accepted fulfilment quotations are : Matt 1:22-23; 2:15, 17, 23; 4:14-16; 8:17; 12:17-21; 13:35;21:4-5 and 27:9-10. The following quotations are debatable because

---

[2] They are usually a combination of LXX and Hebrew texts with a substantial input from the evangelist himself: "They show deviations from all Greek, Hebrew and Aramaic types of texts known to us, while at the same time they intermingle influences from these." See Krister Standahl, *The School of St. Matthew and its Use of the Old Testament*, Second Edition, Philadelphia: Fortress, 1968, p. 97. Cf. Francis W. Beare, *The Gospel According to Matthew, a Commentary*, Oxford: Basil Blackwell, 1981, p. 71.

imperfections in their introductory formula create uncertainty[3] as to whether these should be classified as fulfilment quotations: Matt 2:5-6; 3:3; 13:14-15, and 26:56. Because the present study is primarily an inquiry into the significance of these fulfilment quotations to the theology of the evangelist, I have limited the study to the widely accepted fulfilment quotations. Only the fulfilment quotation at 2:6, among the debatable ones, has been included in this study, because in my opinion its peculiarity can be satisfactorily accounted for by a consideration of the context.

These fulfilment quotations broadly fall into two categories: those found in the infancy narrative and those found in the ministry and passion narrative of the gospel. They are similar in terms of style and theological significance. However, their concentration in the infancy narrative (Matthew 1-2) suggests a deliberate effort on the part of the evangelist to introduce the person of Jesus while the rest of fulfilment quotations scattered in the rest of the gospel appear to emphasize the redemptive work of Jesus Messiah. In the infancy narrative the person of Jesus Messiah is defined by the fulfilment quotations by making reference to his divinity, which, is implied in his virgin birth and his divine call from Egypt (Matt 1:22-23; 2:15, 25) and to his Messianic status as Son of David (Matt 2:15, 17, 23). In the fulfilment quotations found in the rest of the gospel emphasis falls on the saving work of Jesus Messiah which includes his preaching ministry especially in Galilee (Matt 4:14-16), his healing ministry (Matt 8:17; 12:17-21), his teaching ministry (13:35), his kingship (Matt 21:4-5) and his passion (Matt 27:9-10).

The shift in emphasis from person in the infancy narrative to work in the rest of the gospel cannot be satisfactorily accounted for by reference to psychological development. Rather, it is a theological shift for Matthew's primary concern is theological. Matthew writes to Jewish Christians to show them that Jesus is the Messiah right from his birth and that he did not become a Messiah only after performing his redemptive work. The divine authority of Jesus' Messiahship is particularly emphasized by this evangelist.[4]

---

[3] Raymond E. Brown, *The Birth of the Messiah, A Commentary on the Infancy Narrations in the Gospels of Matthew and Luke*, AB, New York: Doubleday, 1993, Ulrich Luz, *Matthew 1-7, A Continental Commentary*, Minneapolis: Fortress, 1985. Also note 1 above.

[4] This aspect of Jesus' Messiahship is thoroughly discussed by Robert H. Gundry in his *Matthew, A Commentary on his Literary and Theological Art*, Grand Rapids: Eerdmans, 1982, especially pp. 58, 137-80.

Methodological Considerations

Most Matthean studies at the beginning of last century employed form-critical approach. Probably the greatest contribution of form criticism to critical scholarship is its attempt to classify literary forms in the Bible. It has been observed, that: "The only abiding interpretative value of form criticism is its classification of the Gospel material into various 'forms'."[5]

However, it is an indispensable help in any sound exegesis: "Since an appreciation of form is necessary for the understanding of any literature, form criticism will remain a basic tool for exegesis of the Gospels."[6]

By the middle of the last century, after the Second World War, redaction criticism came to the front. Probably the most significant contribution of redaction criticism is its focus on the writers as creative authors and theologians who shaped the tradition in accordance with their own theological perspective.[7] With due respect to the positive contribution these approaches have made to critical scholarship in Gospel studies it is important to note that they are limited in certain respects. By assuming that the evangelists read back into the teaching of Jesus what they saw was needed in their own situation, form criticism goes beyond a study of forms and overlooks the fact that topics of the Gospels are not the topics that occupied the early church.[8] Also, by

---

[5] Scot McKnight, *Interpreting the Synoptic Gospels*, Grand Rapids: Baker, 1988, p. 78.

[6] Stephen H. Travis, "Form Criticism," in I. Howard Marshall (ed.), *New Testament Interpretation, Essays on Principles and Methods*, Carlisle: Paternoster, 1985, p. 162. For further positive evaluation of form criticism, see McKnight, *Interpreting the Synoptic Gospels*, pp. 78-9. Cf. Travis, "Form Criticism," pp. 161-62; Robert H. Stein, *Synoptic Problem, An Introduction*, Grand Rapids: Eerdmans, 1978, pp. 139-57, 217-88; Gene M. Tucker, *Form Criticism of the Old Testament*, Philadelphia: Fortress, 1971, p. 18; Donald Guthrie, *New Testament Introduction*, London: Tyndale, 1970, p. 148. For an original and thorough treatment of the whole subject as it relates to the synoptic gospels, see Martin Dibelius' book *From Traditions to Gospel*, Cambridge and London: James Clarke, 1971. Also Rudolf Bultmann's, *The History of the Synoptic Tradition*, Oxford: Blackwell, 1972, for its systematic application to the synoptic tradition.

[7] For a positive evaluation of redaction criticism see, McKnight, *Interpreting the Synoptic Gospels*, pp. 92-3; Stephen S. Smalley, "Redaction Criticism," in I. Howard Marshall (ed.), *New Testament Interpretation*, pp. 188-91; Stein, *The Synoptic Problem*, pp. 139-57. For a brief discussion on the limitations of the historical-critical method which basically includes source, form and redaction criticism, see Terence J. Keegan, *Interpreting the Bible, A popular Introduction to Biblical Hermeneutics*, New York: Paulist, 1985, pp. 30-2.

[8] Leon Morris, *Luke. An Introduction and Commentary*, Second Edition, TNTC, Leicester: Inter-Varsity press, 1988, p. 33. Francis W. Beare's book, *The Gospel According to Matthew, A Commentary*, is an excellent example of a work based on the results of form criticism. He has systematically attempted to bring forward into the setting of the so-called Matthean community almost all references to Jesus' teaching and ministry.

assuming that the tradition was transmitted in isolated units, without any connected narrative and basing its critical judgment on individual phrases, clauses or statements; form criticism blurs the creative role of the evangelist[9] and the significance of the immediate textual context is lost. In form-critical approach each independent unit of tradition (a phrase, a clause, a statement, sometimes a paragraph) is considered to belong to a different 'situation in life' (*Sitz im Leben*) which is often perceived to be different from the textual context in which the unit is found. Attempts are then made to isolate each independent unit from the textual context and associate each of them with other units from other parts of the tradition believed to belong to the same 'situation in life'. The framework of the life of Jesus is considered to be destroyed and the evangelists who wrote the Gospels are viewed as having been confronted with a series of unconnected units[10] which they put together "like beads on a string".

---

[9] That the evangelists do not have a significant creative role in the Gospel tradition is one of the fundamental pillars of form criticism. Martin Dibelius, one of the pioneer scholars to apply this discipline to the Synoptic tradition, has emphasized this point very strongly: "There is a theory that the history of literature is the history of its various forms. This ... has ... special significance when applied to materials where the author's personality is of little importance. Many anonymous persons take part in handing down popular traditions. They act, however, not merely as vehicles, but also as creative forces by introducing changes or additions without any single person having a 'literary' intent. In such cases the personal peculiarities of the composer or narrator have little significance; much greater importance attaches to the form in which the tradition is cast by practical necessities, by usage, or by origin. The development goes on steadily and independently subject all the time to certain definite rules, for no creative mind has worked upon the material and impressed it with his own personality the literary understanding of the synoptics begin with the recognition that they are collections of material. The composers are only to the smallest extent authors. They are principally collectors, vehicles of tradition, editors... Before all else their labour consist in handing down, grouping and working over the material which has come to them. Owing to a philological and theological tradition we ourselves have become accustomed to ascribe to the authors and their prejudices a large responsibility for the tradition as a whole, just as if we were dealing with Belles Letters. This error is ancient." Clearly, here, Dibelius rejects any attempt to attribute creativeness to the evangelists. He, however, attributes any creativeness there is to the early Christian communities in which the tradition arose, i.e, his "many anonymous persons [who] take part in handing down popular traditions" and who act "not merely as vehicles, but also as creative forces." See Dibelius, *From Tradition to Gospel*, pp. 1, 2, 3.

[10] The form–critical assumption that individual units of tradition were passed on in an unconnected form has been vigorously challenged from the beginning, especially by C.H. Dodd who argued that there were different types of materials in the Gospels, namely independent units, larger complexes, and a basic outline of the life of Jesus. He maintained that the latter aspect can be glimpsed in the Marcan summaries (1:14-15, 21-22, 39; 3:7b-19; 4:33-34; 6:7, 12-13, 30) as well as in the early sermons recorded in Acts (2:14-39; 3:13-26; 4:10-12; 5:30-32; 10:37-41; 13:17-41). See C.H. Dodd, "The Framework of the Gospel Narrative," *Expository*

This task of form criticism appears to be an arbitrary one and violates the textual context in which the tradition has come down to us[11]. The assumption that the tradition was transmitted as isolated units overlooks the rabbinic teaching practice of the first century Palestine whereby rabbis cast their teaching into forms suitable for memorization and insisted that their pupils learn it by heart. Contemporary research in Jewish pedagogical practice and the nature of oral transmission in the Jewish milieu either in Palestine or in the Diaspora at the time of the New Testament has shown that the oral transmission of the Gospel tradition is generally reliable:

> My chief objection to the form-critical scholars is that their work is not sufficiently historical. They do not show sufficient energy in anchoring the question of the origin of the Gospel tradition within the framework of the question how holy, authoritative tradition was transmitted in the Jewish milieu of Palestine and elsewhere at the time of the New Testament. During the first four centuries of our era the oral Torah tradition of the Jewish rabbis grew enormously. And it was still being handed down orally. If one wonders how it was possible for such a huge body of text material to be preserved and passed on orally, one must consider the rabbis' pedagogical methods and the technique employed in oral transmission.[12]

Gerhardson then discusses aspects of oral instruction which aided preservation of the tradition that was being passed on by facilitating memorization and understanding of that tradition. These include memorization, the teaching pattern of "text and commentary", use of precise and concise didactic expressions, poetic devices, repetition, "recitation" and taking written notes.[13] Gerhardson then concludes his discussion of these instructional techniques by pointing out the difficulty of the assumption that the early church did not have any interest in the historical Jesus in the light of the unique authority of Jesus over against

---

Times, 43, (1932), pp. 396-400. Cf. McKnight, Interpreting the Synoptic Gospels, p. 78. For a survey of the early scholarly evaluation and use of form criticism, see Edgar V. McKnight, What is Form Criticism? Philadelphia: Fortress, 1969, pp. 38-56.

[11]   George A. Kennedy, New Testament Interpretation through Rhetorical Criticism, Chapel Hill and London: University of North Carolina Press, 1984, p. 4 observes that form-criticism is primarly concerned with the search for the sources out of which the text is constructed and "at its worst seems blind to the finished product."

[12]   Birger Gerhardson, The Origins of the Gospels Tradition, London: SCM, 1979, pp. 8, 19.

[13]   Ibid., pp. 19-48.

the Jewish tradition where many rabbis are referred to while focus and authority remains on and in the Torah:

> If one thinks about it [i.e. the unique authority of Jesus], it beco-
> mes extremely difficult to imagine that there ever was a time
> when Jesus' followers were not interested in preserving his
> teachings and in committing his deeds to memory. And if we
> orient ourselves historically, and remind ourselves how students
> in the Jewish milieu hung on the words of their teachers and
> attentively followed their activities in order to learn how to live
> properly, it then becomes difficult to believe that Jesus'
> disciples could have been less concerned to hear their master,
> to observe his way of doing things, and to store up all of this in
> their memories.[14]

Gerhardson's observation here is all the more significant when it is remembered that one of the fundamental presuppositions of form criticism is that eye witnesses did not play any significant role in the oral transmission of the Gospel tradition.[15] Other scholars have made similar observations. Stein remarks that "One of the greatest failures of the early form critics was that they did not see the central role that the eye witness must have played in the oral transmission of the Gospel traditions. It may be that the heavy sociological emphasis on the early Christian 'community' was not hospitable to this."[16]

> Commenting on the same form-critical assumption, Vincent
> Taylor says, quite ironically, "if the form-critics are right, the
> disciples must have translated to heaven immediately after the
> resurrection."[17] Edward Nielsen makes the following comment:
> As to the problem of reliability of oral tradition, it must be
> strongly emphasised that one would be much mistaken in
> asserting that the oral tradition was subject to no control.
> Especially in those cases where tradition is flourishing i.e.
> where there are many traditionalists of the same text, the
> individual traditionalist has a very small chance of carrying
> through a corrupt recension. His guild brothers, but first of all
> his listeners, have been of immeasurable importance in
> upholding teachers who were to examine the scholars in the
> canonical texts (cf. late Judaism, Pharisaism, Islam), private
> members of the tribe who heard the exploits of their tribe cele-
> brated in the odes of their tribal poets (as the Bedouin do to this

---

[14]   *Ibid.*, p. 48.

[15]   Stein, The Synoptic Problem, An Introduction, p. 183.

[16]   *Ibid.*

[17]   Vincent Taylor, *The Formation of the Gospel Tradition*, London: Macmillan, 1935, p. 41.

day) or those taking part in the annual national and religious festivals (e.g. Israel).[18]

And Wolfgang Schadewaldt relates an incident from an early Christian community which shows how strictly the audience exerted control over the tradition by immediately pointing out if something was presented in a different form:

> We have a similar example from the early Christian communities. A sermon was preached on the story of the paralysed man who was let down through the roof on a bed or a couch. Jesus healed him and said, "Take up your bed and walk" (Mark 2:4-9). Instead of using the word *krabbatos* for bed or couch, the preacher chose a more refined one (*skimpous*). One of his congregation immediately called out, "Are you better than the one who said *krabbatos*?"[19]

It has also been observed that the text *Miqsat ma'ase ha-torah* (4QMMT), probably a letter by the Teacher of Righteousness, shows how important it was for the Qumran community to preserve the teachings of its founder. In this light, it is difficult to see why the first generation Christians should not have preserved in writing the traditions about Jesus until twenty years at the earliest following his death and resurrection as form-criticism presupposes[20].

Thus, the form-critical presupposition that the tradition was transmitted as isolated units falls out of favour in light of the findings of contemporary research in rabbinic teaching methods and the ancient Jewish milieu. The poetic form of much of Jesus' "teaching is probably a reflection of a mnemonic device in Jesus" teaching methodology.

It is partly these limitations which influenced the shift from form to redaction criticism. Gundry, especially, in his work gives as reason for adopting redaction critical approach the form critical assumptions. He observes that in this approach the gospels are a little more than a totality

---

[18]   Edward Nielsen, Oral Tradition, A Modern Problem in Old Testament Introduction, SBT 11, London: SCM, 1954, p. 37.

[19]   Wolfgang Schadewaldt, "The Reliability of the Synoptic Tradition," in Martin Hengel, *Studies in the Gospel of Mark*, London: SCM, 1985, p. 109, quoted in Sozomen I, 11, *Patrologia Graeca* LXVII Col. 889. For a full discussion of oral transmission and its bearing on the realiability of the Gospel tradition, see Stein, *The Synoptic Problem, An Introduction*, pp. 187-216; Gerhardson, *The Origins of the Gospel Tradition*, pp. 19-24; Schadewaldt, "The Reliability of the Synoptic Tradition", pp. 90-113. For a convenient summary of other weaknesses of form criticism, see McKnight, *Interpreting the Synoptic Gospels*, pp. 76-78.

[20]   Otto Betz and Rainer Riesner, *Jesus, Qumran and the Vatican*, London: SCM, 1994, pp. 153, 155.

of isolated units of tradition, and that the evangelists are no more than compilers and editors of a series of unconnected incidents and sayings. These assumptions, he observes, do not reflect an openness to the creativity of the evangelists: "By choosing to make whole passages rather than individual sentences our standard of judgment, we get a higher number of insertions and a lower number of occurrences in unparalleled material. This choice reflects an openness to Matthean creativity as opposed to form critics assigning unparalleled sentences to earlier traditions of a piecemeal sort."[21]

But redaction criticism too is limited in that its "attempt to distinguish sharply between tradition and redaction, and limit the exegetical signifi-cance only to the latter stage is not difficult and arbitrary but undercuts basic canonical function within the gospel."[22]

Further, there is an element of scepticism inherent in both form and redaction critical approaches. "Whereas the form critics hid Jesus behind the community, the redaction critics have hidden him behind the authors. In other words, the Gospels can now [under redaction criticism] be approached with the assumption that we cannot see Jesus as he was, but only as Matthew or Mark or Luke or John saw him."[23] But this kind of scepticism is not necessary since it is possible to see the evangelists as theologians, and still at the same time as men with great respect for history. For instance, while the gospel of John is probably the most theological of the four the many parallels it shares with the Dead Sea Scrolls in its teaching with reference to John the Baptist, as research on these scrolls has shown, indicate that the Fourth Gospel could be regarded as a valuable historical source.[24] The same is true with the

---

[21]   Gundry, Matthew, A Commentary on his Literary and Theological Art, p. 4.

[22]   Brevard S. Childs, The New Testament as Canon, An Introduction, London: SCM, 1984, p. 70.

[23]   Morris, Luke, An introduction and Commentary, p. 32.

[24]   For similarities between the life and teaching of John the Baptist as presented in the Gospel and the life and teaching of the Qumran Community for instance on opposition to temple worship, baptisms and sacred meals replacing temple worship and feasts of Jewish calendar, see Oscar Cullman, "The Significance of the Qumran Texts for Research into the Beginning of Christianity," in Stendahl (ed.), The Scrolls and the New Testament, pp. 22, 28-9. Cf. W.H. Brownlee, "John the Baptist in the New Light of Ancient Scrolls," Stendahl (ed.) The Scrolls and the New Testament, pp. 32-52; Millar Burrows, More Light on the Dead Sea Scrolls, New Scrolls and New Interpretations with Translations of Important Recent Discoveries, London: Secker and Warburg, 1958, pp. 57-62. For general similarities between the Qumran community and the earliest Christian Church, see Sherman E. Johnson, "The Dead Sea Manual of Discipline and the Jerusalem Church of Acts," in Stendahl (ed.), The Scrolls and the New

other evangelists. If the evangelists had great respect for history, then we do not need to suppose that what we have in oral tradition is Jesus as the early church saw him and that we have no means at all of knowing what the historical Jesus really was like.[25]

The approach, therefore, taken in this study is exegetical and literary. It is the grammatical – historical approach[26] in which the meanings of words will be investigated in the light of their historical contexts. I will investigate the literary formulation of these quotations and compare them to their Old Testament counterparts. Both Old and New Testament contexts of these quotations will be investigated in order to determine their theological significance in Matthean usage. The biblical text in the form that it has come down to us in the original languages will be assumed to be genuine, except where there is textual evidence to the contrary. Theological implications will be drawn not only from specifically Matthean additions or omissions or any other changes made in the quoted text as is often the case in redaction criticism but from the whole text- form,[27] these inclusive, as it has come down to us. In addition, the unit of study, especially in the Old Testament context will not be limited to words, phrases, clauses or statements conceived as independent units as is often the case with form criticism, but will be extended to the whole passage from which a citation is drawn. The underlying presupposition to this approach is the assumption that the evangelist had access to the scriptures of his day (just as Paul was, II Timothy 4:13), or at least he had a thorough knowledge of them, including the immediate contexts of the citations he draws, in addition to whatever sources he had at his disposal.

I must stress, here, that the exegetical and literary (grammatical – historical) approach is fundamentally neither more nor less critical towards the biblical tradition than either form-critical method or redaction-

---

Testament, pp. 129-40. Cf. Millar Burrows, The Dead Sea Scrolls with Translations by the Author, New York: The Viking Press, 1961, pp. 111-132.

[25] These are basic assumptions of both form and redaction critical methods.

[26] Henry A. Virkler, *Hermeneutics, Principles and Process of Biblical Interpretation*, Grand Rapids: Baker, 1981, pp. 75-230, has thoroughly discussed this analytical approach.

[27] In a similar vein, Smalley also observes that "the use of the Christian tradition as it stands without editorial shaping, may be just as much an indication of the evangelist's theological outlook. In such a case we must assume that the tradition expressed his intention and understanding so clearly that alteration was unnecessary." See Smalley, "Redaction Criticism," p. 188. Cf. I. Howard Marshall, *Luke, Historian and Theologian*, Exeter: Paternoster, 1970, p. 19; N. Perrin, *What is Redaction Criticism?* London: SPCK, 1970, p. 40.

critical method. For all of these, as methodologies to biblical interpretation, are equally concerned with the task of correctly placing the separate biblical texts into their most likely historical contexts. Thus the intentions are basically the same. However, the methods remain different for each critic first comes to a conscious conclusion regarding the relative merit of the presuppositions underlying the critical method of his choice. One of the assured results of the research in New Testament use of the Old Testament is the understanding that the approach of New Testament writers to biblical interpretation is generally "grammatical – historical plus."[28] "The 'plus' consists in their claim to find specific references to the Christ – event in scriptures where a non-Christian could naturally have a different understanding. It is this 'plus' which makes their approach specifically Christian."[29]

If this conclusion with regard to the New Testament writers interpretive approach to the Old Testament is correct, then it follows that the grammatical – historical (exegetical-literary) approach offers us one of the reliable approaches to a proper understanding of the evangelist's theological grasp of his Old Testament as it bears on the Christ-event. With exegetical-literary method we draw closer to the evangelist's mind for he saw his scriptures as a historical record and applied it to the Christ-event from that perspective. It is this approach that will guide the present research[30]. However, while adopting the grammatical-historical

---

[28]   Dan G. McCartney, "The New Testament Use of the Old Testament," in Harvie M. Conn (ed.), *Inerrancy and Hermeneutic: A Tradition, a Challenge, a Debate*, Grand Rapids: Baker, 1988, p. 102. For New Testament writers' historical view of Scriptures, see E. Earle, Ellis, "How the New Uses the Old," in I. Howard Marshall (ed.), *New Testament Interpretation*, pp. 209-12. Cf. James D.G. Dunn, *Unity and Diversity in the New Testament, An Inquiry into the Character of Earliest Christianity*, Second Edition, London: SCM & Philadelphia: Trinity Press International, 1990, pp. 85-6; Gerhard von Rad, "Typological Interpretation of the Old Testament," in Claus Westermann (ed.), *Essays on Old Testament Hermeneutics*, Richmond: John Knox, 1963, pp. 18-39; John Goldingay, *Approaches to Old Testament Interpretation*, Leicester: Apollos, 1990, pp. 97-102; R.T. France, *Jesus and the Old Testament, His Application of Old Testament Passages to Himself and His Mission*, London: Tyndale, 1971, pp. 38-80. In all these works, New Testament writers' typological view of the Old Testament is underlined. And by definition, typology presupposes historical events viewed as recorded in the Old Testament and finding their ultimate fulfilment in the Christ-event to which they are brought to bear in order to explain its theological significance. See France, *Jesus and the Old Testament*, pp. 38-9.

[29]   Jonathan Nkhoma, "The New Testament Use of the Old Testament," an unpublished MA Module 3, University of Malawi, November 1999, p. 23.

[30] Probably the major weakness of this analytical approach is that it does not address the current hermeneutical concern with what a particular text means "to me". See Walter C. Kaiser, Jr., *Toward An Exegetical Theology, Biblical Exegesis for Preaching and Teaching*, Grand

approach as an analytical tool, the other approaches, as mentioned above, will be consulted.

The methodological procedure of defining a person before his work is quite perplexing to both ancient and modern philosophy. Man as a finite being is said to be:

> Marked by a 'to be not yet', by a dynamic coming to be constantly becoming more itself man is a person in potentiality rather than enjoying the actualised state of being a person. By means of a free project man has to try to become more and more a person. The statement that man 'is' a person does not refer to an established condition but a mandate, a task to be performed it is man's task to make himself a person through his deeds, our consideration of the person will have to pay attention to the specific features of human activity.[31]

It has also been philosophically argued that:

> Both in Greek and Latin culture, up to and including Seneca, the common meaning of the word 'persons'...was that of disguising. Until the advent of Christianity, there did not exist, either in Greek or in Latin. A word to express the concept of person, because in pagan culture such a concept did not exist; these cultures did not recognise the absolute values of the individuals as such, and made their absolute value depend essentially on class rank, wealth and race.[32]

The situation has not changed much in contemporary philosophy, as Mondin further observes: "Many people no longer want the word 'person' to intend the uniqueness, unrepeatability, absolute value, and sacredness of the individual, but wish to assign to this word a merely sociological meaning. Man is not 'man in himself, independently of that which others do' to render him as such."[33]

These philosophical comments indicate that man becomes a person only when he himself and society at large make him such. In line with

---

Rapids: Baker, 1981, pp. 88-9. It is, of course, not the intention of the present study to inquire into what these fulfilment quotations mean to us today. The study, rather, seeks to inquire into what they meant to the evangelist and how they contributed to his theological understanding of the Christ-event. Within this limit, this analytical method appears to be quite satisfactory.

[31] Martin G. Plattel, *Social Philosophy*, DSPS 18, Pittsburgh: Duquesne University, 1965, p. 39

[32] Battista Mondin, *Philosophical Anthropology, Man: an Impossible Project?* Rome: Urbaniana University, 1985, p. 243.

[33] *Ibid.*, p. 244.

this philosophical position, it is logical to see a definition of person before his work as a philosophical contradiction.

However, it has been noted that the definition of the concept of person in terms of his/her uniqueness, concreteness and dignity "is a truth carried, affirmed, and diffused by Christianity. a conquest of Christian thought."[34] This means that in Christian philosophy, man is a person because he/she is a human reality, and not because he is a psychological or social construction.

Because Christian philosophy acknowledges the presence of inherent, dignity and nobility in man, a description of a person prior to and independent of his work does not appear to be contradictory. In fact, it becomes a logical procedure. The present study presupposes this Christian philosophical thought with regard to the concept of person, and structurally proceeds to define the person of the messiah before his redemptive work, as the evangelist himself does.

Literature Review

A review of the literature available to me on Matthew's use of the Old Testament with reference to the fulfilment quotations indicates that although much scholarly work has been done on the literary techniques of the evangelist's use of the Old Testament.[35] Little effort has been made to link his exegesis of the Old Testament and his theology in the light of the Old Testament context of his fulfilment quotations. So far, in my limited research, I have not come across any scholar who has given sufficient attention to the theology of the evangelist in light of the Old Testament contexts of the texts that are quoted. Scholars will be categorized according to the schools of thought in terms of which aspect of the historical – critical method or other has guided their research, e.g. form, source or redaction criticism, Midrashim or grammatical-historical method. It is, however, important to remember that these aspects are often interrelated.

Krister Stendahl

Krister Stendahl wrote his *The School of St Matthew and its Use of the Old Testament* at a time when form criticism was still influential. By

---

[34]   *Ibid.*, pp. 244 - 45.

[35]   In this regard Krister Standahl's, *The School of St Matthew and Its Use of the Old Testament*, and Robert H. Gundry's *The Use of the Old Testament in St Matthew's Gospel*, Leiden: Brill, 1967 remain unsurpassed.

definition form criticism was an attempt to reach back to the pre-literary forms or genres of the gospel tradition and did not consider the Old Testament as direct source for the evangelists. Form criticism viewed words, phrases, clauses, statements etc, of the tradition as independent units with an oral existence whether they reflected an Old Testament text or not. As a son of his time, Stendahl did not consider it plausible that Matthew's fulfilment quotations could have a direct theological relationship to their Old Testament contexts as the evangelist of springs these over in an attempt to define the Christ-event[36].In addition, Stendahl's greatest concern in this work was to study the literary techniques employed by the Matthean "school" in their use of the Old Testament in light of the "pesher" method of biblical interpretation found in the Dead Sea Scrolls, especially the Manual of Discipline (IQS) from Qumran then newly discovered.[37]

In his book Stendahl compares the texts of Matthew's fulfilment quotations with the Masoretic Text (MT), the Septuagint (LXX) and other Greek and Syriac versions. From this comparative study he finds that in contrast to Old Testament citations in the gospels, fulfilment quotations are peculiar to Matthew, follow no single textual traditions, but rather represent a selective targumising process in which interpretation is woven into the text itself; that renderings are not a result of paraphrasing or looseness but have their origin in a scholarly detailed study and interpretation of the texts themselves; and that the Matthean type of midrashic interpretation closely resembled the midrash pesher of the Qumran community. To prove this Stendahl engages into a detailed study of some of the exegetical procedures employed at Qumran. In this examination he finds several variants of the MT after comparing these divergent readings in the Dead Sea Scrolls Habakkuk commentary – with other versions. Then he classifies these variants according to the degree of change they bring into the text, i.e., either a mere alteration of a

---

[36] A similar phenomenon is observed by W.D. Davies in H. Marriott's treatment of the Sermon on the Mount in Matt 5-7. Davies notices that Marriott's pre-occupation with source-critical analysis of the Sermon contributes to his unsatisfactory exegetical theological analysis of it. According to Davies, Marriott devotes 140 pages out of 274 to source and literary problems. See W.D. Davies, *The Setting of the Sermon on the Mount*, Cambridge: University Press, 1963, reprint 1966, pp. 1-2, and note 1 on p. 2.

[37] Stendahl, *The School of St Matthew and Its Use of the Old Testament*, especially pp. 183 - 206

number or a suffix or a more substantial change[38]. To account for these divergent readings,. Stendahl comes to this conclusion, "The peculiar way in which DSH coincides both with those readings differing from MT and with the MT's own makes it inadequate to say DSH's Hebrew text was the one supported by the said texts We must rather presume that DSH was conscious of various possibilities, tried them out and allowed them enrich its interpretation of the prophets' message which in all its forms was fulfilled in and through the teacher of righteousness."[39]

In his study of the Matthean quotations Stendahl finds a similar phenomenon, that is, divergent readings which he accounts for by suggesting that they arose from a "school" who selected from various text traditions. At times the "school" created *ad hoc* readings which best expressed the meaning of a text as they understood it. Thus Stendahl's concern in this book was mainly to see how the distinctive hermeneutical principles and methods of "pesher" interpretation affects the text form of the scriptural passage. He does not relate the theological significance of the fulfilment quotations he studies in the light of their Old Testament context. He is not concerned with the evangelist's theological exposition of these quotations in this study. Stendahl leaves his study at the level of literary parallelism between Qumran commentaries on the scriptural texts and Matthew's scriptural comments in the course of the narrative concerning the advent of Jesus Messiah.

In his later work,[40] Stendahl reiterates his views on the evangelist's use of the Old Testament. Here Stendahl parts ways with form critics by insisting that it would be a mistake to see the evangelist "as a mere redactor who brings together material from different and sometimes conflicting sources as best he can"[41] because the evangelist has played a formative role when handling the tradition and because he works within the context of the life of a church whose needs he intends to serve.[42] Here, Stendahl sides himself with redaction critics. In terms of sources for the evangelist Stendahl only mentions specifically Mark and Q (common tradition this evangelist shares with Luke). The rest is

---

[38] *Ibid.*, especially pp. 39-142

[39] Krister Stendahl, *The School of St Matthew and Its Use of the Old Testament*, p. 190.

[40] Krister Stendahl, "Matthew", Matthew Black and H.H. Rowley (eds.),.*Peake's Commentary on the Bible*, London: Routledge, 1962.

[41] Stendahl, "Matthew", p. 769.

[42] *Ibid.*

attributed to the creativity of the Matthean church and the formative role of the evangelist as he works on the earlier sources interpretively although Stendahl claims not to have offered any specific theory on the evangelist's sources:

> With such confidence in the creative forces of the Matthean church and in the possibilities of analysing and grasping in what manner and for what reasons Matthew presents his materials as he does, the following commentary tries to present Matthew without any specific theory about his sources. The gospel grew out of a 'school' led by a converted rabbi where Jewish methods of teaching and studying were applied to the new cause. From this 'school' originated also the eleven 'formula quotations. In these quotations Matthew applies rules for interpretation similar to those used at Qumran...[43]

On the "eleven formula quotations", Stendahl further comments:

> A study of these suggests that they are the product of Matthean study of scripture applied to Marcan or other material available to Matthew and consequently are neither testimonia, nor quotations chosen by Matthew around which a story was built up.[44]

Thus, Stendahl does not consider the Old Testament as a direct source of the fulfilment quotations that the evangelist employs. He even suggests that the evangelist did not have any role in the choice of these quotations. This, then, implies that according to Stendahl, the evangelist could not be in a position to relate these quotations theologically to their Old Testament contexts in a direct manner. Neither is the Old Testament his direct source nor are the fulfilment quotations his choice.

Robert H. Gundry

Like Stendahl before him, Robert H. Gundry's study of the Matthean fulfilment quotations in his *The Use of the Old Testament in St Matthew's Gospel* leaves them at the level of literary analysis. Gundry enters into a critical dialogue with Stendahl's approach to the subject. He particularly stresses Stendahl's neglect of other more formal quotations and the numerous Old Testament allusions which, Gundry argues, must be taken together in a responsible analysis of Matthew's method. In this study, Gundry observes that the mixed text-form, i.e., use of independent and free translations of Hebrew in place of or together with Septuagint, noted by Stendahl, was not limited to the fulfilment quotations but was also

---

[43]   *Ibid.*, pp. 769-70.
[44]   *Ibid.*

found throughout the gospel except where Matthew draws formal quotations from Mark whose text-form was predominantly Septuagintal.[45]

Gundry concludes his study with the observation that Matthew's use of the Old Testament text was a result of deliberate and responsible study of Scriptures in the trilingual setting of first century AD Palestine. At certain times various textual traditions that were in existence could be used, and at others independent translations from the Hebrew could be made.[46] Gundry also observes that the hermeneutical principles of interpretation used by the evangelist are neither arbitrary nor atomizing. Rather, they are a part of a new hermeneutical tradition that arises from the conviction that in Jesus is the fulfilment of all the messianic promises.

According to Gundry, Stendahl, in his *The School of St Matthew*, is methodologically guilty for limiting his study to the fulfilment quotations and on the basis of that study draw provocative conclusions as he did. However, Grundry's own methodological weakness consists in his choosing an almost limitless number of quotations from and allusions to the Old Testament in the gospel of Matthew as a basis for a study which equally leads him to conclusions that are as provocative as those of Stendahl. Some of the "allusions" to the Old Testament he appeals to in support of the argumentative structure that support his conclusions are of a doubtful significance. Their status as genuine allusions is questionable as they may as well be mere linguistic assimilations to Old Testament phraseology without any conscious or intended reference to it. Even if the allusions are assumed to be genuine, it still remains difficult, whenever an allusion differs from the LXX wording, to know whether a variant textual tradition of the Old Testament lies behind it, or whether it is simply an inexact recollection. It is obvious, therefore, that Gundry' appeal to allusions of this nature weakens his argument. The fulfilment quotations still provide a sufficient basis for the study of the theology of the evangelist. This is not to claim that it is the *only* way to understand the evangelist's theology, nor is it here claimed that it is the *best* way. Rather, it is here maintained that this is one *crucial* way for the proper understanding of the evangelist's theology.

Just as Stendahl, Gundry's work does not address the theological role of the fulfilment quotations, let alone their theological relationship to the

---

[45] Gundry, The Use of the Old Testament in St Matthew's Gospel, pp. 9-150, but especially pp. 89-104.

[46] *Ibid.*, pp. 172-74

Old Testament context. He is content to leave his investigation at the literary level.

In his later work, *Matthew, A Commentary on His Literary and Theological Art,* Gundry is much more explicit with regard to his views on the sources and the evangelist's approach used in the preparation of his gospel. Gundry accepts the view that Matthew's method of writing is "midrash" and the proposal that therefore much of his material is unhistorical. The idea of "midrash" was brought into Matthean studies explicitly by M.D. Goulder in his *Midrash and Lection in Matthew.*[47] Goulder argued that the Gospel of Matthew was an expansion of the gospel of Mark intended for lectionary use and that the evangelist's only source was the gospel of Mark. He also argued that all other material was drawn not from any other existing sources but from the evangelist's own fertile and free imagination that was inspired by his own knowledge of the Old Testament. Thus, for Goulder, whatever was non-Marcan had its origin in the evangelist's creative mind. The role of the Old Testament is clearly relegated to the background. The real source, apart from the gospel of Mark is the evangelist's own creativity.

In terms of sources, Gundry allows for the gospel of Mark as the main source but does not attribute to creativity the status of 'source' in a wholesale manner. He argues that Matthew drew much of his other material, including that of chapters one and two, from an expanded Q source:

> The comparison undertaken here will show that the peculiarities of Matthew derive almost wholly from his own revision of and additions to Mark and the materials shared only with Luke. For Matthew in other words, the need to attempt form – critical extra- polation back to oral tradition reduces nearly to the vanishing point. Both Matthew and Luke used Mark and non-Marcan tradition in common. The shared non-Marcan tradition included not only the material usually designated Q, but also the nativity story and some of the materials usually regarded as peculiar to Matthew (M) and Luke (L). Q included more than is usually thought, in other words, but at times Matthew redacted it so freely that his drawing on Q has gone unrecognised and separate traditions have wrongly been posited.[48]

[47] M.D. Goulder, *Midrash and Lection in Matthew*, London: SPCK, 1974.
[48] Gundry, *Matthew, A Commentary on His Literary and Theological Art*, pp. 2, 4-5.

Gundry views the material that the evangelist draws from these "earlier" sources as more or less historical. However, he sees the evangelist's own contribution as unhistorical. He often finds this unhistorical material in the evangelist's "embellishments" of existing traditions rather than in wholesale creation of stories as Goulder earlier proposed: "Even language that seems historical at first may, on close inspection, look unhistorical If, then Matthew writes that Jesus said or did something Jesus did not say or do in the way described we have to say that Matthew did not write entirely reportorial history. Comparison with midrashic and haggadic literature of his era suggest he did not intend to do so."[49]

Gundry claims that the practice of mixing history and non-history as he holds the evangelist to have done was a normal and regular form of communication. He argues that the evangelist's original readers would, therefore, have no difficulty in recognizing his method and would not have thought of interpreting historically his "midrashic" contribution:

> A mixture of history and non-history should not put us off, then. If each can convey truth separately, there is no presumptive reason to think they cannot convey truth together, provided their mixture was a recognized and accepted mode of communication. Ancient midrash and haggadah show that it was so. History mixed with non-history is still an accepted mode of communication and that unhistorical embellishment can carry its own kind of truth alongside historical truth [50]

Gundry leaves one with the impression that the evangelist's use of midrash, in his attempt to bring out the significance of the tradition has in effect rendered the whole of his gospel so unhistorical even as to threaten the historical base of the Christian faith:

> Classifying elements of Matthew as midrash and haggadah narrow the historical base of the Christian faith. The freedom with which an author treats materials available to him and the measurement of this freedom by the literary conventions of the time must enter our determinations of his intent. The first gospel repeatedly offers data leading to the conclusion that to make certain didactic and hortatory points Matthew edited historical traditions in unhistorical ways and in accord with midrashic and haggadic practices to which he and his first readers were accustomed. Because he intended not only to pass on historical

---

[49]   *Ibid.*, p. 629.
[50]   *Ibid.*, pp. 630-31.

information but also to elaborate on its significance by embellishing it, the judgment "unhistorical" concerning this or that element in his gospel ought not carry negative overtones. In Matthew we have a document that does not match even a selective report of Jesus' words and deeds. Comparison with the other gospels, especially with Mark and Luke, and examination of Matthew's style and theology show that he materially altered and embellished historical traditions and that he did so deliberately and often.... Matthew's intent was to tell the story of Jesus with alterations and embellishments suited to the needs of the church and the world at the time the gospel was written.[51]

For Gundry, the Old Testament is not one of the main sources consulted by the evangelist:

There are differences between the Gospel of Matthew and midrash and haggadah in ancient Jewish literature. For one, those who produced midrash and haggadah were embroidering the Old Testament. Matthew was not. Or was he? In a way we may regard his gospel as a wholesale embroidering of the Old Testament with the story of Jesus. Nevertheless Mark and the further tradition shared with Luke remain Matthew's primary sources. But he treated these sources, which, like the Old Testament, were written and venerated, in much the same way the Old Testament was treated by those who produced midrash and haggadah.[52]

Thus, for Gundry, the evangelist gets all his materials from the Gospel of Mark, the enlarged Q-source and the imaginative embellishments of his own creation. Wherever the evangelist would be expected to be using the Old Testament, Gundry's explanation is almost always that the evangelist is assimilating the tradition to Old Testament models or that "throughout his gospel he subtly conforms phraseology to the Old Testament."[53] Even Old Testament quotations are almost always taken from the tradition, not the Old Testament itself.[54] Indeed, Gundry claims

---

[51]   *Ibid.*, pp. 637-39.
[52]   *Ibid.*
[53]   *Ibid.*, p. 27.
[54]   Gundry's comment on Matt 1:21 is illustrative here: "The Davidic Kingship of Jesus therefore implies that 'he will save his people' as indicated in the personal name... For 'Jesus' Greek form of the Hebrew name 'Joshua' means 'Yahweh is salvation'... To draw out the meaning, Matthew quotes, Ps. 130:8... but replaces the psalmist's 'will redeem' with 'will save'... for a closer link with the meaning of 'Jesus'... 'His people' replaces 'Israel'... 'from their sins' replaces 'from all his iniquities ('lawlessness' in the LXX).' These replacements betray Matthew's source, viz., the tradition behind Luke 1:77; 'to give knowledge of salvation to his people in the

that the evangelist's desire for "parallelism and conformity to the Old Testament offer the most likely reason for his revisions."[55]

In this work, it is clear that Gundry makes too much of what he sees as the evangelist's "midrash". It is important here to note that the term 'midrash' is itself difficult to define and scholars do not always mean the same thing when they use it. In Jewish writings, however, it became a technical term, for a literary composition in a form of an extended "commentary" on a continuous Old Testament text. In this sense it is difficult to see how the gospel could be a midrash when it is not a 'commentary' on any continuous text of the Old Testament unless, probably, it is seen as a commentary on the gospel of Mark. It is also questionable whether the practice of explaining historical accounts with imaginative details under the inspiration of the Old Testament was as widespread as he suggests in the New Testament times. It is even more questionable whether such was indeed a dominant approach to scriptural and historical data. Even if such were the case in non-Christian Jewish practice, it simply does not follow that the evangelist would consider it appropriate for his task. Further, it is difficult to see how "fulfilment" of scriptures would be said to have taken place in the absence of a solid historical occurrence in which that fulfilment is seen as taking place. It is again difficult to see why delight in tracing scriptural connections be in itself incompatible with an interest to relate historical Jesus.[56]

Thus, Gundry in this book does not view the evangelist as in any significant way using the Old Testament. Even the quotations that he uses come to him through other means but especially through the

---

forgiveness of their sins'... As often, Matthew has assimilated the tradition to Old Testament phraseology in order to show fulfilment." See *Ibid.,*. p. 23.

[55] *Ibid.*, p. 116.

[56] France, *Matthew*, pp. 24-6. By definition Midrash and Haggadah as interpretive methods refer to the process of adding creative embellishments to a received tradition, "embroidering history with unhistorical elements." These creative stories, it is held, often derive not from a 'historically based tradition," but from a "scripturally inspired imagination." Gundry, however, takes the view that the use of Midrash by the evangelist results primarily in a mixture of history and non-history in this Gospel. Practically, however, it is difficult to see any history since "in Matthew we have a document that does not match even a selective report of Jesus' words and deeds," *Matthew, A Commentary* (p. 639). For a thorough discussion of the concept of Midrash, see Nkhoma, "The New Testament Use of the Old Testament," an unpublished MA Module 3, pp. 6-11. Cf. Brown, *The Birth of the Messiah*, pp. 557-62; J. Goldingay, *Approaches to Old Testament Interpretations*, Leicester: Apollos, 1990, pp. 146-63; E. Earle Ellis, "How the New Uses the Old," in I. Howard Marshall (ed), *New Testament Interpretation*, Carslie: Paternoster, 1970, pp. 203-6; Gundry, *Matthew. A Commentary on His Literary and Theological Art*, pp. 623-40.

Gospel tradition he uses as a source. This implies that for Gundry the evangelist does not use the Old Testament quotations theologically by consciously relating them to their Old Testament context. Consequently he does not pay sufficient attention to the theological role of fulfilment quotations. Both Stendahl and Gundry have applied redaction critical method in their task.

Francis W. Beare
Francis W. Beare in his *The Gospel According to Matthew, A Commentary*, has approached his Matthean study primarily from form-critical perspective and understands the evangelist's work as midrashic designed in a form of a manual of instruction with a highly developed Christology. Beare suggests that the main source for the evangelist is the gospel of Mark while the rest is legendary:[57] "For the story of the ministry of Jesus against which the teaching is presented Matthew is almost wholly dependent on the narrative of Mark. The few additional anecdotes which he offers are without exception legendary."[58]

For Beare, just like Stendahl and Gundry who are discussed above, the evangelist has employed the method of midrash:

> [Matthew] has the scribe's unshakeable conviction of the divine authority of the scriptures, and he employs the methods of the schools in applying phrases – with no regard for their context or for the meaning which they had for the original writer and his readers – to persons and situations of his own age. For him, this means that he applies them to the person of Jesus and to events of his earthly life. He introduces materials of a midrashic nature.[59]

Governing Beare's interpretation in this book is the form-critical presupposition that the evangelist has read back into the teaching of Jesus what he saw was needed in his own community, and systematically interprets the whole gospel from the perspective that it is anachronistic,[60] and vigorously attempts to re-allocate all the gospel

---

[57] Legends as a form of the Gospel traditional material refers to "religious narratives of a saintly man in whose works and fate interest is taken." See M. Dibelius, *From Tradition to Gospel*, London and Cambridge: James Clarke, 1971 p. 104. For a thorough discussion of this form of the gospel tradition, see *Ibid.*, pp. 104-32.

[58] Beare, *The Gospel According to Matthew, a Commentary*, p. 5.

[59] *Ibid.*, p. 9.

[60] For a critical discussion of the tendency to view the gospel tradition anachronistically, i.e., looking at the gospel tradition as a mere transposition of a religious tradition developed in the Matthean, Marcan, Lucan or Johannine communities to meet their own needs from the setting of these communities back to the earthly ministry of Jesus by the evangelists, see D.A. Carson, "Christological Ambiguities in the gospel of Matthew,"Harold H. Rowdon (ed.), *Christ the Lord,'*

material into the Matthean community in which it was originally developed. This leads him to a "stylistic" understanding of almost all the personalities recorded by the evangelist in this gospel so that they effectively become members of the Matthean community itself:

> The narrative framework of this gospel is not an essentially bio-graphical and historical nature. The writer is primarily concerned with the life and faith of the church of his own time, with the responsibilities laid upon it. His interest in the past is dominated by its bearing upon the present. The whole story is seen in a double perspective. The anecdotes which make it up are formally presented as incidents in a life lived seventy years earlier, but they are at the same time images of the Jesus who lives and speaks to the disciples and the crowds of Matthew's own time. Details of place and time are of no real interest. They are given, for the most part in vague terms; and in an order which has little to do with succession in time. And the words and the deeds are alike presented not simply or primarily as records of the past but as instruction for the present, for Jesus still teach with authority and still acts with healing power in his church. The double perspective in which Jesus is presented is extended to all others who appear in the narrative. The people with whom Jesus has to do are, at once the hearers – followers, interested crowds, enemies, - whom he encountered during his earthly life and are at the same time figures of the people with whom Matthew has to do – the church, the people to whom it proclaims its message, and its opponents. The disciples are under one aspect the immediate followers of the man of Nazareth. and at the same time they are "stylised" as figures of the Christian believers of Matthew's church; there is little interest in them as individuals. The opponents of Jesus – scribes and Pharisees in particular – are not to be seen as historical persons in their individual characters, though of course Jesus was questioned and criticised by scribes and Pharisees. But in Matthew they are much more types or figures of the Jewish rabbis and synagogue authorities with whom Matthew was in conflict in his own day.[61]

Studies in Christology presented to Donald Guthrie, Leicester: Inter-Varsity, 1982, p. 98. With a few exceptions most studies on the gospel of Matthew presuppose that since the evangelist wrote from the perspective of faith and that many decades after the events narrated, he must reflect a theology contemporaneous with his own *Sitz im Leben*. Inevitably, it is presupposed that the gospel of Matthew is studded with Christological anachronisms.

[61] Beare, *The Gospel According to Matthew, a Commentary*, pp. 13-14.

As a midrashic writer, the evangelist is not preparing "a record for the archives."[62] He does not aim at giving exact information but rather to provide practical guidance to members of his Christian community and their leaders. Therefore: "Some of his scenes are artificially constructed settings for sayings of Jesus and are to be regarded rather as a sketch of typical circumstances under which a saying may have been uttered than as a plain account of how and when and where the words came to be spoken."[63] However, this does not imply that the whole story is simply a creation of his fertile imagination:

> There is a nucleus, not inconsiderable, of recollections of the apostles and other hearers of Jesus and spectators of his actions. But these recollections were not committed to writing, except in fragmentary fashion, for some decades, after his resurrection; and they were subject to all the hazards that attend communications. Much was lost, for stories were passed along and words were repeated, only as they were felt to be relevant to the situation and needs of new audiences and changing times. Much was added, both in story and in saying, by unwitting transference from stories and sayings of other persons, and by the imaginative reconstructions of Christian teachers.[64]

To put it simply, Beare is, here, saying that the tradition as we have it is a community construction built on the original tradition which is now lost to us and is beyond recovery. He only reiterates the basic assumption of critical scholarship, which in principle sees no continuity between the Jesus of history and the Christ of faith.[65]

---

[62] *Ibid.*, p.14

[63] *Ibid.*, pp. 14-5.

[64] *Ibid.*, p. 15.

[65] Much has been written on this topic in response to the debate ensured in the wake of the Jesus research. Without entering into the whole debate it is significant here to note that the results have not been very satisfactory. A classical work on this quest is Albert Schweitzer's, *The Quest of the Historical Jesus*, London: A & C Black, 1910. For a critical assessment, see James M. Robinson, *A New Quest of the Historical Jesus*, SBT No. 25, London: SCM, 1959, pp. 26-47, especially, p. 29; Guther Bornkamm, *Jesus of Nazareth*, London: Hodder & Stoughton, 1960, pp. 13-26. For an attempt to reconcile the quest and the *Kerygma* (i.e. that the *Kerygma* contained something corresponding to a life of Jesus), see C.H. Dodd, *The Apostolic Preaching and its Development*, New York: Harper & Row, 1964, pp. 17-56, especially pp. 47-52. Gerhardson has argued for the continuity between Jesus' earthly ministry and the Easter faith stressing that "Jesus already appears with an overwhelming authority in his earthly ministry... [and that this picture] proceeds from this situation to the situation after Easter." See Gerhardson, *The Origins of the Gospel Traditions*, pp. 51-65, especially p. 53. Cf. N.T. Wright,

Beare does not only suggest that "the notion that the tradition was somehow 'guarded' by the apostles is altogether untenable,"[66] but along with Wellhausen and Bultmann, rejects the historicity of Jesus' Twelve disciples who later became pillars of the Apostolic community. Beare finds the arguments of G. Klein and W. Schmithals, who are themselves more radical in their rejection, more "weighty". In commenting on R.P. Meye's book, *Jesus and the Twelve, Discipleship and Revelation in Mark's Gospel* who writes in favour of their historicity, Beare makes the following comment:

> He discuses Klein's argument but is not acquainted with the weighty treatise of Schmithals. He arrives at the hazardous con-clusion that "the New Testament and Marcan, picture of the Twelve as the company of Jesus is not at all open to doubt." But doubts are in fact justified; the arguments of Klein and Schmithals are not to be so lightly dismissed. As Schimthals rightly puts it, "today less than ever can one speak of assured results of the investigation of the Christian apostolate."[67]

With the office of the Twelve Apostles abolished, Beare reiterates the form-critical assumption that the tradition circulated in the form of small independent units and that it was the task of evangelists or of compilers of earlier sources to assemble these units into larger complexes. In this process: "Words which Jesus had spoken to opponents could be adapted and treated as addressed to the disciples (and through them to the church). From time to time the store of sayings kept in memory came to be supplemented by new sayings shaped by teachers of the church, in part at least by prophets speaking 'in the Spirit', which were regarded as words spoken by the risen Jesus."[68]

Who was Jesus?, London: SPCK, 1992, pp. 1-103 for a critical response to the recent developments in this debate including a brief historical survey of the whole question.

[66] Beare, *The Gospel According to Matthew, a Commentary*, p. 22.

[67] *Ibid.*, p. 240.

[68] *Ibid.*, p. 30. But this diminutive view over the role of Jesus' disciples in the upholding of the tradition and the creative role of the church in the production of dominic sayings was never universally accepted since its inception. As early as 1937, T.W. Manson could make the following observations: "The teaching was given by Jesus and passed on by word of mouth from those who first heard it. And at this time the number of such people must have been very great. In the second quarter of the first century there must have been literally thousands of people in Judea and Galilee who had at one time or another seen Jesus, and could tell some story about him or repeat some saying of His. The majority of these people would only have fragments of the whole story; but the tradition is made up by the piecing together of fragments. Some of these eye-witnesses must have become Christians and members of the Palestinian Church, and so their stories and sayings would find their way into the common stock of the

Thus, the community creates the sayings of Jesus while the evangelists only gather them into a connected narrative.

On the "cycle of infancy legends 2:1-23," Beare suggests that they are modeled on the story of Moses and feels that they are simply unhistorical, and that, according to him, does not diminish their significance. He further suggests that the fulfilment quotations are drawn from Matthew's collection of Old Testament oracles.

Hence in his present work, Beare, like those discussed above, does not consider the Old Testament as a direct source for the evangelist. Even his quotations are from a collection of the Old Testament oracles, not the Old Testament itself. The availability of the Marcan gospel and the midrashic method of interpretation the evangelist is said to apply, do not require any direct relationship between the evangelists and the Old Testament as such. Even if the evangelist had used the Old Testament as a source for his quotations, they would still not be understood in light of their Old Testament contexts since the evangelist "employs the methods of the schools in applying phrases with no regard to their context." Consequently, the question of any theological use of the fulfilment quotations by the evangelist in the light of their Old Testament context simply does not arise in Beare's work.

Ulrich Luz
Ulrich Luz in his work, *Matthew 1-7. A Continental Commentary,* categorically denies the possibility of any theological significance to the fulfilment quotations in the Matthean gospel due to his conviction that the evangelist simply lifts these quotations from their sources and does not redact them in any significant manner. For Luz, as for the other scholars discussed above, the evangelists main source is the gospel of Mark. He suggests that Matthew 12-28 is "an altered and enlarged new formulation

---

community's story of its founder... The largest part of the tradition must however, be credited to the disciples. They were most constantly with Jesus during the ministry. They heard what he said when He spoke to the multitude or debated with Scribes and Pharisees, and they heard much besides that He taught them privately. They, more than anyone else, were in a position to know His mind on many points, and to pass on their information to their fellow Christians ... in the first decades of the life of the original Palestinian community the tradition concerning the teaching of Jesus rested on a broader basis than we commonly imagine. We tend to think of it as being in the hands of a few distinguished persons who were leaders of the church, and to forget the common people who had heard Jesus gladly and who also had memories. When this is realized we can see that the Church's task in meeting the problems with the Jewish authorities was not that of creating words of Jesus applicable to these situations, but rather that of selecting what was relevant from the available mass of reminiscences." See T.W. Manson, *The Sayings of Jesus,* London: SCM, 1949, pp. 12-3. Cf. Taylor, *The Formation of the Gospel Tradition,* London: Macmillan, 1935, p. 145.

of Mark 2:12 – 4:34; 6:1 –16:8." [69] He accepts the two-source hypothesis quite unreservedly: "To question this hypothesis is to refute a large part of the post 1945 redaction – critical research in the synoptic, a truly daring undertaking which seems to me to be neither necessary nor possible."[70] However, he acknowledges the difficulty of explaining the minor agreements between Matthew and Luke against Mark, which he admits, "are numerous and in many places not even 'minor'".[71] He rejects the "M" source which, according to Streeter, was a written document[72] and, instead, he suggests the use of oral tradition and argues that linguistic and compositional peculiarities support this view:[73] "The infancy narratives Matt:1:18-2:23 were formulated in writing for the first time by the evangelist himself, on the basis of oral traditions. Even for the fulfilment quotations a written source is not to be assumed."[74] Unlike the writers discussed earlier who attributed so much to the evangelist's creative mind, Luz observes that the evangelist is faithful to his sources both literary and theologically. He sticks to his sources:

> The evangelist was not a "free" author but willingly let himself be influenced to a large extent by his main source, Mark Many vocables of Matthew's preferred vocabulary are not new creations of the evangelist but were suggested by his sources the evangelist even theologically continues to a large extent thoughts of his two main sources. Matthew is the disciple or, better, the heir of his theological fathers, Mark and Q.[75]

On the fulfilment quotations, he reaches the following conclusion:

> The activity of these scribes becomes evident in the background of the gospel of Matthew the "school" which is evident behind the fulfilment quotations is, as I believe, not identical with the evangelist. The evangelist who is influenced by the LXX, is hardly himself responsible for their wording. Since most of the fulfilment quotations belong together with those traditions in which they are found today and since Matthew is not their author, it is to be assumed that in his community many traditions, especially also oral traditions of the uniquely Matthean material, were seen by the scribes in the

---

[69] Luz, *Matthew 1-7, A Continental Commentary*, p. 42.
[70] *Ibid.* p. 46.
[71] *Ibid.* p. 48.
[72] B.H. Streeter, *The Four Gospels*, London: Macmillan, 1924, pp. 150, 232, 249-61.
[73] Luz, *Matthew 1-7, A Continental Commentary*, p. 48, especially note 67.
[74] *Ibid.*, p. 49.
[75] *Ibid.*, pp. 73-4.

light of the Bible. Behind Matthew the work of the scribes becomes visible which were an influence on him.[76]

Thus, for Luz, the fulfilment quotations are merely a received tradition from his sources, in this case an oral tradition current in the scribal "school" of the Matthean community.

The fact that the fulfilment quotations are a received tradition and the manner in which the evangelist handles it, as Luz understands them,[77] have a far-reaching effect on his further conclusions:

> It seems to me that one should not assume that the contribution of the evangelist Matthew to the wording of the formula quotations is higher than to the wording of the remaining quotations. The result of this investigation into the wording of the quotations for the understanding of the theology is minima we see the evangelist as a conservative tradent and interpreter who is obliged to the tradition. He treated the wording of the quotations available to him with the same care as he treated the text of the gospel of Mark or of Q.[78]

Thus, since Luz sees the evangelist as receiving the fulfilment quotations from tradition and then adopting them into his gospel without making any significant changes to them, the logical conclusion is that they have, almost certainly, no theological role. From this position, it is not far fetched to reach its corollary conclusion, namely that any theology that the evangelist reflects has its origin in his sources. From Luz's perspective, therefore, the evangelist cannot be considered to have used the Old Testament in any serious way, and whatever theology he may reflect cannot be said to have developed in the light of the Old Testament contexts of the quotations he draws.

Raymond E. Brown

Raymond E. Brown, however, in his *The Birth of the Messiah* acknowledges the theological significance of the fulfilment quotations: "What they indicate are areas of theological significance which might otherwise be overlooked highlighting the theological character of the

---

[76] *Ibid.*, p. 78.

[77] "The Old Testament quotations from Mark and Q show that the evangelist Matthew changes very little in them. Thus, he quoted the Bible according to Mark or Q. At most, a slight assimilation to the LXX wording can sometimes be observed. All this does not fit the picture of a scribe who would deliberately have produced *only* in his formula quotations a new form of the text which was familiar to him in different versions. The procedure of Matthew with the quotations from Mark and Q, in my opinion, speaks for the view that the formula quotations come from pre-Matthean Christian tradition," *Ibid.* p. 160. Emphasis by Luz.

[78] *Ibid.*, p. 161.

events narrated – events that Matthew has chosen because they are related to the expectations of Israel, and because they fulfil prophecy, as he understands it."[79]

Like many other scholars, Brown approaches his study from the presupposition that Matthew draws upon Mark's gospel.[80] He sees the interpretative approach of the evangelist to his sources as midrashic. This again has far reaching consequences on his conclusions since "midrash" implies a mixture of history and non-history at best, or simply non-history. Commenting on the infancy narratives (i.e., the first two chapters of this gospel in which alone there are five fulfilment quotations), Brown says: "Relative sobriety of the canonical infancy narratives when compared to non-canonical ones has been used as argument for their historicity. But is this a difference of kind (history vs. function) or a difference of degree? One might argue that both canonical and non-canonical narratives result from attempts of Christian imagination to fill in the Messiah's origins, and that in the case of the apocryphal narratives the imagination had a freer and further exercise."[81] For Brown, the midrashic approach to scriptural interpretation accounts satisfactorily for the miraculous events in the infancy narrative of this gospel: "Some of these events which are quite implausible as history, have now been understood as rewritings of OT scenes and themes."[82] Thus, Herod's search for the life of the infant Jesus and the Bethlehem baby massacre becomes a reapplication of the story of the Egyptian wicked Pharaoh who wanted to kill the infant Moses and the massacre of male children that followed. Similarly, Joseph's dream story becomes a mere reproduction of the story of the Patriarch Joseph and his dreams, both of whom found security in Egypt. The story of Zechariah and Elizabeth is likened to that of Abraham and Sarah.

Commenting further on an outline, which supposes the evangelist's preservation of his intention in the two-fold divisions of the infancy narratives, i.e., chapters one and two, Brown reaffirms the evangelist's midrashic practice:

> This situation reflects the history of the composition of Matthew's infancy narrative. In my judgment, Matthew has

---

[79] Brown, *The Birth of the Messiah*, p. 22.
[80] *Ibid.*, pp. 45, 48.
[81] *Ibid.*, p. 33, note 21.
[82] *Ibid.*, p. 36.

incorporated into the final narrative several different kinds of raw materials: lists of names of patriarchs and kings, and a messianic family tree; an annunciation of the messiah's birth *patterned* on OT annunciation's of birth; a birth story involving Joseph and the child Jesus, *patterned* on the patriarch Joseph and the legends surrounding the birth of Moses; a magi-and-star story *patterned* on the magus Balaam who came from the East and saw the Davidic star that would rise from Jacob.[83]

It is important to note that according to Brown, much if not all of the infancy narratives are products of the evangelist's creative imagination triggered off not by the historical events surrounding the birth of Jesus but the evangelist's knowledge of Old Testament miraculous childbirth stories. As creative stories patterned on Old Testament ones they are simply unhistorical. Indeed, Brown concludes that his own: "Previous investigation with all its "hard-nosed" probing of historicity discovered that probabilities were more often against historicity than for it."[84] It is, of course, difficult to see how the Old Testament can be fulfilled in a birth story that is no more than a mere imaginative creation of the writer. By definition, the concept of scriptural fulfilment cannot be divorced from historical events or realities.[85] It requires an acrobatic imagination to see any meaningful fulfilment of the Old Testament in these fictitious stories as Brown holds them to be.

Since Mark is the major source of this evangelist and since his imagination plays an essential role in the creation of the infancy narratives and the miraculous stories, any serious study of the Old Testament with a view to understand the context of his Old Testament fulfilment quotations in order to relate them theologically to the Christ-event cannot be expected. Such a serious application of the Old Testament to the Christ-event could only be meaningful if the evangelist believed that he had factual information concerning the birth of Jesus Messiah. It is obviously much easier to engage into some creative imagination than it is to engage into a serious scriptural study and historical reflection in an attempt to discern the theological relationship of the two. If the evangelist did the first it is very unlikely that he practiced the second. Therefore, it can be said that Brown does not see the evangelist as using the fulfilment quotations in the light of their Old

---

[83] *Ibid.*, p. 52 .Emphasis mine.

[84] *Ibid.*, p. 37.

[85] R.T. France, *Jesus and the Old Testament*, London: SCM, 1971, p. 83: "To claim a prediction is fulfilled is not simply to affirm a discernible correspondence, but to assert that the Old Testament passages concerned... pointed forward to that which has occurred."

Testament contexts and then apply them theologically to the Christ-event, although he sees the evangelist as assimilating his creative stories to Old Testament phraseology.[86]

Willoughby C. Allen

Willoughby C. Allen, in his *Gospel According to St. Matthew*[87], also does not see the evangelist as applying the fulfilment quotations to Jesus Messiah in the light of their Old Testament contexts. In Allen's day the widely held scholarly opinion over the manner of the authorship of the gospels was that the evangelists functioned as mere compilers or editors of a received tradition. In this perspective it is not quite easy to see the evangelists as theologians who responsibly apply the divine promises recorded in the Old Testament to the Christ-event. Moreover, it was a time when form criticism was now applied to New Testament research and one of the assured results of that research was that the gospel tradition circulated in independent units. Form critical studies were just beginning to dominate New Testament research over against source criticism whose most assured result had been the establishment of Marcan priority. Both source and form criticism did not provide a suitable scholarly environment for the conception that the evangelists could apply the Old Testament to the Christ-event theologically since both of these critical approaches saw the evangelists as mere compilers or editors of received tradition.

Allen avoids critical questions: "Considerations as to the historical character of the incidents which the gospel records, have for the most part been carefully avoided, and no attempt has been made to discuss the question whether the teaching here put into the mouth of Christ was a matter of fact taught by him."[88] He accepts the priority of Mark[89] but rejects the use of a common written source apart from Mark as an explanation for the Matthew – Luke agreements against Mark.[90] He

---

[86] Although Brown acknowledges the theological significance of the fulfilment quotations, he does not develop the idea further because he is concerned first and foremost with the infancy narratives as a whole. Neither is the limited development he offers along the lines I have indicated. He disregards the role of the Old Testament context of these quotations in the evangelist's theological reflections. However, he provides valuable background information to the study of the fulfilment quotations in the infancy narrative. See *Ibid.* pp. 96-104, 143-53, 184-88, 219-25.

[87] Willoughby C. Allen, *A Critical and Exegetical Commentary on the Gospel According to S. Matthew*, ICC, Third Edition, Edinburgh: T & T Clark, 1912.

[88] *Ibid.*, p. ix.

[89] *Ibid.*, p. xxxv.

[90] *Ibid.*, p. xxiv.

further suggests that the matter common to Matthew and Luke comes "not from written sources, but from oral traditions or from independent written sources."[91] He finds the common written source theory (we now call Q) unsatisfactory since it fails to account for the variations in order, context and language.[92]

On the fulfilment quotations, he suggests that they are quite earlier in their date,[93] and that those in the infancy narratives together with the one at 27:9 appear to be an integral part of the narrative while those in the infancy narratives appear to be insertions into or appended to a Marcan text by the evangelist:[94] "It seems therefore probable that the eleven quotations introduced by a formula ... were already current when the editor compiled his work in a Greek form. They may come from a collection of Old Testament passages regarded as prophecies of events in the life of the messiah."[95] Thus Allen sees the evangelist as a compiler of received tradition. The fulfilment quotations are part of this received tradition. Obviously, the evangelist does not play any significant theological role in this picture. We can therefore conclude that Allen does not see the evangelist as making a theological use of these quotations in the light of their Old Testament contexts in their application to the Christ-event.

Charles H. Dodd

The first major study to attempt a serious consideration of the Old Testament quotations in the light of their Old Testament setting was undertaken by Charles H. Dodd in his *According to Scriptures*.[96] The study, however, received a remarkably cool reception from critics.[97] Nevertheless, Dodd's study is quite impressive. After a systematic analysis of Old Testament texts quoted in the New Testament, he successfully establishes that the unit of reference for these quotations is wider than the words actually quoted and that the citation by different

---

[91]   *Ibid.*, p xlii.

[92]   *Ibid.*, pp. xlvi - xlviii.

[93]   *Ibid.*, p. lx.

[94]   *Ibid.*, pp. lx - lxii.

[95]   *Ibid.*, p. lxii.

[96]   Charles H. Dodd, *According to Scriptures*, London: Nisbet, 1952, and New York: Scribner, 1953.

[97]   W.F. Albright and C.S. Mann, *Matthew*, AB, New York: Doubleday, 1971, p.lxi.

New Testament writers of adjacent or contiguous passages within a single context indicates a common pre-canonical tradition.[98]

He further examines the contexts from which the fifteen attested quotations come in an attempt to define the probable extent of the context which for their (New Testament Writers) purpose was treated as a unit. He then concludes that certain sections of the Old Testament scriptures, especially from Isaiah, Jeremiah, the Minor Prophets and the Psalms were considered as "wholes" and that particular verses or sentences were quoted from them as "pointers" to the whole context than as constituting testimonies in and for themselves, independently of their Old Testament context.[99]

While Dodd has shown us the necessity of relating New Testament quotations to their Old Testament contexts, he does not specifically discuss Matthean fulfilment quotations. He is concerned with those quotations commonly used by New Testament writers in their attempt to interpret the Christ-event, although the evangelist Matthew shares in the usage of these common traditions even in his fulfilment quotations (e.g. Jer 31:15 = LXX 38:15 in Matt 2:18, a quote which is in the same context as Jer 31:31-34 quoted partly in Luke 22:20; 1 Cor 11:25 and almost fully in Heb 8:8-12; 10:16-17. Also Zech 9:9, in Matt. 21:4-5).

Conclusion

Although the number of works surveyed in this chapter is limited, this review has sufficiently revealed that contemporary scholarship available to me has not addressed adequately the link between the evangelist's exegesis of the Old Testament and his theology in the light of the Old Testament context of his fulfilment quotations. In this regard, a hiatus still remains in the field of Matthean fulfilment quotations research. This literary survey has shown that Matthean scholarship has primarily concerned itself with the literal techniques applied by the evangelist in his use of Old Testament material (K. Stendahl, R.H. Gundry). Further,

---

[98] The Old Testament texts cited by New Testament writers which Dodd analyses for this purpose are Ps. 2:7; 8:4-6; 110:1 (LXX 109:1); 118 (LXX 117):22-23; Isa 6:9-10; 28:16; 40:3-5; 53:1: Gen. 12:3; Jer. 31 (LXX 38): 31-34: Joel 2:28-32; Zech 9:9; Hab. 2:3-4; Isa 61:1-2 and Deut 18:15, 19. See Dodd, *According to Scriptures*, pp. 30 - 58. Dodd finds the clearest example for illustrating that the position of scripture in the writer's mind is not necessarily restricted to the amount quoted in Acts 2:17-21 where Joel 2:28-32 is cited. The Joel quotation ends at Acts 2:2 in the middle of verse 32 (in Joel) while the latter part of verse 32 is quoted later at Acts 2:39. See *Ibid.*, p. 47, especially note 21.

[99] Dodd, *According to Scriptures*, pp. 61-110, 126.

the approaches taken by most scholars have not yielded much fruitful results with regard to the theological relationship between the fulfilment quotations that the evangelist applies to the Christ-event and their Old Testament contexts because the presuppositions governing their methodological procedures rule out, *a priori*, any possibility of direct use of the Old Testament by the evangelist. Form-critical and midrashic approaches (F.W. Beare, R.E. Brown) do not, by definition, allow for any direct and meaningful use of the Old Testament as a source. Also the multiplicity of sources supposedly used by the evangelist, for instance the sources, Mark, Q, (K. Stendahl, R.H. Gundry, F.W. Beare, U. Luz, R.E. Brown, W. Allen) and the manner in which these sources were supposedly used, for instance, simply copying (Luz) or simply compiling the received tradition (Allen) militate against the possibility that the evangelist may have used the Old Testament itself as one of his sources.

But Dodd has broken new ground by successfully establishing the principle that New Testament writers theologically used Old Testament quotations by applying them to the Christ-event in the light of their Old Testament context. By making reference to Old Testament context, Dodd logically presupposes, to some extent, direct use of Old Testament books or potions in which the quoted texts are originally found, or at least some thorough knowledge of these contexts that would enable a theological application of some text from them to the Christ-event. Such a view of New Testament writers' use of the Old Testament is almost unattainable if one begins with the approaches whose presuppositions require that the evangelist be denied any meaningful access to the Old Testament, the only authoritative scriptural corpus for both Jews and Christians at the time.

However, Dodd's main interest was on quotations commonly used by the New Testament writers in their efforts to define the *Kerygma*. It is at this very point that Dodd fails to address Matthean fulfilment quotations as they do not fall within the range of his academic interest. Matthean fulfilment quotations are not a part of those quotations that are commonly used by New Testament writers, and as such, Dodd does not sufficiently address the question as to how the evangelist uses these fulfilment quotations in the light of their Old Testament contexts. Hence, the hiatus still remains. And it is toward the filling of this gap that the present study is undertaken. But it is by proceeding along the direction that Dodd has indicated that we can probably come to a balanced understanding of Matthean theology, especially in terms of his Christological outlook. It is my contention that, contrary to the tendency to reject any possibility of direct and meaningful use of the Old Testament by the evangelist in modern Matthean scholarship, the evangelist Matthew, like other Jewish and Christian writers of his age, used biblical quotations theologically in an attempt to articulate and interpret certain theological teachings that were relevant to their contemporary society with respect to the Old Testament contexts of the quoted texts. In the case of Christian writers, the subject for their theological articulation and interpretation was the Christ-event. The next task here is, therefore, to investigate whether the claim that biblical quotations were generally used theologically could be substantiated by the evidence from late Judaism and early Christianity

Chapter 2

THE ROLE OF QUOTATIONS IN ANCIENT JUDAISM AND EARLY CHRISTIANITY

Introduction

In the previous chapter, it has been shown that previous research on Matthean fulfilment quotations largely focused on literal; techniques in its study of Matthean usage of the Old Testament. It has been clearly revealed that the theological significance of the fulfilment quotations in light of their prophetic context has not been sufficiently addressed. The chapter has also shown that the failure to address the theological aspect of the quotations in view of their prophetic light is partly due to methodological considerations. The chapter has, however, concluded at an optimistic note, showing that a quotation in the New Testament points to an Old Testament context in which it first appears. This was then noted as a profitable guide to a fruitful theological investigation of the fulfilment quotations.

In the present chapter, I have investigated the use of biblical quotations in Jewish religious literature and patristic writings in order to see whether these writings used biblical quotations theologically. The results reveal that, with a few exceptions, these writings use biblical quotations theologically, and that this provides a literary background to Matthean usage of fulfilment quotations.

The theological use of biblical quotations is a phenomenon well attested by ancient Jewish religious literature. A study of biblical quotations (including, in some cases, quotations from apocryphal books) in the *Mishnah*, the *Dead Sea Scrolls*, the patristic writings and the Old and New Testament apocryphal books shows that quotations are used to support certain doctrinal teachings. These theological teachings cover a wide spectrum of issues ranging from practical issues of daily life in the *Mishnah* to the highly abstract questions of a philosophical nature in the patristic writings. Almost in every case an attempt is made to support a particular theological teaching with a biblical quotation. Such theological use of biblical quotations is widely used in the literature that has a strong legal element, as it is the case with the *Mishnah*, or a strong apologetic element as it is the case with the *Dead Sea Scrolls* and the patristic writings. In general, the apocryphal writings of the Old and New Testament do not share these two characteristics very strongly. They are of course not completely missing.

There is, however, another way in which biblical quotations are used. For lack of a proper term, I will simply refer to this type of usage as a *literary use* of biblical quotations as over against the theological use of biblical quotations, which is the subject of this chapter. This usage applies to cases where the quotations are not used directly to support a specific theological teaching or practice but rather are used to bring a particular narrative to a literary completion. Such quotations can further be divided into two forms. First, they can take the form of direct quotations. This form is greatly used in New Testament apocryphal writings where it is used, usually, to complete a literal sense of a narrative or a dialogue. Secondly, they can take the form of linguistic or historical allusions. This usage is particularly prominent in Old Testament apocryphal writings. One significant feature of both forms of *literary use* of quotations is that the writer is usually not conscious of using any quotations at all. They appear to arise simply from the writer's familiarity with the biblical traditions he quotes although direct use might have been made. Examples of the literary usage of biblical quotations will be provided as specific cases arise. However, the major concern here is to show that wherever the writer is conscious of using a biblical quotation, it is almost always the case that such a quotation is used theologically.

In this chapter the theological use of biblical quotations in the ancient Jewish milieu and early Christianity will be demonstrated by looking at such usage in the *Mishnah,* the *Dead Sea Scrolls,* the patristic writings and the apocryphal traditions.

The Mishnah

The *Mishnah* is a deposit of Jewish religious and cultural practice that cuts across four centuries ranging from the earlier half of the second century BC to the end of the second century AD.[1] This suggests that the *Mishnah* has a substantial amount of pre-Christian traditional material. The similarities it shares with our evangelist in the use of quotations, therefore, point to an early date for the composition of his gospel. Its chief purpose is to provide a theological interpretation of the Mosaic Law so that the Law continues to have relevance on contemporary Jewish society as ages pass by[2]. Since the Law is alone the principal doctrine of Jewish religion,[3] its interpretation constitutes more than a mere legal enterprise. It is a theological process in which almost every legal decision is validated by Scriptural authority. This is a theological use of biblical quotations and is manifest throughout the *Mishnah*. For our purpose, it is sufficient to look at how biblical quotations are employed to support various rabbinical doctrines in some of the tractates. Even here I do not pretend to be exhaustive. The examples cited are, however, sufficient to show the theological role of biblical quotations in the *Mishnah*.

Berakoth (Benedictions)

In Ber 1:3 the schools of Shammai and Hillel develop a teaching on the appropriate body posture when one is reciting the Shema based on Deut 6:7. By emphasizing different phrases in that verse, the two schools develop different teachings on the subject. The school of Shammai teaches that in the evening all worshipers should recline but in the morning they should stand up "for it is written, 'And when thou liest down and when thou rises up." On the other hand, the School of Hillel teaches that they may recite it everyone in his own way "for it is written, 'And when thou walkest by the way." In Ber 1:5, the quotation from Deut 16:3 provides a theological explanation as to why the "going-forth from Egypt" is almost always rehearsed at night. In Ber 7:3, the quotation from Ps 68:26, "By congregations bless ye the Lord", provides the theological basis for the liturgical practice of varying the benediction formula according to the number of the people who have gathered for worship. In Ber 9:5, the quotation from Deut 6:5 provides the theological basis for the teaching that man is obliged to bless God regardless of the circumstances in which he finds himself.

A series of quotations are further used to suggest a rabbinic doctrine concerning greetings which is apparently contradictory to another teaching regarding the Holy Name:

---

[1] Herbert, Danby, *The Mishnah*, London: Oxford University Press, 1993, p. xiii

[2] *Ibid.*, pp. xiii-xiv.

[3] *Ibid.*, p. xiv.

> And it was ordained that a man should salute his fellow with the
> use of the Name of God; for it is written, "and, behold, Boaz
> came from Bethlehem and said unto the reapers, the Lord be
> with you. And they answered, the Lord bless thee" (Ruth 2:4).
> And it is written: "the Lord is with thee, thou mighty man of
> valour" (Judg 6:12). And it is written, "And despise not thy
> mother when she is old" (Prov 23:22). And it is written, "it is time
> to work for the Lord: they have made void thy law"(Ps 119:
> 126). R. Nathan says: they have made void thy law because it
> was a time to work for the Lord.[4]

The traditional Law prohibits any vain use of the Name of God (Yahweh) (Exod 20:7).[5] It is, however, theologically argued here by the use of these quotations that the prohibition on the mentioning of the Holy Name may be suspended in times of need or emergency in order even to serve Him better. In such cases the Law could be served better by breaking it. This is especially supported by the quotation from the Psalms, which R. Nathan accordingly interprets.[6]

Peah (Gleanings)

On the one hand, this tractate concerns itself with the biblical laws that allow the poor to glean in the fields (Lev 19:9; 23:22; Deut 24: 19-21), and also with the "poor man's tithe" (Deut 14:28) which takes the place of Second Tithe[7] in the third and sixth years of the seven-year circle. On the other hand, in Peah 8:9, the quotation, "Blessed is the man that trusteth in the Lord, and whose hope the Lord is", from Jer 17:7 is employed as a theological basis for the view that those who forgo the privilege of a poorman's tithe even when they qualify for it become blessed of God. God provides them with resources so that they are able not only to support themselves but also to support others out of their own wealth before they die in old age. To die in old age is itself a special kind of blessing. The quotations from Prov 1:27, "But he that searcheth after

---

[4] *Ibid.,* p. 10.

[5] By the later period of the Second Temple the personal name of god, YHWH, had become "unspeakably holy and therefore unsuitable for use in public reading, although it continued to be used privately". See G. Jones Botterweck and Helmer Ringgren (eds), *Theological Dictionary of the Old Testament,* vol. V, Grand Rapids: William B. Eerdmans, 1986, p. 500.

[6] George F. Moore, *Judaism in the First centuries of the Christian Era,* vol. 1,. New York: Schocken, 1971, p. 259 for the view that Ps 119:126 is frequently cited as a theological basis for the liberty of suspending laws in the Pentateuch on rabbinic authority when circumstances demand it.

[7] For a brief definition of "Second Tithe", see Danby, *The Mishnah,* p. 73, note 6. For a thorough treatment, see the tractate, "Maaser Sheni" which is wholly devoted to that subject in *Ibid.,* pp. 73-82.

mischief it shall come unto him", and from Exod 23:8, "And thou shalt take no gift, for a gift blindeth them that have sight" are used as a theological basis for the teaching on the curses and misfortunes that befall, even in this life, those who obtain the poor man's tithe through false pretence and those who pervert the course of justice. These become poor, ill health and are not blessed with a long life.

Terumoth (Heave – Offerings)

Terumah is the portion (between sixtieth and fortieth) that must be given to the priests from the produce of the harvest. Non-priests would not start eating their produce until the Terumah has been set aside (Num 18:8, Deut. 18:4) and only those of a priestly status would eat it (Lev 22:10). Terumah is highly susceptible to uncleanliness and as such there are elaborate instructions on how to go about it. In Ter 6:6, a single biblical quotation is used as a theological basis for two different teachings concerning its restitution. On the one hand, from the text, "And he shall give unto the priest the holy thing", in Lev 22:14, R. Eliezer rules that restitution may be made from one kind instead of from another kind provided it is from a better instead of from a worse kind. On the other hand, R. Akiba rules that restitution could be made only from the like kind. For Eliezer, whatever is holy is suitable while for Akiba, it must be the same kind of holy thing that had been eaten.[8]

Maasar Sheni (Second Tithe)

In this tractate at 5:10-13 there is an avowal, which was made at the time of the afternoon offering on the last Festival day. It consists of word for word quotation of Deut 26:13-15. It could only be cited by one who has fulfilled the sacrificial demands stipulated in vv 13-14 and upon that fulfilment of the sacrificial law is based the prayer for the land blessing recorded in v.15 which every eligible worshipper recites. Here, a biblical quotation has not only a liturgical function but also a far-reaching theological implication over the land promise made to Abraham and his descendants as constituting a type of the totality of the blessings of God that are in store for his people. The exclusive nature of these divine promises is reflected in the fact that only Israelites and bastards could make the avowal, but not proselytes and freed slaves who had no share in the land (Maaser Sheni 5:14)

---

[8] The Terumah is one of the most significant themes in *The Mishnah*. There are almost six hundred references to it in *The Mishnah*. The right to eat of it is a mark of priestly status. See *Ibid.*, p.797.

Hallah (Dough-Offering)

In Hallah 4:10, after a citation of rejected dough-offerings from Be-ittur, Alexandria and Zeboim, all of which are outside the land of Israel the quotation, "And the feast of harvest, the first fruits of thy labours which thou sowest in the field", from Exod 23:16 is used to support the view that dough-offerings should only come from the first fruits grown by Israelites within the land of Israel.

Bikkurim (First-Fruits)

In Bikk 1:2, the quotation, "the first fruits of thy land" from Exod 23:19 is used as a theological basis for the view that the first-fruits offering must come only from fruits grown on each one's land, not from leased or hired land (Deut 26:1-2), and that only those who offer such fruits are eligible to recite the avowal (Deut 26:13-15). In Bikk 1:1, there is an outline of categories of people whose first-fruits do not qualify for such offering specifically because the growth of their fruits is not "wholly from thy land".[9] In Bikk 1:9, the quotation "The first of the first fruits of thy land thou shalt bring into the home of the Lord thy God" from the same Exod 23:19, provides the basis for the view that the worshipper is responsible for his first –fruit offerings until they are presented at the Temple. Should they become unclean at anytime before that moment, the worshipper remains obliged to making a restitution for them.

Shabbath (the Sabbath)

In this tractate at 6:4, the quotation from Isa 2:4, "And they shall beat their swords into plowshares, and their spears into pruning –hooks: nation shall not lift up sword against nation, neither shall they learn war any more" is used in support of the view that to go out[10] with any weapon of war like a sword, a bow, a shield, a club or a spear on the Sabbath day is a reproach. In the Old Testament context this verse refers to the eschatological hope for Israel when all Israelites including those among the nations would come to Zion and be used as a divine instrument for bringing world peace bringing an end to disputes among the nations. This would render military weapons obsolete and necessitate their

---

[9] "Bikkurim" 1:2, in Danby, *The Mishnah*, p. 93.

[10] The phrase "going out" is a technical term based on Exod 16:29, "Let no man go out of his place on the seventh day". It also refers to "carrying a burden" from one place to another (Jer 17:22). For types of "going out", see 'Sabbath 1:1', in Danby, *The Mishnah*, p. 100. Cf. *Ibid.* note 2.

adaptation to non-violent usage[11]. Thus in the context of the Old Testament the verse is understood theologically as a reference to the eschatological role of Israel among the nations and its implications on world affairs. In the context of rabbinic theology, the verse is used in no less a theological way. The difference is rather in their concern. While the Old Testament context concerns itself with the eschatological hope of Israel, the rabbinic context concerns itself with the Sabbath and the maintenance of its holiness. This concern is more existential and practical but in no way less theological for keeping the Sabbath holy is a matter of theological concern. In rabbinic theology the Sabbath is a heavenly gift that, in a special way, expresses God's infinite love and mercy which are bestowed upon his children as a foretaste of the blessings that await the righteous in the world to come.[12]

At Shabb 9:1 the quotation from Isa 30:22 is used to define the manner in which an idol conveys uncleanliness, namely, by carrying, "like a menstruant thing".[13] At Shabb 9:2 the quotation from Prov 30:19 is used to support the rabbinic view that a ship, like the sea, is incapable of contracting uncleanliness.

Pesahim (Feast of Passover)

The mention of the words "assembly", "congregation" and "Israel" in Exod. 12:6 quoted at Pes 5:5 is used as the theological basis for the tradition that the passover offerings be slaughtered in three groups. At Pes 10:5 it is taught that any worshipper at the Passover who does not mention the three things in the verses he recites has failed to fulfil his passover obligation. The three things are passover, unleavened bread and bitter herbs. In these three aspects the whole salvific drama of the original passover is recapitulated and re-enacted in the present worshipper so that its efficacy is applied to him. Further, Exod 13:8, "And thou shall tell thy son in that day saying, it is because of that which the Lord did for me when I came forth out of Egypt", is quoted as a theological basis for the teaching that the Passover experience must be

---

[11]   R.E. Clements, *Isaiah 1-39*, NCBC, Grand Rapids: Wm. B. Eerdmans and London: Marshall, Morgan and Scott, 1980, pp. 40-2. For the view that the text is eschatological not in the sense of an end to world and human history but in the sense of a fundamental change in earthly conditions whether within or outside history, see Otto Kaiser, *Isaiah 1-12, a commentary*, London: SCM, 1972, p. 29.

[12]   Solomon Schechter, *Aspects of Rabbinic Theology*, New York: Schocken, 1961, pp. 153-54. Cf. A. Cohen, *Everyman's Talmud*, London: J.M. Dent and New York: E.P. Dutton, 1949, pp. 155-56.

[13]   See Lev 15:19-33. Cf Kelim 1:3, in Danby, *The Mishnah*, p. 604.

relived in every generation, that is, that every Jew must personally participate in the passover experience, and thus appropriate for himself the redemption it affords to God's people, a redemption which in turn becomes a springboard for praises and thanksgiving to God.

Yoma (The Day of Atonement)

At Yoma 8:9 the writer of this tractate cites Ezek 36:25, "And I will sprinkle clean water upon you and ye shall be clean", and Jer 17:3, "O Lord, the hope of Israel", as the theological basis for the doctrine of atonement, that God cleanses his people from sin.

Rosh ha-shanah (Feast of the New Year)

The writer of this tractate at 3:8 uses the quotations from Exod 17:1 which refers to Moses' raising of hands during Israel's war with Amalek, and Num 21:8 which refers to the fiery serpent which was to be a means for healing to those who after being bitten by snakes looked at it for a healing. This is the basis for the doctrine that Israel can be healed or blessed, or prevails, only when she trusts in the Lord, keeping their hearts in subjection to him.

Taanith (Days of Fasting)

During the Feast of Tabernacles which usually takes place in the latter half of the month of October, a time when the first rain usually falls in Israel, rain is considered as a sign of divine displeasure because it renders it impossible to observe the command to stay in booths.[14] At Taan 1:7 the writer uses the quotation, "Is it not wheat harvest today? I will call unto the Lord that he send thunder and rain, and ye shall know and see that great is your wickedness which ye have wrought in the sight of God to ask for yourselves a king", from I Sam 12:17. The quotation is applied to support the view that drought (i.e., lack of rain between the months of October and April) and late rain (i.e., rain in the month of May, which is otherwise a harvest time) indicate divine displeasure upon Israel, which consequently signifies to the nation a call for repentance. At Taan. 2:1, quotations from Jonah 3:10 and Joel 2:13, set in a liturgical context, are used as the theological basis for the appeal for moral uprightness over against the mere ritual of fasting:

How did they order the matter on the last seven days of fasting? They used to bring out the Ark into the open space in the town and put wood—ashes on

---

[14]   Rosh Ha-Shanah 1:2; Tannith 1:1; Sukkah 2:9. Also Danby, The Mishnah, p. 175, note 7.

the Ark and on the heads of the President and the Father of the court, and every one took of the ashes and put them on his head. The eldest among them uttered before them words of admonition: Brethren, it is not written of the men of Nineveh that "God saw their sack cloth and their fasting", but "and God saw their works that they turned from their evil way" (Jonah 3:10); and in his protest the Prophet says, "Rend your heart and not your garments" (Joel 2:13).[15]

Moed Katan (Mid-Festival Days)

The use of the quotation, "He hath swallowed up death forever, and the Lord God will wipe away tears from off all faces; and the reproach of his people shall be taken away from off all the whole earth, for the Lord hath spoken it", from Isa 25:8 indicates that rabbinic theology shared the Old Testament eschatological hope of Israel.[16] Set in the context of a funeral ceremony during or at certain appointed feasts like the Feast of Dedication, the quotation is used as a definition of the eschatological hope of Israel when Yahweh will bring an end to the years of suffering and sorrow, inaugurating a period of salvation for Israel and the nations.

Sotah (The Suspected Adulteress)

One of the major teachings in this tractate is the view that the measure a man metes with shall be measured to him also whether it is for the better or for the worse. Samson and Absalom are cited as those who meted out a poor measure while Miriam, Joseph and Moses are cited as those who meted out a better measure. At that point the writer adduces Deut 34:6, "And he buried him in the valley", and Isa 58:8, "and thy righteousness shall go before thee; the glory of the Lord shall gather thee in death" to support the rabbinic view that the righteous are as great as Moses for just as Moses was buried by the Lord the righteous are gathered by the Lord's glory in their death.[17]

At Sotah 9:15, the quotation, "For the son dishonored the father, the daughter riseth up against her mother, the daughter –in-law against her mother-in-law: a man's enemies are the men of his own house", from Micah 7:6 is used as a theological springboard for a discussion on the eschatological signs which are to herald the coming of the Messiah at the end of the time of exile.[18]

---

[15]   Taanith 2:1, in Danby, The Mishnah, p.195.

[16]   See my discussion of Isa 2:4 under the tractate "Shabbath" above.

[17]   Sotah 1:7-9.

[18]   For a discussion of the footprints of the Messiah, see Sotah 9:15, in Danby, The Mishnah, p. 306.

Sanhedrin (The Sanhedrin)

At San 10:1, there is the quotation, "thy people also shall be all righteous, they shall inherit the land forever, the branch of my planting, the work of my hands that I may be glorified", from Isa 60:21. It is used to support the view that all Israelites shall be saved except those who reject the doctrine of the resurrection of the dead, those who deny that the Law is from heaven, those who read heretical books, those who are superstitious and those who are licentious and sceptical.[19]

At San 10:3, several quotations are used to support the view that some generations have no share in the world to come. Gen 6:3 is quoted as the theological basis for the view that the generation of the flood has no share in the world to come. Gen 11:8 is similarly applied to the generation of the dispersion; Gen 13:13 is applied to the people of Sodom; Num 14:37 to the Spies, Num 14:35 to the wilderness generation, and Deut.29:28 to the Ten Lost Tribes of Israel. But R. Akiba finds a theological basis for the salvation of the wilderness generation in a quotation from Ps 50:5, "Gather my saints together unto me, those that have made a covenant with me by sacrifice."

Eduyoth (Testimonies)

At Eduy 8;7, the quotation, "Behold, I will send you Elijah the prophet and he shall turn the heart of the fathers to the children and the heart of the children to their fathers," from Mal 4:5-6 provides the theological basis for the teaching that Elijah will not come to change the law but to bring an end to injustice and introduce peace into the world as a prelude to the Messianic age.

Aboth (The Fathers)

At Aboth 3:2 there are quotations which are used to support the rabbinic view of the Divine Presence, namely, that wherever the Law is being meditated the Lord's presence is guaranteed, whether the meditation is done individually or in a group, while where the Law is not meditated, the Shekinah does not rest. The quotation, "nor sitteth in the seat of the scornful" from Ps 1:1, is the basis for the postulation that where the Law is not meditated, the Lord absents himself, while the quotation, "Then they that feared the Lord spoke one with another: and a book of remembrance was written before him for them that feared the Lord, and that thought upon his name", from Mal 3:16 supports the view that where two people meditate the Law the Shekinah presents himself. The

---

[19]   Danby, The Mishnah, p. 397 and notes 4 and 5.

quotation, "Let him sit alone and keep silence, because he hath laid it upon him", from Lam 3:28 is then used to support the view that the Lord is present even to an individual who meditates upon the Law.

At About 3:6 the writer provides the theological basis for the view that the *Shekinah* is also present in a congregation of any size (a congregation has a minimum of ten people[20]). The quotation, "God standeth in the congregation of God", from Ps 82:1 supports the view that the Lord is present even in the minimum - size congregation. But further quotations support the view that the Lord presents himself even to congregations with less than ten people. Amos 9:6 supports the view that the Lord is present even among five worshippers; Ps 82:1, "he judgeth among the judges", supports Divine Presence among three worshippers; Mal 3:16 supports the Presence among two worshippers as indicated above; and the quotation, "In every place where I record my name I will come unto thee and I will bless thee", from Exod. 20:24 argues for the Presence to a single worshipper.

At About 3:7, the quotation, "For all things come of thee, and of thine own have we given thee", from I Chron 29:14 is cited by R. Eleazar b. Judah of Barlotha to support the view that people must give to God what is his own since the people themselves and whatever they have belong to him.

The writer uses some quotations at 6:8 which serve as a theological springboard for the discussion of the "Seven qualities" which in rabbinic theology are "reckoned as comely to the righteous".[21] The quotations are drawn from Prov 16:31; 20:29; 14:24; 17:6 and Isa 24:23. The blessings of the righteous include strength, riches, honour, wisdom, long life and children.

At About 6:9, the writer applies quotations from Ps 119:72; Prov 6:22 and Haggai 2:8 to support the rabbinic view that the Law is better and superior and more lasting than worldly riches, and that the Law protects and guides the righteous even after death.

At About 6:10, the writer applies quotations in order to define, in accordance with rabbinic theology, the five possessions which the Lord took to himself. These holy possessions are: the Law (Prov 8:22); heaven and earth (Isa 66:1; Ps. 104 :24); Abraham (Gen 14:19); Israel (Exod 14:16; Ps 16:3), and the Temple (Exod 15:17; Ps 78:54).

---

[20]   The number is based on Num 14:27. See Sanhedrin 1:6.

[21]   Danby, *The Mishnah*, p. 460.

Also at About 6:11, the writer has used quotations to support the view that all things were created for God's glory. The quotations from Isa 43:7 and Exod 15:18 have been cited to serve this purpose. And the quotation, "It pleased the Lord for his righteousness sake to magnify the Law and make it honourable", from Isa 42:21 has provided a theological basis for the rabbinic multiplication of the Law for Israel.

This analytical study of the use of biblical quotations in the *Mishnah* has revealed that biblical quotations have been consciously cited, with full scriptural authority,[22] in order to support rabbinic theological views on different aspects of religious interest. These quotations are almost always introduced by some introductory formula, for instance, "It is written", "And it says", "It says", "The prophet says", " Rabbi says, but the sages say'. Such formulas indicate that the quoted texts are not mere historical or linguistic allusions, but that they are consciously and carefully quoted to serve a specific theological purpose. This is a theological use of biblical quotations and serves as one possible background to Matthew's theological use of his fulfilment quotations.

The Dead Sea Scrolls

While the legal element characterizes the rabbinic theology reflected in the *Mishnah*, the apologetic element pervades all the Dead Sea Scrolls, an element shared with the New Testament writings. As it is with the *Mishnah*, it is often the case in the Dead Sea Scrolls that where a writer consciously and clearly cites a biblical quotation, a theological use of it can often be attested. The sectarian nature of the Dead Sea Scrolls helps to bring this phenomenon into sharp relief. Since the earliest Christian movement could from the point of view of official Judaism, be viewed as a sectary, similar use of biblical quotations could be expected from the New Testament writers. That the Dead Sea Scroll writers were conscious of using certain biblical quotations, and hence in many cases putting them to a theological use, is attested by the various introductory formulas with which they introduce such quotations. The most common introductory formulas are "It is written", and "interpreted this concerns", or its variant: "interpreted this means". Other introductory formulas include, "as God ordained by the hand of the Prophet. saying", "as he spoke by

---

[22]   For the view that Jewish scholars ascribed full scriptural authority of the basic Old Testament text regardless of the variants they might have introduced themselves into that text to better account for their own theological views, see Matthew Black, "The theological appropriation of the Old Testament by the New Testament", *Scottish Journal of Theology* Vol. 39, No1 (1986), pp. 3, 10-2.

the hand of . saying", "which is written", "and concerning the saying", "for this is what he said", "and as for that which he said", etc.

It is generally taken that the Dead Sea Scrolls and the community that used them are pre-Christian in their origin and dating.[23] This pre-Christian character of the scrolls would further suggest that the similarities they share with the evangelist Matthew in the theological use of quotations[24] point to an early date for the origin of his gospel.

The Community Rule (IQS)

The Doctrine of "Second Degree" Separation[25]

The Community Rule does not only teach that members of the covenant community turn away from sin but also teaches that covenant members disassociate themselves from all sinful people, which practically referred to all non-members of the covenant community. In support of the teaching on "second degree" holiness, the writer of this scroll quotes

---

[23]   For a brief discussion on the historical development of the Qumran Community, see Nkhoma, "The Significance of the Dead Sea Scrolls (Qumran Literature)", pp.1-2. Also, Black, "The Dead Sea Scrolls and Christian Origins", *Theological Collections II*, pp. 97-8; Albright and Mann, "Qumran and the Essenes", *Theological Collections II*, pp. 16-20; Kurt Schubert, *The Dead Sea Community, Its Origins and Teachings*, Westport: Greenwood, 1959, p. 25; Gaalyah Cornfeld, *Archaeology of the Bible*, London: Adams and Charles Black, 1977, p. 258; A. Powell Davies, *The Meaning of the Dead Sea Scrolls*, New York: The New American Library, 1956, pp. 25-42, especially p. 42 for the pre-Christian origin and character of the Scrolls and their community.

[24]   Similarities in literary techniques in the use of Old Testament quotations between the evangelist and the Dead Sea Scrolls was a major focus in previous Matthean quotations research, especially as carried out by Stendahl as I have argued in Chapter 1. For a discussion on the hermeneutical principles practiced by the Qumran Community in their interpretation of Scripture, See F.F. Bruce, *Biblical Exegesis in the Qumran Texts*, London: Tyndale, 1960, especially pp. 8-17, 75-88. For a more recent discussion on the similarities between the Qumran Scrolls and the New Testament in general, see James C. VanderKam, *The Dead Sea Scrolls Today*, Grand Rapids: Wm. B. Eerdmans, 1994, pp. 163-84. For the opposing view that these similarities do not go very far and that the evangelist must be seen as commenting on the Marcan Gospel rather than the prophetic writings, see A.R.C. Leaney *et al.* (eds.), *A Guide to the Scrolls, Nottingham Studies on the Qumran Discoveries*, London: SCM, 1958, p. 95.

[25]   The term 'second degree separation', is used by Klaus Fiedler to describe the Christian groups or movements that actively and formally endeavour not only to keep away from any known sin but also to keep away from any known sinners or any corporate institution that deals with such sinners. Fiedler further suggests that in terms of the history of Christian missions this attitude goes back to John Nelson Darby. See Klaus Fiedler, *The Story of Faith Missions*, Oxford: Regnum and Lynx, 1994, p. 22 and note 20, also pp. 119-20.

Exod 23:7, "Keep away from the man in whose nostrils is breath, for wherein is he to be accounted of ?"[26]

The Doctrine of the Council of the Community

The Council of the covenant community is portrayed in eschatological terms, as an embodiment of the eschatological Elijah who returns at the end of time to prepare Israel, the people of God, for the imminent coming of the Messiah. It is vested with messianic qualities and powers:

> In the council of the community there shall be twelve men and three priests, perfectly versed in all that is revealed of the Law, whose works shall be truth, righteousness, justice, loving-kindness and humility. They shall preserve the faith in the land with steadfastness, and meekness, and shall atone for sin by the practice of justice and by suffering the sorrows of affliction... when these are in Israel the council of the community shall be established in truth. It shall be an Everlasting Plantation, a House of Holiness for Israel, an Assembly of Supreme Holiness for Aaron. They shall be witness to the judgment, and shall be the elect of Good Will who shall atone for the land and pay to the wicked their reward.[27]

In support of this view of the Council of the community the quotation, "precious corner-stone", probably from Zech 4:7, is cited to provide the theological basis for the eschatological and messianic character that is attributed to it. Then the quotation "prepare in the wilderness the way of . make straight in the desert a path for our God", from Isa 40:3 is then adduced to serve as a theological basis for its preparatory role for the coming Messiah. The preparing of the way in the wilderness for the Messiah is understood by the covenant community as referring to the ardent study of the Law and its scrupulous application in the life of the covenant community, away from the habitation of the ungodly men.

The Damascus Rule (CD)

The Doctrine of Salvation

In support of the sectarian teaching on salvation the writer of this scroll uses the quotation from Amos 5:26-27 as a theological basis for the promise of salvation that God has made to the covenant community. Ordinarily in the Old Testament context, this Amos text serves as a

---

[26] G. Vermes, *The Dead Sea Scrolls in English*, Third Edition; London: Penguin, 1987, pp. 67-8, cf. *p.* 86-7.

[27] IQS viii, *ibid.* p. 72.

threat to Israel. The people of Israel are threatened to go into exile along with their idols because they have forsaken the Lord.[28] The biblical text reads, "You shall take up Sakkuth your king and Kaiwan your star-god, your images which you made for yourselves, for I will take you into exile beyond Damascus". The Damascus rule, however, changes the threat into a promise of salvation to the covenant community. To achieve this end the biblical text is reworked changing some words and leaving out others so that the new text now reads, "I will exile the tabernacle of your king and the bases of your statues from my tent to Damascus". A symbolic meaning is then accorded to the key phrases so that now the word "tabernacle" refers to the books of the Law, the word "king " refers to the congregation of the covenant community and the phrase "bases of statues" refers to the book of the prophets. In this way, the biblical quotation is made to apply, not to the exile of apostate Israel, but rather to the "exile" of the covenant community to the land of Damascus where this community develops into a truly saved remnant of Israel, the only true Israel through which the promises of God are to find their eschatological fulfilment.[29]

The transformation of the text of this verse by the writer of this scroll, in order to adapt it into a form that serves the writers' intended theological purpose, provides us a good example of a biblical text which is forced by the interpreter to speak on issues of his interest regardless of its Old Testament context. In such cases, the theological view that the interpreter holds becomes a determining factor of the final text to appear in his work. In the present case, it is the eschatological nature of the community to which the writer or interpreter belongs that has determined the final form of his quoted text. In the case of a New Testament writer similar considerations relating to the *Kerygma* would account for some textual variants in a biblical quotation.[30]

The Doctrine of the "Age of Wrath" and the Remnant
The writer of this scroll uses the quotation, "Like a stubborn heifer thus was Israel stubborn", from Hos 4:16 as a theological definition of the

[28]   Jacob M. Myers, *Hosea, Joel, Amos, Obadiah, Jonah*, LBC, Vol. 14, Richmond: John Knox, 1959, p.132.

[29]   Vermes, *The Dead Sea Scrolls in English*, p. 82.

[30]   Black, "The Theological Appropriation of the Old Testament by the New Testament", p. 6. cf. C.F.D. Moule, *The Birth of the New Testament*, London: Black, 1962, p. 79.

period of apostasy in Israel during which the covenant community was born, and he calls this period, "the age of wrath":

> And in the age of wrath, three hundred and ninety years after he had given them into the hand of King Nebuchadnezzar of Babylon, He visited them and He caused a plant root to spring from Israel and Aaron to inherit his Land and to prosper on the good things of His earth.[31]

While the apostate state of Israel was a long-standing problem, the crucial issue in the age of wrath was the rise of opposition to the teaching of the covenant community and its subsequent persecution by these opponents:

> When the Scoffer arose who shed over Israel the waters of lies. He caused them to wander in a pathless wilderness... abolishing the ways of righteousness ... that he might call down on them curses of his covenant and deliver them up to the avenging sword of the covenant . and they justified the wicked and condemned the just ... they banded together against the life of the righteous and loathed all who walked in perfection.[32]

In these difficult circumstances, however, the remnant, following their repentance, persevered even before a strong leadership developed among them, "for twenty years they were like blind men groping for the way."[33] At the end of the "twenty years", however, God raised for them a leader, the Teacher of Righteousness, who organized the remnant into a well-established, eschatological covenant community:

> But with the remnant which held fast to the commandments of God he made His covenant with Israel forever, revealing to them the hidden things in which all Israel had gone astray. He unfolded before them his holy Sabbaths and his glorious feasts, the testimonies of his righteousness and the ways of his truth, and the desires of his will which a man must do in order to live... and he built them a sure home in Israel whose like has never existed from former times till now. Those who hold fast to it are destined to live forever and all the glory of Adam shall be theirs. [34]

To support this bold claim to the state of being an eschatological community, the only true remnant of Israel in whom all the promises of God find

---

[31] CD1, in Vermes, *The Dead Sea Scrolls in English*, p. 83.
[32] *Ibid.*
[33] *Ibid.*
[34] CD III, *ibid.*, p. 85.

their ultimate fulfilment, the writer uses the quotation, "The priests, the Levites and the sons of Zadok who kept the charge of my sanctuary when the children of Israel strayed from me they shall offer me fat and blood", from Ezek 44:15. He then interprets the key words and phrases, "priests", "Levites", and "sons of Zadok", as referring to the converts and the elect of Israel who are, in fact, the members of the covenant community themselves.

The age of wrath is at the same time the period of grace for those who repent and join the covenant community. But there will come a time when grace shall be no more for God shall no longer forgive their sins and let them enter into his covenant community:

> Until the age is completed, according to the number of those years, all who enter after them shall do according to that interpretation of the Law in which the first were instructed. According to the covenant which God made with the forefathers, forgiving their sins also. But when the age is completed there shall be no more joining the house of Judah, but each man shall stand on his watchtower.[35]

The theological basis for this teaching that the period of grace will come to an end and there after none will be saved is the quotation from Micah 7:11, "The wall is built the boundary far removed".

During the age of wrath a great temptation will befall Israel. Satan will set up three nets, namely, fornication, riches and profanation of the Temple. The Devil will present these three forms of righteousness, and thus cause many to fall. The theological basis for this teaching on the "three nets" is the quotation, "Terror and the pit and the snare are upon you, O inhabitants of the land", from Isa 24:17.[36]

The Doctrine of Marriage

The reference to fornication as one of the great temptations leads to the theological consideration of the institution of marriage. Here, the writer uses some quotations in support of monogamy as a divinely instituted form of marriage. He quotes Gen 1:27, "male and female created he them", as a definition of the principle of creation with regard to marriage. This means marriage can only be entered into by one man and one woman, just as God in the beginning created only one man and one

---

[35] CD IV, *ibid.*, pp. 85-6.
[36] *Ibid.*

woman. Then the quotation, "there went in two and two unto Noah into the ark, the male and the female, as God had commanded Noah", from Gen 7:9 is referred to in support of the same position on marriage. He further argues that this divine principle applies even to kings, "And concerning the prince it is written, 'he shall not multiply wives to himself'", from Deut 17:17.[37]

On the law of marriage concerning relations of forbidden degrees the covenanters come to a quite distinctive theological position in spite of the fact that the covenanters, the Pharisees and the rabbis based their teaching on the same text. The text is used as a theological support to a marriage between an uncle and his niece in Pharisaic and rabbinic Judaism. But the covenanters, by not only applying the laws of incest to men but also to women, they conclude that the text, which is Lev 18:13, is a theological basis for condemning such forms of marriage:

> And each man marries the daughter of his brother or sister, whereas Moses said, "You shall not approach your mothers sister, she is your mother's near kin" (Lev 18:13). But although the laws against incest are written for men, they also apply to women. When therefore, a brother's daughter uncovers the nakedness of her father's brother, she is (also) his near kin.[38]

The Doctrine of the Covenant Law

I have already made reference to the establishment of the covenant community by the Teacher of Righteousness when discussing the doctrines of the Council of the community and the age of wrath above. Here, it will be sufficient to look at the chief aim of the community. In response to God's gracious establishment of their covenant community as the only valid form of eternal relationship between God and Israel, the community made the observation of the Law, as interpreted by its founder and leader, the chief aim of its existence. They committed themselves to the observance of the Law with absolute faithfulness:

> Everyman who enters the Council of Holiness (the Council of those) who walk in the way of perfection as commanded by God, and who deliberately or through negligence transgresses one word of the Law of Moses, on any point whatever, shall be

---

[37] To defend David's involvement in polygamy, and thus violating this principle, the writer argues that David never saw the sealed book of the Law which was in the Ark of the Covenant because it remained sealed and hidden from the days of Eleazer and Joshua to the days of Zadok when it was revealed. See CD.V, in Vermes, *The Dead Sea Scroll in English*, p. 86.

[38] *Ibid.*

expelled from the Council of the Community and shall return no more.[39]

Thus, their chief purpose was "the study of the Law which he commanded by the hand of Moses, that they may do according to all that has been revealed from age to age, and as the Prophets have revealed by His holy spirit."[40] Hence, in the theology of the covenanters knowledge of the Law is itself a gift from God. But this theological principle is expressed in a poetic language which strongly alludes to the Old Testament poetic language of the Psalms, a language which is so characteristic of biblical poetic literature that it is almost impossible to consider it as a specific biblical quotation:

> From the source of his righteousness
> Is my justification
> And from his marvelous mysteries
> Is the light in my heart
> My eyes have gazed
> On that which is eternal,
> On wisdom concealed from men
> On knowledge and wise design
> (hidden) from the sons of men;
> On a fountain of righteousness
> And on a store house of power
> On a spring of glory
> (hidden) from the assembly of flesh.
> God has given them to his chosen ones
> As an everlasting possession.[41]

This is an example of *literary use* of biblical quotations, taking the form of linguistic allusions to the Old Testament. We cannot classify this as a theological use of a biblical quotation since it is almost impossible to show that the writer is quoting any specific biblical text in the first place. What might be considered as quotations in such a passage (a somewhat common scholarly practice in dealing with Old Testament apocryphal books) might actually have risen from the writer's mere familiarity with Old Testament poetic language.

Due to their knowledge of the Law, the covenanters regard themselves as "men of discernment men of wisdom" and find their own

---

[39]   IQS viii, *ibid.,* p.73.

[40]   IQS viii; 14-16, *ibid.,* Vermes, *The Dead Sea Scrolls English,* p. 73.

[41]   IQS xi, Vermes, *ibid.,* p. 78-9.

embankment on the Law as a theological (eschatological) fulfilment of the quotation, "the well which the princes dug, which the nobles of the people delved with the stave", from Num 21:18. They understood the word "well" as referring to the original members of the covenant community who fled to Damascus who God honoured by designating them as "princes", while the term "stave" is applied to the Interpreter of the Law to whom is also applied the quotation, "He makes a tool for his work" from Isa 54:16.[42]

The Doctrine of the Divine Visitation

In the age of wrath, the covenant community will continue to abide by the Law of Moses as interpreted by the Interpreter of the Law or Teacher of Righteousness. However, at the end of days God shall visit the land. The members of the covenant community shall have a long blessed life extending to thousands of generations. This eschatological blessing is based on the quotation, "keeping the covenant and grace with those who love me and keep my commandments, to a thousand generations", from Deut 7:7. The eschatological fate of those who despise the covenant law of the community will experience the retribution of the wicked. This finds a theological ground in the quotation, "He will bring upon you, and upon your people, and upon your father's house, days such as have not come since the day that Ephraim departed from Judah", from Isa 7:7 . In a variant text, the visitation is based on a quotation from Zech 13:7, "Awake, O Sword, against my companion, says God. Strike the shepherd that the flock may be scattered and I will stretch my hand over the little ones". This is understood to mean that the "little ones" are those who wait for Him and will be saved while others will be given to the sword at the coming of the Anointed of Aaron and Israel. The visitation is further clarified by the precedence it has in a former visitation which was itself a fulfilment of the quotation, "they shall put a mark on the foreheads of those who sigh and groan", from Ezek 9:4. Thus the quotations cited are theologically used to highlight the nature of the eschatological visitation of the messianic ruler (s) of Aaron and Israel.

The former visitation that the writer refers to is the incident of the division of the Kingdom of Israel after the reign of Solomon:

> When the two houses of Israel were divided, Ephraim departed from Judah. And all the apostates were given up to the sword, but those who held fast escaped to the land of the north, as God said, "I will exile the tabernacle of your king and the bases of your statues from my tent to Damascus" (Amos 5:26-27).[43]

---

[42]   CD vi, Vermes, *ibid.*, p. 87.
[43]   CD vii, Vermes, *ibid.*, p. 88.

The quotation from Amos 5:26-27 is used as a theological basis for the salvation promised to the members of the covenant community who probably founded the Damascus group of the covenanters.[44]

The Doctrine of Election

Just as Israel considered herself the elect of God, his special possession (Deut 7:6, 11), the Qumran covenant community was convinced that it was only its members that were to be conceived as the "new covenant" community (Jer 31:31-33; Isa 54:13), the true Israel and the only elect of God. Their election is, in the present scroll, defined in poetic language that is reminiscent of the Old Testament poetic books:

> (God) has caused (His chosen ones)
> To inherit
> The lot of the Holy Ones
> He has joined their assembly
> To the sons of heaven
> To be a Council of the Community
> A foundation of the Building of Holiness,
> And eternal plantation throughout all
> Ages to come.[45]

This is another instance where the theology of the community is defined in terms of language which alludes to or even quotes the biblical texts.

---

[44]   For further discussion of the Amos 5:26-27 quotation, see the section 'the Doctrine of salvation", above. But the suggestion that the verse refers to the establishment of the Damascus group of the covenant community must only be taken as a tentative one. It is not even clear whether the name, Damascus, was meant to be understood literally. Any attempt to link the historical allusions in the Dead Sea Scrolls to attested historical events remains an issue of great difficulty although broadly speaking the sect is often linked with the Hasidim, a group of pious Jews which probably first appeared in the Maccabean period. For a discussion on the historical question of the covenanters, see Vermes, *The Dead Sea Scrolls in English*, pp. 19-35; Schubert, *The Dead Sea Community, its origins and teachings*, pp. 25,31-41; Frank M. Cross, *The Ancient Library of Qumran and Modern Biblical Studies*, Wesport: Greenwood, 1958, reprint 1976, pp. 42-8. For a critical evaluation of the generally accepted dates and in favour of a late date of origin, probably in the first century AD, see G.R. Driver, *The Judean Scrolls, the Problem and Solution*, Oxford: Basil Blackwell, 1965, especially pp. 359-439. For a more recent assessment of the historical question, see James C. VanderKam, "Calendrical Texts and the Origins of the Dead Sea Scroll Community", in Michael O. Wise *et.al.* (eds), *Methods of Investigation of the Dead Sea Scrolls and the Khirbet Qumran Site, Present Realities and Future Prospects*, New York: the New York Academy of Sciences, 1994, p. 384, who observe that "the combination of data lying behind the thesis that a community began to live in the area of Qumran – a community that had brought scrolls with them, copied some, and obtained more in other ways – in the mid-second century B.C.E. and continued there until the first revolt against Rome remains convincing and that no rival theory is close to it in plausibility".

[45]   IQS xi, in Vermes, *The Dead Sea Scrolls in English*, p. 79.

However, it is almost impossible to determine with certainty any passages that are specifically used, rendering it impossible for us to verify the theological use of any particular texts in the passage, if any specific text is being quoted at all. This is what I have referred to as a *literary use* of biblical quotations. In such cases not only is the quotation's theological role not obvious but also the determination of whether any quotation really exists can be no more than a mere conjecture. It is, therefore, hazardous to treat such passages as quotations, let alone as quotations with a specific theological function. They would best be referred to as mere allusions.

The Doctrine of the Community's Discipline

The quotation, "You shall not take vengeance on the children of your people, nor bear any rancour against them," from Lev 19:18 is used as a theological basis for an orderly presentation of grievances within the community. On the basis of this quotation, members of the community are not allowed to accuse a fellow member personally or privately before presenting one's grievance against the offender in the presence of witnesses. Further, none is allowed to denounce his offender in the heat of his anger, or report the incident to elders in a manner that makes him appear contemptible. On the basis of the quotation, "You shall rebuke your companion and not be burdened with sin because of him," from Lev 19:17, the teaching is developed that no member should keep his anger until the following day without making any immediate effort to resolve the matter on the same day it arises.[46]

To support the teaching that no one who is past sixty years of age should hold the office of judge in the community, a quotation is cited from the book of Jubilees 23:11, "Because man sinned his days have been shortened and in the heat of His anger against the inhabitants of the earth God ordained that their days are completed".[47]

The quotation from Exod 18:25, "thousands, hundreds, fifties and tens", is also used as a theological basis for the ecclesiastical principle that the members of the covenant community have to be divided into groups of at least ten men including a priest who is to assume, almost automatically, the leadership role within the group.[48]

This Rule concerning members of the covenant community who dwell in camps has a binding character and it is administered by the Guardian of the Camp. Its binding force will remain throughout the age of

---

[46] CD ix, Vermes, *ibid.*, p. 93.
[47] CD ix, Vermes, *ibid.*, p. 94.
[48] CD ix, Vermes, *ibid.*, p. 97.

wickedness until the end of days when the Messiah of Aaron and Israel shall come when the final reward shall be meted out to each according to his ways: retribution of the wicked to those who do not hold fast to these precepts and salvation to those who walk in these statutes. As before, [49] the eschatological distribution of rewards finds its theological basis on the quotation, "There shall come upon you, and upon your people, and upon your father's house, days such as have not come since Ephraim departed from Judah', from Isa 7:7.

---

[49]   See my discussion under "The Doctrine of Divine visitation" above.

The Doctrine of the Sabbath

On the basis of the quotation, "Observe the Sabbath day to keep it holy", from Deut 5:12, a whole series of Sabbath regulations are developed. Members were to abstain from labour from sunset on the sixth day and throughout the seventh, i.e., the Sabbath Day. They could not engage in any monitory transaction and could not go out of the house on any financial business. In fact, they were never to go beyond 500 yards (450 meters) from their house, although they would pasture their beasts at a distance of 1000 yards (900 meters) away from their town. They could not pick up and eat fruit or anything edible lying on the ground or from a tree plant in the field. They could not draw water and carry it but drink from where it was. One could not whip his beast or reprimand his servant. None could carry a child, apply perfume or even sweep the house. An animal in labour could not be assisted nor could one that falls into a pit. However, they could rescue a man out of water or fire using a ladder or a rope.[50] The quotation, "Except your Sabbath offering," from Lev 23:38 is used as the theological basis for the teaching that no man could offer any offering on the Sabbath except the Sabbath burnt offering. And on the basis of the quotation, "The sacrifice of the wicked is an abomination, but the prayer of the just is an agreeable offering", from Prov 15:8 is founded the doctrine that no one should send any burnt-offering or cereal offering or incense "by the hand of one smitten with any uncleanliness, permitting him thus to defile the altar",[51] i.e., through someone who is ritually unclean.

The War Rule (IQM, 4QM)
The Doctrine of the Messiah
(1) The War of the Messiah

The theological basis for the view that the eschatological battle in which Satan will suffer an ultimate defeat shall be fought by the Lord's Messiah and that the covenant community totally depended on his success is found in the quotation, "A star shall come out of Jacob and a sceptre shall rise out of Israel. He shall smite the temples of Moab and destroy all the children of Seth. He shall rule out of Jacob and shall cause the survivors of the city to perish. The enemy shall be his possession and Israel shall accomplish mighty deeds", from Num 24:17-19. This defines

---

[50]   CD x-xi, in Vermes, *The Dead Sea Scrolls in English*, p. 95.

[51]   CD xi, *ibid.*, p. 96

the ultimate salvation of the covenant community.[52] The hour of this eschatological war when God will deliver the mighty Kittim and the whole world into the hands of the covenanters is said to be theologically foretold in the quotation, "Assyria shall fall by the sword of no man, the sword of no mere man shall devour him", from Isa 31:8.[53]

The Blessings of Jacob (4QP Bless)

(2)   The Reign of the Messiah

In this scroll is found a quotation which serves as a theological basis for the Davidic covenant in which it is ensured that a Davidic heir will always occupy the throne of Israel until the Messiah of Righteousness, himself from David, comes. The quotation is, "The sceptre shall not depart from the tribe of Judah, nor the rulers' staff from between his feet, until he comes to whom it belongs. And the peoples shall be in obedience to him", from Gen 49:10. "The sceptre From the tribe of Judah" finds an initial fulfilment in Davidic kingship, which will be maintained by Davidic heirs until the Davidic heir par-excellence occupies the throne forever. The commentator, thus implies that all non-Davidic rulers are only usurpers to the throne. If the historical context of this scroll is the Hasmonean period, the implication would be that the Hasmonean rulers occupy the throne illegally.[54] Since the covenant community is now the only true remnant of Israel, the only chosen ones of God, this Davidic covenant will now be ultimately fulfilled in the Messiah of Israel who will accompany the Messiah of Aaron at the end of days. The duty of the community, as the only true Israel, is thus to prepare for the coming of the Messiahs.

Commentaries of Isaiah (4Q161-4)

The eschatological reign of the Davidic Messiah is further supported by the quotation from Isa 11:1-3:

---

[52]   IQM, 4QM xi, in Vermes, *The Dead Sea Scrolls in English*, p. 116; cp, p.82 where the star is understood as the Messianic Interpreter of the Law who will at the end of time come with his Messianic companion, the Prince of the Congregation.

[53]   *Ibid.*

[54]   4QP Bless, *ibid.*, p. 260.

4Q 161:

> And there shall come forth a rod from the stem of Jesse and a Branch shall grow out of its roots. And the Spirit of the Lord shall rest upon him, the spirit of knowledge and of the fear of the Lord. And his delight shall be in the fear of the Lord. He shall not judge by what his eyes see, or pass sentence by what his ears hear; he shall judge the poor righteously and shall pass sentence justly on the humble of the earth.[55]

Thus, the Davidic Messiah shall be vested with divine royal powers through his anointment by the Spirit of God and shall rule with wisdom and authority all the nations of the world.

Despite these royal powers, however, the Davidic Messiah shall occupy a secondary position to his priestly counterpart since the latter will teach him the art of government: "interpreted, this means that (the priests) . As they teach him, so will he judge; and as they order, (so will he pass sentence)." This is the covenanters' theological understanding of the section, "he shall not judge by what his eyes see or pass sentence by what his ears hear", of the Isaiah text quoted above.

4Q162: The Doctrine of the Divine Visitation

The view that the land of Israel shall be devastated by the sword and famine in the last days is here derived from the quotation, "For ten acres of vineyard shall produce only one (bath), and an (omer) of seed shall yield but one (ephah)", from Isa 11:10. The fate of apostate Israel, especially the "Scoffer in Jerusalem", is further seen in Isa 11:11-14, 24-25. Thus because Israel has despised the Law as given to the covenanters, its people together with its misguided leadership will go into exile and the land will lie desolate.[56]

4Q163:

Here the verses in Isa 30:14-18 are quoted to further define the eschatological fate of apostate Israel and its leaders who despise the Law as revealed to the covenant community. Despite the proclamation of doom, there is a promise of salvation, even for "those who seek smooth things in Jerusalem" once they repent because the Lord is a gracious God. This promise of salvation is derived from the quoted text of Isa 30:19-20.

---

[55] 4Q 161 xi, 1-3, *ibid.*, p. 268

[56] *Ibid.*, pp. 268-69

O people of Zion who live in Jerusalem, you shall weep no more. At the sound of your crying He will be gracious to you; He will answer you when He hears it. Although the Lord give you bread of oppression and water of distress, your Teacher shall be hidden no more and your eyes shall see your teacher.[57]

4 Q 164: The Doctrine of the Council of the Community

In this fragment the quotation, "And I will lay your foundations with sapphire," from Isa 54:11c is applied to the founders of the covenant community. This further indicates that the covenanters viewed themselves as an eschatological community of the elect of God in whom scriptures find their eschatological fulfilment.[58]

Commentaries on Hosea (4 Q 166-7)

The Doctrine of Divine Visitation on Apostate Israel

The quotation, "She knew not that it was I who gave her the new wine and oil, who lavished upon her silver and gold which they used for Baal", from Hosea 2:8, is again applied to apostate Israel pictured as an unfaithful wife to her husband going after other men. Israel has been led astray by her lovers, that is Gentiles and their idols.

Israel has become apostate through the influence of secularism from other nations. The consequence of this unfaithfulness to her true husband, Yahweh, will be divine judgment upon her, in full view of those who led her away, that is, Gentiles. This divine visitation upon Israel finds its theological basis on verses 9-12, which the writer also fully quotes.[59]

Commentary on Micah (1 Q 14)

In a commentary on this prophetic book preserved in tiny fragments, the writer finds that the text in Micah 1:5-6 defines and foretells the two eschatological groups that are deadly opposed to each other, namely, the leader or founder of the covenant community and the "Spouter of Lies", the enemy of the sect, especially in the reference to Samaria and Jerusalem:

All this is for the transgression of Jacob and for the sins of the House of Israel. What is the transgression of Jacob? Is it not

---

[57]   *Ibid.*, p. 269.
[58]   *Ibid.*
[59]   4Q166-7, *ibid.*, pp. 276-77.

Samaria? And what is the high place of Judah? Is it not Jerusalem? I will make of Samaria a ruin in the fields, and of Jerusalem a plantation of vines.[60]

The interpretation implies that the reference to Samaria concern the Spouter of Lies who had led many astray. The reference to Jerusalem is clearly interpreted as concerning the Teacher of Righteousness who interprets the Law to all so that those who accept his teaching and join the community can be saved on the Day of Judgment.

Commentary on Nahum (4Q169)

In this scroll the writer continues a discussion concerning the divine visitation. The quotation, "The prowler is not wanting, noise of whip and noise of rattling wheel, prancing horses and jolting chariot, charging horsemen, flame and glittering spear, a multitude of slain and a heap of carcases. There is no end to the corpses; they stumble upon their corpses", from Nahum 3:1-3 continues to define, in the theological understanding of the covenanters, the divine judgment that will fall on apostate Israel, that is the seekers of "smooth things" (those who despise the covenanters) in a form of military invasions, killings and captivity by foreign nations:

> Interpreted, this concerns the dominion of those who seek smooth things, from the midst of whose assembly the sword of the nations shall never be wanting. Captivity, looting, and burning shall be among them, and exile from dread of the enemy. A multitude of guilty corpses shall fall in their days; there shall be no end to the sum of their slain. They shall also stumble upon their body of flesh because of their guilty counsel.[61]

Similarly, a quotation from Nahum 3:4, fully quoted, is applied to false teachers and enemies of the community who lead many away from God in Israel with many families and cities and people from various levels of the social structure perishing. Nahum 3:7b is again fully cited as a theological basis for the same view that the eschatological wrath will fall upon the seekers of smooth things who lead people astray while the simple will repent and join the covenant community. To the same theological use are put the quotations from Nahum 3:9b; 3:10, 11a, 11b, among others. The wicked of Judah (i.e., the opponents of the community) who join Manasseh and Ephraim themselves shall suffer an

---

[60]   IQ14, *ibid.*, p. 278.
[61]   4Q169, II, *ibid.*, p. 281.

eschatological defeat under Israel (i.e., members of the covenant community).[62]

Commentary on Habakkuk (IQP Hab)

The Habakkuk scroll has been one of the most important sources for scholarship on Qumran literature. The theology of the scroll centers on the same theme of divine judgment or visitation. The enemies of the covenant community will be condemned while there will be salvation for the covenant community itself. The enemy is presented in the form of "Wicked Priest", "Spouter of Lies". Judgment is seen in terms of an eschatological military invasion by the "Kittim", a mighty nation chosen by God as an instrument of judgment. The covenant community is represented in the person of its leader-founder, the "Teacher of Righteousness", also known as the chosen "Priest". The biblical quotations in this scroll are mainly applied theologically to these three groups of players in the eschatological drama, namely: the *enemies* of God, the *elect* of God, and the *instrument* for God's judgment.

The quotation in Hab 1:3b – 4b is applied to the opponents of the covenant community who despise the Law of God and Hab 1:1-3a provides the basis for a theological explanation for the cries of the founding members of the community at its very beginning as it sought God's intervention to its persecution: "How long, O Lord, shall I cry for help and thou will not hear? Or shout to Thee 'Violence', and Thou wilt not deliver? Why dost thou cause me to see iniquity and to look upon trouble? Desolation and violence are before me. For the wicked encompasses the righteousness" (Hab 1:1-3a, 4c).

The quotation at Hab 1:5, "Behold the nations and see, marvel and be astonished, for I accomplish a deed in your days, but you will not believe it when told", provides a theological explanation for three distinctive groups of non-believers in the theology of the covenanters:

> Interpreted, this concerns those who were unfaithful together with the Liar in that they did not listen to the word received by the Teacher of Righteousness from the mouth of God. And it concerns the unfaithful of the New Covenant (i.e., unfaithful members of the covenant community) in that they have not believed in the covenant of God and have profaned his holy name. And likewise this saying is to be interpreted as concerning those who will be unfaithful at the end of days. They, the men of violence and the breakers of the covenant, will not believe when they hear all that is to happen to the final generation from the Priest in whose heart God set

---

[62]   4Q169, II-IV, *ibid.*, pp. 281-82.

> understanding that he might interpret all the words of His servants, the prophets, through whom he foretold all that would happen to His people and His land.[63]

Thus, the three groups are those who never accept the teaching of the Teacher of Righteousness, those who accept it but remain unfaithful to its covenantal terms, and those who shall be unfaithful to the covenantal provisions at the end of time.

In order to explain the military prowess and the terrible eschatological devastation that will be caused by the Kittim, the chosen instrument for divine judgment, quotations are drawn from Hab 1:6, 7, 8-11.[64] The quoted text in Hab 1:12-13a theologically defines the view that the covenant community shall itself be used as a tool for divine judgment for the nations.[65]

The quotation, " O traitor, why do you stare and stay silent when the wicked swallows up one more righteous than he", from Hab 1:13b is theologically applied as an explanation for a group which did not support the Teacher of Righteousness in his struggles with his enemies at the very beginning of the covenant community.

The focus shifts from the community back to the Kittim in the interpretation to Hab 1:14-16, 17, where it is further portrayed as a great army which swiftly conquers nation after nation, destroying devastatingly many lands and many lives, amassing great wealth in the process for themselves and glorifying their idols.[66]

Several other quotations have been used theologically in this commentary. The quotation from Hab 2:1-2 provides a theological basis for the view that the biblical prophet Habakkuk received the vision of what would happen to the last generation, i.e., the generation of the covenanters themselves and their contemporaries. However, it is held that God did not make known to the prophet the time when the world would come to an end. But it is taught that the portion which says, "that he who reads may read speedily", in the verses just referred to, does show that God has made known all the mysteries of the words that he

---

[63]   IQP Hab, II, *ibid.*, pp. 283-84.

[64]   IQP Hab, II-III, *ibid.*, pp. 284-85.

[65]   This abrupt change in the theological meaning regarding their divine instrument for judgment from the "Kittim" to "His elect" temporarily disrupts the view that the instrument for the eschatological judgment is the "Kittim", a view that is maintained elsewhere in this commentary. See *Ibid.*

[66]   IQP Hab, V, in Vermes, *The Dead Sea Scrolls in English*, p. 286.

spoke through his servants the prophets to the Teacher of Righteousness who, inspired, now engages in the interpretation of these prophetic messages which now begin to be fulfilled in this eschatological generation. Hab. 2:3a is quoted to support the view that the final age shall be prolonged and exceed all the prophetic sayings. Hab 2:4b, "But the righteous shall live by faith", is applied to all who observe the law who shall be delivered from judgment because of their suffering and faith in the Teacher of Righteousness.

The quotations from Hab 2:5-6, 7-8a, 8b, 9-11, 15, 16 and 17 are rather forcedly made to theologically define the Wicked Priest who is the contemporary archenemy of the Teacher of Righteousness, founder of the covenant community. In the Old Testament context, this prophetic passage refers to the Great Power of Babylon, a Power which God had chosen as an instrument for administering his divine judgment upon nations. After its mission, this Great Power would then be accounted responsible for their ruthless and devastating behaviour so that it gets its own share of divine judgment in a measure equal to the one it meted out to other nations.[67] In the Qumran commentary, however, this part of the text is applied to a local oppressor, the Wicked Priest. The text, however, appears to favour the application to an external oppressor in which case its application to the Kittim would be more appropriate.[68] It provides a theological basis for the teaching of the covenant community regarding the false teachings of the Wicked Priest and the divine wrath that awaited him.[69] The quotations from Hab 2:18 and 2:19-20 provide the basis for the teaching that on the judgment day idols will not deliver anyone from divine punishment.[70]

Commentary on Psalms (4Q171, 4Q173)
4Q171

In this scroll the theme of divine visitation or judgment continues. The major portion of this fragment is a commentary on Psalms 37. It outlines the fate of the righteous and the wicked in terms of the story of the

[67] Maria E. Szeles, *Wrath and Mercy, A commentary on the Book of Habakkuk and Zephaniah*, Grand Rapids: Wm B. Eerdmans and Edinburgh: Handsel, 1987, pp. 35-9. Cf. David E. Baker, *Nahum, Habakkuk and Zephaniah, An Introduction and Commentary*, Leicester: Inter-Varsity, 1988, pp. 61-8.
[68] For the view that both applications are implied in the text and that the references to both a local oppressor and a foreign oppressor are inseparably twinned together, see James H. Galley. Jr: *Micah, Nahum, Habakkuk, Zephaniah, Haggai, Zechariah, Malachi*, LBC Vol. 15, Richmond: John Knox, 1962, pp. 63-5.
[69] IQP Hab viii-xiii, in Vermes, *The Dead Sea Scrolls in English*, pp. 287-89.
[70] IQP Hab xii-xiii, *ibid.*, p. 289.

covenant community and its opponents, especially the struggle between the Teacher of Righteousness and the Wicked Priest. Since the community is already living in an eschatological period, it is the final generation and consequently all Scriptures find their ultimate fulfilment in the life of the covenant community and its contemporaries.

The quotation from Ps 37:7a finds its eschatological fulfilment in the Liar (i.e., the Wicked Priest) who has led many people astray, away from the Teacher of Righteousness, to the destruction by sword, famine and plague of those who are led away. The quotation from Ps 37:8-9 is applied to those who return to the Law and join the covenant community while those who do not repent are cut off from the people of God, and are subjected to complete destruction. Similarly the texts quoted from Ps 37:10, 11, 14-15, 18-19a, 19b-20a, 20b, 20c, 21-22, 23-24, 32-33 are all used to highlight theologically on the condemnation of the wicked and enemies of the covenant community and on the salvation of the members of the covenant community and those who repent and join it.[71]

4Q173

The quotation, "Vain is it for you to rise early and lie down late. You shall eat the bread of toil, he shall feed those who love him in their sleep", from Ps 127:2 is used as a theological springboard for the teaching that at the end of the age people will anxiously seek the Teacher of Righteousness. In the Old Testament context, the Psalm teaches that God is the ultimate source of everything, without denying the significance of human efforts in the support of human existence.[72] Thus knowing the ultimate source of all things is the first step in the process of salvation, and hence, one's search for God. By making reference to a search for the Teacher of Righteousness at the end of the age, the writer of this scroll indicates a recognition of the fact that God is the ultimate source for all things and that he will be sought by all as knowledge of him deepens in the Messianic era.

Florilegium: a Midrash on the last Days (4Q174)
The Doctrine of the Messiah

Before introducing the subject of the two Messiahs, the covenant community writer uses quotations from II Sam 7:10 and Exod 15:17-18

---

[71] 4Q171 I-1V, *ibid.*, pp. 290-92.

[72] Carroll Stuhlmueller, *Psalms 2: Psalms 73-150*, Wilmington: Michael Glazier, 1983, pp. 166-67 . Cf Arnold B. Rhodes, *The Book of Psalms*, LBC, Vol. 9, Richmond: John Knox, 1960, pp. 170-71.

as the basis for the covenant community doctrine that identifies the community itself and the Temple. The covenant community is itself the Lord's living temple, a sanctuary of holy men dedicated to meticulous observance of the Law, replacing the physical temple destroyed by foreign armies. In commenting on the quotation, "I will appoint a place for my people Israel and will plant them that they may dwell there and be troubled no more by their enemies. No son of iniquity shall afflict them again as formerly, from the day that I set judges over my people Israel", from II Sam 7:10, the writer offers the following theological interpretation:

> This is the House which he will build for them in the last days, as it is written in the book of Moses, 'In the sanctuary which Thy hands have established, O Lord, the Lord shall reign forever and ever' (Exod 15:17-18). This is the house, into which the unclean shall never enter, nor the uncircumcised, nor the Ammonite, nor the Moabite, nor the half-breed, nor the foreigner, nor stranger, ever, for there shall my Holy Ones be. And strangers shall lay it waste no more, as they formally laid waste the Sanctuary of Israel because of its sin. He has commanded that a Sanctuary of men be built for Himself, that there they may send up, like smoke of incense, the works of the Law.[73]

Thus the community itself is the eschatological temple. To join the covenant community is to enter into the very presence of God.

The quotation, "And I will give you rest from all your enemies", from II Sam 7:11 is then applied to the community and the eschatological peace it will enjoy when all the wicked men are destroyed by the consequences of their own sins.[74]

Then the Davidic covenant is applied theologically to the covenant community so that the community itself as the remnant of Israel constitutes that Davidic house through which God will, at the end of time, raise from it "the Branch of David" who, along with the Interpreter of the Law shall rule in Zion. This eschatological appearance of two Messiahs is based on the Davidic covenant as stated in the following quotations: "the Lord declares to you that he will build you a house (II Sam 7:11c). I will raise up your seed after you (II Sam 7:12). I will establish the throne of his kingdom forever (II Sam 7:13). I will be his father and he shall be

---

[73] 4Q174 I, in Vermes, *The Dead Sea Scrolls in English*, p. 293.
[74] *Ibid.*

my son (II Sam 7:14) ... I will raise up the tent of David that is fallen (Amos 9:14)".[75]

Over against the picture of eschatological peace portrayed in the theological interpretation of II Sam 7:11 above the writer reverts to a picture of eschatological conflict in his interpretation of Ps 2:1 and Dan 12:10. This latter eschatological view is the one that is characteristic of the theology of the Qumran covenant community. The quotation, "Why do the nations rage and the people meditate vanity, the kings of the earth rise up, and the princes take counsel together against the Lord and against his Messiah", from Ps 2:1, provides the basis for the view that there will be an eschatological opposition to the Messiah coming from the nations of the world. However, the quotation from Dan 12:10, "But the wicked shall do wickedly and shall not understand, but the righteous shall purify themselves and make themselves white", is used to support the view that despite the universal opposition to the Messiah and his remnant community, the covenant community shall remain spiritually strong and maintain its practice of righteousness through its committed obedience to the Law.[76]

The Heavenly Prince Melchizedek (11 Q Melch)
In this scroll, the general restoration of property of the year of jubilee (Lev 25:13) takes an eschatological twist in which the proclamation of liberty to the captives occurs at the end of days (Isa. 61:1, Deut 15:2). Melchizedek, who is identical with the archangel Michael, heads a delegation of heavenly hosts the "sons of heaven" or "gods of Justice". He is referred to as "Elohim" or "El", i.e. God, a term which in this context implies "Judge". He presides over the final judgment in which Satan and all evil forces are condemned and thus freeing the world from all influences of evil, thereby establishing a Messianic age. All this is portrayed as taking place on the Day of Atonement.

Thus the quotations in this scroll fragment provide a theological basis for the covenant community's teaching on eschatological judgment. It has already been noted above that the quotations from Levi 25:13; Deut 15:2 and Isa 61:1 define the eschatological salvation or atonement by making reference to end –time remission of debts, the proclamation of forgiveness and the assignment of the former captives to the ranks of Melchizedek for an inheritance.

The quotation, "Elohim has taken his place in the divine council; in the midst of the gods he holds judgment", from Ps 82:1 and the quotation

---

[75]   4Q174 I, *ibid.*, p. 294.
[76]   *Ibid.*

from Ps 7:7-8, "return to the height above them, EL (god) will judge the peoples", and Ps 82:2, "How long will you judge unjustly and show partiality to the wicked? Selah", are theologically used to portray Melchizedek as an eschatological judge vested with divine powers in order to "avenge the vengeance of the judgment of God".

The peace, i.e. salvation, that goes forth on the day of end-time judgment is said to be a theological fulfilment of a prophecy that came through Isaiah saying, "How beautiful upon the mountains are the feet of the messenger who proclaims peace, who brings good news, who proclaims salvation, who says to Zion: your Elohim reigns" (52:7). The word "messenger" in this quotation and the phrase "an anointed one" in the quotation "until an anointed one, a prince" in Dan 9:25 are theologically applied to Melchizedek to define his Messianic status, and thus he becomes a divine figure.

In conclusion with regard to the use of biblical quotations in the Dead Sea Scrolls, this study has revealed that they were used theologically to support various theological doctrines of the Qumran covenant community. As it is the case with the *Mishnah,* the quotations in the Dead Sea Scrolls are almost always introduced by an introductory formula, a factor which further attests to a theological use of quotations, consciously adduced to support a particular doctrinal position. Thus, the theological use of biblical quotations in the Dead Sea Scrolls, like that of the *Mishnah,* serves as a background to Matthew's theological use of biblical quotations which, in his gospel, comes into sharp relief in his fulfilment quotations.

The Early Christian Fathers
The patristic writings share an apologetic motif with the Dead Sea Scrolls. The patristic writings often arose in the context of theological debates with personalities holding contrary views on theological questions from the established views of the Church. Although philosophy plays a significant role in the method and substance of their argumentation, almost all theological positions are supported by specific biblical quotations to enhance their authoritative value.

The apologetic interest is not lacking in the New Testament. Just as the early Church fathers sought to show their Christian opponents (heretics) and other interested peoples, especially the learned in the Greco-Roman world, the reasonableness of the official Church's theological position, the New Testament sought to show the reasonableness of the claim that Jesus is the Messiah promised to Israel and Saviour of the world to both the learned and the not-so-learned of the Jewish-Greco-Roman world. While the New Testament writers turned to the Old Testament for a theological light on the meaning of the Christ-event, having accepted the Old Testament as an authority on theological issues, the patristic writers looked to both the Old and the New Testaments as authorities on theological questions that concerned them. As it is the case with the *Mishnah* and the Dead Sea Scrolls discussed above, conscious use of biblical quotations is indicated by the use of introductory formulae such as "For the scripture says", "just as the Holy Spirit said of him", "The Scripture bears witness when it says", "For on this point the Lord said", "For this reason John says in the Apocalypse", "For he (the Lord) says", "It is he himself who says to Moses", "Therefore Paul says", "and this the Apostle shows in the Epistle. when he says', "God said", "This was the Apostle's meaning when he wrote", "For the saying ... is more applicable here", "as the prophet says", "it is written", "For that is the meaning of the scriptural passage", etc. Thus various doctrines of the early Church are supported or defined by the theological use of biblical quotations.

Clemens Romanus (Clement of Rome)
Clement was the Bishop of Rome at the end of the first century. On the doctrine of the Person and Work of Christ, Clement teaches the humility of Christ: "Christ is with those of humble mind, not those who exalt them-selves over his flock. Our Lord Jesus Christ, did not come with the pride of pretension and arrogance – though he has the power – but in humility of mind, just as the Holy Spirit said of him". Clement, then, rests this teaching on the basis of the quotation from Isa 53:1-12, "Lord who has believed our report? And to whom is the arm of the Lord revealed?.", and the same idea in Ps 21(22): 5-8.[77] Using a quotation which ends with Ps 50:23, "The sacrifice of praise will glorify me, and there is the way by which I shall show him the salvation of God", Clement supports the theological view that Christ is the way of salvation, and that he is our High Priest through whom we get access to God and the knowledge of

---

[77] Clement of Rome, "First Epistle to the Corinthians xvi", in Henry Bettenson (ed. and transl.), *The Early Christian Fathers, A Selection from the Writings of the Fathers from St Clement of Rome to St Athanasius*, London: Oxford University Press, 1969, p. 29.

him: "this is the way, beloved, in which we found our salvation, Jesus Christ, the High Priest of our offerings, the protector and helper of our weakness. Through him we see as in a mirror the spotless and excellent face of God through him the Ruler willed that we should taste the immortal knowledge."[78]

On the doctrine of Church and ministry, Clement finds a theological ground for the orderly process of passing on the Christian tradition (i.e. Christian fundamental teachings) which begins with the Lord Jesus Christ himself, who passes it to the disciples who in turn pass it to elected officers of the Church (bishops and deacons) in a quoted text from Isa 60:17.[79] By using this Isaiah text as a theological basis for the establishment of the ecclesiastical offices in the Church, Clement equates the Church to an eschatological community in which its leaders guide the flock in peace and righteousness.[80]

Writing on the doctrine of Church liturgy, Clement further supports the view that oneness and peace and order must prevail during worship by quoting Isa 6:3, "Ten thousand times ten thousand were doing service to him, and they cried out, Holy, holy, holy Lord Sabaoth; the whole creation is full of his glory". The earthly Church is a replica of the heavenly hosts and hence must conform to its oneness and peace and order.[81]

On the doctrine of eschatology, Clement argues that the eschatological return of Christ is imminent over against the view probably stated in the *Book of Eldad and Modad* which Clement quotes as Scripture:

> Let the passage of Scripture be far from applying to us, where it says 'Wretched are the double –minded who doubt in their soul, and say: We have heard these things also in our father's time,

---

[78] Clement, "Corinthians xxxvi", in Bettenson, *The Early Christian Fathers*, p. 29.

[79] The biblical text of the Isaiah reference depicts an eschatological establishment of peace and justice, a time when there will be no more wars from without and corrupt practice from within. Peace and righteousness themselves will reign. This is a state of ultimate peace and righteousness. For a discussion of the difficulty in translating this verse into English and the variations in its text form between the Septuagint and the Masoretic Texts, see Bettenson, *The Early Christian Fathers*, p. 32, especially note 5; John L. McKenzie, *Second Isaiah*, AB, New York: Doubleday, 1968 p. 176; George A.F. Knight, *The New Israel, A Commentary on the book of Isaiah 56-66*, ITC, Grand Rapids: Wm B Eerdmans and Edinburgh: Handsel, 1985, pp. 47-8.

[80] Clement, "Corinthians xliii", in Bettenson, *The Early Christian Fathers* p. 32.

[81] Clement, "Corinthians xix-xx, xxxiv", *ibid.,* p. 34.

and look, we have grown old and none of them has happened to us.[82]

Clement asserts that the return of Christ will be fulfilled quickly and suddenly. To support this view of the imminent return of Christ, he provides, as a theological basis the quotation, "He shall come quickly and not linger, and the Lord will come suddenly to his temple, even the Holy One whom you expect", which combines Isa 13:22 and Mal 3:1.[83]

Ignatius

Ignatius was Bishop of Antioch and probably was martyred in 115 AD. The theological use of quotations come out very clearly in his *Letter to the Smyrnaeans* where he discusses the doctrine of physical resurrection. To support the teaching that Jesus rose physically and bodily he uses the quotation, "Take hold and feel me, and see that I am not a bodiless phantom",[84] placed in the context when the Risen Lord appeared to Peter and his fellow disciples who then touched him to attest his physical and bodily existence, though in a spiritual form.[85]

The Didache : The Teaching of the Apostles

In its teaching on the doctrine of baptism it appears that it is the Trinitarian baptismal formula which authenticates the ritual of baptism as a Christian rite. The novitiate must be baptised 'in the name of the Father, and of the Son, and of the Holy Ghost', a formula quoted from Matt 28:19. This is the most important feature although there are certain requirements like the recital of certain words or prayers and a day or two of fasting prior to baptism. The nature and amount of water required and the method of baptising are not tied to a specific mode. It could be in "running water" or in "other water"; it could be "cold water" or "warm water" and "if you have neither, pour water on the head thrice."[86]

On the doctrine of Eucharist, the *Didache* teaches the view that those who are not baptized should not partake in the Eucharist. The theological

---

[82] Clement, "Corinthians xxiii", Bettenson, *ibid.,* p. 36. Also note 1.

[83] *Ibid.*

[84] Although the incident resembles the one that is recorded at Luke 24:36-53, the source of this quotation cannot be identified with certainty. Jerome ascribes it to the Gospel according to the Hebrews, but Eusebius is unable to find it in that gospel, while Origen who also knew that gospel assigns the quotation to the teaching of Peter. See Bettenson, *The Early Church Fathers*, p. 48, note 4.

[85] Ignatius, "To the Smyrnaeans iii-iv", in Bettenson, *The Early Christian Fathers*, p. 48.

[86] Didache vii, *ibid.,* p. 50.

basis for this view is found in a quotation from Matt 7:6, "Do not give what is holy to the dogs". The theology of the Eucharist itself is not expressed in terms of the suffering and death of Jesus as narrated in the passion narrative of our Gospels. Rather it appears to be based on the feeding miracles. The broken bread symbolizes the gathering of the Church into God's kingdom as the recorded prayer of the broken bread of Eucharist shows:

> We give thanks to thee, our Father, for the life and knowledge which thou did make known to us through Jesus thy Son: thine be the glory forever. As this broken bread was scattered upon the mountains and was gathered together and become one, so let thy Church be gathered from the ends of the earth into thy kingdom.[87]

This variant theological understanding of the Eucharist shows that various theological views concerning aspects of the Christ-event existed in the early Church before some of them were adopted as the standard teaching of the Church.[88]

Justinus (Justin Martyr)

Justin was probably martyred in 165 AD. His teaching on the Church-State relationship is based on a quotation from Matt 22:21. The Church is to obey and pray for the state and its leadership while praise and worship are reserved for God alone:

> The Lord said, "Pay to Caesar what belongs to Caesar; to God what belongs to God" (Matt 22:21). Therefore we render worship to God alone, but in all other things we gladly obey you, acknowledging you as kings and rulers of earth, and praying that in you royal power may be found combined with wisdom and prudence.[89]

Irenaeus

On the doctrine of immortality, Irenaeus quotes Ps 81 (82): 6, 7, "I have said, you are gods, and all of you children of the Highest. But you will die like men", to support the view that man was first made mortal and that only later was his nature raised to immortality to make clear both God's

---

[87]   Didache ix-x, *ibid.,* p. 50. Cf. Mark 8:4-9; Matt 14:15-21.

[88]   For the view that the New Testament apocryphal writings developed to accommodate theological views and teachings which did not find a place in the standard teaching of the early church, see E. Hennecke, *New Testament Apocrypha,* vol. II, London: SCM, 1965, pp. 63-4.

[89]   Justin Martyr, "Apologia I. Xvii", in Bettenson, *The Early Christian Fathers*, pp. 59-60.

generosity and man's weakness. The latter had first to be shown and then be overcome.[90]

Concerning the doctrine of human freedom and God's design he uses the quotations, "How often did I wish to gather your sons and you refused?" from Matt 23:37 and "Let it happen to you according to your faith" from Matt 9:29 to support the view that man is free and responsible:

> In saying this the Lord made plain the ancient law of man's freedom; for God from the beginning made man free. Man had his own power of decision, just as he had his own life, so that he might freely fall in with God's intention, without compulsion from God. he equipped man with the power of choice.... And not only in actions but in faith also God has preserved man's free and unconstrained choice.[91]

In his discussion on Christology, he argues for the pre-existence of Christ, the Logos. To support this view he quotes Rom 10:4, "Christ is the end of the Law to obtain justification for every believer". Rather rhetorically and philosophically, Irenaeus questions the apostolic claim that Christ is "the end of the Law" unless he were also its beginning. Then from the theological assumption that Christ is also the beginning of the Law, he concludes that it was Jesus himself who appeared to Moses and said, "I have surely seen the affliction of my people in Egypt, and I have come down to rescue them", quoting Exod 3:7. From this, he finds the theological basis for the teaching that Christ is pre-existent and that he occasionally appeared to God's people before his incarnation in order to save them: "From the beginning he was accustomed, as the Word of God, to descend and ascend for the salvation of those who were in distress."[92]

---

[90]   Irenaeus, "Adversus Haereses iv. Xxxviii. 2-3", Bettenson, *ibid.*, p. 68. This view of man's acquired immortality is contrasted in the Didache where it is taught that before the Fall man was naturally immortal, "God set man certain limits so that provided he kept God's commandment, he should remain in his original immortality: otherwise he should become mortal and dissolve into the earth from which he was created". See the Didache, xv, in Bettenson, *The Early Christian Fathers*, pp. 68-9. This theological difference on their understanding concerning the doctrine of immortality in the early Church further indicates that a variety of theological views existed on certain theological questions before or even after some of them were elevated by the Church to a status of orthodoxy.

[91]   Irenaeus, "Adversus Haereses iv. Xxxvii 1", in Bettenson, *The Early Christian Fathers*, p.72.

[92]   Irenaeus "Adversus Haereses, iv. Xii. 4", *ibid.*, p. 75.

To support the view that the Son is divine, Irenaeus argues that since as the Word he is one with the Father, he proclaims the Father. This is supported by the quotations, "My name is IAM. And you shall say to the Israelites, 'HE WHO IS has sent me to you'", from Exod 3:14 and, "I have come down to rescue this people," from Exod 3:8. Although it is the pre-existent Son who descends and appears to Moses, he announces the Father. The Father in turn proclaims the Son. The theological basis for this is Isa 43:10, "I am witness, says the Lord God and so is the child (servant) whom I have chosen, that you may know and believe and understand that IAM". This mutual proclamation of Father and Son shows that the Father is in the Son and the Son is in the Father. This means they are one in divinity and hence, the divinity of the Son.[93]

Irenaeus also argues for the pre-existence of the Holy Spirit. Understanding the Holy Spirit as "Wisdom", he finds theological support for the view that the Holy Spirit existed before creation and that he was then with the Father and the Son in the quotations from Prov 3:19, "The Lord established the earth by his Wisdom", and Prov 8:22, "The Lord created me for his works at the beginning of his ways; he established me before the ages".[94]

On the sacrament of baptism, Irenaeus quotes the phrase "a dry tree" from Isa 56:3, "Neither let the son of the stranger, that hath joined himself to the Lord, speak, saying the Lord hath utterly separated me from his people: neither let the eunuch say, Behold, I am a dry tree". In the Old Testament context the verse is part of an assurance of salvation to those who are sanctified and keep his commandments. In this context, the phrase "a dry tree" refers to one who is not saved. Thus beginning from the theological understanding that man is naturally "a dry tree", i.e. mortal and lost in sin,[95] he uses this quoted phrase to support the view that our bodies and souls receive the unity that brings us to immortality through the washing of the body by the baptismal water (likened to 'willing rain' which turns the dry tree into a fresh and fruitful one, and thus bringing it to life. Cf. Isa 30:23, "Then shall he give the rain of thy seed..." which he might have had in his mind) and the washing of the soul through the gift of the Spirit both of which are needed for salvation:

---

[93]   Irenaeus, "Adversus Haereses, III. Vi. 2", *ibid.,* p. 75.
[94]   Irenaues, "Adversus Haereses, iv. Xx. 3", *ibid.,* p. 85.
[95]   See my discussion on Iranaeus' views on the doctrine of immortality above.

> And as dry earth does not produce fruit unless it receives mois-
> ture; so we, who are at first "a dry tree' would never have
> yielded the fruit of life without the "willing rain" from above. For
> our bodies have received the unity which brings us immortality,
> by means of the washing of baptism; our souls receive it by
> means of the gift of the Spirit.[96]

Discussing the sacrament of Eucharist, Irenaeus draws quotations from Hos 6:6: Matt 12:7 and Mal 1:14 to establish the view that since God requires faith, obedience and righteousness over against mere ritual in offering burnt offerings it is the Eucharist which the Church offers, that is, "bread of the natural creation" and "the cup of wine belonging to the creation of which we are part" which constitutes a pure sacrifice of thanksgiving and praise to God. This pure sacrifice "the Church receives from the Apostles and throughout the whole world she offers it to God." Thus in using these quotations to establish the view that true thanksgiving and worship is only offered by the Church, Irenaeus attacks both Jewish sacrificial practice and Gentile conceptions of the created matter. The condemnation of ritual-oriented burnt offerings (Mal 1:14) indicates that the Church's system of thanksgiving supercedes and renders obsolete the Jewish sacrificial system of thanksgiving while the cosmic character of the Church offering of this pure sacrifice and its use of resources from natural creation like bread and wine implies the purity of creation over against Gnostic views that see creation as generally evil.[97]

With regard to the doctrine of resurrection, Irenaeus uses the quotations, "firstborn from the dead", from Col 1:18; "the lower parts of the earth", from Eph 4:9 and, "departed in the midst of the shadow of

---

[96]   Irenaeus, "Adversus Haereses III. Xvii. 2", in Bettenson, *The Early Christian Fathers*, p. 94.

[97]   Irenaeus "Adversus Haereses iv. Xvii. 4", *ibid.,* p. 95. It is noteworthy that this interpretation of Eucharist as a "pure sacrifice" is also shared with other early Church fathers like Justin, Tertullian, Chrysostom and Augustine, see *Ibid* note 3. It should also be noted that the emphasis on the cosmic character of the effects of Eucharist implies corporate and universal character of the salvation it effects. This accounts for the reason why the Lord's supper was central in Christian worship in the early Church, while in the period between the early Church and the Reformers, Eucharist became a monopoly of the ordained priests, while after the reformers, the preaching of the word became central. This emphasis on corporate and universal character is set over against the emphasis on the salvation of the individual through the washing of his sins by the blood of Christ, symbolized in the latter ages of the Christian Church when salvation focused more on the individual Christian (i.e. through his faith) than on the corporate Church. See Timothy George, *Theology of the Reformers*, Nashville: Broadman, 1988, pp. 145, 156-57.

death", from Ps 22 (23):4 to support physical and bodily resurrection over against the immortality of the bodiless soul. Just as Jesus who is the "first-born from the dead" resurrected bodily after his soul had sojourned "in the midst of the shadow of death" before he rose bodily and went to heaven, the souls of his disciples will remain in:

> An unseen region set apart for them by God, and will dwell there until the resurrection which they await. Then they will receive their bodies and arise entire, that is in bodily form as the Lord arose, and thus will come into the presence of God.[98]

He further supports the doctrine of physical resurrection by using the quotation, "as in Adam all die", from I Cor 15:22:

> What then was it which perished? Clearly it was the substance of flesh, which lost the breath of life . the Lord came to restore this flesh to life, that "as in Adam all die", as possessing merely sensual life, we may live " in Christ" as having spiritual life, putting away not the handiwork of God but the lusts of the flesh, and receiving the Holy Spirit.[99]

To support the view that the creation will be restored to its pre-fall condition at the last day, he quotes Rom 10:12, "rich in all things", and Rom 8:19-21. "The earnest expectation of the creation awaits the revelation of the sons of God."[100] This understanding of the restoration of creation develops into the concept of milleniarism. To support the view that a millennial age will be established in which Christ himself will reign together with the saints and enjoy the fruits of the restored creation before a final translation to heaven takes place, he quotes Matt 26:29, "I will no more drink the fruit of the vine until I drink it new in my Father's kingdom", and Ps 103 (104) :30, "shall renew the face of the earth":

> And he thus indicates two things: the inheritance of the earth in which the new fruit of the vine will be drunk and the physical resurrection of his disciples. For it is the body which arises new which receives the new drink. We cannot understand him as drinking the fruit of the vine when he has taken his place with followers in the regions above the heavens; and those who drink it are not disembodied: for to drink wine belongs to the body rather than the Spirit.[101]

---

[98]   Ireneaus, "Adversus Haereses v.xxxi. 2", in Bettenson, *The Early Christian Fathers*, pp. 97-8.

[99]   Ireneaus, "Adversus Haereses v. xii.3", *ibid.*, p. 98.

[100]   Ireneaus, "Adversus Haereses v. xxxii, 1", *ibid.*, p. 99.

[101]   Ireneaus, "Adversus Haereses v.xxxiii. 1", *ibid.*, p. 99.

A full blown doctrine of millennial reign finds its theological basis in Gen 27:27-29 where reference is made to the blessings of Isaac.

> This blessing indisputably refers to the time of the kingdom, when the righteous shall rise from the dead and reign; when creation, renewed and liberated, shall produce food of every kind, in abundance, thanks to the dew of heaven and the fertility of the earth. and all the animals, enjoying these fruits of the earth shall live in peace and harmony, obedient to man in entire submission.[102]

Quintus Septimius Florens Tertullia (Tertullian)

He was a Church Father around 200 AD. On the doctrine of God, Tertullian begins with the assumption that God is substantial. From that philosophical premise he proceeds to argue that the Son is substantial and then concludes that the Son is a Person with a special form of a body. To support this teaching, he quotes III John 1:3, "Without him nothing was made". On the basis of this quotation, he argues that since the Son proceeds from the Father who is substantial and created all things which are also substantial, he cannot himself be unsubstantial. Therefore, the Word of God who is the Son is not insubstantial and void. This argument is further strengthened by a quotation from Exod 20:7, "Thou shalt not take the name of God for nothing". The phrase "for nothing" literary means for a void thing or for unreality. Thus God is in a substantial form and not in no form, and in that substantial form he is God. Then he argues that the Son is in that form in which God is by quoting Phil 2:6, "Who, being in the form of God, thought it not a prize to be equal with God". He then proceeds to argue that, since God is in a form, that form is his body, although that body is Spirit (quoting John 4:24), since even spirit is a body of its own kind. He then concludes that since the Son is substance, a body in the form of spirit, he is a person distinct from the Father. Therefore, the Word of God is a person with the name Son.[103]

Regarding the doctrine of man, Valentinus and his followers had taught Gnostic determinism using the quotation from Matt 7:17, 18, "a good tree does not bear bad fruit, nor a bad tree good fruit; and can one

---

[102]   Ireneaus, "Adversus Haereses v. xxxiii. 3-4", *ibid.,* p.100.

[103]   Tertullian's argument for the doctrine of the personhood of God the Son, here, reveals that although classical philosophy played a major role in the theology of the early Church fathers, biblical quotations remained the basis for any theological construction. See Tertullian "Adversus Praxean 7", in Bettenson, *The Early Christian Fathers*, p. 104.

reap figs from thorns or grapes from thistles".[104] Against this position, Tertullian uses phrases quoted from Matt 3:7-9 to support the doctrine of human freedom and responsibility. Man is free to chose to repent or not. The worst sinner can become the best saint if he decides to repent:

> But the sayings of Scripture will not prove inconsistent. A bad tree will not yield good fruit without grafting, and a good tree will give bad fruit if not tended. Stones will become sons of Abraham if trained in Abraham's faith: the offspring of vipers will produce fruit of repentance if they expel the poison of malignity. This will be the power of the grace of God, more powerful surely than nature, having under it in us the free power of choice, which is called "self determination". This faculty belongs to our nature and is capable of change; and thus whithersoever it inclines, our nature inclines the same way.[105]

Over against Gnostic heretics who ascribe the creation of the material world, including human flesh, to an inferior deity, Tertullian, on the basis of a quotation from Gen 2:7, "God made clay from the earth into man," supports the view that all God's purposes and promises to man are for the benefit not of the soul alone but of the soul and the flesh. From that quotation, Tertullian argues that an entire man consists of flesh and spirit and hence, neither of those elements can constitute man separately according to God's design.[106]

On the doctrine of man's inherited guilt, he uses quotations to support the view that during the period of the Law and people's hardness of heart, the blessings as well as the curses of the fathers were visited on the sons to the third and fourth generations. This is based on the quotation, "bringing home to the sons the transgressions of their fathers", from Exod 20:5.[107] However, after the hardness of the Law and the hardness of the people had been overcome through Christ in fulfilment of the prophecy : "men shall not say, The fathers have eaten a sour grape and the children's teeth have been set on edge," from Jer 31:29,[108] each individual will be responsible for his own sins. This is individual responsibility for sin. Hence, sin will no longer be inherited. But there is one exception. For Jews who still apply the Law, sin continues to be an

---

[104] The quotation is a transposition of Matthean verses.
[105] Tertullian, "De Anima 21", in Bettenson, *The Early Christian Fathers*, p. 110.
[106] Tertullian, "De Resurrection Carnis, 5-6", *ibid.*, p. 113.
[107] Cf. Numb 14:18.
[108] Cf. Ezek 18:2-3.

inherited phenomenon. This exception is theologically based on the quotation, "His blood (be) on our head and on the heads of our sons", from Matt 27:25.[109]

In his discussion of the doctrine of incarnation, he supports the view that the Son is begotten of the Father, as the Father's Reason or Discourse or Wisdom in eternity. To support this view he applies the quotation. "The Lord created me as the beginning of his ways for his works", from Prov 8:22.[110] That is, the Father first created and begot His own Consciousness in eternity. The initial outward manifestation of the Son or Word is seen in his utterance of the word of creation. To support his view that this was his initial manifestation, Tertullian quotes Gen 1:3, 'Let there be light", and defines this as:

> The entire nativity of the Word, when it proceeded from God, who created it for thinking with the title of Wisdom. and begot it to put the thought into effect . then the Word makes God his Father, since by proceeding from him he became the first-born Son: first-begotten as begotten before all things; only begotten, as begotten uniquely from the womb of his heart.[111]

He further supports the doctrine that the Son proceeded from the Father by using the quotation from Ps 4:1, "My heart has thrown up a good Word".[112] In further support for the doctrine that the Son proceeded from the Father and that the Son is united with him, he quotes I Cor 2:11, "For who knows the things that are in God, except the Spirit which is in him". Since Spirit is the body of the Word, that is the Son, the Word is always in the Father. The quotation, "I in the Father", from John 14:11 and, "with the Father", from John 10:20, are all used to define the theological teaching that the Son proceeds from the Father but he is not separated from him.[113] He further argues in support of the view that the Son is distinct and subordinate to the Father and finds the theological support for this view in the quotations, "The Father is greater than I am", from

---

[109]   Tertullian, "Adversus Marcionem, ii. 15", in Bettenson, *The Early Christian Fathers*, p. 115.

[110]   For the quotation from Prov 8:22 concerning the origin of "wisdom" as used by Irenaeus to explain the proceeding of the Holy Spirit, not the 'begottenness' of the son, see my discussion of his theology above.

[111]   Tertullian, "Adversus Praxean 5-7", in Bettenson, *The Early Christian Fathers*, p. 119.

[112]   *Ibid.*

[113]   Tertullian, "Adversus Praxean 8", *ibid.*, p. 120.

John 14:28 and, "For you have made him a little lower than the angels", from Ps 8:5.[114]

The doctrine of the two natures of Christ, namely, that Christ is both human and divine finds theological support in the quotations, "What is born in flesh is flesh; and what is born of the spirit is spirit", from John 3:6, and, "mediator of God and man", from I Tim 2:5. Tertullian suggests that the name Son of God refers to his divine nature while the name Son of man refers to his human nature.[115]

On the doctrine of the impassability of God, he held a view which, though similar to that of Monarchians was fundamentally different from theirs. The Monarchians, on the basis of Matt 27:46, "My God, my God, why hast thou forsaken me?" formed the teaching that at the cross, at the time of the cry of suffering, the Christ-God departed from the man Jesus, since God could not suffer. Some of the early theologians shared this view. For instance, Hilary of Poitiers says concerning the cry of dereliction: "The voice of the human body proclaims the departure of the Word".[116] While sharing the view that God could not participate in the suffering at this moment, Tertullian rejects the suggestion that the divine Christ deserted the human Jesus at this point. Rather he supports the view that Jesus remained both divine and human even at the cross but that the cry was a human cry, not of the Word or Spirit, and that it was uttered for the purpose of showing the impassability of God who thus forsook his Son in delivering his humanity to death. That it was the humanity of Jesus that suffered finds a theological basis in the quotation, "If the Father did not spare his Son", from Rom 7:32 and, "The Lord had delivered him up for our sins", from the prophecy of Isaiah (53:6 LXX):

> You find him crying out in his suffering...Then either the Son was suffering, forsaken by the Father, and the Father did not suffer; or if it was the Father who was suffering to what God was he crying? But this was the cry of flesh and soul (that is, man), not of the Word and the Spirit (that is God); and it was uttered for the very purpose of showing the impassability of God who thus forsook his Son in delivering his humanity to death.[117]

---

[114]   Tertullian, "Adversus Praxean, 9", *ibid.,* p. 121.

[115]   Tertullian, "Adversus Praxean, 27", *ibid.,* p. 122.

[116]   This quotation is taken from Hilary of Poitiers, "Commentary in Matthew 33" and is quoted in E. Evans, *Tertullian's Treatise against praxeas* (1948). Probably Bettenson gets it from Evans. See Bettenson, *The Early Christian Fathers*, p. 124. Note 3.

[117]   Tertullian, "Adversus Praxean 30", in Bettenson, *The Early Christian Fathers*, pp. 124-25.

And to support this view that the Father did not forsake the divinity of the Son, he points out to the fact that the Son entrusted his spirit into the Father's hands (Luke 23:46). Over against the Monarchian argument, Jesus' voluntary surrender of his spirit, that is the word "into (the Father's) hands" indicates that his divinity did not leave at the moment of his cry of dereliction. Rather at the moment of his physical death when the whole principle of his life, that is both human and divine, left his physical body, his human nature entered into the state of death. At the same time his spirit, that is, his divine nature immediately passed into the hands of God:

> He forsook him in not sparing him, he forsook him in delivering him up. Yet the Father did not forsake the Son, for the Son entrusted his spirit into the Father's hands. In fact, he thus entrusted it, and straightway died. For while the spirit remains in the flesh it is utterly impossible for the flesh to die. Thus to be forsaken by the Father was death to the Son. The Son therefore both dies at the Father's hand.[118]

On the doctrine of the Holy Spirit with regard to his relationship to the Father and the Son, he supports the view that there is a coherent and dependent relationship between the Father, Son and Spirit and that there is unity of substance. To support the doctrine of a coherent and dependent relationship, he makes an allusion to John 16:7 where the Son promises to request the Father for the Paraclete and then sends him. In this allusion he notes that the Paraclete is "another" and therefore distinct from either Father or Son. This noted, he further quotes from John 16:14: "He will take of mine, as I of what is the Father's." And then to support the view that the three are one in essence, not in number or person, he quotes John 10:30, "I and the Father are one thing."[119]

In support of the doctrine of Trinity, Tertullian claims that all the scriptures support the view that there are Three Persons in the Godhead, Father, Son and Holy Spirit. From the passages in which, it is claimed, the doctrine finds clear support, a principle is said to be deduced:

> All the scriptures give clear proof of the Trinity, and of its distinction; and it is from these that our principle is deduced, that speaker and spoken of and spoken to cannot be thought of as one and the same. the distinction of the Trinity is quite clearly displayed. For there is the Spirit himself who utters the

---

[118] *Ibid.*

[119] Tertullian, "Adversus Praxean 25", *ibid.*, p. 129.

statement; the Father, to whom he speaks; the Son of whom he speaks.[120]

Among the many references that support the doctrine are Isa 42:11; 45:1; 49:6; 53:1 and 61:1. In these references, it is held by Tertullian, the Spirit speaks from the stand point of a third person. He specifically quotes, 'The Lord said unto my Lord', from Ps 110:1 as a clear example of such cases.[121]

In further support of the same doctrine, he quotes, "let us make", "in our image", "as one of us", from Gen 1:26 and 3:22, and from these he argues that there was attached to the Father and second person, the Word; and a third person, the Spirit as a theological explanation of the use of plural in these quoted phrases. And basing on Heb 9:24, where it says of Jesus, "the image and likeness of the real", Tertullian draws the theological conclusion that the Father had the Son as his model when he was creating man.[122]

In his teaching on the doctrine of the Last Things, Tertullian also applies quotations theologically. In the quotations, "in the heart of the earth", from Matt 12:40 and, "ascend to the heights" and "descended into the depths", from Eph 4:8, 9, Tertullian finds the theological basis for the view that the underworld is the abode of the souls of both the righteous and the wicked during the intermediate state and the basis of the more or less scientific view of the underworld, namely, that it is a "vast space in the deep pit beneath the earth'.[123]

On the doctrine of the millennium, Tertullian uses theological quotations from Gal 4:26, "our mother from above", from Phil 3:20, "our citizenship is in heaven", and also quotations from Ezek 48:30 and Rev 21:2 to support the view that after the first resurrection saints shall live in new Jerusalem sent from above for a thousand years. On the basis of Ezek 48:30, he argues that the Prophet Ezekiel knew this city, while Rev 21:2 is the basis for the claim that the Apostle John saw it. The one thousand years are intended to enable the saints to enjoy spiritual good in the very place they suffered affliction because of their faith (i.e. on earth), while they await completion of the resurrection of the saints (who rise sooner or later according to their degrees of merit). After this, destruction and

---

[120]   Tertullian, "Adversus Praxean, 11", *ibid.*, p. 135.
[121]   *Ibid.*
[122]   Tertullian, "Adversus Praxean 12", *ibid.*, p. 136.
[123]   Tertullian, "De Anima 55", *ibid.*, p. 160.

judgment of the world will take place and the saints, changed into angelic substance will be translated to heaven. The change of substance into angelic form and the translation find theological support in a quotation from I Cor 15:52, 53.[124]

Titus Flavius Clemens Alexandrinus (Clement of Alexandria)
He wrote about 200 AD. Of all the early Church fathers, Clement made the greatest efforts to present the Christian faith in terms of Alexandrian philosophy. And yet even in this case, biblical quotations still stand out as the basis for his theological construction. He still uses biblical quotations to save as a springboard for his philosophical theology. Thus, even his work reflects a theological use of biblical quotations.

On the doctrine of God the Father, Clement finds the theological basis for his teaching on the incomprehensibility of God in a quotation from Acts 17:22, 23, where Paul refers to God as the Unknown God as the Athenian philosophers themselves did. From that premise, Clement teaches that God is infinite, inexpressible, without form (*contra* Tertullian) and nameless, and that he cannot be apprehended by natural wisdom or knowledge but by divine grace through the Word that proceeds from him.[125] On the basis of the pronoun "Thou" in a quotation from John 17:21, Clement finds the basis for the teaching that God is one and beyond one. He further finds, in that emphatic pronoun, the basis for the view that the one really existing God is, and was and will be. This fits the three categories of time which are also expressed in the name IAM. He further finds the basis for the attribute of the goodness of God in his character as Father, and the basis of his attribute of justice in the mutual relationship between the Father and the Son-his Word – who is in the Father.[126]

Concerning the doctrine of the Fall, Clement supports the view that the Fall was not connected with sex over against the Gnostic Julius Cassianus who attacked marriage as evil. On the basis of the quotation, "I fear lest, as the serpent deceived Eve", from II Cor 11:3, the Gnostic theologian argued that human generation arose as a result of Eve's deceit by the serpent, and thus degrading the human soul through its entering the human body at birth (that is, the soul moves from a higher to

---

[124]   Tertullian, "Adversus Marcionem iii. 24",*ibid.*, p. 164.
[125]   Clement of Alexandria, "Stromateis, v.xii (82,4)", *ibid.*, pp. 169-70.
[126]   Clement Alex, "Paedagogus I. Viii. (71)", *ibid.*, p. 170.

a lower state of life). Thus by joining the body at birth, the soul is "going astray". Support for this going astray of the soul is, for the Gnostics, found in Matt 18:13, "What is going astray". Over against this Gnostic teaching, Clement argues that while the soul was "straying", it was not straying from a higher sphere to a lower sphere through birth on earth, since generation is part of God's creation and does not involve any degrading of the soul. Hence, the Fall is not connected with sex. Using the same quotation of Matt 18:12, Clement supports the teaching that the "straying" does not refer to the degrading of the soul as it moves from a higher sphere to a lower one through birth but refers to the corruption of our minds through disobedience:

> But the Lord came, admittedly, to "what was going astray" but not "straying" from a higher sphere to birth on earth. For generation is part of the creation of the Almighty, and he would not degrade the Soul from a higher state to a worse. Rather it was to us who had strayed in our minds that the Saviour came, minds which had been corrupted because through our love of pleasure we disobeyed the commandments.[127]

On the doctrine of inherited sin, Clement supports the view that there is no inherited sin: "Let them say where the new-born child committed fornication, or how that can have fallen under Adam's curse which has not yet performed any action. They should logically go on to say that not only the birth of the body is evil but also that of the soul on which the body depends."[128] He rejects the quotation, "I was conceived in sins, and in lawlessness my mother bore me", from Ps 50 (51) :7 as a theological basis for inherited sin, and understands the phrase "my mother" in this verse as a mere prophetic reference to Eve as "the mother of all living" in Gen 3:20. It is not, he argues, a reference to David's actual mother. Hence, the Psalm quotation does not refer to David's actual pollution through his real mother:

> When David says "I was conceived in sins, and in lawlessness my mother bore me" (Ps 50 (51) :1), he refers prophetically to Eve as his mother. But Eve was 'the mother of all living' (Gen 3:20), and if he was conceived in this sense still he is not himself in sin nor is he himself sin.[129]

---

[127] Clement Alex. "Stromateis xiv (94, 1)", *ibid.*, p. 173.
[128] Clement Alex. "Stromateis III. Xvi (100 5)", *ibid.*, pp. 173-74.
[129] *Ibid.*

The theological use of biblical quotations is also clear in Clement's discussion of the doctrine of the work of Christ. Regarding the teaching on salvation, Clement supports the view that since God is love, Christ saved us through his example of love through his incarnation and passion and urges us to be likewise instruments for salvation to others. The theological basis for this teaching on salvation through the example of love, is found in the quotation from John 13:34, "I give you my love". Clement calls this a "new testament".[130]

Concerning the universalism of Christ's saving power, he supports the view that the power of the Lord to save is universally operative: it reached those who had died and were in Hades-even gentiles-and converted them. To support this view, he quotes Matt 27:53; I Pet. 3:19 and I Cor 1:29.[131]

On the deification of man, Clement supports the view that man will be deified. The quotation from Matt 13:12 serves as a theological springboard for a discussion of a number of attributes that are to be added to man in the deification process including such attributes as knowledge, love, and inheritance. The process of perfection moves on until man conforms to God's will and develops such a close intimacy with the Lord that he (i.e. man) now awaits "a restoration to eternal contemplation" and is destined to be enthroned as one of the "gods", ranked next to the Saviour.[132] In connection with the deification of man, Clement further argues that the Son who is himself God became man in order to raise man to a divine status. This Christological mission, Clement finds expressed in Phil 2:18, "Who being in the form of God, thought of his equality with God not as a prize to be grasped, but abased himself".

> This is the God of compassion, yearning to save man; and the Word himself at this point speaks to you plainly, putting unbelief to shame; the Word, I say, of God, who became man just that you may learn from a man how it may be that man should become God.[133]

---

[130]   Clement Alex. "Quis Dives Salvetur 37", *ibid.*, p. 174.

[131]   Clement Alex. "Stromateis, vi.vi (47)", *ibid.*, p. 176.

[132]   Clement Alex, "Stromateis, vii. X. (55-6) ", *ibid.*, p. 177. Clement probably alludes to Ps 81 (82):6,7, which Irenaeus uses to support the doctrine of immortality. See my discussion of Irenaeus' theological use of biblical quotations above. But Clement here puts into the argument a strong element of Gnostic philosophy.

[133]   Clement Alex, "Protrepticus I (8 4)", in Bettenson, *The Early Christian Fathers*, p. 177.

Clement's attempts to marry Gnostic philosophy and the Christian faith come out quite clearly in his discussion of the doctrine of salvation by enlightenment. Beginning with the philosophical antithesis of darkness and enlightenment, he argues that, on one hand, darkness is ignorance which leads into sin through a poor perception of the truth. On the other hand, enlightenment comes through knowledge and as knowledge grows the bounds of ignorance diminish, while knowledge takes up a corrective role in one's perception of the truth. Having said this, Clement links up these philosophical tenets to the principles of the Christian faith, namely, man's faith and God's grace. He asserts that the process of knowledge growth is speeded up by faith on the part of man and by grace on the part of God, leading to far beyond a mere correction of man's perception of the truth (as philosophically true knowledge would), to the forgiveness of sins through faith in Christ, expressed in one's acceptance of the spiritual medicine of baptism.[134]

While this philosophical exposition could as well be taken as sufficient ground for his doctrine, Clement still feels compelled to rest the doctrine on biblical foundation and, hence, in another place, he contrasts the Gnostic and the Jewish pietists, basing the contrasts on a quotation from Matt 5:20, "exceeds the Scribes and the Pharisees." Since Jesus says for one to be saved his righteousness must go beyond that of the Scribes and the Pharisees, and in his (Clement's) judgment the piety of the Gnostic goes far beyond that of the Scribes and the Pharisees, he finds in this very Gnostic piety and apprehension of the truth an assurance for salvation. "The 'Gnostic' is saved, we may suppose, owing to his apprehension of the good and bad life, for as well in knowledge as in activity he 'exceeds the Scribes and the Pharisees'" (Matt 5:20).[135]

In his discussion of the sacrament of baptism, Clement supports the view that the cleansing effect of baptism is to make believers immortal and gods – as sons of the Most High. To support this view of the immortality of man, he quotes Ps 81(82):6, 7, "I said, you are gods, and are all sons of the Highest" (cf. John 10:34), then says, "Being baptized, we are enlightened; being enlightened we are adopted as sons; being

---

[134]   Clement Alex, "Paedagogus, I. Vi 929)", Bettenson, *ibid.*, p. 178.
[135]   Clement Alex, "Stromateis vi.xv (115)", *ibid.*

adopted we are made perfect; being made complete, we are made immortal".[136]

He discusses the sacrament of Eucharist in symbolic terms as signifying faith and hope which, he asserts, are nourishment to the soul, and thus meat for the soul. This is based on the quotation "milk" and "meat" from I Cor 3:2. From the quotation, "eat my flesh and drink my blood" from John 6:53-58, he suggests that the metaphor of drinking applies to faith. Thus faith is both meat and drink, that is, a nourishment for the soul. Faith is therefore a nourishment for the Church which is thus refreshed and grows. Hence, faith and hope are the body and blood that together nourishes the Church.[137]

In another place, Clement provides a more Gnostic interpretation of the elements of the Eucharist. While understanding the reference to "milk" in I Cor 3:2 as meaning instruction or preaching as before, the reference to "meat" is no longer applied to faith and hope (concepts of the Christian faith), but is now applied to mystical contemplation (concepts of Gnostic philosophy). With this change in conceptual meaning, the flesh and blood of the Word are now understood as "the apprehension of the divine power and essence for the eating and drinking of the divine Word is the knowledge of the Divine essence."[138] Thus the Eucharist is now defined not in terms of faith that nourishes the Church but in terms of mystical knowledge that saves. Although the doctrine of mystical knowledge is derived from Gnostic philosophy, Clement gives it a theological basis by quoting Ps 33 (34):9, "Taste and see that the Lord is Christ". It is noteworthy that in this quotation Clement substitutes the word 'Christos' (i.e. Christ) for the original 'chrestos' (i.e. kind),[139] and yet he attributes full biblical authority to the resultant text. In this way, he allows the quotations to speak directly on the subject of his interest, namely, Christ, the Word, not the mere attribute of kindness which the original suggests, and thus refers to the totality of his divine essence and power. In this way, Clement makes the quotation speak

---

[136] Clement Alex, "Paedagogus, I. Vi (26)", *ibid.,* p. 180. Irenaeus has used the same Psalm quotation to support the same doctrine of man's immortality. See my discussion of his use of biblical quotations above.

[137] Clement Alex, "Paedagogus, I. Vi (38)", in Bettenson, *The Early Christian Fathers*, p. 180. Cf. "Paedagogus I. Vi. (42-43)"; "II.ii (19-20)", *ibid.* p. 181

[138] Clement Alex, "Stromateis, v. x. (67)", *ibid.,* p. 181.

[139] *Ibid.,* note 3.

about knowledge of the Divine essence and power of Christ and not about knowledge of a single attribute of his being.

On the doctrine of the Last Things, Clement discusses heavenly rewards. On the basis of a quotation from the Apocryphal book of Solomon, which he apparently holds as Scripture, he develops the teaching that the heavenly reward one will get depends on the degree of perfection he attained. This is based on the quotation, "There shall be given to him the chosen grace of faith, and a more delightful portion in the temple of the Lord", from Wisdom 3:14. From the comparative reference "more delightful", he finds support for the teaching that the heavenly rewards are distributed in accordance with one's degree of attainment of righteousness, participating in the inheritance of the lords and gods once he reaches perfection. In further support of this doctrine, Matt 13:8 is used to support the view that there are three mansions in heaven; Eph 4:13 is used to show that those who attain to the perfection of man get to the perfect inheritance; while Matt 10:28 and Matt 5:48 are used to support the view that those who are appointed to adoption and friendship with God share in the inheritance of the lords and gods, if they are perfect in accordance with the Gospel.[140]

Clement further supports the view that the believers who reach perfection (John 1:47; Matt 5:8) go to the eighth heaven (Ps 14(15):1), while others go to other mansions (John 10:16).

And using John 10:27, "My sheep hear my voice" and Mark 5:34, "Your faith has saved you", Clement teaches the need for Gnostic Christians to practice works worthy of redemption:

> "My sheep hear my voice" (Jn 10:27), comprehending the commandments "gnostically" that is, nobly and worthily understanding them and responding with the actions that result from them. So that when we hear the words, "your faith has saved you" (Mk 5:34), we do not take him to mean simply that those who believe in any way will be saved without any resulting action. This saying was addressed to Jews who lived blameless lives in obedience to the Law and merely lacked faith in the Lord.[141]

Origenes Adamantius (Origen) (185-255 AD)
On the doctrine of the omnipotence of God, Origen uses the quotation, "Everything is possible to God," from Matt 19:26 and the quotation, "If

---

[140]   Clement Alex, "Stromateis Vi. Xvi (114)", *ibid.*, p. 183.
[141]   Clement Alex. "Stromateis vi.xiv (108)", *ibid.*

God does anything shameful, he is not God," from the secular writer Euripides (Euripides, *frg.* 292) to support the view that the omnipotence of God does not extend to his doing impossible and inconceivable things, for instance, shameful things.[142]

On the doctrine of divine passability (passion or suffering), Origen supports the position that God participates in the sufferings and passions of his people (*contra* Tertullian). To support this view of divine passability, he quotes Ps 86:15 which says that the Father and God of the universe is "long-suffering, full of mercy and pity", and Deut 1:31, "For the Lord thy God bare thy ways, even as a man bares his own son". Origen comments:

> Some of this sort I would have you suppose of the Saviour. He came down to earth in pity for human kind, he endured our passions and sufferings to assume flesh. For if he had not suffered he would not have entered into full participation in human life the Father himself is not impassable. If he is besought he shows pity and compassion, he feels, in some sort, the passion of love. And for us men he endures the passion of mankind.[143]

In further support of the view that God participates in human passion, he appeals to the text which suggests that there is joy in heaven for one sinner who repents (Luke 15:7) and logically concludes that, since God can experience joy together with his angels, he can also experience suffering and lament for our sinful life. To root this divine passability theologically, he quotes the following texts which he considers to be divine cries of lamentation: "I repent me that I have made man on earth", from Gen 6:8; "Jerusalem, Jerusalem!", from Matt 23:37, and, "Woe is me, for I am like one who gathers stubble in harvest and as a grape cluster in the vintage, because there is no ear, nor first-born cluster for eating! Ah, woe is me, my soul, for the godly man has perished from the earth and there is no one among men to chasten them", from Mic 7:1, 2 (LXX loosely quoted).

But in his concluding statements on the doctrine of divine passability, Origen contradicts himself, or at least makes his position quite dubious if not difficult for one to understand:

> These are the cries of the Lord, grieving for mankind. now all these passages where God is said to lament, or rejoice, or hate,

---

[142] Origen, "Contra Celsum v. 23", *ibid.*, p. 186.
[143] Origen, "Hom in Ezechielem vi 6", *ibid.*

or be glad, are to be understood as spoken by Scripture in metaphorical and human fashion. For the divine nature is remote from all affection of passion and change, remaining even unmoved and untroubled in its own summit of bliss.[144]

It is, however, interesting that Origen does not support his concluding suggestion of an unmoved, untroubled and affectionless God with any biblical reference. This view is probably more philosophical than biblical. For our present purpose, his intentions to use biblical quotations to support his theological teaching is clear.

On the doctrine of creation, Origen held the view that creation came about by a descent from a higher to a lower state, i.e., from the higher and invisible to this lower and visible realm, not only for the souls which deserved it by various motions of their will (because of the excessive failure of their intelligences) but also for those who were brought low for the service of the whole world. It is important here to note that the former (i.e. failing souls) deserved this lowering while the rest of rational beings did not. He finds the theological basis for the view that rational beings had originally an eternal status on the higher plane of existence in the quotation, "Those things which are not seen and are eternal", from II Cor 4:17. The view that the rational beings were, in creation brought down from that higher plane to a lower, some deservedly others forcedly, finds a theological basis in the quotation, "For creation was made subject to vanity, not willingly, but by reason of him who subjected it in hope", from Rom 8:20-21.[145]

In the discussion on the doctrine of Providence with regard to the question of foreknowledge and freedom, Origen's opponents, Celsius and his followers, use the quotations, "Set apart for the gospel of God", from Rom 1:1; "But when God who separated me from my mother's womb, was pleased to reveal his Son in me", from Gal 1:15; and, "We know that all things work together for good for those that love God", from Rom 8:28 to support their doctrine of absolute determinism, i.e., that God's foreknowledge of someone is the cause for the future events in the life of that person and that God introduces men into the world who are already by nature (i.e. by divine foreknowledge) equipped for salvation. This position rules out human freedom and responsibility. Origen, in reply uses the same text of Rom 8:28 to support his view that

---

[144]   Origen, "Hom in Numeros xxx iii.2", *ibid.*, p. 187.
[145]   Origen, "De Principiis III v. 4-5", *ibid.*, p. 190.

human responsibility is the cause of God's predestination and foreknowledge:

> This text clearly makes us responsible causes of the predestination and foreknowledge of God. For it is as much as to say that all things work together for good because those who love God are worthy of this cooperation... if we grant that God foreknows, we ask our opponents, "if we grant human responsibility, is God's foreknowledge the cause of future events? Or did he foreknow because it will happen thus?" In this case his foreknowledge is not the cause of what happens as a result of the responsible actions of each individual. Therefore the freedom bestowed by the Creator is able to choose which to realize, of various possibilities, which arise.[146]

In similar fashion, Origen uses quotations from Gen 1:26, 27 and John 3:2 to support the view that man was created in the image of God but that his likeness of him will appear at consummation, after he has appropriated it by his own efforts.[147] Quotations from Rom 2:14, 15; Tobit 4:15, Matt 7:12; I Cor 2:11 and Rom 8:12 are used to support the view that natural law or conscience or spirit is present in all men and that it corresponds to the laws of the gospel.[148] Quotations from Ps 50:6, 52:4; Rom 3:4 are used to support the view that the presence of natural law in men justifies God's judgment on such men,[149] while quotations from Rom 2:10, 15; John 3: 5; 17:3 show that only faith in Christ leads to salvation despite the fact that everyman is capable of doing good works.[150]

On the doctrine of Sin the view that sin is a perversion of man's nature and that the good that remains in man is not reckoned as good because no man is able to bring goodness to its complete fulfilment, and that only Christ the Good Shepherd managed this task is supported by quotations from Rom 3:12 (quoting Psalms 19) : "They have all gone out of the way", and "I am the good shepherd" (John 10:2).[151] Origen also holds the view that original sin was inherited from Adam by imitation (i.e. "not only from his seed but also from his instruction"), but it only reigned over those who walk in the way of their fathers (quoting I Kgs 15:26 and meaning those who follow their own desires and subject themselves to

---

[146] Origen, "Comm In Ep. Ad. Romanos 1 (Greek in Philocalia, xxv.1)", *ibid.*, p. 195.
[147] Origen, "De Principiis III. Iv. 1", *ibid.*, p. 199.
[148] Origen, "Comm. in Ep. Ad. Romanos, ii. 9", *ibid.*
[149] Origen, "Comm. in Ep ad. Romanos iii.6", *ibid*", p. 200.
[150] Origen, "Comm in Ep. ad. Romanos, ii. 7", *ibid.*, p. 200.
[151] Origen, "Comm, in Ep ad, Romanos, iii. 3", *ibid.*, p. 202.

sin whole-heartedly) and not those who walk along the way of the Lord their God (quoting Gen 18:19 meaning those who are faithful to God).[152] To show that all sinned because all are generically identified with Adam, he uses Rom 5:18.[153] Origen also teaches innate sin. He teaches that our body is sinful not because of its corporal nature (Gnostic view) but because of the Fall; and that Christ's body is not sinful because he was not conceived through man's seed. He backs up this teaching through a theological use of quotations from Rom 6:6; Phil 3:21; Ps 50(51):5; and Job 14:4.[154]

On the doctrine of Providence, regarding human freedom, he further uses Rom 9:19; Gal 6:16; II Cor 5:17 and II Tim 2:2 to support the doctrine of human freedom and responsibility. It is man's acts that determine whether he becomes a vessel of honour or dishonor in the house of God, i.e., whether he is saved or not.[155] Origen's opponents used the quotation, "then it is not the result of man's will or effort (running) but of God's mercy", from Rom 9:16, to support the view that human freedom and responsibility is not involved in our salvation. Salvation is a matter of our constitution for which the Creator is alone responsible. Over against this position, Origen uses Ps 126 (127):1; Phil 2:13; 3:14 to show that it is a matter of both human responsibility and freedom and God's grace.[156]

Discussing the doctrine of incarnation, Origen uses quotations from John 17:5; Phil 2:7 and I Cor 15:25 including a quotation from Virgil's Aeneid ii 521 to show that the Son subordinated himself to the Father by abasing himself, leaving his former glory to become man, and being obedient to death, and thereby restore the world to himself.[157] He also supports the teaching that Christ is the image of God, the "radiance" of God, not only enabling men to receive the Light (i.e. God), but also as Mediator between man and the Light who, being in the form of God, displayed to us the fullness of godhead through his self abasement. This teaching is theologically supported by references to Heb 1:3; I John 1:5;

---

[152]   Origen, "Comm. in Ep. ad. Romanos, v.1", *ibid.*, p. 204.

[153]   Origen, "Comm. in Ep. ad Romanos v. 4", *ibid.*, p. 204.

[154]   Origen, "Comm. in Ep ad. Romanos, v. 9", *ibid.*, p. 205.

[155]   Origen "De Principiis III. 21 (Philocalia, xxi.22)", *ibid.*, pp. 208-9.

[156]   Origen "De Principiis, III.i. 18-9 (Philocalia, xxi. 17-18)", *ibid*, pp. 209-10.

[157]   Origen "De Principiis III. V. 6", *ibid.*, p. 213.

Luke 6:42, and Phil 2:8.[158] The view that Jesus and the Word have become one in the incarnation and yet he remained as "soul" and not limited as if he had no actual existence outside the body of Jesus, i.e., that he remained universally present, is supported by quotations from John 1:26; 14:6; Matt 18:20; 19:6; I Cor 6:17; Col 1:15; Gen 2:24; Ps 148:5.[159] And to support the unity of the two natures with Jesus' soul as a uniting factor between God and flesh, hence becoming God-man, Origen applies quotations from Gen 2:24; Matt 16:27; 19:5-6; Mark 8:38.[160]

On the doctrine of Atonement, Origen applies the quotation, "The heavens will perish; and they shall grow old, like a garment, and they will be changed", from Ps 101 (102):27 (26) to support the view that even heavens need propitiation. Then he uses the quotation, "take away the sin of the whole world", from John 1:29 to support the view that Jesus provides such propitiation.[161] The view that the sacrificial role of saints supplement Christ's sacrifice is theologically grounded on quotations from Num 18:1; II Cor 12:15; II Tim 4:6; and Rev 6:9 as well as Ps 105:15; I John 2:18; and Ps 45:7.[162] The cosmic nature of Jesus' sacrifice is further supported by references from Lev 1:3, 5 and quotations from Heb 12:23 and Col 1:20 where emphasis is on Christ's sacrifice for both heavenly and earthly things,[163] while the quotation from Job 25:1 is quoted to emphasize that Christ's sacrifice is for every rational being that is involved in sin beside man.[164] The vicarious nature of Jesus' sacrifice or suffering is supported by quotations from Isa 53:7-8; Phil 2:8 and Heb 2:9.[165] The view that in Jesus man is reconciled to God and God reconciled to man is supported by quotations from Rom 3:25; 5:1.[166]

With regard to the doctrine of the Holy Spirit, the quotations from John 3:8; I Cor 12:11; and Acts 13:2; 15:21; 21:10, which refer to the will and speech of the Holy Spirit, are used to show that the Holy Spirit has a per-

---

[158] Origen, "De Principiis I. Ii. 7-8", *ibid.*, p. 214.
[159] Origen, "Contra Celsum ii. 9; vi.47", *ibid.*, pp. 215-6.
[160] Origen, "De Principiis II. Vi. 3", *ibid.*, p. 217.
[161] Origen, "Hom in Numeros, xxiv. 1", *ibid.*, p. 221.
[162] Origen, "Hom in Numeros x. 2; Contra Celsum, vi.79", *ibid.*, pp. 222-3.
[163] Origen, "Hom in Leviticum i.3", *ibid.*, p. 224.
[164] Origen, "Comm in Ioannem i. 40 (35)", *ibid.*, p. 225.
[165] Origen, "Comm in Ioannem xxviii. 19 (14)", *ibid.*, p. 225.
[166] Origen, "Comm in Ep. ad Romanos, iii. 8; iv.8", *ibid.*, p. 225-26.

sonality over against the view that it is a mere activity of God.[167] The quotation from John 1:3 is used to support the view that the Holy Spirit proceeds from the Father through the Son, being the first of all that was created through the Son; while the quotation from Matt 12:32 is used to define the clear distinction between the Son and the Holy Spirit. In a quotation from I Cor 12:4, Origen finds a theological springboard for the view that the Father, Son and Holy Spirit work in a coordinated manner, with the Spirit providing matter to the spiritual gifts which are then ministered through the Son, having been put into operation through the Father. Thus, through these quotations, Origen defines the relationship of the Spirit to the Father and to the Son.[168] Using the quotation, "moved over the water", from Gen 1:2 which refers to the Holy Spirit, Origen argues that the Spirit is not created, and asserts that even the quotation from Prov 8:22 where Solomon speaks of Wisdom as being created does not prove that the Holy Spirit was created.[169] In his teaching on sanctification, he applies the quotations, "the righteousness of God", from I Cor 1:30; "In the midst of two living beings thou shalt be known", from Hab 3:2 (LXX) and also allusions to Matt 11:27; I Cor 2:10; and John 16:12, 13 to define the role of Christ and the Holy Spirit in causing the knowledge of the Father in people.[170] The quotations from Ps 103 (104):29, 30; John 20:22; II Cor 5:17; Eph 4:24, Col 1:18 are applied to support the view that the Holy Spirit dwells only in those who are renewed by himself.[171]

Concerning the doctrine of Trinity, Origen applies Wis 7:25; Col 1:15; Heb 1:3 to support the view that Jesus is Son by nature, not by adoption of the Spirit.[172] While Origen's opponents, on the basis of the quotation, "My heart has disgorged a good word", from Ps 44 (5):1 argue that the Son has no individuality but is rather a mere probation of the Father, Origen, to the contrary insists that the Son or Word has its own life distinct from the Father and is endowed with concrete existence (Gr. *ousia*).[173] To support the view that the Son was begotten in eternity, he

---

[167] Origen, "Ioannem Fragmenta, 37", *ibid.*, p.227.
[168] Origen, "Comm. in Ioannem, ii.10 (6) ", *ibid.*, pp. 227-8.
[169] Origen, "De Principiis, I. Iii.3", *ibid.*, p. 229.
[170] Origen, "De Principiis, I. Iii. 4,8", *ibid.*, pp. 229.
[171] Origen, "De Principiis, I.iii.7", *ibid.*, p. 230.
[172] Origen, "De Principiis, I. Ii.4-5", *ibid.*, p. 231.
[173] Origen, "Comm. in Ioannem, i.24 (25)", *ibid.*, p. 231.

uses quotations from John 1:5, "God is light", and Heb 1:3, "the radiance of eternal light", where Christ is compared to the figure of light from the Father, the Father's radiance: "Therefore, as light can never be without radiance, how can it be said that there was a time when the Son was not?"[174] On the subordination of the Son, Origen uses the quotation, "The Father who sent me is greater than I", from John 10:29; 14:28 to support the teaching that the Father is known to himself more fully, clearly and completely than he is known by the Son.[175] On the distinctive spheres of the three Persons, Origen applies the quotation from Ps 32(33):6, "By the word of the Lord the heavens were set fast, and the whole power of them by the spirit (breath) of his mouth", to show that there is no question of lesser or greater in the godhead, although each person has a distinct sphere of operation. The Holy Spirit operates only in those who are sanctified, while the operations of the Father and the Son extend to both the good and the bad. But the quotations from I Cor 12:4-7 and I Cor 12:11 are used to support the view that, although each person has a sphere of operation, their functions are complementary so that there is no divergence in the Trinity.[176] The quotations from Exod 3:14; Luke 17:21 and John 15:22 are applied to show that the operations of both the Father and the Son concern both sinners and saints.[177]

That Origen also used philosophy as a hand maid to theology is seen in his quotation from Plato (*Republic*, 509 BC) with reference to the problem of whether God "is transcendent over 'being' in dignity and power" and that he imparts being to those to whom he imparts it or whether, God is himself "being". Here, Origen only defines the problem, and on the basis of Col 1:15, which speaks of "the image of the invisible God", leaves the question unresolved as to whether Jesus is to be called by such titles as "being of beings", "idea of ideas" and "the source", while the Father is spoken of as transcending all these titles.[178] In support of the unity between the Father and Son, Origen applies John 4:34; 10:30; 14:9, and also John 17:22, 14:11 and Acts 4:32. For the Son's pre-

---

[174]   Origen, "De Principiis iv. 28", *ibid.*, p. 232.
[175]   Origen, "De Principiis iv.35 (Greek in Justinian, Ep. ad. Menam [Mansi, ix. 525])", *ibid.*, p. 233.
[176]   Origen, "De principiis i.iii. 7", *ibid.*, pp. 239-240.
[177]   Origen, "De Principiis i.iii. 6", *ibid.*, p. 240.
[178]   Origen, "Contra Celsum vi.64", *ibid.*, p. 241.

existence with the Father, Origen applies John 8:58, 14:6 and Heb 1:3.[179]

In his discussion of the doctrine of the Church, Origen alludes to Joshua 2, Rahab's story and then quotes Matt 27:25 and Luke 2:34 to support the view that there is no salvation outside the Church since, the blood of Christ effects condemnation for those outside and effects salvation for those who believe in Christ's blood as a sign for redemption.[180] He also shows that the Church is as old as creation, that it has its origin before the foundation of the world, built on the foundation of not only the apostles but also the prophets one of whom is Adam. Christ loved the Church even before he gave himself for her. To do this, Origen applies the quotations from Eph 1:4, 5; 2:20; 5:25; 26, 32.[181] Regarding ordination into the ministry of the Church, Origen applies the quotation from Lev 8:5 to show that the congregation has a role of witnessing the ordination process. Thus he supports public witness for ordination.[182]

On the doctrine of the Last Things, Origen applies quotations from Ps 102(103):26; Isa 66:22; I Cor 7:31; 15:28 to show that the final consummation will not be utter annihilation of all things but a change of quality of matter.[183] He further explains that the eschatological end of the devil will not be an annihilation of his substance (i.e. being) but the perishing of his evil purposes. The eschatological view is grounded on a quotation from I Cor 6:26.[184] And on the eschatological punishment, Origen teaches that each sinner will be tormented by the fire which arises from the accumulation of his own sins. He also supports the view that God's purpose in such a divine punishment will always be corrective so that the sinner can sooner or later be restored. To provide a theological framework to this view, Origen applies the quotation from Isa 50:11, "the fire which you have kindled", and makes further allusions to Isa 10:17; 47:15; 66:16; Mal 3:3.[185] Origen's view here might as well be

---

[179]   Origen, "Comm. in Ionannem xiii. 36; Contra Celsum, viii. 12", *ibid.*, p. 242.
[180]   Origen, "Hom in Lib Iesu Nave, iii.5", *ibid.*, p. 243.
[181]   Origen, "Comm in Canticum, Canticorum ii", *ibid.*, pp. 244-45.
[182]   Origen, "Hom in Leviticum ix.9", *ibid.*, p. 246.
[183]   Origen, "De Principiis I. Vi. 4", *ibid.*, p. 256.
[184]   Origen, "De Principiis III. Vi.5", *ibid.*, p. 256.
[185]   Origen "De Principiis II. X 4, 6", *ibid.*, p. 258.

an early version of the doctrine of purgatory in the contemporary Roman Catholic Church.

This study of Origen's use of biblical quotations, in addition to the fathers already discussed, indicates that despite the strong philosophical background that the early Church fathers had, their theological discussions were always rooted in a theological use of biblical quotations.

Thascius Caecilius Cyprianus (Cyprian)
He was the Bishop of Carthage in the years 248-258 AD. In his teaching on the doctrine of the Church, Cyprian quotes as Scripture, Cant vi. 9, "My dove is one the favourite of her mother", and Eph 4:4, "There is one body, one Spirit, one hope of our calling, one Lord, one faith, one baptism, one God", in defining the sacrament of the unity of the Church.[186] The doctrine is further developed by the use of quotations from Matt 12:30; John 10:30 and John 5:7. On the basis of these quotations, Cyprian supports the view that divine unity is the source of the unity of the Church, and that failure to keep unity of the Church implies failure to keep God's Law and that this is tantamount to failure to keep hold on life and salvation.[187] The quotation from John 6:67-9 which is said to be Peter's representative speech on behalf of the Church is used to support the view that the Church is the bishop and the bishop is the Church and that not to be with the bishop means not to be in the Church:

> The Church is made up of the people united to their priest, the flock cleaving to its shepherd. Hence you should know that the bishop is in the church, and the church in the bishop, and that if anyone is not with the bishop he is not in the church.[188]

On the choice of bishop, Cyprian supports the view that the choice of bishops must be public in the Church. It must be made by the bishops with the approval of both the clergy and laity. The basis of this ecclesiastical teaching is the quotation from Num 20:25. There may also be an allusion to the election of Matthias in Acts 1:5-26 and the appointment of deacons of Acts 6:2.[189] Concerning Christian initiation, Cyprian shows that the administration of baptism and the seal of the

---

[186]   Cyprian "De Catholicae Ecclesiae Unitate 7", *ibid.*, p. 264.
[187]   Cyprian "De Catholicae Ecclesiae Unitate 7", *ibid.*, p. 265.
[188]   Cyprian "Epistle lxvii 7", *ibid.*, p. 266.
[189]   Cyprian "Epistle lxvii.4", *ibid.*, p. 269.

laying on of the hands are necessary for full sanctification. In the argument Cyprian suggests that the practice of laying on of hands invokes the Holy Spirit to come. In support of this view concerning these initial Christian rites, Cyprian makes allusions to the practice of laying hands by Peter and John, and then specifically quotes John 3:3, 5:

> Men can only be fully sanctified and sons of God if they are born of both sacraments; since Scripture says, "unless a man is born again of water and spirit he cannot enter the kingdom of God" (John 3:3;5).[190]

Athanasius

He lived from 296 to 373 AD. He was Bishop of Alexandria in the years 328-373. In his discussion of the doctrine of Man, Athanasius supports the view that God created "ex-nihilo" over against the Stoic concept of spontaneous generation, the Platonic notion of pre-existent matter and the Gnostic idea of the demiurge. Rather, God created man in his own image giving him a share in the power of his Word so that they become "shadows of the Word", and thus becoming "rational" (i.e. spiritual). To support the concept that man was created "ex nihilo", Athanasius applies quotations from Gen 1:1; Heb 11:3, and Hermas (Mandate).[191] To support the view that man is naturally mortal but the "likeness" of God imputed immortality on him, he applies quotations from Exod. 3:14; Ps 81 (82):6; and Wis 6:18.[192] On the basis of Wis 2:23, "God created man for incorruption", Athanasius strengthens the support for man's immortality that he had at creation, but lost through the Fall.[193]

On the doctrine of the Incarnate Son, Athanasius supports the view that since the Father is eternal, the Son is also eternal. To support this view, he alludes to the divine Name in Exod 3:14, 'Who Is', and appeals to the light-radiance metaphor[194] to support his theological position.[195] To show that the Son is perfect, and unchangeable, since capabilities to change and develop would imply imperfection, Athanasius applies quotations from John 14:9 and John 10:38. If the Word is capable of change and alteration, then it is difficult to see in which of his states man

---

[190] Cyprian "Epistle lxxiii.9 lxii 1", *ibid.*, 1, 269.

[191] "Athanasius "De Incarnatione, 3", *ibid.*, p. 274.

[192] "Athanasius "De Incarnatione, 4", *ibid.*, p. 275.

[193] Athanasius "De Incarnatione 5", *ibid.*, p. 276.

[194] Compare with my discussion of Origen's views on the doctrine of Trinity above.

[195] Athanasius, "Contra Arianos i. 24-5", in Bettenson, *The Early Christian Fathers*, p. 277.

is able to "see the father" in him (John 14:9) and it is difficult to see how he would be wholly "in the Father" (John 10:38). In this case, the moral character of the Son would largely remain undetermined.[196] Thus the Son must be perfect in order to be equal to God. Regarding the exaltation of Christ as man, he supports the position that Christ was exalted for us, that is as man and for man, not in his capacity as God, for in that capacity, the Word was already exalted:

> The exaltation is of the mankind. It is said after the incarnation of the Word to make it clear that "humbled" and "exalted' refer to the human nature. The Word being the image of the Father and immortal, "took the form of a servant" (Phil 2:7) and as man endured death for our sake in his own flesh, that thus he might offer himself to the Father on our behalf, therefore also as man he is said to be exalted because of us and on our behalf, that as by his death we all die in Christ, so also in Christ himself we may all be exalted, being raised from the dead and ascending into heaven.[197]

To support this exaltation of Christ as man and for man, Athanasius applies Phil 2:7, 9 and Heb 6:2. Thus in the process, humanity is deified (i.e. what he put on) for our sake.[198] Contrasting the Son with the creation and comparing him with the Father, Athanasius applies quotations from Heb 1:8, 10, 11 to support the eternal nature of the Son and the temporal nature of creation, while John 14:28 is used to show the subordination of the Son to the Father, not in substance and nature but in begetting.[199] That the creative Word was himself not created is supported by quotations from John 14:6, "I am the truth", Prov 8:30, "I was by his side ordering", and John 5:17, "my Father works hitherto, and I work".[200] Consequently, he is worshipped as God for the Son is not created but is proper to the substance of the Father. This is further supported by quotations from Heb 1:6; Isa 45:14; John 12:13; 16:15; and 20:28.[201]A quotation from Col 1:16 is applied to support the view that the Word was not created for us but we for him.[202] The view that the Son as the substantial Word of God has an eternal and distinctive personal

---

[196] Athanasius "Contra Arianos i.35", *ibid.*, p. 278.
[197] Athanasius "Contra Arianos i.41", *ibid.*, p. 278.
[198] Athanasius "Contra Arianos i.42", *ibid.*, p. 279.
[199] Athanasius "Contra Arianos i. 58", *ibid.*, pp. 280-81.
[200] Athanasius "Contra Arianos ii. 19-20", *ibid.*, pp. 281-82.
[201] Athanasius "Contra Arianos ii. 24", *ibid.*, p. 282.
[202] Athanasius "Contra Arianos, ii. 31", *ibid.*, p. 283.

existence, unlike man's word which is impersonal and inactive and without independent existence, is supported by quotations from Judith 8:16 quoted as Scripture, Exod. 3:14 and Heb 14:12.[203]

On the teaching concerning the begottenness as Son and createdness as man, the Arians who are Athanasius' opponents have theologically used Prov 8:22: "the Lord created me the beginning of his ways, for his works", to support the view that the Son was created. Over against this position, Athanasius argues that the phrase "created me" only refers to Jesus' humanity, not his divinity. It only applies to the incarnation. To support this view, he applies the quotation, "All things were made through him", from John 1:3, and, "are established in him", from Col 1:17, and argues that these scriptural references require that the Son exists before his incarnation, otherwise to say that he was before all things does not make much sense. In a further attempt to draw Christological clues from the disputed quotation of Proverbs, he observes that Christ calls the Father, "Lord", not because he was a servant as the term would generally mean, but rather because he "took the form of a servant", itself a quotation from John 4:34. Thus, in this manner, Athanasius accounts for the incarnation which is a mere dispensation of his being not the creation of his substance:

> The Word of God is not a creature but Creator, and says in the fashion of proverbs "he created me" at the time when he put on created flesh. if he says that he was "created for the work" it is clear that he means to signify not his substance but the dispensation which happened "for his work" and this dispensation is subordinate to being.[204]

To support the view that the Father and the Son are coherent, each being full and perfect in himself, each being life in himself, Athanasius applies the quotation from John 14:10 over against the Arians. The same quotation is used by the Arians to support the view that the Father and the Son are, taken separately, not full and perfect, because their perfection depends on each filling the emptiness of the other. Athanasius argues otherwise and finds the fullness and perfection of the Son in the expression "the fullness of the godhead" from Col 2:9. He further rejects the view that the Son is in the Father in the sense that "we live and move and exist in him", quoting Acts 17:28, since the Son is the life with

---

[203] Athanasius "Contra Arianos, ii. 34-35", *ibid.,* pp. 283-84.
[204] Athanasius, "Contra Arianos, ii. 50-51", *ibid.,* pp. 284-85.

substantial existence, and since "life does not live in the life, for then it would not be life".[205]

The quotations from John 10:30, "I and the father are one thing", and from John 14;10, "I in the Father and the Father in me", are used as a theological basis for the view that there is unity of substance between the Father and the Son, the Son being distinct from the Father as his offspring but identical with him as God.[206] On the two natures of Christ, Athanasius applies the quotations from Col 2:9; John 8:40; 10:30; 14:1; and Isa. 53:4 to show that although he was God, he had body for his own which he used as an instrument for our sakes. The properties of the flesh were in him. At the same time the works belonging to the Word (divine) were also performed through his body of flesh.[207] The Son's limitation of knowledge in his capacity as man is shown through a quotation from Mark 13:32, "Not even the Son knows", while his human weakness is also shown by a quotation from Matt. 26:39, "Let this cup pass".[208]

On the doctrine of Trinity, Athanasius shows that mutual relations of the Persons exist within the Godhead. Theological support for this view is found in the quotations, from John 3:16 where the Son is sent by the Father; John 16:7, where the Son sends the Spirit; John 17:4 where the Son glorifies the Father; John 8:26 where the Son speaks to the world what he heard from the Father, and John 14:26 where the Father sends the Spirit in the name of the Son.[209]

To show that the Spirit is not created but partook in the work of creation, Athanasius applies the quotation from Ps 103(104):29, 30, "Thou shalt take away their spirit and they shall fail, and return to their dust. Thou shalt send forth thy spirit and they shall be created". This quotation supports the view that the Spirit is not created. Rather, the Spirit takes part in the work of creation. To support the position that the Father creates all things through the Word, in the Spirit, he uses the quotation from Ps 32(33):6, "By the word of the Lord the heavens were set fast, and by the spirit of his mouth all the power of them."[210]

---

[205]   Athanasius "Contra Arianos, iii. 1", *ibid.*, p. 286.

[206]   Athanasius "Contra Arianos iii. 3-4", *ibid.*, pp. 286-87.

[207]   Athanasius "Contra Arianos iii. 31. Ep. ad. Serapionem iv.14", *ibid.*, pp. 288-89.

[208]   Athanasius "Contra Arianos iii. 43, 57", *ibid.*, p. 290.

[209]   Athanasius "Ep.ad. Seraionem i. 20-21", *ibid.*, p. 295.

[210]   Athanasius "Ep.ad Serapionean, iii.4", *ibid.*, p. 296.

On the doctrine of the Eucharist, Athanasius defines Eucharist as heavenly food and spiritual nourishment. To support this theological definition of Eucharist, he applies a quotation from John 6:61-63:

> The reason for his mention of the ascension into heaven of the Son of man was in order to draw them away from the material notion; that henceforward they might learn that the flesh he spoke of was heavenly food from above and spiritual nourishment given from him. For he says, "What I have spoken to you is spirit and life", which is as much as to say "what is displayed and given for the world's salvation is the flesh which I wear but this flesh and its blood will be given to you by me spiritually as nourishment, so that this may be bestowed spiritually on each, and may become for individuals a safeguard to ensure resurrection to eternal life".[211]

This discussion on the use of biblical quotations in the early Church reveals that the early church fathers applied biblical quotations theologically in order to either defend, or propound certain theological views. That they made conscious use of those quotations is clear from the fact that introductory formulas to biblical quotations are almost in every case maintained. Thus, the evidence from early patristic writings supports the thesis that biblical quotations are used theologically to support certain theological views. *Literary use* of biblical quotations is not a feature of this category of ancient religious writings. The cumulative effect of the results of the present investigation in the religious literature so far studied, namely, the *Mishnah*, the *Dead Sea Scrolls,* and the patristic writings, is the establishment of a strong case in favour of the thesis that biblical quotations were used theologically[212] in ancient Judaism and early Christianity. This strongly attests to the claim that the Evangelist Matthew used the Old Testament quotations theologically as this would be in keeping with the literary religious tradition that has come down to us from an age more or less contemporary with him.

---

[211] Athanasius "Ep. ad Serapionem, iv. 19", Bettenson, *The Early Christian Fathers*, p. 299.

[212] Hilary B.P. Mijoga, *Separate But Same Gospel, Preaching in African Instituted Churches in Southern Malawi*, Blantyre: Claim, 2000, pp. 91-93 finds that biblical quotations are used as sources of authority to support discussions in the course of preaching in both African Instituted Churches and mainstream churches in contemporary Malawian Christianity. It should be noted, however, that this is in the context of sermon preaching, and not in the context of a systematic theological discussion, a situation that obtains in the literature now under study. As such, we may not consider this contemporary usage as a theological usage of quotations in the sense that usage is understood in the present study.

The Apocryphal Writings

The Old Testament Apocryphal Writings

With a few exceptions, biblical quotations are not used theologically in the Old Testament apocryphal writings in the sense defined in this study. Over against theological use as defined at the beginning of this chapter, biblical quotations are in these writings used *literary*. The usual forms in which this *literary usage* take are direct quotations made without an expressed intention to quote which usually, as in the case of the writings discussed above, is indicated by an introductory formula. Introductory formulae are remarkably lacking in these writings, although direct quotations may be detected in some cases. The most common forms in which the Old Testament is used in these writings are the forms of linguistic and historical allusions. Linguistic allusions often take place through poetic expressions that are patterned on Old Testament language. Historical allusions to Old Testament tradition often appear in historical narratives in these writings. Sometimes the narratives take visionary, apocalyptic, and dialogue forms.

To say that quotations are not used theologically in these writings is not to imply that there is no theological expression on the whole. Rather, it means that specific theological teachings are not directly and centrally supported by the scriptural authority of specifically quoted biblical texts. Instead, their theology is expressed through the historical narratives or poetic expressions themselves without recourse to specific biblical texts to support the theological position that is taken at that point in the narrative. In these cases, the intention to quote is almost always lacking. However, where an intention to quote is clearly expressed through an introductory formula, it is often the case that the quotation which follows has been used theologically. These isolated instances of theological use of quotations in these apocryphal books further attest to the thesis that quotations were used theologically in ancient Judaism and early Christianity, and thus, providing literally background to Matthew's theological use of the fulfilment quotations in his Gospel.

These aspects of the use of biblical quotations in the Old Testament apocryphal books will now be demonstrated through the selected apocryphal books discussed below.

1 I Esdras

A clear example of the non-theological use of biblical quotations is provided by I Esdras chapter 1. The historical events that are alluded to in this chapter are recorded in II Chron 35; II Kings 23:21-25:30; and the relevant portions of the Book of Jeremiah.[213]Although the writer of I Esdras does not say that he is using this tradition, it is highly probable, if not quite obvious, that he is using or even quoting from them. If this observation is correct, then we are here provided with an example of *literary use* of biblical quotations where the intention to quote is lacking and the quotations are not drawn to serve a specific theological role. They are mainly drawn in order to bring the literal sense of a narrative or story to its dramatic completion.

The theological use of a biblical quotation at I Esd 1:58 is more of an exception than a norm in this category of apocryphal literature:

> Carried them away unto Babylon. And they burnt the house of the Lord and broke down the walls of Jerusalem and burnt the towers
>
> thereof with fire; and as for her glorious things, they never ceased till they had brought them all to naught: and the people that were not slain
>
> with the sword he carried unto Babylon; and they were servants unto him and to his children, till the Persians reigned, to fulfil the word of the
>
> Lord by the mouth of Jeremy: until the land hath enjoyed her Sabbath, the whole time of her desolation shall she keep Sabbath to fulfil three score and ten years.
>
> (cf. Chron 36:17-21)

The Jeremiah quotation sums up the whole historical narrative which reaches a climax in the evil reign of the last Judean kings and culminates into the Babylonian invasion and exile. The quotation puts these historical events into a prophetic perspective so that all that has been narrated was leading to the fulfilment of God's word. Thus the historical developments that culminate into exile and the exile itself are seen not as mere historical events, but as divine judgment for Judah's sins in

---

[213]   See R.H. Charles (ed), *The Apocrypha and Pseudepigraph on the Old Testament in English, Vol.1, Apocrypha*, Oxford: Clarendon, 1913, reprint 1971, p. 21. Chapter 1 corresponds to II Chron 35:1-36; chap 2:1-15 corresponds to Ezra 1:1-11; chap 2:16-30 corresponds to Ezra 4:6-23. See *Ibid.*, pp. 21-28. For a discussion on sources, see *Ibid.*, pp. 8-19.

which period God's people are denied the land blessing and all that it stood for. It would be seventy years before this blessing could be restored, and this for Israel meant salvation. Thus, the verse does not only refer to divine judgment upon people, but also contains a promise of salvation for once the land has enjoyed its sabbatical rest, God would bring back his people.

2   The First Book of Maccabees

In this book, we find instances where biblical quotations – quotations if they are – are expressed in poetic forms whose language is borrowed from the Old Testament poetic books. A good example of this is I Macc 1:25-28:

> And there was great mourning in Israel in every place
>
> And the rulers and the elders groaned; virgins and young men languished; and the beauty of the woman faded away
>
> Every bridegroom took up his lament, she that sat in the bridal-chamber mourned
>
> And the land was moved for her inhabitants and all the house of Jacob was clothed with shame.

Also I Mac 3:45:

> And Jerusalem was uninhabited like a wilderness, there was none of her offspring that went in or went out. And the Sanctuary was trodden down, and the sons of strangers (dwelt) in the citadel, a lodging- place for Gentile (it became); and joy was taken away from Jacob, and the pipe and the harp ceased.

Other examples are I Macc 1:37-40; 2:8-12. Although it is extremely difficult to show that these are quotations from the Old Testament-and they need not be – it cannot be doubted that the language of these passages is full of Old Testament thought-forms and expressions. Despite this, however, they might as well be original compositions by a writer who is very familiar with Old Testament poetic language. Indeed, it has been suggested that the main source of I Maccabees is eyewitness reports.[214]

Since we can not be certain whether the writer is directly using or quoting from Old Testament or whether he is creating his own material, it cannot be established whether any theological use of quotations is at stake.

---

[214]   See R.H. Charles (ed), *The Apocrypha and Pseudepigraph on the Old Testament,* p.61 for this view.

3   The Second Book of Maccabees

This book has its theology expressed through the historical narratives themselves without recourse to clear quotations, although its relationship to the First Book of Maccabees is similar to the relationship of the books of Chronicles to the books of Kings.[215] This being the case, it is probable that the writer of II Maccabees used I Maccabees as one of his sources.

At 2 Macc 12:43-45, the theological significance of prayers for the dead is intermingled with the doctrine of resurrection within the context of the story of Judah's military campaigns:

> He then collected from them, man by man, and the sum of two thousand drachmas of silver, which he forwarded to Jerusalem for sin-offering. In this he acted quite rightly and properly, bearing in mind the resurrection – for if he has not expected the fallen to rise again, it would have been superfluous and silly to pray for the dead – and having regard to the splendour of the gracious reward which is reserved for those who have fallen asleep in godliness – a holy and pious consideration! Hence he made propitiation for the dead, that they might be released from their sin (12:43-45).

Thus, in this extract, the theology of resurrection and the theology of propitiation for the dead through prayer are expressed within the context of this historical narrative.

Similarly, the writer's theology on the intercession of the saints is expressed at 2 Macc 15:16; that on retribution and chastening is expressed at 6:12-17; that on divine punishment is expressed at 4;38; 5:8-10; 7:29-36; 9:5-6; 13:4-8; 15:32-36. The doctrine of the bodily resurrection of the righteous is expressed at 7:11, 21-23; 14:44-46, as they rise to eternal life in the Messianic kingdom on earth. The doctrine of the millennial kingdom is expressed at 7:29, 33, 37; 14:15.

4   The Book of Tobit

Of interest to us in this book is that at Tob 2:6, there is a quotation from Amos 8:10 which has been used theologically. The quotation, "your feasts shall be turned into mourning, and all your ways into lamentation", is originally applied to define the divine judgment that came upon Israel through the Assyrian exile. It is important to note that Tobit is a hero who is said to have lived "in the days of Shalmaneser king of the Assyrians

---

[215]   *Ibid.*, p. 130.

(and) was carried away captive out of Thisbe".[216] Thus the story is set within the context of Assyrian exile which is itself a divine fulfilment of Amos' prophecy. In causing this exile, God has acted in accordance with the prophetic word that he gave to his servant Amos the prophet. By using this quotation, the writer of this book intends us to see the exile not as a mere historical accident but as a divine punitive act necessitated by the sins committed by Israel. This is a theological use of a biblical quotation.

Although the writer may have depended on the Book of Genesis and the other historical books of the Old Testament for much of his material,[217] the narrative only alludes to those sources so that any real quotations can only be identified with great difficulty except in those few cases where both the intention to quote and the quotations themselves are clearly indicated. As was the case with I Esdras 1:58, this clear theological use of a biblical quotation is more of an exception than a norm in this apocryphal writing.

5   The Book of Judith

Although it has been suggested that the writer has quoted Num 23:19 at 8:16; Exod 15:3 at 9:7 and 16:3; Gen 14:19, 20 at 13:18,[218] it can be shown that these are mere allusions than clear quotations. The supposed quotation at Judith 8:16 is introduced by the conjunction, "For", a term that could naturally introduce a quotation. But the context in which the quotation occurs indicates that the writer has used the same conjunction over eight times within 16 verses, and almost none of the others has anything to do with a clear quotation. Therefore, we cannot simply conclude that the conjunction is in that verse alone intended to introduce a clear quotation.

The alleged quotations at Judith 9:7 and 16:3 from Exod 15:3 also turn out, upon examination, to be mere allusions. The supposed quotation at 9:7 is simply a literary integral part of the historical narrative without any hint that a biblical text is being quoted. The alleged quotation at Judith 16:3 is actually part of a speech made by Judith presented in a poetic fashion. There is no indication that any biblical text is being quoted either.

---

[216]   *Ibid.*, p. 202.
[217]   *Ibid.*, p. 192.
[218]   *Ibid.*, p. 246.

The claim that there is a quotation at Judith 13:8 is also lacking in substance. The supposed quotation is really no more than a literary integral part of the dialogue between Ozias and Judith. Again there is no indication that a biblical text is being quoted at this point. This mistaken identity of biblical quotations indicates not only the fact that this category of apocryphal books rarely uses clear biblical quotations, but also the fact that quotations can in many cases only be identified with great difficulty. Undisputably, clear quotations are relatively few. However, in such cases it can almost always be shown that such quotations are used theologically as the isolated cases of I Esdras 1:58 and Tob 2:6 have shown.

6   The Book of Sirach

It is almost certain that the book is based on the biblical book of Proverbs. The writer has used the Old Testament material for the construction of his work. A comparison of Sir 24:1-34 with Prov 8:22-9:12 is sufficient to show this. However, the material is dressed into poetic language in which personified Wisdom is the character speaking. Thus, while the book alludes to the canonical book of Proverbs in language and content, the writer, through the speaker, does not often use the borrowed material for specific theological purposes in the form of quotations. There is in many cases no expression of the intention to quote. This kind of use of biblical material further illustrates *literary use* of borrowed material over against theological use of quoted sources. There is no attempt to clarify particular theological questions through the use of specific and direct quotations.

7   The Wisdom of Solomon

The book has a lot of allusions to the Old Testament. However, its poetic language taking the form of either direct speech by Wisdom herself or reported speech concerning her by Solomon, makes any attempt to determine biblical quotations an extremely difficult task, although allusions to Old Testament are quite numerous. Its theology is also mainly expressed within the same poetic context without much recourse to direct and theological use of quotations. For instance, the transcendence of God is the main teaching of Wisdom 1-11, necessitating his performance through an intermediary who turns out to be Wisdom herself (9:10). The intermediary is herself vested with divine qualities like omnipotence (7:27); omniscience (8:8; 9:11); she is an agent of creation (9:9); and administrator of all things (8:1). Thus, through the poetic narratives, Wisdom is theologically defined in Messianic terms.

8   The Book of Baruch

Like the other books discussed above, allusions to the Old Testament abound, but not many can be regarded as biblical quotations. Some examples of allusions in this book are Bar 4:7 which alludes to Deut 32:16, 17; Bar 4:15 which alludes to Deut 28:49, 50; and Bar 4:20 which alludes to Isa 52:1. The author's familiarity with the canonical texts may sufficiently account for both linguistic and historical parallels that exist, and direct quoting need not be posited.

9   The Book of Jubilees.[219]

This book, again testifies to the expression of theology through the narratives without much support from theological use of biblical quotations, despite the abundant allusions to the Old Testament. A casual reading of any part of this book is sufficient to impress upon the reader that the book is probably a re-writing of the Genesis story.

That the writer has borrowed the Genesis material is almost certain. However, the writer comes to his task as if the story was being written for the first time and makes no conscious attempt to acknowledge the quoted material. Neither does he use the borrowed material theologically in support of specific theological doctrines.

Its theology, like the other apocryphal books, comes to us through the historical narrative itself. The doctrine of pre-determination with regard to the ways of man is expressed in this way: "And the judgment of all is ordained and written on the heavenly tablets in righteousness – even judgment of all who depart from the path which is ordained for them to walk in (5:13)."

The doctrine of human freedom and responsibility is also expressed in 5:13, "If they walk therein, judgment is written for every creature", and in 5:17-18, "if they turn to him in righteousness, he will forgive all their transgressions and pardon all their sins".

The doctrine of human depravity is not based on the effects of the Fall, which, according to the writer of this book, is limited to Adam and the animal world, but is based on the moral failure of the daughters of

---

[219]   See R.H. Charles (ed), *The Apocrypha and Pseudepigrapha of the Old Testament*, vol. II, Pseudepigrapha, Oxford: Clarendon, 1913, reprint 1969, pp. 1-82.

men who failed to resist seduction from the angels who had been sent down to teach men (5:1-4). The eternal validity of the moral and ritual Law is indicated by its being written on the "heavenly tablets":

> On this account, it is prescribed on the heavenly tablets as touching all those who know the judgment of the Law, that they should cover their shame (3:31). For this reason it is ordained and written on the heavenly tablets, that they should celebrate the feast of weeks in this month once a year, to renew the covenant every year (6:17).

The doctrine of the final judgment is again defined in a narrative style without apparent recourse to biblical quotations. The Lord will judge all without regard of their persons. Both heaven and earth are subject to this judgment. This will take place at the end of the Messianic Kingdom (5:10,14,15; 23:30).

This study of selected Old Testament apocryphal books reveals that biblical quotations were not often used theologically, although in relatively a few exceptional cases such usage may be attested. Although on the surface quotations appear to abound, upon closer investigation many of these simply turn out to be mere historical or literary allusions to the Old Testament. The theology of these books is not predominantly defined by the use of biblical quotations, but rather it is often expressed through the historical narratives themselves in the case of historical books, and through the poetic expressions in the case of the poetic books. Unwillingness to use biblical quotations clearly and consciously in support of the theological tenets enshrined in these books is one of their characteristic features.

The New Testament Apocryphal Writings

The New Testament apocryphal writings broadly fall into two different categories. The earliest New Testament apocryphal writings like the Gospel of Peter, the Gospel of Egyptians, Papyrus Oxrhynchus 840 and Papyrus Egerton 2 use the New Testament books, especially the gospels, in the manner the Old Testament apocryphal books use the Old Testament. What is significant for us is that they do not use quotations theologically. Their theology, like that of the Old Testament apocryphal books is expressed through the narrative which often takes the form of a dialogue between the Risen Lord and some members of his Church, or retrospectively, between the earthly Jesus and his disciples. While verbal reminiscences and historical allusions to the canonical gospels abound, there is no effort to use quotations theologically. In a sense, the Risen Lord who speaks directly takes over the authority that would otherwise be accorded to a quoted portion of canonical Scripture.

However, the latter New Testament apocryphal books progressively begin to acquire features of a theological treatise – like the patristic writings – of which the most significant one was their theological use of biblical quotations. This feature can be seen developing in *Kerygma Petrou*, which is one of the apocryphal writings that has transitional features that obtained as this literary genre moved from the apocryphal style of the early Christian literature to apologetic writing similar to the patristic writings.[220] Within the New Testament apocryphal genre, this process can be seen to have reached maturity in the *Pseudo Titus* type of apologetic writing. Thus, in terms of theological use of biblical quotations, the latter New Testament apocryphal books fall into the same category as the *Mishnah,* the Dead Sea Scrolls, and the patristic writings, while the earliest New Testament apocryphal writings fall into the category of Old Testament apocrypha. The former category expresses its theology mainly through the theological use of biblical quotations, while the later expresses its theology mainly through historical narratives, and poetic expressions which take the forms of dialogue, visions, stories etc. In the New Testament apocryphal books discussed below, I have attempted to show these characteristic features.

The Earliest New Testament Apocryphal Writings

1 The Gospel of Egyptians

This apocryphal gospel was known and was used as Scripture by Clement of Alexandria, although he did not consider it to be at par with the four canonical gospels. His opponents similarly used this apocryphal gospel. A few extracts from it have reached us through quotations found in Clement's *Stromates III.*[221]

The Gospel of the Egyptians is extremely difficult to reconstruct. However, the extracts from Clement indicate that one of its main features was the presence of the dialogues of the Risen Lord with other saintly personalities and had some Gnostic elements, elements which in Egypt set into the gospel tradition at the earliest period. Clement writes:

---

[220]   See E. Hennecke, *New Testament Apocrypha* vol. II, London: SCM, 1965, p. 90.

[221]   See E. Hennecke, *New Testament Apocrypha vol.*, I, London: SCM, 1962, pp. 166-178.

> When Salome asked, "How long will death have power?" The Lord answered, "So long as ye women bear children" – not as if life was something bad and creation evil, but as teaching the sequence of nature.[222]

And also:

> Those who are opposed to God's creation because of continence, which has a fair-sounding name, also quote the words addressed to Salome which I mentioned earlier. They are handed down, as I believe, in the gospel of the Egyptians. For, they say: the Saviour himself said, "I am come to undo the works of the female", by the female meaning lust, and by the works birth and decay.[223]

A study of these quotations from Clement and the others that follow[224] show that, while the Gospel of Egyptians itself does not use theologically quotations from any canonical gospel, the words of the Lord in his dialogues and the responses of the saints addressed by him, form the theological basis for the arguments between Clement and his opponents over the question of marriage and sexuality. Thus, it is Clement and his opponents who use quotations theologically not the *Gospel of the Egyptians* itself.

2   The Gospel of Peter

It has indications of further development of the gospel traditions found in the four canonical gospels,[225] and there is an attempt to show through these additional details that Christ is Lord, "the testimony of belief is replaced by apparently direct proof of truth."[226] The gospel has a lot of allusions to the four canonical gospels which, however, appear as integral part of the narrative for literary completeness rather than for any specific theological function. There is no evidence of any intention to consciously and clearly quote from the gospel tradition, and then follow such a clear quotation with a theological explanation. Any theology there is finds expression through the historical narrative itself as the writer

---

[222] *Ibid.*, p. 166

[223] Ibid., pp. 166-67

[224] *Ibid.*, pp. 166-78

[225] *Ibid.,* p. 180.

[226] *Ibid.,* p. 181.

retells the Gospel story. Even the only Old Testament quotation from Deut 21:23 at Pet. 2:5 and 5:15 is not used theologically.[227]

3 Papyrus Egerton 2[228]

The two synoptic periscopes which come second and third (Ll. 32-59 of f.1[r] and f.2[r]) show close contact with all the three synoptic Gospels. There are verbal reminiscences which indicate that the writer knew the parallel canonical texts but that he had none of them before him as he wrote. The first periscope is Johannine (Ll. 1-31 of f1[v] and f1[r]). The fourth periscope describes an apocryphal miracle which Jesus performs along the banks of the River Jordan (LL 60-75 of f2[v]). Both the historical allusions to the canonical gospel and the linguistic style of the narrative as a whole are reminiscent of the canonical traditions. Even if one took them for quotations, they could not be said to have been used theologically. The first two periscopes presented below should suffice to show this point:

f. I[v] (LL 1-20)

(I) to the lawyers "everyone who acts contrary to the law, but not me! (5) . what he does, as he does it". And having turned to the rulers of the people he spoke the following saying, "ye search scriptures in which ye think that ye have life; these are they (10) which bear witness of me[a]. Do not think that I came to accuse you to my Father! There is one that accuses you even Moses, on whom Ye have set your hope."[b]. And when they said (15): "We know that God hath spoken to Moses, but as for thee, we know not whence thou art",[c] Jesus answered and said unto them, "Now already accusation is raised[d] against your unbelief (20). No one otherwise."

f. I[r] (LL 22-41)

> to gather stones together to stone him[e]. And the rulers laid (25) their hands on him that they might arrest him and deliver him to the multitude. But they were not able to arrest him because the hour of his betrayal was not yet come[f]. (30) But he himself, the Lord, escaped out of their hands[g] and turned away from them.
>
> (II) And behold a leper drew near him and said, "Master Jesus, wandering with lepers and eating with them was I? Publicans art thou? (35) in the inn; I also became a leper. If thou therefore

---

[227] *Ibid.*, pp. 183 - 84, especially p. 184 for a similar view in contrast with the way the same quotation has been used at John 19:31 in the New Testament.

[228] *Ibid.*, pp. 94-97

wilt, I am made clean". And thereupon the leprosy departed from him. And the Lord (40) said to him, "Go thy way and show thyself to the priests[h]

[a. John 5:39, b. John 5:45; c. John 9:29; d. cf. John 12:31; e. John 10:31; f. John 7:30; g. John 10:39; h. Mark 1:40-44; Matt 8:2-4; Luke 5:12-14]

Looking at these quotations – if quotations we might call them – it is clear that they are not used to define any specific theological teaching. Rather they are used as integral literary parts of the narrative which has taken the form of a dialogue between the Lord and his Jewish opponents. They have no distinctive theological function. This is yet another case where quotations (or better still, allusions) are used *literary* in order to complete the literal sense of the narrative. Even the intention to quote is lacking.

4   Papyrus Oxrhynchus 840

This is an unknown gospel of the synoptic type. Its first seven lines contain Jesus' conclusion to a discourse given in Jerusalem in which he warns his disciples against false confidence. Then there is recorded a visit to the Temple where Jesus engages into a sharp debate with a Chief Priest called Levi. Jesus' critical rejoinder in the debate is in substance paralleled in Matt 22:27. The subject concerns ritual purification which was absolutely necessary before one visited the Temple court. There are allusions to John 4:14; 13:10; Matt 7:6; 15:14; 23:16-39.[229] Again, these are allusions to the canonical gospels, not biblical quotations used theologically. They are used merely to complement the narrative.

The Late New Testament Apocryphal Writings

In contrast to the earliest New Testament apocryphal writings, which did not use biblical quotations theologically, these later apocryphal writings progressively use biblical quotations as they become more and more apologetic in tone. Two of these should be sufficient to demonstrate this point. The first one, *Kerygma Petrou,* represents a transitory stage from early Christian literature to full-blown apologetic writing comparable to the patristic fathers. In the realm of apocryphal writings, the mature stage of apologetic development is represented by *Pseudo Titus*:

---

[229]   *Ibid.,* pp. 92-4.

5   Kerygma Petrou

This book has features of both early Christian missionary discourse and late apologetic Christian literature.[230] The following extracts[231] show non-theological use of biblical quotations:

> Neither worship him in the manner of the Jews; for they also, who think that they alone know God, do not understand, worshipping angels and archangels, the months and the moon (Gal 4:10; Col 2:16, 18). And when the moon does not shine, they do not celebrate the so-called first Sabbath, also as they do not celebrate the new moon or the feast of the unleavened bread or the feast of Tabernacles or the great Day of Atonement. (Clem. Alex., Strom, vi. 5.39-41)

Here, the references to Gal 4:10; Col 2:16,18 are not used theologically but *literary*. They only, at this point, illustrate the manner in which Jews worship. That the writer is not applying theologically any specific passage is seen in the fact that the phrase "worshipping angels, and archangels, the months and the moon" is not found in any single passage. Gal 4:10 only mentions "days" and "months" and "times of the years". The word "moon" is found in Col 2:16, but in the phrase "new moon" in a context of judgment and is paralleled by "meat", "drink" the sense being that of a warning that no one should be allowed to judge believers on the basis of their ritual observations with regard to these issues. The word "angels" is found at Col 2:18, but the word "archangels" is completely missing in these references. This means that the writer was only making a list of things that are influential in determining Jewish worship, and hence, he collects these items from a number of biblical references.

Again in the following extract, there is no theological use involved:

> If now anyone of Israel wishes to repent and through my name to believe in God, his sins will be forgiven him (Lk 24:47; Acts 5:31; 10:43). And after twelve years go ye out into the world that no one may say, "We have not heard it" (Clem. Alex., Strom vi. 5.43).

Here, again, the references to Luke 24:47; Acts 5:31; 10:43 with regard to the idea of forgiveness are not used theologically. Peter merely records the Lord's discourse to the disciples without making any theological application.

---

[230]   Hennecke, *New Testament Apocrypha*, vol. II p. 97.

[231]   For a detailed study of the extracts from *Kerygma Petrou*, see *Ibid.*, pp. 94-104.

But theological use is also attested in this latter apocryphal writing. This is clear in the following extract:

> Learn then, ye also, holily and righteously what we deliver to you and keep it, worship God through Christ in a new way. For we have found in the Scriptures, how the Lord says, "Behold, I make with you a new covenant not as I made (one) with your fathers in Mount Horeb" (cf. Jer 31 [38]: 31; Deut 29:1). A new one has been made with us. For what has reference to the Greeks and Jews is old. But we are Christians, who as a third race worship him in a new way. (Clem. Alex., Strom vi. 5. 39-41).

Clearly, the quotations in this extract provide the basis for the definition of a new relationship to God through Jesus on which a new form of worship is to be based. Thus the quotations here provide a theological basis for the new form of worship, namely, the Christian worship.

There is also a general attestation to the Christological (and therefore theological) use of Old Testament quotations in defining Christ's passion and resurrection in the manner of I Pet 1:10-12.

The writer says:

> But we opened the books of the prophets which we had, which partly in parables, partly in enigmas, partly with certainty and in clear words name Christ Jesus, and found his coming, his death, his crucifixion and all the rest of the tortures which the Jews inflicted on him, his resurrection and his assumption to heaven before the foundation (? better doubtless, before the destruction) of Jerusalem, how all was written that he had to suffer and what would be after him. Recognizing this, we believed God in consequence of what is written of (in reference to) him. (Clem. Alex., *Strom* vi. 15.128).

6 Pseudo Titus

This apocryphal writing does not only have biblical quotations but also has made a *literal use* of other apocryphal writings. The writer, throughout the document, commends the life of chastity as the ideal way of life for the ascetic Christian believer.[232]

In the following extract the quotation from I Cor 2:9, which also recalls Isa. 64:4, is used by the writer to define the divine wisdom from the Spirit which is here theologically interpreted as the celibate life of the ascetic believer:

---

[232]   *Ibid.,* p.142.

> Great and honourable is the divine promise which the Lord has made with his own to them that are holy and pure, "He will bestow upon them what eyes have not seen nor ears heard, nor has it entered into any human heart" (I Cor 2:9). And from eternity to eternity there will be a race in comparable and incomprehensible.[233]

The "holy and pure" are those who practice celibate life and God will make them into a special race "incomparable and incomprehensible" through the spiritual knowledge he bestows upon them concerning the virtue of celibacy. This is further clarified in the following extract:

> Blessed then are those who have not polluted their flesh by craving for this world, but are dead to the world that they may live for God! To whom neither flesh nor blood has shown deadly secrets *but the spirit has shone upon them and shown some better thing* so that even this. and instant of our pilgrimage on the earth they may display an angelic appearance. As the Lord says, "Such are to be called angels" (Mk 12:25 par).[234]

This quotation from Mark 12:25 provides a theological linchpin for the whole epistle. The "better thing" which the Spirit has "shown" to the ascetic believer is the blessedness of celibate life. And the rest of the epistle develops this theme. The writer then continues:

> Those then "who are not defiled with women" (Rev 14:4) he calls an angelic host. Those who have not abandoned themselves to men, he calls virgins, as the apostle of Christ says, "the unmarried think day and night on godly things" (I Cor 7:34), that is to act properly and to please Him alone, why should a virgin who is already betrothed to Christ be united with a carnal man?[235]

The quotations from Revelation and Corinthians further provide a theological definition of the "better thing" which the Spirit has shown to those that are pure and holy. Hence, according to this special spiritual knowledge, the holy and pure are those who are not defiled by either men or women, and are members of the angelic host.

In a similar fashion the quotation, "one cannot serve two masters, for he obeys the one and despises the other", from Matt 6:24 is applied to show that married life robs God of his glory. The quotation, "That in the mountains throughout sixty days they might bewail her virginity", from

---

[233]   *Ibid.*, p. 144.

[234]   *Ibid.* Emphasis mine.

[235]   *Ibid.*

Judg 11:38 concerning Jephthah's daughter, is used to provide a theological explanation of the passions that go with celibate life. Further, this quotation (the mention of the figure sixty) and those from II Cor 4:8 and 11:23 are used to support the teaching that the suffering of the ascetic brings the sixtyfold reward of holiness, and that a man attains to glory through much suffering. The quotation, "Whom I love, I rebuke and chasten", from Rev 3:19 is applied to support the view that the sufferings of the ascetic believer are chastisements aimed at making the ascetic pure.

The following apocryphal quotation:

> Oh! As a virgin, as a woman, so is the mystery of resurrection (which) you have shown to me, you who in the beginning of the world did institute vain feasts for yourselves and delighted in the wantonness of the Gentiles and behaved in the same way as those who take delight therein.[236]

Is used to define the mystery of resurrection life as a virgin life, a life of ultimate blessedness and purity. Quotations from I Cor 15:50; Jer 9:23; 17:5, and Ps 118:8 are used to support the view that it is vanity to trust in man:

> Where then art thou, now who has passed the time of thy youth happily with a sinner, the apostle testifying moreover that "neither flesh nor blood will possess the kingdom of God?" (I Cor 15:50). And again the Law runs, "Let not a man glory in his strength, but rather let him trust in the Lord" (Jer 9:23) and Jeremiah says, "Accursed is he who puts his hope in man", (17:5). And in the Psalms it is said, "it is better to trust in the Lord than to rely on men" (118:8). Why then art thou not afraid to abandon the Lord and to trust in a man who in the last judgment will not save thee but rather destroy.[237]

By the phrase "trust in man", the writer of this epistle implies that trust which develops between a man and a woman in the context of a mutual love relationship whether or not such a relationship is marital.

Thus the epistle *Pseudo Titus* is clearly an apologetic writing comparable to the patristic writings and uses biblical quotations (and apocryphal ones) theologically in support of the doctrine of celibacy.

---

[236] The source of this quotation is not known. See *Ibid.*, p. 146, note 4.
[237] *Ibid.*, p. 146.

Conclusion

This study on the role of quotations in ancient Judaism and early Christianity has revealed that biblical quotations were used theologically to support particular theological teachings in mainline Judaism as the *Mishnah* shows, in sectarian Judaism as the *Dead Sea Scrolls* indicate, and in early Christianity as the early patristic writings reveal. The only exception to theological use of biblical quotations is found in the apocryphal writings, especially the Old Testament apocryphal writings and the early New Testament apocryphal literature, where biblical quotations, or better allusions (with a few exceptions) are in the main used *literary*. These apocryphal writings express their theology mainly through the narrative and poetic expressions. But the cumulative effect of the common theological use of biblical quotations in the *Mishnah,* the *Dead Sea Scrolls*, and the Patristic writings is so strong that one would be compelled to see theological use of biblical quotations as a common feature in ancient Judaism and early Christianity. It can, therefore, be concluded that the literary background to the Evangelist Matthew's work attests very strongly to a common Jewish style of religious literary presentations in which the Old Testament was considered as an authority from which support for various theological teachings could be drawn.

The apocryphal exception can be satisfactorily accounted for by the presence in them of strong apocalyptic interests and an apparent lack of clear apologetic concerns. That apologetic motives played a significant role in the use of biblical quotations is attested by the difference between early and late New Testament apocryphal writings that has been observed in this study. As this type of apocryphal writings became more apologetic, the theological use of biblical quotations also increased. The apologetic factor explains why biblical quotations are used theologically in the late New Testament apocryphal writings and not in the earliest New Testament apocrypha.

The New Testament in general and the Gospel of Matthew in particular is closer to the common Jewish style of religious literary presentations presented by the *Mishnah*, the *Dead Sea Scrolls*, and the patristic writings than it is to the apocryphal writings,[238] and this

---

[238]   W. Scheemelcher, in the introduction to a chapter on Apostolic Pseudepigrapha, makes a similar observation with regard to New Testament epistles which he finds to be closer to the theological treaties in their orientation than to apocryphal writings, "It is a fact, to which in my

closeness extends to the theological use of biblical quotations. The thesis that the Evangelist Matthew used the fulfilment quotations, therefore, better suits the evidence, for as a religious writer, he should be expected to follow the literary customs of his day, and one of the significant customs of that day was the theological use of biblical quotations wherever legal, apologetic and kerygmatic considerations were determinative.

I therefore conclude that the Evangelist Matthew, like most religious writers of his day, used biblical quotations theologically. The manner in which he did this with regard to the fulfilment quotations in his Gospel is the subject of my investigation in the next two chapters of this work.

---

opinion sufficient attention has not yet been paid, that the real letters of the New Testament do not live on in the apocryphal literature that the epistles of the New Testament shade into the theological treatise literature, and that the few apostolic Pseudepigrapha...which we possess represent no pure type, but are either theological treatises which make use of certain elements of a letter, or literary experiments that have deliberately been made pseudonymous". See Hennecke, *New Testament Apocypha*, Vol. II., p. 91. And I add that it is not only the New Testament epistles that resemble the theological treatises (represented in this study by the patristic writings) but also the rest of the New Testament resemble the theological treatises, and that this similarity extends to the manner in which biblical quotations are theologically used in both the New Testament and the patristic writings. It is also important to note that the later New Testament apocryphal writings are an exception within the apocryphal family in that they share this feature as it has already been shown in this chapter.

Chapter 3

Fulfilment Quotations in the Infancy Narrative

Introduction

Although it has been argued that the fulfilment quotations we find in the Gospel according to Matthew "are not an absolutely special case within Matthean Old Testament quotations" so that "one may not consider the formula quotations as a unique theological problem,"[1] the fact that fulfilment quotations have attracted much scholarly attention points in the opposite direction. In fact, while their extent and characteristics are widely agreed, "their origin and function are keenly contested."[2] It is therefore not a surprise that the subject continues to draw scholarly interest to the effect that most recent studies on Matthew's use of the Old Testament have concentrated on them and the findings have been used to support widely diverging views on the origin and purpose of the Gospel according to Matthew itself.[3] In the present inquiry on the origin and function of the infancy fulfilment quotations, the evidence appears to favour the view that these fulfilment quotations have their origin in the evangelist himself and that he employs them in order to introduce distinctive theological themes in his gospel which in their totality, show that Jesus is indeed the Messiah, according to the scriptures.[4]

---

[1] Ulrich Luz, *Matthew 1-7, A Continental Commentary*, pp. 156,157.

[2] Graham N. Stanton, *A Gospel for a New People, Studies in Matthew*, Edinburgh: T & T Clark, 1992, p. 349. Cf. R.T. France, *The Gospel According to Matthew*, p. 39.

[3] *Ibid.*, pp. 349, 355.

[4] For a good summary of the background and development of the concept of Messiah, see James Hastings, *Dictionary of the Bible,* revised by Frederick C. Grant and H.H. Rowley, Second Edition, Edinburgh: T&T Clark, 1963, pp. 646-55. For a brief discussion of the Messianic texts in the Old Testament in relationship to the ancient Near Eastern cultural context, see Helmer Ringgren, *The Messiah in the Old Testament*, Studies in Biblical Theology No. 18, Chicago: Alec R. Allenson, 1956. The messianic theme in the context of prophetic promise and Christological fulfilment is worthy of a fresh investigation because, as Reventlow observes, "More recent research has brought considerable changes to exegetical knowledge

They identify the person of Jesus as that of the Messiah who was long foretold in Old Testament Scriptures and hence emphasize that Jesus is the fulfilment of the Old Testament.

The task before me, therefore, is to show that the fulfilment quotations have their origin in the evangelist and that they serve specific theological interests. The study will show that they define the person of Jesus, the Messiah by referring to his divinity implied in the virgin birth and his divine call from Egypt, and by referring to his Messianic status implied in his Davidic Sonship.

There are four clear fulfilment quotations in the infancy narrative, namely: 1:22-23; 2:15; 17, and 23. Although the quotation at 2:5-6 does not possess all indications of a fulfilment quotation, it will be treated as a fulfilment quotation here because the differences it has in comparison with the clear fulfilment quotations appear to be necessitated by the context in which it is found.

Almost all the distinctive themes that the evangelist presents in the Gospel are found in the first two chapters of the Gospel.[5] They appear to be concentrated in these first two chapters in order to serve as a theological prologue to the rest of the Gospel narrative. The *person* of the Messiah has to be identified before his *work* can be understood.

The Origin and Character of the Fulfilment Quotations

The Problem of the First Century Biblical Textual Tradition

Before I consider the origin and character of the fulfilment quotations, it is probably in order, first, to reflect on the nature of the first century biblical textual tradition and the manner in which New Testament writers used it. This would shed some light on the problem of their origin and character.

Two theories have been suggested to explain the origin of the LXX. The first postulates that there was an archetypal text which originated around 300 BC as a Greek translation of the Torah in a Jewish community in Alexandria and that it had three major recensions: Hesychian (Egyptian), Lucian (Syrian) and Origen's Hexapla (Palestinian). The difficulty with this theory is that it can not explain the

---

both with respect to the so-called 'messianic' sections in the Old Testament and to the New Testament. Both the time of origin and the character of 'the Messianic prophecies' like Isa 9 1-6; 11:1-5; Micah 5:1-5 are still disputed". The present study however, takes for granted the Messianic character of such Old Testament texts. See Henning Graf Reventlow, *Problems of Biblical theology in the Twentieth Century*, London: SCM, 1986, p. 48.

[5] Stanton, *Studies in Matthew*, p. 360.

textual variations of the Old Testament citations in Jewish writings (e.g. Philo), in the New Testament and in early church fathers. This led to its abandonment.

The other theory postulates that there was no archetypal text. Rather, the LXX started life as oral renderings of the Hebrew text in the form of Aramaic targums in various synagogues. These oral targumic versions were later reduced to writing which then developed into an official targum, that is the LXX.[6] Thus Kahle sees variant traditions behind Origen's Hexapla, in Old Latin version and to some extent in Philo and Josephus while Manson sees similar Greek texts developing along regional lines. For instance, behind the Theodotion is seen a Greek Targum of Asia while Targums of Syria and Egypt are thought to lie behind Lucian and the LXX.[7] It is in the light of this theory that Manson suggests that the LXX we now possess "is the debris of primitive diversity only very imperfectly overcome rather than the record of sporadic lapses from a primitive uniformity."[8] And Kahle concludes, "The task which the LXX presents to the scholar is not the 'reconstruction' of an imaginative Ur-text, nor the discovery of it but a careful collection and investigation of all the remains and traces of earlier versions of the Greek Bible which differ from the Christian standard text."[9]

In recent LXX studies, however, the theory of multiple and simultaneous development of Greek targumic texts leading to subsequent compilation of the LXX has suffered on two counts, first, Kahle's treatment of Aristeas tradition[10] and the quotations from Philo is highly questionable. Extant Greek Targums are lacking, and the manner he relates the New Testament quotations to the Greek Old Testament betrays a radical treatment.

Secondly, the Qumran evidence favour an archetypal view of LXX origin. F.M. Cross regards this evidence from the Dead Sea Scrolls as "decisive evidence for the older view".[11] This view is further strengthened

---

[6] Earle E. Ellis, *Paul's Use of the Old Testament*, London: Oliver Boyd, 1957, pp. 16-17.

[7] *Ibid.*, p.18.

[8] *Ibid.*

[9] *Ibid.*

[10] *Ibid.*, p 19. For the Letter of Aristeas, see R.H. Charles, *The Apocrypha and Pseudepigrapha of the Old Testament*, Vol. II, Oxford: Clarendon, 1969, pp. 83-122.

[11] Quoted in Ellis, *Paul's Use*, p. 19 note 3. For a thorough discussion of the "decisive evidence" from Qumran with regard to its probable witness to a "Ur-text", probably an old Palestinian text lying behind both the MT and the LXX itself, see Frank Moore Cross, Jr. *The*

by the observation by most New Testament scholars that not only did New Testament writers often approximate their quotations to LXX but also did that in relation to a Palestinian form of LXX, that is MSS A, Q and Lucian, as over against the MSS B and X (Aleph). They also agree that New Testament writers did not make their own translations into Greek under normal circumstances. Similarly, Josephus, Philo and early Christian writers approximated their Greek texts to these MSS.[12]The Letter to the Hebrews appears to be an exception to this general tendency of textual conformity to a particular extant witness to LXX.[13]

Thus, while there is a tendency for quotations to appropriate certain text-type, it is still uncertain whether these were independent texts or merely, revisions within a LXX family of a textual tradition. The evidence

---

Ancient Library of Qumran and Modern Biblical Studies, Westport: Greenwood, 1976, pp. 124-45, especially pp. 133-34. 141-42. Driver, in spite of his vigorous rejection of any pre-Christian dating of the Qumran Scrolls, shares the view that the substantial agreement in the Qumran text with the text of the LXX, especially in the text of the Book of Samuel found in Cave IV, over against the text of the MT, offers a strong witness to the probable existence of a Ur-text, an Old Palestinian text predating both the LXX and the MT. see G.R. Driver, *The Judean Scrolls, The Problem and a Solution*, Oxford: Basil Blackwell, 1965, pp. 145-48, especially p. 445: "The influence of the Septuagint on the Hebrew text as represented by the scrolls is further illustrated by two portions of I and II Samuel found in Cave IV... for their text not only differs frequently from the Massoretic text but also for the most part agrees, where it so differs, with that underlying the translation of the Septuagint. This text, whose superiority to the Massoretic text in this book has long been recognized, seems to have originated in Palestine so that it must go back to a time before the Jewish migrations to Egypt out of which the need for a Greek translation of the Scriptures must have arisen".

[12] John W. Wenham, *Christ and the Bible*, London: Tyndale, 1972, p. 95. Cf. David F. Hinson, *Theology of the Old Testament, Old Testament Introduction 3*, London: SPCK, 1976, p. 135; R.T. France, *Jesus and the Old Testament*, p. 31. For the view that even the Qumran sectarians did not deliberately change their received Hebrew text to suit their convictions, but rather employed received textual variants since the Hebrew text was still in a fluid state, see W.F. Albright and C.S. Mann, *Matthew, Introduction, Translation and Notes*, AB, New York: Doubleday, 1971, p. LIX.

[13] See Harold W. Attridge, *The Epistle to the Hebrews, A Critical and Historical Commentary on the Bible*, Hermeneia, Philadelphia: Fortress, 1989, p. 23. Efforts to identify the LXX behind the Epistle to the Hebrews has become even more complicated by recent development in LXX textual studies. For instance, the recognition of the need to judge every book of LXX or groups of books, or even part of a book on its own merit, implying that what is true with one book or part of a book or a group of books in the LXX is not necessarily true of all the others; the recognition that uniformity of text-type in any book cannot be assumed; disagreements among scholars as whether to speak of different forms of LXX text or different translations of LXX, have all contributed to this problem of identification. For a discussion of these and other difficulties related to textual criticism of the LXX in contemporary scholarship, see Paul Ellingworth, *The Epistle to the Hebrews, A Commentary on the Greek Text*, NIGTC, Grand rapids: Wm B. Eerdmans and Carlisle: Paternoster, 1993, p.37.

does not point to any great number of independent textual traditions or to a great majority of Greek Targums. We might as well conclude with Sanday's observation that "(there is) no sufficient evidence to say whether this (narrative) arises from a reminiscence of Hebrew text. or from an Aramaic Targum or from the use of an earlier form of LXX text."[14] It would appear to us that the greatest difficulty is not only the question of the text behind Paul's quotations as Ellis observers[15] but indeed, the text behind the New Testament writers in general.

The question of the Hebrew text of the first century AD is even more uncertain. While the Qumran discoveries vindicated the trustworthiness of the Massoretic text,[16] pushing our knowledge of the Hebrew text a thousand years back and revealing a wonderful fidelity in scribal transmission of the text in the subsequent centuries, the case is not one of complete uniformity of the Hebrew text in the first century AD.

Readings appear in the Qumran texts which have so far only been known through the LXX, especially in the historical books. Other readings appear which are only preserved in the Samaritan Pentateuch text and not found in the Hebrew.[17] This inquiry on the text-form of the first century biblical text leads us to the conclusion that the New Testament writers are themselves an early witness to important text-types found at the time. If this is correct, then while these writers could modify the quoted texts to fit their purpose or contention, such modifications are likely to be usually of a grammatical nature while important variants would be drawn from other textual sources. It is doubtful that a biblical writer could base a serious argument on a text of his own creation and make everyone else believe it was scriptural.

Krister Stendahl, in a preface to the second edition of his book, *The School of St Matthew and its Use of the Old Testament* acknowledges that research that followed the first publication of his work has shown that both Hebrew and Greek textual traditions were much more fluid in the first century AD than had been assumed earlier:

---

[14] Quoted in Ellis, *Paul's Use*, p.20.

[15] *Ibid.*, p. 19.

[16] Albright and Mann hold the view that the Hebrew originals on which the Greek text of the Old Testament (LXX)was based were more reliable than the present Hebrew text (MT). See Albright and Mann, *Matthew*, p. LX and Cross, Jr., *The Ancient Library*, p. 133, and note 24.

[17] Wenham, *Christ and the Bible*, p. 97.

New data are about to allow new and better founded hypotheses about text forms available in the first Century AD. Such... state of affairs. makes it more probable that readings found in Matthew could witness to text forms actually available in Greek prior to Matthew. It makes the recourse to testimonies less compelling as an explanation of textual peculiarities.[18]

Raymond E. Brown also refers to the "multiplicity and fluidity of Hebrew and Greek textual traditions in the first century, as well as Aramaic turgums" and quoting Stendahl, he adds, "When we add to these the possibility of a free reading by the evangelist himself the avenue of deciding what citation is Matthew and what is pre-Matthew on the basis of wording becomes uncertain".[19]

The foregoing discussion on the nature of first century biblical textual tradition has shown that the task of classifying variants in terms of sources is a difficult problem. However, there is sufficient evidence in favour of the view that both the introductory formula and the mixed-text form of the fulfilment quotations derive from the evangelist himself.

The Introductory Formula to the Fulfilment Quotations

The evangelist introduces his fulfilment quotations with a more or less stereotyped introductory formula. There is a broad scholarly consensus that these come from the evangelist himself and that they reflect linguistic features that are peculiar to the evangelist.[20] The variations that occur among the introductory phrases can satisfactorily be accounted for by the nature of the Matthean context in which they are found.[21]

In the fulfilment quotations of the infancy narrative the following introductory phrases are employed:

Matt 1:22. "That it might be fulfilled which was spoken of the Lord by the prophet saying" (*hina plērōthę to rēthen hypo kyriou dia tou prophētou legontos*)

---

[18] Quoted in Stanton, *Studies in Matthew*, p. 35.

[19] Brown, *The Birth of the Messiah*, p.103.

[20] Luz, *Matthew*, p. 157; Stanton, *Studies in Matthew*, p. 359; Brown, *The Birth of the Messiah*, p. 103, note 17. For a discussion of Matthean linguistic features in the introductory formula, see G. Strecker, *Der Weg der Gerechtigkeit, forschungen zur Religion und Literatur des Alten und Neuen Testaments 82*, 2nd ed., Gottingen: Vandenhoeck, 1966, p. 50, to whom Brown here refers.

[21] For a thorough discussion of the minor variations in the introductory formula, see R. Pesch, "Der Gottessohn im Matthaischen Evangelienprolog (Mt 1-2) Beobachtungen zu den Zitations - formeln de Reflexionszitate", *Biblica 48* (1967), pp. 397-400, to whom Brown, *The Birth of the Messiah*, p103, note 17 also refers.

Matt. 2:5. "For thus it is written by (liter "through") the prophet" (*houtōs gar gegraptai dia tou prophētou*)

Matt. 2.15 (as in Matt 1:22 above)

Matt. 2:17. "Then was fulfilled that which was spoken by Jeremiah the prophet saying" (*tote eplērōthę to rēthen dia Ieremiou to prophētou legontos*)

Matt. 2:23. "That it might be fulfilled which was spoken by the prophets" (*hopōs plērōthę to rēthen dia tōn prophētōn*).

In these introductory phrases, it may be observed that in 1:22 and 2:15, the Lord is introduced as the "Speaker" and the prophet is named as a mere human instrumentality. Thus the real author of the word of prophecy is not the prophet but God himself and this consistently applies to all references that mention a prophet as having either said or written.[22] By beginning the introductory formula with *hina* (in order that) in 1:22; 2:15 or *hopōs* (that) in 2:23, the evangelist presupposes that the thing which is fulfilled was already reported.

In 2:5 the evangelist deviates from this pattern because the quotation from Micah 5:2 is quoted by the high-priests and the scribes and that it is

---

[22]   Cf. Rom 1:2; Luke 18:31; Acts 2:16; 28:15. Luz has the view that although this is exemplified in early Christian tradition, it could be rooted in Greek-speaking Judaism. This suggestion leads him to the conclusion that the Gospel of Matthew is not rooted directly in Hebrew exegesis, and hence the evangelist himself cannot be a converted Jewish rabbi. See Luz, *Matthew*, p. 159. But Luz's supposition that the introductory phrases which portray God as real speaker and the prophet or other prophetic means as mere instrumentality find their origin in Greek-speaking Judaism cannot be justified since similar phrases are found in typically Jewish writings. They are found in the Old Testament, in Qumran literature, in Philo's writings as well as in rabbinic works. The formula "it is written" in secular Greek culture referred to the terms of an unalterable agreement. For the Jew it referred to the unalterable nature of the Word of God. Although the human author could be cited, for instance, "Moses says" (Rom 10:19) "Isaiah says" (Rom 10:20) it is the word of God that is quoted. For the New Testament writers such formulas as "God says", "Scripture says", "Moses says", "the Law says" are just alternative ways of expressing the same thing. To them the Old Testament is inspired and as such it was the very Word of God despite their acknowledgement of the human or other means through which it was spoken. See Ellis, *Paul's Use*, p.23. For the view that such formulas emphasize the divine authority of the Old Testament, the "revelational 'word of God' character" of Scripture that is present within their current interpretation as over against its absence in the rival rabbinic traditional interpretations (Matt 22:29), see E. Earle Ellis, "How the New Uses the Old" in I. Howard Marshall (ed.), *New Testament Interpretation,* p. 200. For a discussion of the New Testament writers' view on verbal inspiration of scriptures, see Wehnam, *Christ and the Bible,* pp. 86-9, 101-103. For a more detailed study on verbal inspiration see H. Wheeler Robinson, *Inspiration and Revelation in the Old Testament,* Oxford: Clarendon, 1962. Also Benjamin B. Warfield, *The Inspiration and Authority of the Bible,* Philadelphia: Presbyterian and Reformed, 1948; C.H. Dodd, *The authority of the Bible,* London: Nisbet, 1928, reprint 1947, especially pp. 35-85.

woven into the narrative itself. In 2:17 the evangelist does not introduce the introductory formula with an adverb of purpose (*hina* or *hopōs*). Rather he uses an adverb of time (*tote*).[23] Here the evangelist does not emphasize God's intention in bringing about the massacre of the infants but rather his permissiveness to evil that is brought about through human sinfulness. It is human evil intention that comes into sharp relief here.

Luz draws conclusions which to me appear to be far-fetched from his study of these introductory phrases. From the plural reference "through the prophets" (*dia tōn prophētōn*) in 2:23 he concludes that the evangelist was unable to identify the specific source of the quotations he received from earlier Christian tradition. A similar conclusion is drawn from 13:35 where the evangelist omits the name of the prophet when in reality the quotation is drawn from Ps 78:2, and from 21:14 and 27:9 where the evangelist quotes Zechariah, one time without a name, the other timed "incorrectly" naming Jeremiah instead. But a more plausible explanation to these peculiarities is not lacking. At this point it is sufficient to note that France, for instance, suggests that the evangelist in 2:23 does not intend to quote a specific passage, but rather "a summary of a theme of prophetic expectation".[24] From these observations, Luz is able to conclude that the evangelist had no access to a copy of the minor prophets because his community did not have one. In this deduction Luz, further, finds confirmation to the view that the evangelist's community no longer lived within synagogue union, otherwise he should have a ready access to the synagogue library. Luz also concludes that the evangelist had access to a scroll of Isaiah which was available in his community. However, no other prophetic scroll can be assured to have been available. In this supposed lack of the larger portion of the Bible in the community, Luz further finds grounds to question the theory that the Matthean community was a "well to-do city church".[25]

The chain of conclusions that Luz draws here appear to be forced, for they greatly outrun the evidence. They appear to be determined more by the presuppositions that Luz holds regarding the nature and context of the Matthean community than the evidence he adduces. His conclusions can only be sustained with great difficulty when the evangelist's interest

---

[23]   Barclay M. Newman, Jr., *A Concise Greek English Dictionary of the New Testament*, Stuttgart: Deutsche Bibelgessel-schaft, 1994, pp. 86, 126, 183 respectively.
[24]   France, *Matthew*, pp. 88-89.
[25]   Luz, *Matthew*, pp. 157, 158.

and knowledge of the Old Testament, his scholarly resourcefulness which is evident throughout his work, and the great mobility of the early Christians who usually carried their biblical scrolls and parchments with them (2 Tim. 4:13) are taken into consideration. Luz, however, provides a good illustration of how results from research into the fulfilment quotations have been used to support divergent views over the synoptic problem, especially the reconstruction of the Matthean community and its dating.

The Formation and Textual Character of the Fulfilment Quotations
With regard to the origin, the fulfilment quotations are generally attributed to the evangelist in recent scholarship. However, there is no scholarly consensus as to the manner in which they came into existence. There are two main competing theories here. The first theory argues that these fulfilment quotations gave rise to infancy stories. That is, it was on the basis of these quotations that the evangelist imaginatively created the infancy narratives.[26] The second theory postulates that these fulfilment

---

[26] Some scholars have viewed the Gospel of Matthew as belonging to the genre midrash which basically, by definition, imply something unhistorical or at best a mixture of both history and non-history. Thus D.M. Goulder, also quoted in France, *Matthew*, p. 24, argues that the process of midrash "has resulted in the creation of stories about Jesus and teaching attributed to him which derive not from any history-based tradition, but from a scripturally-inspired imagination". This view is later adopted by Robert H. Gundry, in his *Matthew, A Commentary on his Literary and Theological Art*, who sees in *Matthew* not only "non-history" but rather a combination of both history and "non-history": "Matthew did not write entirely reportorial history. Comparison with midrashic and haggadic literature of his era suggests he did not intend to do so... what Matthew wrote bears the stamp of inspiration in the meaning he intended – be it historical, unhistorical or a mixture of the two" (p. 629). In this view the virgin birth, the magi, the flight to Egypt and the massacre of Bethlehem infants become a fictitious production of Matthew's creative imagination. But the incidents narrated in the infancy narrative are not historically impossible in light of the historical circumstances of the time. From what we know through non-biblical sources about the cult of astrology, about Herod's character in terms of his cruelty and political instability particularly towards the end of his long reign, and about the oppressive rule of Archelaus, there is nothing that can be said to be incompatible with the biblical account. Even the choice of Egypt as a place of refuge makes much historical sense since the Egyptian boarder at the time was very close to Judah and there were many Jews living in Egypt. See France, *Matthew*, p. 70. Cf. William Hendriksen, *An Exposition of the Gospel According to Matthew*. Grand Rapids: Baker, 1973, pp. 150, 156-65, 187; Albright and Mann, *Matthew*, pp. 13-16, 17, 19; Allen, *A Critical and Exegetical commentary on the Gospel According to Saint Matthew*, p. 14. It is over the question of the moving star and the angelic warnings that would pose a real difficulty to historians. Even these can only be "unhistorical" in the sense of being non-empirical and unrepeatable. But as realities that took place at some point in the past, their historical probability still remains. To reject a supernatural element *a priori* is just as unscientific as its uncritical acceptance. Rudolf Bultmann, *The History of the Synoptic Tradition*, Oxford: Basil Blackwell, 1972, pp. 209-244, 302-317 and Martin Dibelius, *From*

Tradition to Gospel, pp. 70-103, suggest that the framework of the miracle stories is such that it fits almost exactly the pattern of Hellenistic wonder-stories and hence conclude that both Greek and Jewish wonder-stories, including the New Testament miracle –stories arose in the same atmosphere. The identification with Hellenistic wonder-stories effectively robs the gospel miracle-stories of their credibility. They simply become a product of the fertile imagination of the early Christian communities or at best an assimilation of both Jewish and Gentile heroic stories that depict the exploits of the gods with the story of Jesus in order to improve his public image following his shameful death on the cross, an execution not befitting one who is acclaimed to be a Saviour: Albright and Mann, *Matthew*, pp. CXXVI-CXXX. Most studies on the Gospel of Matthew presuppose that since the evangelist wrote from the perspective of faith and that he did so many decades after the events narrated, he "must reflect a theology contemporaneous with his own *Sitz im Leben*. Inevitably, it is presupposed that the gospel of Matthew is studded with Christological anachronism". See D.A. Carson, "Christological Ambiguities in the Gospel of Matthew", in Harold H. Rowdon (ed.), *Christ the Lord, Studies in Christology presented to Donald Guthrie*, p. 98. In this view the evangelist presents a gospel of Jesus that is so altered in order to fit the theological needs of his community that in the process it loses touch with the ministry of Jesus. Such renowned Matthean scholars as Luz, Gundry and Beare, to name a few, assume that the evangelist is anachronistic in his presentation, and therefore not historical. Luz, (*Matthew*, p. 86) suggests that the evangelist who "is obliged to his community works with its own normative traditions and contemplates them anew in the light of the gospel of Mark." Gundry, (*Matthew*, p. 639) says "Matthew's intent was to tell the story of Jesus with alterations and embellishments suited to the needs of the church and the world at the time the gospel was written", while Beare, (*Matthew*, pp. 13,14) has the following comment: "The narrative framework of this gospel is not of an essentially biographical and historical nature. The writer is primarily concerned with the life and faith of the church of his own time, with the responsibilities laid upon it, and with the conduct required of all who profess faith in Jesus... His interest in the past is dominated by its bearing upon the present. Jesus is depicted, from birth to death and resurrection, not alone in his historical character as a man who lived in Palestine in the early decades of the first century, but also and above all, as the Lord who teaches and governs his church in the present time. The whole story is seen in a double perspective. The anecdotes which make it up are formerly presented as incidents in a life lived seventy years earlier, but they are at the same time images of the Jesus who lives and speaks to the disciples and the crowds of Matthew's own time. Details of place and time are of no real interest. They are given, for the most part, in vague terms: and in an order which has little to do with succession in time... The evangelist is not preparing a record for the archives. His primary aim is not to give exact information, but to provide practical guidance for the Christians of his own time, and for their leaders". Common to all these scholars is the assumption that Matthew is more concerned to write a gospel *for the community* rather than a gospel *about Jesus* and that he sacrifices the historical truth about the latter in order to serve the interests of the former to the effect that what Matthew writes as reflecting the life time of Jesus is really a reflection of his own contemporary world many decades after the earthly ministry of Jesus. But Carson, "Christological Ambiguities", has convincingly called into question these assumptions. He asks: "Was Matthew himself unaware of his putative anachronisms? If so, then must we assume he was anachronistic only sometimes? And exactly how may we distinguish genuine anachronisms, material that is not anachronistic yet not historical, and material that is historical and therefore not anachronistic. On the other hand, if Matthew was aware of his alleged anachronisms, then we must adjust our understanding of what a *Gospel* is, and we would have to ask whether he intended to be consistently anachronistic, reflecting his own time, or selectively so; and if the latter, we would need to know how (or if!) he, expected his readers to tell the difference" (p. 98). Carson then suggests that if we start with the assumption that Matthew primarily chose to write quotations were added to existing infancy narratives. There are a number of factors which favour this postulation. First, it is very difficult to see how the fulfilment quotations in 2:13-23 could lead to the creation of that part of the story since the fulfilment quotations do not deal with major aspects in the story outline. While in 2:5-6 the quotation could be said to have led to the creation of the reference to Bethlehem, it is difficult to see how it could lead to the creation of the reference to the Magi. Similarly, while it could be understandable for the quotation in 1:22-23 to influence the creation of the reference to virgin birth, it is not easy to see why the Joseph story should be created at this point.

Secondly, there is a clear indication in 1:18-25 and 2:13-23 that the fulfilment quotations are appended in that a reading of the text while omitting these quotations provides quite a smooth flow to the narrative, not to say a better one. This undoubtedly shows that the quotations in 1:22-23; 2:15, 17 and 23 are added to the narrative. The quotation in 2:5-6 is not only added but also woven into the plot of the narrative.[27]

---

a Gospel *about Jesus*, that is primarily reflecting Jesus' own life time, the results could be quite different. This questioning becomes particularly significant when it is remembered that what critical scholarship has come to designate as "Matthean community" is itself "a fairly speculative 'historical' *Sitz im Leben* which are reconstructed almost exclusively on the grounds of form and redaction criticism ... reconstructions that are no more than deductions based on debatable judgments about why he wrote" (*Ibid.*, p. 99). This is not to belittle the role of form and redaction criticism in critical scholarship but rather to recognize them as valuable tools while keeping in mind their limitations. Equally convincingly, Carson has demonstrated in his article that the evangelist carefully avoids Christological anachronisms but rather holds that the seemingly ambiguous Christological confessions and claims of Jesus' day point to the full understanding of them by the Church in the post-resurrection period (*Ibid*). Thus, although Matthew writes from a post resurrection perspective, he still writes a Gospel *about Jesus*. The widespread scholarly opinion that the evangelist tells the story of Jesus "with alterations and embellishments" because he was more interested in the needs of his Christian community than in the story of Jesus himself is quite unconvincing, unless one accepts the view that the whole story of Jesus is unhistorical and that it was primarily created to address the needs of the community at this point. But to hold this view creates the difficulty of how to account for the establishment of the Church itself. If the historical Jesus was almost completely unknown at this earliest period of the Church, then it must be asked why the Church attributed to him the Messianic status and function. Without any meaningful knowledge of the historical Jesus, the Christ of faith is not only incomprehensible but also totally meaningless. The Risen Christ only makes sense as indisputable proof that God has vindicated the Jesus of history and his Messianic claims. In other words, the evangelist is not simply creating stories nor is he merely distorting facts or arranging information to suit the theological needs of his community. Rather he primarily reflects on what he knows to be historical realities that transpired during the period of Jesus' earthly life. The biblical narrative is a fair reflection of the historical realities it presents.

[27] For the same view that the evangelist has added these quotations to an existing tradition, see Allen, *Matthew*, p. LXI.

Thirdly, there are instances where Matthew has appended fulfilment quotations to existing common synoptic tradition. For instance, all the synoptic gospels relate Jesus' entry into Galilee at the dawn in his public ministry (Mark 1:14; Luke 4:14; Matt. 4:12). But it is only Matthew who appends a fulfilment quotation at Matt 4:14 drawn from Isa 8:23-9:1 (RSV, AKJV, Isa 9:1). It can be assumed that the evangelist does the same in the infancy narrative.[28] Thus, with regard to the origin of the fulfilment quotations, it can be concluded at this point that they come from the evangelist himself.

Probably, a more difficult problem is how to account for the mixed-text form of the fulfilment quotations. With the publication of J. Rendel Harris, *The Testimonies*, it was generally accepted that the evangelist drew his quotations from this source. But this theory was soon overtaken until it was revived with the discovery of testimonies at Qumran in the Spring of 1947. In contemporary scholarship, the theory has again fallen into disfavour largely because the frequency of this literature among the Dead Sea Scrolls remains unclear, and J. Allegro is probably mistaken in his identification of testimonia in 4Q Florilegium and 4 Q Testimonia.[29]

With the abandonment of the Testimonia theory, scholars have sought to trace their origin by investigating the possibility of a wider use of these quotations in early Christianity, the wording of the quotations in relation to the Hebrew and Greek Old Testament, and the relationship of the quotations to the theology of the evangelist.[30]

It is probable that the evangelist bears witness to well-known passages to Christians. For instance, both Mark 4:1 and Matt 13:13-15 relate the stubbornness of the heart of the Jews, but it is only Matt 13:14 that appends a fulfilment quotation from Isa 6:6-10. While only Matthew appends a fulfilment quotation from Zech 9:9 to his narration of Jesus triumphal entry in the synoptics, the evangelist John simply associates the entry with the same prophecy but does not employ any fulfilment quotation at this point (John 12:15-16). Despite such evidence, however, it is still difficult to know whether the evangelist has borrowed his fulfilment quotations in the infancy narrative, not only because of the lack

---

[28] For a thorough discussion of these theories, see Brown, *The Birth of the Messiah*, pp. 99-101.

[29] *Ibid.*, p. 101, especially note 10.

[30] For the analysis of these scholarly attempts, I am gratefully indebted to Raymond E. Brown. For a thorough discussion, see Brown, *The Birth of the Messiah*, pp. 101-104.

of material to compare with but also because of the difficulty in seeing how else other Christians could use the quotations that the evangelist employs other than the way he does.

In a comparative study with the Hebrew and Greek Old Testament Bibles, Stendahl finds that in the common synoptic tradition excluding the fulfilment quotations, the use of the Old Testament conforms to the LXX. The evangelist tends to follow Mark in this usage who himself attests to LXX usage. However, in his fulfilment quotations the evangelist does not correspond to the LXX. Rather, he draws closer to the Hebrew and other text-types. From this observation, Stendahl concludes that these quotations are original with the evangelist. But Gundry challenges Stendahl's observations and claims that the evangelist follows the LXX only in the fulfilment quotations he copies from Mark. In his non-Marcan use of scripture, Gundry claims, be it in fulfilment quotations or not, the evangelist exercises much freedom in his usage of the LXX.[31]

Gundry suggests a "targumic" explanation for the evangelist's quotations from Scripture. He holds that various forms of the Hebrew text were in circulation and that preachers rendered the texts of their choice into either Aramaic or Greek for use in their ministry to fellow Jews. These renditions could sometimes be original. Sometimes they could reflect existing Aramaic and Greek translation. Following this line of argument Gundry concludes that the evangelist made his own translations.[32]

But Luz has in turn challenged Gundry rejecting the idea that it is only in those quotations drawn from Mark that the evangelist follows the LXX. From a study of quotations which, for Luz, are drawn from Mark and source Q he concludes that the evangelist transfers the text of his sources without or at most with very slight modifications to resemble the LXX families which Luz presumes were known to him through worship.[33] Since the evangelist makes no significant alterations to his sources (Mark and Q), Luz concludes that the fulfilment quotations are drawn from a pre-Matthean tradition. For Luz, therefore, the evangelist's use of his sources does not favour the theory that he is responsible for the mixed form of the text selecting variants from a number of LXX

---

[31]   Ibid., p. 102.

[32]   See Ibid., especially note14. For the opposing view that New Testament writers as well as the Qumran covenanters did not primarily use their own translations, see Ibid., note 12.

[33]   Luz, Matthew, 1-7, p. 159.

recessions. Rather, for Luz, the mixed form of the text in the fulfilment quotations which are generally at variance with the LXX is better accounted for by the theory that the wording of these quotations is not made by the evangelist, selecting variants from different sources, but that this wording already exists in the source that the evangelist uses such as Aramaic Targum of Mark, the Testimonial and oral tradition.[34]

Logically this understanding leads Luz to the conclusion that:

> One should not assume that the contribution of the evangelist Matthew to the wording of the formula quotations (i.e. fulfilment quotations) is higher than to the wording of the remaining quotations. A large number of recessions out of which he could have made his own was not available to him. We see the evangelist as a conservative trident and interpreter who is obliged to tradition. He treated the wording of the quotations available to him with the same care as he treated the text of the Gospel of Mark and Q.[35]

Understandably Luz also objects to the claim of redaction critics that the evangelist has edited redactionary his sources to serve his intentions. He argues that the amount of material that is demonstrably redactional is relatively small. Luz, consequently, concludes that a study of these fulfilment quotations does not substantially contribute to our knowledge and understanding of Matthean theology: "The result of this investigation into the wording of the quotations for the understanding of the theology of Matthew is minimal."[36]

> However, when we consider the multiplicity and fluidity of textual traditions of scripture and the possibility of free rendering by the evangelist himself, it seems appropriate to conclude, with Brown that:

> If one maintains that sometimes Matthew introduces as a formula quotation (i.e. a fulfilment quotation) a passage that was already known in Christian usage, one would expect that he would reproduce the familiar wording, a wording that may or

---

[34]   *Ibid.*

[35]   *Ibid.*, p. 161.

[36]   *Ibid.*, This view is reiterated in his more recent work, *The Theology of the Gospel of Matthew*, Cambridge: Cambridge University Press, 1995, p. 9: "Furthermore, a large number of basic theological ideas of Matthew's Gospel derive from Mark. I need only mention the imitation of Jesus' path of suffering, the Church as an assembly of disciples, the 'Son of David' title for a central Christological concept, the passions of the son of man, the fulfilment of scripture, and, above all the openness toward the Gentile mission. Many key theological terms of the first Gospel ultimately derive from Mark."

may not reflect the LXX, depending on when and where the tradition entered into circulation. On the other hand, when Matthew himself was the first to see the possibility of an Old Testament fulfilment, he would presumably choose or even adopt a wording that would best fit his purposes.[37]

However, where to draw the line between a variant from a source and a variant which is the evangelist's own contribution to the text remains an unresolved difficulty.[38]

In the light of the preceding discussion, it can, at this point, be safely concluded that the evangelist was responsible for the choice of the text form that appears in the fulfilment quotations from whatever sources he had.[39] If this is correct, then Luz's thesis does not stand.

The Purpose of Fulfilment Quotations

Scholars have assessed the purpose of these quotations quite differently. Lindars has argued that the primary purpose of these fulfilment quotations, including those to be discussed in the next chapter, is apologetic against the synagogue.[40] But this argument fails to account for the concentration of these quotations in the infancy narrative (5 in all when 2:5-6 is included) rather than in the passion narrative which is the real stumbling block for the Jews (1 Cor 1:23) (There are only 2 undisputed fulfilment quotations in the passion, that is 21:4-5 and 27:9-10. 27:35 is textually dubious).[41] Brown considers that the primary purpose is didactic and argues that they are intended for Christian leaders, informing them and giving support to their faith at a time when, possibly, the Church had become less missionary in zeal.[42] For

---

[37] Brown, *The Birth of the Messiah*, p. 103.

[38] J.M. Allegro, *The Dead Sea Scrolls*, Harmondsworth: Penguin, 1959, p. 134 calls this difficulty a "puzzle" in the study of Matthean citations of scriptures and specifically mentions the quotations at 2:6; 13:35 and 21:5 as examples.

[39] Such sources could include not only the standard Hebrew Text (MT) which may as well have been not yet standardized at the time and the Greek Text (LXX), but also variant Hebrew textual traditions, Aramaic targums and other Greek translations some of which were closer to the MT than the LXX.

[40] Barnabas Lindars, *New Testament Apologetic, the Doctrinal Significance of the Old Testament Quotations*, London: SCM, 1961, p. 259.

[41] The phrase "cast lots" (*ballontes klēron*) appears not to be part of the original text of Matthew and is believed to be an interpolation in some later MSS from John 19:24. See Stanton, *Studies in Matthew*, p. 349. The word "cast" (*ballontes*) literary "throw" is missing in Alph, A, D, Theta, f^1 and the Bohairic (a coptic version) manuscripts. See the Critical Apparatus on these variants in *Nestle-Aland, Novum Testamentum Graece*, Stuttgart: Deutsche Bibelgesellschaft, 1979.

[42] Brown, R, *The Birth of the Messiah*, p. 98.

Kilpatrick, it is liturgical. For him, liturgy influenced the choice of the quotations for preaching to the community and sometimes to enhance the context of eucharistic celebrations.[43] The main purpose, however, was not apologetic, didactic or liturgical as these scholars suggest. It was kerygmatic,[44] designed to either cause or nurture faith in whoever would dare to listen.

Exegetical: Theological Analysis of the fulfilment Quotations
This section attempts a grammatical-historical analysis of the fulfilment quotations in an effort to bring out their theological contribution to an understanding of the evangelist's Christology. It will be shown that the manner in which the evangelist applies them to the Christ-event reveals that the evangelist was aware of their Old Testament context and that he applies them to the Christ-event in the light of their original context.[45] In that way the evangelist shows that the whole history of Israel together with all of its institutions and representative personalities find its ultimate fulfilment in the person of Jesus. Jesus as the Messiah is Israel par excellence. The fulfilment quotations in the infancy narrative that will be discussed in more detail in this chapter define the Person of Jesus Messiah as understood through Old Testament prophetic light as that personality manifests itself through the Christ-event.

---

[43] *Ibid*, p. 98. Also note 6.

[44] In this I agree with W.D. Davies. But while Davies suggests that such a *Kerygma* was not directed to the non-believers but rather to the believers, I am of the view that it is directed to both types of audience, either to cause faith in the person of Jesus as the Messiah or to strengthen it among believers, just the way the passion *Kerygma* would function. Brown agrees with Davies in holding that the primary audience is the Church and that the goal was to "expand the mystery of the Lord through his birth" but hesitates to call this "Kerygmatic". His major objection being that the systematic presentation of fulfilment quotations and the inclusion of the numbered genealogy are not indicative of a proclamation that is intended to cause faith. Brown, here fails to see that the basic motive of the evangelist right from the beginning, especially in the first two chapters of his gospel is to proclaim, to all who would dare to listen, that Jesus is the Messiah, according to Scriptures. Obviously, such a bold claim can only be accepted by faith, and this could only be the result of a kerygmatic function of the fulfilment quotations. See Brown, *The Birth of the Messiah* p. 144. Cf. W.D. Davies, *The Setting of the Sermon on the Mount*, pp. 66-67; Hendriksen, *Matthew*, p. 133.

[45] This phenomenon is not limited to our evangelist here. In - Gyu Hong, *The Law in Galatians*, JSNT 81, Sheffield: Sheffield Academic Press, 1993, pp. 80-83 has shown that a proper understanding of the original context of Deut. 27:26 is essential for a proper understanding of the Pauline quotation from that text at Gal 3:10b, a quotation which resembles our fulfilment quotations in that it has a mixed text form and does not fully agree with either the Septuagint or the MT. Hong's success in showing this suggests that Paul also applied this quotation to the Gospel in the light of the Deuteronomic context of Deut. 27:26.

The Fulfilment Quotation in Matt 1:23

Matt.　Behold the virgin (*parthenos*) will be with child (*en gastri hexei*) and will give birth to a son and they will call (*kalesousin*) his name Emmanuel. (Isa 7: 14)

LXX.　Behold the virgin (*parthenos*) will be with child (*en gastri hexei*) and will give birth to a son and you (sing) will call his name Emmanuel. (Isa 7: 14)

MT.　Behold the young girl (*'almâ*) is (will be) with child, and will give birth to a son, and she will call his name Emmanuel:

Textual Observations

The reading *hexei* ("will have") found in the Matthean quotation is also found in the LXX reading of Codices Alexandrinus and Sinaiticus. This is a more reliable reading than *lēpsetai* ("will receive") which Brown finds in the LXX version he uses. Probably *lēpsetai* is a later scribal interpolation of the LXX to make it conform to the evangelist's version.[46] Where Matthew has "they will call", the LXX has "you (sing) will call", while the MT has "she will call", *qārā'th*. Thus, for the evangelist, it s not only Mary who would call the "son" Immanuel but all who believe in him will in him find the Presence of God, that is "God with us".[47] But the difficult problem in this quotation is the use of the word "virgin" (*parthenos*) in both the Matthean version and the LXX as a translation of the word "young woman" (*'almâ*) in the Hebrew. This problem is further compounded by the fact that the Hebrew text is not clear as to whether the *'almâ* already "is" with child or "will be" with child.[48] It has been suggested that Isaiah was probably using mythological terms current in his own time to demonstrate the birth of an expected deliverer, that the LXX translators probably understood the passage in a similar way, and that only later did Greek translators of the Hebrew adopted the word *neanis* ("young maiden") instead of *Parthenos* ("virgin")[49]. If this is correct, then the sense of a supernatural birth is the original one. Scholarly opinion

---

[46] Brown, *The Birth of the Messiah*, p. 145, especially, note 34.

[47]　Hendriksen, *Matthew*, p. 134.

[48] Brown, *The Birth of the Messiah*, pp. 147-48. Cf Bernard W. Anderson, *The Living World of the Old Testament*, Harlow: Longman, 1963, pp. 331-32. For the view that the Hebrew perfect tense "has conceived and will bear a son" is better understood as implying that the conception was in the past while the birth was still in the future, see R.E. Clements, *Isaiah 1-39*, NCBC, Grand Rapids: Wm. B. Eerdmans and London: Marshal, Morgan and Scott, 1980, reprint 1982, p. 87. The ambiguous time reference is also noted in the RSV.

[49] Albright and Mann, *Matthew*, p 8; Allen, *Matthew*, p.10.

remains sharply divided over the term and its theological implications. A detailed discussion of this debate is beyond the scope of the present inquiry. It will be sufficient at this point to note the main line of argument. One theory argues that the *'almâ* of Isa 7:14 does not refer to the virgin birth of Christ and therefore cannot be the basis for the doctrine of the virgin birth of Christ. In this view, it is argued that the reference is to the wicked king, Ahaz (735-715), intended to be a sign to this unbelieving monarch during the Syro-Ephramitic war of 734 BC so that the reference must be to an event that year or shortly after. It is also argued that the child to be born could not be the Messiah since the idea of a single Messianic king was not yet fully developed. It is also said that the word *'almâ* does not emphasize virginity: that the presence of the definite article "the" (*ha*) implies a reference to a definite girl probably known at the court, and that from the Hebrew participial construction it is difficult to know whether the young woman was already pregnant or was still to become pregnant. The other theory holds that the *'almâ* refers to the virgin birth of Jesus. Some of these arguments are accepted by both schools of thought. For instance, immediate reference to Ahaz is not denied, the definiteness of the young woman is accepted as well as the vagueness caused by the participial construction with reference to time. However, it is insisted that the reference is to the Messianic figure. Probably, the strongest argument for this theory is that Isa 7:14 prepares for the development of a Messianic theme which is further developed in the Immanuel concept in Isa. 8:8, 10 and in the child deliverer of Isa 9:6-7; 11:1-9, which, it is maintained, cannot be fully realized in a child of purely normal child-birth. In commenting on the word *'almâ* which is, according to France, nowhere used with reference to childbirth or marriage, France observes that perhaps this indicates that Isaiah was thinking of a birth outside the normal pattern of childbirth within marriage which led the LXX to use *parthenos*.[50]

Looking at both arguments, the theory that supports virgin birth appears to be stronger and more consistent with the rest of Christian revelation. The observation of Benjamin B. Warfield at the beginning of last century remains worth noting: "The supernatural Christ and the

---

[50] France, *Matthew*, p. 79. For a discussion of this position, see France, *Matthew*, pp. 79-80. For a thorough response to the first theory, see Hendriksen, *Matthew*, pp. 133-44. Cf. Allen, *Matthew*, p. 9. For a brief reference to the scholarly dispute surrounding Isa 9:1-6; 11:1-5; Micah 5:1-5 with respect to their Messianic status, see note 44 in this chapter.

supernatural salvation carry with them by an inevitable consequence the supernatural birth".[51] If the foundational Christian claims, like the bodily resurrection of Jesus, are a historical reality, the virgin birth is not impossible. In a similar vein, Argyle observes that:

> There is no adequate reason to doubt that the virgin birth is historical. No convincing motive has yet been suggested for inventing the story. Many would argue that a supernatural birth of Jesus' body best accords with the miracle of resurrection and ascension.[52]

The Historical Context of Isa 7:14

The historical setting is the Syro-Israelite crisis of 733-732 BC. Rezin of Syria and Pekah King of Israel conspired to stop by force Assyrian western advance as they had successfully done at Qarqar more than a century earlier.[53] When Ahaz, king of Judah, refused to join the coalition, they decided to attack him in order to force him out of the throne and install a puppet king, a son of Tabeel who was of non-Davidic descent. Jerusalem was surrounded. As Isaiah approached Ahaz, the latter was contemplating either to accept defeat from the coalition or to appeal to Assyria as he inspected Jerusalem's water system. Ahaz decided to appeal to Assyria for help. But Isaiah opposed this, for, while the enemies of his kingdom would be destroyed, Judah would lose her independence and become a vassalage. This would mean that Judah would be forced to worship the Assyrian gods. An appeal to Assyria was, for Isaiah, an indication of lack of faith and trust in Yahweh's deliverance. Having opposed the decision for an appeal to Assyria, Isaiah demanded that Ahaz should trust Yahweh for deliverance. In this connection, the king would ask for any sign, and it would be given from Yahweh. When the king refused, Isaiah simply went on to announce, angrily, the sign from God: a virgin shall be with Child and shall call his name Immanuel.[54]

---

[51] Benjamin B. Warfield, *Christology and Criticism*, New York: Oxford University Press, 1929, p. 452. Also Hendriksen, *Matthew*, p. 143.

[52] A. W. Argyle, *The Gospel According to Matthew*, Cambridge: University Press, 1963, p. 27.

[53] Anderson, *The Living World of the Old Testament*, p. 329.

[54] For a brief treatment of the historical context, see the Excursus in Otto Kaiser, *Isaiah 1-12, A Commentary*, Second Edition, London: SCM, 1983, pp. 148-50. For further discussion of the Immanuel prophecy, see *Ibid.*, pp. 151-72; George Buchanan Gray, *The Book of Isaiah, A Critical and Exegetical Commentary*, vol. 1, ICC, Edinburgh: T & T Clark, 1912, reprint 1975, pp. 122-36. For the view that the manner in which this citation is used, i.e., its single occurrence in this gospel contrasted with its prominence and widespread usage in later Christianity, reflects

The Theological Significance of the fulfilment Quotation

Some scholars have not seen any theological significance in these fulfilment quotations for the understanding of Matthean theology. For instance, Luz is of the opinion that a study of the fulfilment quotations does not contribute much to the understanding of the evangelist's theology. But this position is a natural consequence of his views on the origin of these quotations. Luz holds that the evangelist does not make any significant changes in these quotations which he receives from an earlier tradition. Hence, the little modification that the evangelist makes, according to Luz, are too insignificant to account for his theological emphases.[55] But a careful study of these quotations both in their Old and New Testament contexts indicate that they are theologically pregnant. It has been argued by some scholars, like Anderson, that a sign does not need to be extraordinary. The supernatural aspect in the virgin birth narrative is played down, understanding it merely as one of similar supernatural birth-stories in Hellenistic Judaism.[56] Schweizer emphasizes that the evangelist's focus is not on the virgin birth of the Messiah but on his normal human birth except that this particular birth is in accordance with God's will:

> Bethlehem as the place of Jesus' birth and the prophecy of his birth by a virgin were already given to the Christian community by their Bible, the Greek Old Testament. Naturally the Christians thought in terms of the ideas of their period. It was assumed of many great men at the time, from Plato to Alexander, that they had been born without human father. The fact of such a birth therefore did not single Jesus out as unique, it simply placed him in the company of all great men of the age... the story of a birth without a human father, even the idea of God's creative power that performs an act of generation, was widespread outside the Christian Community... the idea did not signify much more than that a certain person was given to the world by God. The focus of the story therefore is not the physical, biological process, but the theological watershed. The biology did not appear unique to Matthew and his contemporaries... The focus is God's offer in Jesus, of salvation to man, and man's response in obedience. What the text asks

an early stage of Christian doctrine preceding the patristic pre-occupation with the nativity and the Virgin Birth, see John F.A. Sawyer, *The Fifth Gospel, Isaiah in the History of Christianity*, Cambridge: Cambridge University Press, 1996, p. 31.

[55] See Luz, *Matthew*, p. 161. Also, note 377 above.

[56] For example, see Anderson, *The Living World of the Old Testament*, p. 331

is therefore not whether we can consider a virgin birth physically possible, but the same question put by Mark in his statement that the word became a human being (1:4), by Paul in his use of the term 'Son of God' (Gal 4:4); whether in this birth we can see God's own and unique intervention for man's salvation. And if this is the case, then we can also say what this story of the virgin is further meant to say: that this birth stands not merely as one among many in the long series of millions of births, that it took place not merely through the creative will or drive of a man, but through God's own will as creator.[57]

Thus, for Anderson and Schweizer and many others of their number, the question of virgin birth is a peripheral one and lacking in substantiality. It is a mere claim, parallel to similar Hellenistic mythical claims, but without any historical credibility.

A careful study of chapters 7, 8, 9 and 11 of Isaiah suggest that the prophet speaks undoubtedly of a child whose birth, person and function were no less than miraculous. Indeed, the use of the word "sign", not only in Isaiah but also in all biblical writers, refers to divine interventions in human history through which God declares himself and his purposes to men. Such extra-ordinary happenings, by their very nature lie beyond ordinary human experience.[58]

As reflected in the historical setting of Isa 7:14 discussed above, the context of Isa 7:14 reveals a situation in which men are faithless, fearful and hopeless. It is a time of testing to the nation. Yet it is also a time of calling to faith and trust in Yahweh. Will the nation and its king trust in Yahweh at this time when the nation faces a fatal danger of an imminent military invasion? The faith of many vacillates and fails, including that of the king. It is at this point that God takes the initiative and promises a child as a pledge for his promised deliverance.

That the prophet is referring to an eschatological child who will bring salvation and not merely an ordinary king is indicated by the eschatological language which, like a thread, runs through this section of Isaiah's prophecy. There is a prophetic reference to the end-time, a time of both testing and calling to trust (Isa 7:15-25). The reference to the

---

[57] Edward Schweizer, *The Good News According to Matthew*, London: SPCK, 1976, pp. 33-5. Cf. Gerald O'Collins, *Interpreting Jesus*, London: Geoffrey Chapman and Ramsey: Panelist Press, 1983, pp.54-9, 195-99 on the centrality of the miraculous and the theological significance of the virginal conception even in the Gospel of Mark although he tends to attach a greater importance to theological significance in a way that overshadows its historical probability.

[58] Albright and Mann, *Matthew*, p. LXXV.

end-time is further indicated by the constant references in the same context to the Day of the Lord,[59] here depicted as a Day when Israel shall be experiencing divine judgment. Thus the most striking feature about the Immanuel prophecy in Isaiah is probably the promise of the exercise of God's initiative in bringing salvation in the face of people's faithlessness, hopelessness and fear.[60] It is significant, here, to note also that the name Immanuel describes the person and, in an unspecified manner, the role of the child. It does not focus on the faith of the mother as she confesses trust in God that He would still provide for his people and protect them from their enemies in their troubled times. Through the promised child, God will be among his people[61] both in person and in function.

In the Matthean context, we notice that the reference to the virgin birth is noteworthy. The evangelist sees a typological correspondence between the child Immanuel of Isaiah's prophecy and the child Jesus of the Gospel tradition. Just as the miraculous birth of the child Immanuel in the Old Testament context points to both the extraordinary nature and function of the one to be born, in the Gospel context it points to both the divinity of Jesus Messiah and the supernatural function he is to play in salvation history. In this way, the evangelist sees an ultimate fulfilment of the Immanuel prophecy in Jesus. Hendriksen rightly points out that to account for all the miraculous works that he did without recourse to supernatural origin would be difficult let alone his sinless life.[62] His birth meant that God, had come to dwell among his people, and that ultimately implied that Yahweh's salvation had come. Thus we see that this

---

[59] The Day of the Lord was associated with special times of judgment and blessing. However, there was one great Day of the Lord that was yet to come on which the Lord would bring salvation and judgment "either by inaugurating a covenant or by enforcing its provisions". This is an eschatological expectation. See O. Palmer Robertson, *Joel: the Day of the Spirits Restoration of all Things*, 1994, a personal copy of a commentary then unpublished, p. 16. Cf. Gerhard von Rad, *The Message of the Prophets*, London: SCM, 1968, p. 95: "Special consideration needs still to be given to the expectation of the Day of Yahweh, which has often been regarded as the very heart of the prophetic eschatology... Wherever it occurs in prophecy, the statements culminate in an allusion to Yahweh's coming in person".

[60] Albright and Mann, *Matthew*, p. LXII.

[61] Hendriksen, *Matthew*, pp. 135, 135-39. Hare, like many other scholars, holds that the miraculous birth and the name Immanuel have little to do with the nature of the person to be born but rather identify only his function or role in the history of redemption. See Douglas R.A. Hare, *Matthew, A Bible commentary for Teaching and Preaching, Interpretation*, Louisville: John Knox, 1993, p. 10.

[62] Hendriksen, *Matthew*, pp. 143, 144. Cf., France, *Matthew*, p. 79.

fulfilment quotation contributes to the evangelist's understanding of both the person and, by implication, the function of the Messiah, with special emphasis on his divinity, for he is born without a father's help. The Messiah is the son of God.

The evangelist's understanding of Jesus as the Messiah is so closely related to the Immanuel prophecy that it is difficult to imagine that the evangelist did not know the wider Old Testament context of the text he quotes as a fulfilment quotation. The specific text is quoted and applied to Jesus in an attempt to define his person, and by implication, his mission. In Jesus' birth, the evangelist sees a God-given sign *par excellence*. The primary purpose is at this point, however, to define the person of Jesus Messiah so that the reader is prepared in advance for the supernatural work of redemption that is narrated later in the Gospel.

The fulfilment Quotation in Matt 2:6

Matt. And you, O Bethlehem (in the) Land of Judah are by no means
    least among the rulers (*hēgemosin*) of Judah;
    for from you will come forth a ruler (*hēgoumenos*)
    who will shepherd my people Israel.

LXX. And you, O Bethlehem, house of Ephrathah
    are too small to be among thousands (*chiliasin*) of Judah;
    from you there will come forth for me a leader (*archonta*) of
    Israel
    you will shepherd my people Israel (Micah 5:1).

MT. And you, O Bethlehem Ephrathah,
    small to be among the clans (lit. thousands) of Judah;
    from you there will come forth for me one who is to be a ruler in
    Israel,
    you will shepherd my people Israel (Micah 5:1).

Textual Observations

In the Matthean version certain exegetical modifications can be observed. In line 1 reference to Ephrathah[63] is omitted and is replaced by the well-known terms "the land of Judah". The term "land of Judah" not only differentiates this Bethlehem from the one in Galilee (Josh 19:15), but also serves to emphasize Jesus descent from a royal tribe, the tribe of Judah. It has been suggested that the original reading of Micah 5:1 was probably "O Beth-Ephrathah".[64] In line 2 the evangelist rejects the

---

[63] For the ancient clan of Ephrathah, see I Chron 2:19, 24, 50; for the city which received this name, see Gen 35:19; 48:7; Ruth 4:1.

[64] Brown, *The Birth of the Messiah*, p. 185. Cf. France, *Matthew*, p. 83.

insignificance of Bethlehem, although the reference to the lowliness of Bethlehem in the MT and the LXX is clear. It has been asked whether this change could be a deliberate one or is due to a variant. Allen and Lohmeyer have argued for the latter.[65]Another difference in this line is the translation "rulers" *('allupe)* where the MT and the LXX have "clans or thousands" *('alpe)*. Some scholars suggest that this could be possibly a variant.[66] Lindars suggests that the evangelist could have been influenced by Ps 68:28 (27): "There is little Benjamin with their ruler, the princes of Judah and their council".[67] But these changes do not make much difference in Hebrew. The phrase "small to be or too small to be" could become "by no means" by simply substituting *lhyyt* for *lhywt*, and the word "rulers" is a legitimate rendering of the same Hebrew consonants as for "thousands or clans" *('lpy)*.[68] Hendriksen suggests that in both cases the meaning is "though you, Bethlehem, are but little, yet you are by no means least."[69] Although the MT and the LXX mention the insignificance of Bethlehem, they anticipate and enhance the greatness to come as the line that follows shows. In essence, therefore, it is the greatness of Bethlehem that is the point of Micah's prophecy which the evangelist only makes explicit.[70] In line 3, the evangelist does not mention Israel, probably because it is to be mentioned in line 4 where he appends a line from II Sam 5:2. He also skips the phrase "for me" which Fitzmyer suggests is a representation of a more ancient construction.[71] In line 4 the evangelist does not make any significant changes except those that are grammatically necessary for joining the two texts of Micah 5:1 and II Sam 5:2.

While the text form of the line appended from II Sam 5:2 is almost identical to both standard Hebrew and standard Greek, the text form of Micah 5:2 is a mixed one. Of the 22 words in the LXX form of Micah only 8 are found in Matthean version. It has been asked whether Matthew received it in a fixed form. It has been argued by some that the lack of conformity between "Bethlehem of Judah" in 2:1, 5a (Matthean) and

[65]   *Ibid.,* especially note 21. Also Allen, *Matthew*, p. 13.
[66]   *Ibid.*
[67]   Lindars, *New Testament Apologetic*, p. 193.
[68]   France, *Matthew*, p. 83.
[69]   Hendriksen, *Matthew*, p. 167.
[70]   France, *Matthew*, p. 83. Cf. Brown, *The Birth of the Messiah*, p. 185.
[71]   J.A. Fitzmyer, *Catholic Biblical Quarterly* 18 (1956), pp. 10-13, quoted in Brown, *The Birth of the Messiah*, p. 186, especially note 23.

"Bethlehem (in the) land of Judah", in 2:16 (pre-Matthean) can best be explained if the quotation was received by him already in a fixed form.[72] Allen, however, suggests that it was an independent rendering of the Hebrew text.[73] The suggestion that Matthew is responsible for this mixed text-form appears to be more probable.

The status of this quotation as a fulfilment quotation has been doubted by some. It lacks the usual formula: "(All) this was done that it might be fulfilled which was spoken of the Lord by the prophet", or its variant form. It is also not quoted as the evangelist's comment. It is woven into the plot of the passage. However, the lack of the usual introductory formula can be explained by the fact that the quotation is spoken by the priests and the scribes and could therefore not carry it. Like the other fulfilment quotations it could be omitted without affecting the smooth flow of the passage. It also mentions a geographical place name like the other three fulfilment quotations in this chapter. Matthew has recorded these words from the Jewish leaders to emphasize their hardness of heart despite their knowledge of scriptures.

The historical context of Micah 5:2 and II Sam 5:2

(i) Micah 5:2

The prophet Micah was a young contemporary of the prophet Isaiah of Jerusalem, but, like Amos, he was coming from a rural background. His ministry probably covered the reigns of Ahaz (733-721 BC) and Hezekiah (720-693 BC). The ministry was probably at its height from the time of the fall of Samaria (721 BC) to the arrival of the Assyrians (701 BC) when King Sennacherib of Assyria invaded Judah. This fateful situation provides the background to the prophecies.[74]

Critical scholarship has, however, denied him chapters 3 to 7 where, it is claimed, there is pre-exilic, exilic and post-exilic tradition. 5:2 falls into the second category of the book which is said to be in the main exilic and

---

[72]   Brown, *The Birth of the Messiah*, p. 186.

[73]   Allen, *Matthew*, p. 13.

[74]   D. Winton Thomas, "Micah" in Matthew Black and H.H Rowley (eds.), *Peakes' Commentary on the Bible*, London: Routledge, 1990, p. 630. For the gross social injustice that formed the background sinful state and provided justification for divine judgment in the form of the Assyrian invasion, and a more detailed discussion of the historical context, see Bruce K. Waltke, "Micah, An Introduction and commentary", in David W. Baker *et al. Obadiah, Jonah and Micah*, TOTC, Leicester: Inter-Varsity, 1988, pp. 138-45. Cf. John M.P. Smith, *et al. Micah, Zephaniah, Nahum Habakkuk, Obadiah, and Joel, A Critical and Exegetical Commentary*, ICC, Edinburgh: T & T Clark, 1911, reprint 1974, pp. 19-23.

post-exilic in origin. In this section only 4:9-10; 5:5-6; and possibly 4:6-8 and 5:10-15 are said to be pre-exilic.[75]

But matters of introduction do not need to delay us here. What is significant for our purpose is the message that the prophet gave or was attributed to his name by his "school".[76] The message of Micah is one of judgment and renewal. Because of the sin of Judah and Jerusalem which is associated with Samariah, God will visit them with divine judgment through the instrumentality of the Assyrians (1:2-9). But beyond the approaching destruction there is renewal for God will raise a Messiah from the house of David (cf. Ezek 34:23-24; Amos 9:11) who will come out of "Bethlehem-Ephrathah", despite its insignificance (5:2-4). Until his birth, Israel will have no shepherd from Yahweh. When he comes, he will restore Judah and Israel and establish peace and security throughout the world.[77]

(ii)   I Sam 5:2

The historical setting of this text is the accession of David as king over Israel at the demand of the people who reminded him what God had told him before, saying: "You shall feed my people Israel and you shall be a captain over Israel". Matthew appends to his quotation the first half of this statement in order to define the person of the Davidic Messiah. The symbol of a shepherd to represent a ruler and the duties that are bound to that office was well known in the ancient Near Eastern world. In the context of the Old Testament, this symbol was extended to Yahweh, the personal God of Israel and His caring love. As a shepherd, God was a model of faithfulness, justice and loving kindness.[78] Since the Davidic Messiah was also a "Son" of God, he was Israel's king *par excellence*, an embodiment of divine faithfulness, justice and loving kindness. But while popular Davidic covenant theology "guaranteed the permanence of the Davidic dynasty and the security of the Davidic city", the coming ruler

---

[75]   Thomas, "Micah," p. 630. Cf. Anderson, *The Living World*, p. 339. For a brief history of the textual criticism of the Book of Micah see Smith *et al.*, *Micah*, pp. 8-12, especially p. 12 for the irrefutability of the argument that Micah 4-5 have prophet Micah as their author except for the tradition in Micah 4:14; 5:9-12.

[76]   Anderson attributes the Book of Micah as we have it to a "Prophetic school" that preserved and expanded the "poems" of the eighth century BC prophet. See his *The Living World*, p. 337.

[77]   Thomas, "Micah", pp. 630, 632.

[78]   Joyce G. Baldwin, *1 & 2 Samuel, An Introduction and Commentary*, TOTC, Leicester: Inter-Varsity, 1988, pp. 194-95.

would not be born at the royal court of Jerusalem but from remote and insignificant Bethlehem.

The Theological Significance of the Fulfilment Quotation

The prophetic context of Micah 5 is marked by its promise of national up-heaval until the birth of one who is to come and feed his flock in the strength of the Lord. However, this royal birth and the promise of a future return of those who are in dispersion to Zion, followed by a lasting peace, is to be gained at a great cost. The nation must reject all its secular and religious means, including sorcery, upon which Israel has so much relied all along. Hence, judgment for the people of God as well as their enemies is drawing near. This judgment will be followed by a spiritual renewal. The appended line from II Sam 5:2 only emphasizes that both the judgment and the renewal of the people of God have a divine origin and will be administered through the rightful king of Israel, the Davidic Messiah.[79]

In the Matthean context, the evangelist sees in the birth of Jesus, in the midst of royal anxiety for a dynastic future in the family of Herod, in the widespread political discontent partly arising from the mismanagement of Herod the Great and the oppressive Roman rule, and in the midst of secular, almost magical, calculations of the priestly establishment on matters of national and religious importance, the fulfilment of what was prophesied in the days of prophet Micah. The evangelist sees in the birth of Jesus the embodiment of judgment over the royal administration, the religious establishment and Israelite society. At the same time he sees the dawning of spiritual renewal over Israel.

By associating Jesus' birth with the town of Bethlehem, the ancestral home of David (Ruth 4:11; I Sam 16:1; 20:6; Luke 2:4), the evangelist is here emphasizing the royalty of the Messiah as a "Son of David", a royalty already implied in the genealogy (Matt 1:1-16).[80] The evangelist sees in David a type of Jesus Messiah. Like David, Jesus is born in Bethlehem, he is beloved of God (the name David means "the beloved one"), he is anointed or set apart for a special purpose in the history of redemption, and like David, Jesus passes through humiliation to glory. Hence, David becomes a type of the Messianic king who, after a period of suffering and humiliation, is raised to power and glory.

---

[79]   Albright and Mann, *Matthew*, p. LXII.

[80]   *Ibid.*, p. 5.

But there is also a negative emphasis in the prophetic change of the birth-place of the messiah from Jerusalem, which was the centre for both political and religious establishment and now sanctioned by popular Davidic Covenant theology. Jerusalem was now the city of David. This prophetic change of the birth-place of the Messiah from Jerusalem, now the royal city, in favour of a return to the ancestral home of David, Bethlehem, stresses the sad fact that Jerusalem with its royal court and temple administration had lost its spiritual direction. In this sense the change itself becomes an integral part of her divine judgment for her sinfulness. Jerusalem can no longer effectively be a spiritual heart and mentor for the nation. Thus here, especially in the quotation from Micah 5:2, the evangelist defines the royal status and the incomparable spiritual stature of Jesus Messiah.

Also, by attributing to him a Davidic descent through Joseph, the evangelist emphasizes the humanity of Jesus.[81] By appending a line from II Sam 5:2 to the Micah quotation, the evangelist shifts his focus from the royalty of the person of Jesus Messiah and his humanity through Davidic descent to the function of Jesus Messiah. He now defines the function and purpose of his presence. It is to shepherd God's people. He will restore Israel and Judah and establish peace and security throughout the world.[82] But as usual in the infancy fulfilment quotations, the specific nature and form of this redemptive activity is not pressed further. The primary interest is on the *person* of the messiah. The specific nature and form of his ministry are left undefined. The *work* of the Messiah becomes an issue of primary concern in the ministry-passion section of his narrative and it is thus left to be defined by fulfilment quotations used in that part of the Gospel narrative.

The Fulfilment Quotation in Matt 2:15

Matt   Out of Egypt have I called (*ekalesa*) my son (*ton huion mou*).

Lxx   Out of Egypt have I summoned (*metekalesa)* his children (*ta tekna*

        utou) (Hos 11:1)

MT   From (or "out of") Egypt have I called my son (Hos 11:1)

---

[81]   In the Lucan infancy narrative, the humanity of Jesus Messiah is emphasized, not through Joseph but through Mary, his mother.

[82]   France, *Matthew*, p. 84.

Textual Observations

The evangelist inserts the quotation at a peculiar place. The quotation depicts the Exodus, the coming "out of Egypt", and its natural place would be at 2:21, following the return from Egypt. However, the evangelist inserts it as a comment where Joseph takes the child and his mother to Egypt. It has been suggested that, probably, this was done because he wanted to give "a different geographical thrust to the return journey – not so much a journey from Egypt, but a journey to Nazareth".[83] While this is possible, it does not appear to be probable. It is unlikely that the evangelist would emphasize Egypt when he intended to stress Nazareth.

In the MT the word "son" is a collective one for Israel. But the LXX has plural "children" (*tekna*) probably because subsequently Hosea treats Israel as a plural entity.

The evangelist's quotation is certainly not from the LXX, but prefers Greek translations that are close to the MT. This explanation is more probable than that the evangelist uses the LXX but changes "his children" to "my son" in order to stress Jesus' divine Sonship.[84] In fact, the evangelist comes very close to the Greek translation of Aquila, a translation generally faithful to the MT, which has "from (*apo* instead of Matthew's *ex*) Egypt have I called (*kalein*) my son (*huios*)".[85]

That this quotation could come from existing Christian tradition is not impossible since the Exodus motif was a popular one in early Christianity. However, it is difficult for us to see how this Exodus "from Egypt" could apply to Jesus ministry[86] in a way different from the one envisaged by the evangelist.[87] It is also hard for Christians using the LXX to see any reference to Jesus in the word "children". And the context of the Hosea passage does not favour the application to Jesus either, since

---

[83] Brown, *The Birth of the Messiah*, pp. 219-20.

[84] *Ibid.*, p. 220. Cf. Allen, *Matthew*, p. 15.

[85] *Ibid.*, especially note 20.

[86] It is probably in view of this problem that Gundry sees the evangelist's point of this quotation in the preservation of the "son" in Egypt rather than in the Exodus itself. See Gundry, *The Use of the Old Testament in St Matthew's Gospel*, pp. 93-4.

[87] Lindars' suggestion that the Hosea text was used in pre-Matthean Christian tradition with reference to the resurrection in light of Revelation 11:8 is hardly convincing. The spiritual interpretation of the death and resurrection of Jesus in terms of their redemptive significance as "spiritually, called Sodom and *Egypt*" (Rev 11:8) appears to be a late tradition and probably non-existent in pre-Matthean tradition if an early date for this tradition is maintained. [emphasis mine]. See Lindars, *New Testament Apologetic*, p. 217.

it speaks of punishment for their disobedience (especially 11:2,5-7). Only verse one of Hosea 11 is clearly applicable to Jesus.[88]

It appears to me, therefore, that the probability favours the view that the evangelist, was original in his application of this text to Jesus.

The Historical Context of Hosea 11:1
Hosea prophesied during the last troubled years of the kingdom of Israel. His message falls into two major themes: (1) the intimacy of relationship between God and his people and (2) the inevitability and seriousness of God's judgment. In our text, the themes of divine call and Israel's disobedience recur with allusions to the Exodus. In the present circumstance, the imagery changes from the relationship between husband and wife to the relationship between parent and child. Israel, Yahweh's "son", has fallen into apostasy both politically and religiously, rejecting "his" covenant with Yahweh. The prophecy, therefore, depicts the creative and caring love of Yahweh which lies behind the whole history of Israel right from the beginning of "his" life as a people called to divine Sonship (Exod 4:22:23), the time he was redeemed from Egypt (11:1-4). But now, since Israel has rejected the covenant, Yahweh will repudiate "him" and bring judgment upon "him" through the instrumentality of Egypt and Assyria (11:5-7). However, "his" punishment will not be destructive, but rather reformatory (11:9-9). For Yahweh will not abandon his people and his fatherly love will never cease. Yahweh would afterwards restore to Israel "his" Sonship status, "They shall come trembling like birds from Egypt. And like doves from the land of Assyria. And I will return them to their homes, says the Lord" (11:11).[89]

The Theological Significance of the Fulfilment Quotation
By quoting the text of Hos 11:1, the evangelist portrays his presentation of the childhood history of Jesus as "the dawning of Messianic age." Even to Hosea himself within the Old Testament context, the ancient Exodus from Egypt already acquires Messianic dimensions. Israel as a "son" of God becomes a type of the Messiah and "his" Exodus from Egypt prefigures messianic salvation.[90] In the context of Hosea

---

[88]   Brown sees only the first line of this verse, "When Israel was a child, I loved him", as applicable to Jesus, see Brown, *The Birth of the Messiah*, p. 220.

[89]   P.R. Ackroyd, "Hoseah" in Black and Rowley (eds.), *Peake's Commentary on the Bible*, pp. 603-604, 611. Cf. Anderson, *The Living World*, pp. 301-316, but especially p. 313.

[90]   France, *Matthew*, p. 86. Cf. Hendriksen, *Matthew*, p.178; Hare, *Matthew*, pp. 15-16.

prophecy, the emphasis in Hos 11 falls on the close relationship which Israel, God's son (cf. Exod 4:22) enjoyed with God in the formative years of desert wanderings. The prophet pictures Israel as a beloved Son of God whom Yahweh has cared and provided for since "his" birth from the womb of desert wanderings, having saved "him" from the death of Egyptian slavery. The evangelist here sees Jesus as Son of God *par excellence* who relives the spiritual experience of Israel in leaving the bondage of Egypt for freedom. Jesus in his complete obedience is to relive Israel's experience and reverse Israel's failure to resist temptation in the wilderness. Just as Israel experienced the Exodus, that is, salvation from Egypt, so now Israel's history is capitulated in Jesus as he brings a new Exodus, that is, the dawning of Messianic salvation.

In the early Church, the concept of Son of God as applied to Jesus involved the ideas of his pre-existence, his mediation at creation and his being sent into the world through the incarnation.[91] By using the concept of "Son of God," the evangelist emphasizes the unique relationship of Jesus, now as the exalted Christ, to God. The Son belongs together with the Father.[92] Thus, the evangelist through this concept of divine Sonship, attempts to define the person of Jesus in his relation both to God and to Israel, an issue which called for an explanation in order to encourage the

---

[91] For discussion of these ideas and their Jewish origin over against the History of Religion School which finds their sources in Greek and Hellenistic tradition, see Martin Hengel, *The Son of God, the Origin of Christology and the History of Jewish Hellenistic Religion*, London: SCM, 1976, pp. 7-15, 66-76, especially his introductory comment: "It is possible and indeed probable that they were first developed among those Greek – speaking Jewish Christians who were driven out of Jerusalem and began the mission to the Gentiles in the Hellenistic cities of Palestine, Phoenicia and Syria. On the other hand, Paul already uses these expressions (e.g. Phil 2:6-8; Rom 8:3; Gal 4:4; Rom 8:32; Gal 2:20) as though they had established forms. Direct pagan influence is extremely improbable, if only because of the ethic composition of these earliest mission communities. The Jewish Christians were always the spiritual driving force which determined the content of the theology. In fact they put their stamp on the whole of first-century church. Unfortunately the History of Religions School paid too little attention to this decisive point" on p. 67. The very thesis of this little book by Hengel is to demonstrate, in my opinion quite convincingly, that the origin of the concept of "son of God", must be sought within the Jewish religious milieu rather than in Hellenistic parallels as the History of Religions School still holds. The school maintains that the introduction of a "son of God" theology into early Christianity represents "acute Hellenization of Christianity" (quoting Harnack), quite "un-Jewish and a kin to heathen ideas of the time" (quoting Schoeps) (Hengel, *The Son of God*, p. 5). To this, Hengel replies: "The constantly repeated view that the development of the Son of God Christology is a typically Hellenistic phenomenon and represents a break in primitive Christianity hardly bears closer examination" (p. 25). In the rest of the book, he carries out this closer examination to prove his thesis. Cf. Hastings, *Dictionary of the Bible*, pp. 142-143.

[92] Hengel, *The Son of God*, pp. 9, 10, 14.

development of Christian awareness.[93] The close identification of the Messiah and his people in this quotation develops into an identification with his Church in the New Testament, the new people of God, the new Israel.[94]

Thus, the Sonship of Jesus is defined in terms of the evangelist's theological understanding of the concept of Sonship as it applies to Israel within the Old Testament prophetic context. It is again difficult to see how the evangelist could apply this concept to Jesus without seriously taking into account the Old Testament context of the concept he applies.

The Fulfilment Quotation in Matt 2:18

Matt   A voice was heard in Ramah
weeping and loud mourning
Rachel crying for her children (*tekna*);
and she would not be consoled
because they are no more.

LXX.B. A voice was heard in Ramah
of lamentation and weeping and mourning
Rachel was crying,
would not cease on behalf of her sons (*huiois*)
because they are no more. (Jer 38:15)

LXXAA voice was heard on high
of lamentation and weeping and mourning
of Rachel's crying over her son (*huiois*);
and she would not be consoled, because they are no more. (Jer 8:15)

MT   A voice is (or was) heard in Ramah,
lamentation and bitter weeping,
Rachel weeping over her sons (*'al baneyah*)
refusing to be consoled over her sons
because he is no more. (Jer 31:15)

Textual Observations

The following aspects can be observed in Matthew's version. In line 1, Matthew, the MT and the LXXB consider "Ramah" as a proper name and

---

[93]   Albright and Mann, *Matthew*, p. LXIII.

[94]   See Matt 10:25; Mark 13:13; John 15:18-21; II Cor 1:5-10; Gal 6:17; Col 1:24; Heb 11:26; Rev 3:12, 21; 4:4; 12:13; 14:1, 14; 17:14; 19:11; 19:14; 20:4.

do not translate it as do LXXA, Codex Sinaiticus, the Aquila translation and Targumic tradition.[95] In line 2 Matthew agrees with the MT in understanding the grammatical relationship of the nouns involved. In Hebrew there are three nouns of which the last two are jointed by a construct so that one of them is better translated as an adjective. This aspect is lacking in the LXX. Also Matthew agrees with the MT in considering the nouns as nominative appositives to the "voice" of the first line, while the LXX shifts them into a negative construction. Matthew also appears to have reversed the order of the Hebrew nouns, preserved in the first two nouns of the LXX. In line 3 *huiois* of the LXX is closer to *banim* of the MT than Matthew's *tekna,* although the latter is used elsewhere in the Gospel to translate the Hebrew *ben* (son). If Matthew is responsible for the Greek of Jeremiah, it is surprising that he chose the plural of *teknon* (child) rather than the plural of *pais* (boy) or else p*aides* which could include both male and female. This probably could be explained if it is assumed that the evangelist adapts certain quotations to his context, while with others he retains the standard Greek way of rendering Hebrew.[96] In line 4, the evangelist's, "She would not be consoled" is identical with LXX A and both are close to MT's "refusing to be consoled" while LXX B diverges significantly with its "would not cease". Also in the repetition of "sons", LXX B agrees with the MT: while the evangelist and LXX A omit it. However, this divergence is only apparent than real since it appears that the original Hebrew did not have the second reference to "sons". This could therefore be an interpolation in the MT text.[97] In line 5, the ambiguous reading of the MT is not followed by any known Greek translation. It has again been suggested that this could be an interpolation in a more original Hebrew. Probably, the original Hebrew read "her son" (singular) in line 3 so that "he is no more" in line 5 could be understandable.[98]

In summary, it is clear that the evangelist's quotation is closer to the MT than LXX B and its similarities to LXX A are easily understood when it is realized that LXX A itself resembles the MT. Probably the few

---

[95] See the Critical Apparatus in *Septuaginta*, Stuttgart: Deutsche Bibelgesellschaft, 1979 on Jer 31:15, 38:15 in Septuaginta.

[96] Brown, *The Birth of the Messiah*, pp. 222 for a thorough discussion of this textual problem.

[97] *Ibid.*

[98] *Ibid.*, p. 223.

differences between the evangelist and the MT can be accounted for if the evangelist's Greek rendered a better text than is now presented in the MT.

The Historical Context of Jeremiah 31:15 (LXX 38:15)

Jeremiah lived in the second half of the 7th Century BC when Assyria was on the verge of collapse and Babylon was rising to an international superpower status. At the same time Judah was declining and would soon fall. The focus of his message is the vision of a new people in a new age that lie beyond the imminent catastrophe. He was called to the prophetic ministry in 627 BC. Coming from Anathoth near Ramah, the traditional sight for the tomb of Rachel, the prophet figuratively visualizes Rachel watching the defeated Jews and Israelites as they are gathered at Ramah by the Babylonian conquerors in readiness for a long match into a gloomy exile in 586 BC, an experience that Jeremiah personally shared in 588 BC. Rachel breaks down at the sight of the helpless defeated exiles and weeps for her dying children.[99]

Both Ramah and Rachel could represent both Israel and Judah. Ramah was located on the border between Israel and Judah (I Kgs 15:17; II Chron 16:1), five miles north of Jerusalem. And, as I have indicated, this is the traditional sight for the tomb of Rachel[100] and is the place where the exiles gathered for their march into exile. Similarly Rachel could represent both kingdoms. She bore Joseph who was the father of Ephraim and Manasseh. And Israel was known as Ephraim simultaneously, hence she could represent her "son". Also she was the mother of Benjamin whose descendants, and those of Judah, formed the southern Kingdom of Judah. Thus she could also represent Judah.

The Theological Significance of the Fulfilment Quotation

The focus of Jeremiah's message was the blessing that would come in the future after the present catastrophe. This is a cause for rejoicing. For there is comfort for both Israel and Judah (Jer 31:27, 31), that is the entire remnant (31:7). Yahweh has loved his people with an everlasting

---

[99]   John Paterson, "Jeremiah", in Black and Rowley (eds.), *Peaker's Commentary on the Bible*, p. 537, Cf. Anderson, *The Living World*, p. 419.

[100]   Possibly, the late tradition that Rachel's tomb is at Bethlehem (Gen 35:16-20; 48:7) influenced the evangelist's choice of Bethlehem. However, since the text locates Rachel's weeping at Ramah, an earlier traditional site, this is probably unlikely. See France, *Matthew*, p. 87. Cf. Jack Finegan, *The Archeology of the New Testament, the Life of Jesus and the Beginning of the Early Church*, Princeton: Princeton University press, 1969, pp. 24, 25.

love (31:3). Therefore, he who is scattering them will also gather them (31:10). Hence, Rachel should not weep any longer (31:16) because Ephraim is Yahweh's dear child (31:20) and Yahweh will make a new covenant with his people (31:31).[101] The remnant will return so that through it Yahweh will cause "a righteous Branch to spring forth for David" who will administer, "justice and righteousness in the land" (33:15). The prophet here obviously refers to the Messianic age.[102]

Thus, in the prophetic context of Jeremiah 31 the evangelist sees the ideas of both suffering and healing presented side by side. The idea of the Exodus and of the grace that Israel enjoyed in the betrothal times of the desert wanderings is not far removed from the substance of this fulfilment quotation. The testing which inevitably follows God's initiatives also brings suffering in which both the innocent and the guilty share. The whole of this chapter focuses on the hope of return that is held out to Israel by God's promise: those who survive the sword will receive grace and enjoy eternal love in the wilderness. Thus the suffering is not only a temporally experience, but also an inevitable prelude to their entering into the realities of the blessings of God. There is also a reference to God's shepherding of his scattered people. To Ephraim in the north and to Judah in the south, the promise of healing and restoration is held out. God's planting and building will follow his sifting and judgment (Jer 30:28). Once this sifting and judgment are over, God will establish a New Covenant with his people Israel.[103]

In all this, the evangelist sees the principle of God's out-workings through disaster and blessing, death and life.[104] The temporary suffering of the exiles, which is a cause for Rachel's weeping in the context of the book of Jeremiah, is only a prelude to a greater blessing. Yahweh will not abandon his people, but will make a New Covenant with them and cause a righteous branch from David to administer justice and righteousness. Therefore, Rachel should mourn no longer for her children will return.

---

[101] For a through discussion of the nature and character of the New Covenant promised in Jeremiah's prophecy including the relational tension of some of its aspects, see O. Palmer Robertson, *The Christ of the Covenants*, Phillipsburg: Presbyterian and Reformed, 1980, pp. 271-300.

[102] Hendriksen, *Matthew*, p. 185.

[103] That the concept of new covenant was very important to New Testament writers is reflected in the many references to it, for instance Matt 26:28; Mark 14:24; Luke 22:19 – the longer text; 1 Cor 11:25 and Heb 12:24.

[104] France, *Matthew*, p. 87.

Beyond the present catastrophe there is hope for joy. Similarly, the evangelist sees in the deaths of Bethlehem infants, as the prophet saw in the suffering of the exiles before him, a temporary prelude to Messianic blessings. For Jesus, like the remnant of the prophetic vision, will be preserved and will usher in the blessings of the Messianic age. This points to the theme of Jesus' humiliation and suffering before he was raised to glory in the resurrection, one of the central themes in the Gospel. Thus, rather than cry with sorrow because of the present suffering, the people of the Messiah must rejoice for their salvation will soon come, and now is.

It is again difficult here to see how the evangelist would apply this fulfilment quotation to the person of Jesus the way he does without taking into serious consideration of the Old Testament prophetic context. His use of the fulfilment quotation here further indicates that the evangelist defines the person of Jesus Messiah in light of its Old Testament prophetic context.

The Fulfilment Quotation in Matt 2:23

Matt   He will be called a Nazorean (*Nazōraios klēthēsetai*).
LXX   (Isa. 4:3) They will be called holy (*hagioi klēthēsontai*)
MT   (Isa 4:3) He will be called holy (*qādôsh*).
LXX B. (Judges 16:17) I am a holy one (*hagios*) of God.
LXX A. (Judges 16:17) I am a Nazirite (*Naziraios*) of God.
MT   (Judges 16:17) I have been a Nazirite (*Nazîr*) of God.

Critical Observations

Brown has called this quotation "the most difficult formula in the gospel."[105] Likewise, Allen thinks it is "still unexplained difficulty".[106] Albright, while admitting that there is no clear Old Testament source from which the evangelist might have derived this fulfilment quotation, he suggests that Jer 31:6 might be a possible source. In this text, not only do the consonants *nsr* appear but also its meaning in both the MT and the LXX was either lost or obscured. It also provides, according to Albright, the necessary context against which the incidents of vs. 19-23 can be understood.[107] While Albright's theory remains a possibility, it does not appear to be probable. The fact that he bases his theory on the obscurity

---

[105]   Brown, *The Birth of the Messiah*, p. 223.
[106]   Allen, *Matthew*, p. 16.
[107]   Albright and Mann, *Matthew*, p. 20-22.

of the text weakens his argument. It is based on a prophetic text "where a form of the Hebrew Consonants nsr appeared, but where also the meaning had been *lost* or *obscured* both in the Hebrew Masoretic text (MT) and in the Greek of LXX".[108] This is highly conjectural. However, it has been suggested that the term "Nazorean" that the evangelist has applied to Jesus is nevertheless appropriate not only because Jesus stayed in Nazareth but also because the word appears to allude to the word *netser*, a branch of the house of David, and it also appears to allude to the word *Nazir*, the consecrated or holy one.

Brown is of the opinion that the evangelist has *Nazir* more in mind and is citing two definite passages: Isa 4:3, "He who is left in Zion and remains in Jerusalem will be called holy", and Judg 16:17, "I have been a Nazarite to God from my mother's womb." Although he admits that the relationship between these texts and the evangelist's version is a complicated one, he further argues that the word *Nazir* also means both *hagios* (holy one) and *Naziraios* (Consecrated one) in Greek. He finds added support to his position in that during his ministry, Jesus was also known as "the Holy One" (a title only found in Judg 16:17 with reference to Samson), and the fact that the book of Judges was part of the former prophets in the Jewish Bible. The association of *Hagios Theou* (holy one of God) title with *Naziraios*, in turn, Brown argues, echo *Nazoraios* (that is Nazareth). The association would also remind the evangelist another passage, Isa 11:1, which refers to a shoot from the stamp of Jesse, *netser*, a branch that would grow from his roots, that is a Messianic branch of David.[109]

Without doubt, Brown's theory is quite a genius in character. But the evidence he adduces and the procedure he follows appears to be rather shaky. There is no etymological connection between the word *netser* and Nazareth. Also the context connects Nazarene with Nazareth and not any special consecration.[110] Moreover, Jesus was never a Nazirite in the sense that this Old Testament reference implies.[111] Besides all this, it is quite unsafe to build such a towering theory on the basis of a single occurrence of a term throughout the whole of the Old Testament where

---

[108] *Ibid.*, p. 21, Emphasis on "lost", "obscured" is mine.
[109] Brown, *The Birth of the Messiah*, p. 227.
[110] Hendriksen, *Matthew*, pp. 189, 190.
[111] France, *Matthew*, p. 88.

the term is applied to an individual person, in this case, Samson. Every other reference is plural and general.[112]

Other explanations are also not fully satisfactory. While many see allusions to both *netser* (Isa 11:1) and *Nazir* (Judg 16:17), some see Isa 11:1 as a more plausible reference.[113] Others are of the opinion that the evangelist has employed a complicated word-play at this point.[114] Since the evangelist does not appear to have quoted any specific passages, we may conclude with Hendriksen that the fulfilment is not, however, of one particular passage but the prophets in general.[115] This means that we cannot completely reject any of the proposed texts. Equally, we cannot endorse any of them with complete certainty[116] although, in the words of Allen, some would be "more plausible" than others.

The Theological Significance of the Fulfilment Quotation
The fulfilment quotation in Matt 2:23 has given us a special difficulty because we have not found any convincing claim as to its specific source, although passages such as Isa 4:3; 11:1; Jer 31:1; Judg 13:5; 16:17 have been suggested by various scholars. However, what is significant for our purpose here is that to Matthew, the point is that the Nazareth residence, like every stage of the coming and work of Jesus, was directed by God and fulfilled His purpose and promise.[117] By emphasizing Jesus' stay in Nazareth as fulfilment of Scripture, the evangelist stresses a line of thought which underlies the whole of this gospel, namely, that all stages of Jesus' life were a fulfilment of scripture. If the passages that have been appealed to as sources of this quotation are its real sources, then we would find at least three significant theological emphases in this quotation. First, the evangelist would be emphasizing the Davidic royalty of Jesus Messiah (*netser* – branch, Isa

---

[112]   John Metcalfe, *The Messiah, the Apostolic Foundation of the Christian Church*, vol. 3. Penn: John Metcalfe, 1978, p. 39.

[113]   Allen shares this opinion: "Attempt to connect the word (Nazirine) with the Hebrew Nazir has little in its favour", See Allen, *Matthew*, p. 16.

[114]   Hare, *Matthew*, p. 17. Cf. Allen, *Matthew*, pp. 16-17. The wordplay is not obvious in Hebrew and is completely lacking in Greek. See France, *Matthew*, p. 88.

[115]   Hendriksen, *Matthew*, p. 189.

[116]   It is for this reason that I have omitted a discussion on the historical context of any of the suggested texts. However, the fact that the evangelist would see in them a typological relationship to Jesus quite naturally is clear. There is a typological correspondence between these prophecies and the person of Jesus.

[117]   Floyd V. Filson, *A Commentary on the Gospel to St Matthew*, London: Adam and Charles Black, 1971, p. 62.

4:3; 11:1). The second emphasis would be on his holiness which would partly account for his sinlessness (*nazir* – the consecrated one, Judg 13:5; 16:17), as he was indeed the Holy One of God. The third emphasis would be on his mission of proclaiming salvation to the world (Jer 31:6). If this is the case, then the fulfilment quotation defines the person of Jesus Messiah. Not only is he the long-awaited Messiah, but he is also the Holy One of God entrusted with the mission of proclaiming salvation to the world.

Although we cannot trace the real source of the quotation with complete certainty, it is clear that its application to the Christ event by the evangelist rests on his understanding of the Old Testament prophetic context of whatever texts he draws his quotation from. The very difficulty we have in locating the exact source of this quotation suggests that the evangelist had such a thorough knowledge of the Old Testament contexts of the texts he had in mind as to enable him draw synthetically their theological implication and apply them to the Christ-event in a manner that we cannot easily comprehend.

Conclusion

In this chapter, it has been demonstrated that New Testament writers witness to earlier textual recensions. That they make their own extensive translations is very unlikely. However, it is clear that they made necessary grammatical modifications to received textual traditions and selected variants from them that better served their theological purpose. This is not surprising at a time when the biblical text was still in a fluid state and existed in multiple textual traditions.

Although it is generally difficult to tell whether a citation is Matthean or pre-Matthean on the basis of wording, in the case of fulfilment quotations, the evidence largely suggests Matthean construction and modification. The evidence also shows that Matthew has added these special quotations to the traditions he reports. It has also shown that Matthew is responsible for the mixed-text form of the fulfilment quotations. He is responsible for the choice of the text-form that now appears in these quotations.

The discussion has further demonstrated that the evangelist applied these Old Testament quotations to the Christ-event in full awareness of their Old Testament prophetic context in order to define the Person of the Messiah. He is defined in terms of his royalty implied in his Davidic Sonship. This at the same time implies his humanity, for he is a royal descendant of the Davidic dynasty. He is also defined as divine. He is the Son of God. This is implied in his virgin birth and the divine call from Egypt. Thus the Messiah is not only invested with human royalty but also transcends the human plane in his intimate relationship to God. As the Son of God, his redemptive mission transcends time and space in its effects and acquires cosmic dimensions and eschatological finality.

But the specific forms of this redemptive mission are left undefined. The primary focus at this stage in the narrative is on the Person of the Messiah. The nature and form of the redemptive activity that this messiah will undertake are yet to be defined by the fulfilment quotations which fall under the mission-passion section of his Gospel narrative. Hence, in the final chapter of this work, I shall turn to these fulfilment quotations to see how they define the *work* of the Messiah.

Chapter 4

Fulfilment Quotations in the Ministry and Passion Narratives

Introduction

In the preceding chapter, it has been demonstrated that the fulfilment quotations in the nature and form they have come down to us are the work of the evangelist. It has also been demonstrated that the fulfilment quotations in the infancy narrative define the person of Jesus Messiah as both human and divine. He is the Son of David and at the same time the Son of God with a redemptive mission that transcends the limits of time and space. It has been, however, noted in that chapter that the fulfilment quotations in the infancy narrative leave the specific forms of this redemptive mission largely undefined. It is the fulfilment quotations that are found in the mission-passion section of the gospel that shed light on specific forms that the redemptive mission of the Messiah will take. The task before me in this chapter, therefore, is to show how these special Old Testament quotations in the mission-passion section of the gospel narrative contribute to the evangelist's understanding of the nature and forms that the Messiah's redemptive mission will take. It will also be argued, as it was the case in the previous chapter, that the Old Testament contexts of the fulfilment quotations provide the conceptual framework for the evangelist's understanding of the mission of the Messiah. It is in light of the conceptual categories that are found in the Old Testament contexts of those fulfilment quotations that the evangelist applies the specific texts he quotes, albeit in a modified manner, to the mission of Jesus Messiah. It will thus be demonstrated that the Old Testament background to these quotations is crucial for any proper assessment of the evangelist's understanding of the nature and role of the Messiah's redemptive mission. Critical scholarship has generally disregarded or even actively undermined the role of the Old Testament background in its search for an understanding of Matthean theology. It has largely attributed Matthean Christological understanding to the evangelist's supposed sources, especially the Gospel of Mark.[1]

The fulfilment quotations to be examined in this chapter are Matt 4:14-16; 8:17; 12:17-21; 13:35; 21:4-5 and 27:9-10. These are spread across the whole period from the beginning of Jesus public ministry in Galilee (4:14-16) to his condemnation by the Jewish Sanhedrin and the Roman Governor in Jerusalem (27:24). They focus on the theological significance of Galilee as the base for Jesus' ministry; on the theological implications of his healing ministry (8:17); on the theological implications of his humble attitude as an approach to his mission (12:17-21); on the theological significance of parables as a means for teaching divine truth (13:35); on the theological significance of his triumphal entry into Jerusalem (21:4-5); and on the theological significance of the "Lordly price" for which he was betrayed (27:9-10). The underlining concept in the mind of the evangelist is that the prophetic word of God (i.e. the Old Testament) not only defines the nature of the person of the Messiah, but also defines the mission of that Messiah. Thus the whole life and ministry of the Messiah is not only set in eternity, but it is also revealed in time through the prophetic word. It is the fact that the life and work of Jesus fulfills the prophetic word that establishes him as the Chosen One of God, the Messiah. There were many who took God's word to Gentile – dominated areas; and there were many who healed and preached his word. There were many who attempted to rule with a humble heart; and there were many whose sacrificial attempts in their leadership career went unrecognized and unappreciated. One thing makes all these individuals different from the Matthean Messiah, namely, that their efforts, good or even Godly as they were, were not a direct fulfilment of his prophetic word in the sense that this Messiah is.

The idea of fulfilment is crucial to the understanding of the evangelist's Christology. It is for this reason that the evangelist finds fulfilment quotations an appropriate tool for expounding the redemptive meaning of Jesus' life and work in which he sees no less than the life and work of the Messiah as foretold in the prophetic word of God. This chapter attempts, as I have already indicated, to show how that prophetic

---

[1] For example, see Luz, *The Theology of the Gospel of Matthew*, p. 9, who attributes Matthean Christology to the Gospel of Mark.

word sheds light on the work of the Messiah with full regard to the Old Testament context of the prophetic word.

Exegetica: Theological Analysis of the Fulfilment Quotations in the Mission Narrative

This section continues the grammatical- historical analysis of the fulfilment quotations. The focus here is on those fulfilment quotations that are found in the missionary narrative of the Gospel according to Matthew. These are found at 4:14-16; 8:17; 12:17-21 and 13:35. The introductory formula for the fulfilment quotations at 4:14 and 12:17 includes the words *hina plērōthę to rēthen*. The introductory formula at 8:17 and at 13:35 includes the words *hopōs plērōthę to rēthen.* The words *hina* and *hopōs* in this context are used as synonyms. Both mean "in order that", "so that" or "that" and are used as conjunction of purpose. Thus, the use of the one or the other does not lead to any substantial difference in meaning. In this section, it will be again argued that the way in which the evangelist applies these fulfilment quotations to the Christ-event reveal, his awareness of their Old Testament context, and that he applies them to the Christ-event while taking full account of their Old Testament setting.[2] All the fulfilment quotations in the mission narrative define the work of Jesus Messiah, although the emphasis on the work of

---

[2] Many critical scholars do not acknowledge the significant impact that the Old Testament background to specific fulfilment quotations would have on the mind of the evangelist as he wrote the Gospel. Allen, *A Critical and Exegetical Commentary on the Gospel According to S. Matthew*, p. 34, has the view that the evangelist whom he sees as an editor, "tears the words from their context, because he saw in them a prophecy of the fact that Christ went to Galilee to begin his ministry." In Allen's opinion, the geographical references in the fulfilment quotations at 4:14, for instance, have no relevance to the evangelist's application of that quotation to the Christ- event, especially to the fact that Jesus established his ministry in Galilee with Capernaum as its headquarters: "We need not inquire as to the exact signification of the geographical terms in the original", p. 34. Daniel J. Harrington, *The Gospel of Matthew*, Sacra Pagina Series Vol. 1, Collegeville: The Liturgical Press, 1991, p. 73, sees the evangelist more preoccupied with the Gospel of Mark, one of his supposed sources so that the account of Jesus' move to Galilee is created out of the brief references to it at Mk 1:14a and 1:21 which he then saw as the fulfilment of Isa 8:23-9:1. The evangelist is basically portrayed as seriously considering the Marcan text. There is little reason to think that, in Harrington's view, the evangelist would apply the same seriousness in his consideration of the Old Testament context of his fulfilment quotation: "his use of Mark illustrates some of his editorial techniques: In the first pericope (i.e. 4:12 – 17) Matthew has shaped the account of Jesus movement from Nazareth to Capernaum from Mk 1:14a and 1:21, reinforced the idea of that movement as being in accord with God's will by the quotation from Isa 8:23-9:1, and shortened Mark 1:14b – 15 and brought it into line with the summary of John's preaching (i.e. Matt 3:2)". For the view that even the evangelist's basic theological ideas are derived from Mark, see Luz, *The Theology of the Gospel of Matthew*, p. 9.

the Messiah in itself further defines his person. His extraordinary work of redemption as specifically defined by these fulfilment quotations follows as a corollary to his extraordinary personality as defined by the fulfilment quotations of the infancy narrative.

The Fulfilment Quotation in Matt 4:14-16

> Land of Zebulun and land of Naphtali,
> Toward the sea, beyond the Jordan,
> Galilee of the Gentiles.
> The people sitting in darkness
> Have seen a great light
> and upon those sitting in the land of the shadow of death
> Light has dawned.

Textual Observations

In the Hebrew original of Isa 9:1-2 (Heb 8:23-9-1) the first items, "The land of Zebulun and the land of Naphtali" are separated from the three, "toward the sea, beyond the Jordan, Galilee of the nations". All of these five items are in an objective position. The first two items are objects of the verb "brought into contempt" or "degraded" (Hebrew qal). The other three items are objects of the verb "will glorify" or "will cause to be honoured" (from Hebrew kaved)

The evangelist has brought all the items into the position of nominative in apposition with "the people sitting in darkness", the predicate being "have seen a great light". The last two lines beginning with "And upon" (Greek kai tois) are in a parallelistic relationship to the preceding items. Here "light" is the subject, and "has dawned... and upon those sitting in the land of the shadow of death" is the predicate.

It has been argued that the evangelist was probably quoting a Greek version otherwise he would not have rendered the Hebrew word derek by the accusative hodon (Greek). It is said that if the evangelist were translating directly from the Hebrew, he would have rendered that word by the nominative hodos just as he has "the land of" (Hebrew. Artsah) rendered by the nominative "gē" (Greek), not the accusative "gēn" (Greek). It is then concluded that the accusative rendering hodon can only be the result of "careless copying from a version before him."[3] However, to draw such a bold conclusion of source criticism out of this simple grammatical element does not seem quite convincing. It is one

---

[3] Allen, *Matthew*, p. 34.

thing to say that the evangelist made a grammatical error here since *hodos* would be more appropriate as the phrase *hodon thalasses* has in his quotation taken a nominative position. It is, however, quite another thing to see this as sufficient evidence for the assumption that the evangelist was carelessly copying from a Greek version. Whether this was the case or not, it is clear that the present evidence does not offer any sufficiently conclusive proof. It is, however, sufficiently clear that the evangelist is not simply following a literal translation of the Hebrew text. The evangelist, in his own original way, has quite successfully reproduced Isaiah's thoughts. Essentially, Isaiah and Matthew are in agreement: light has dawned or shines brightly upon the people who were formerly in darkness.

When compared with the Septuagint, significant textual differences that rule out the possibility of literal reproduction of its text also appear. Where the evangelist has *gē Zaboulōn kai gē Nephtalim* (land of Zebulun and land of Naphtali), the Septuagint has *kōra Zaboulōn he gē Nephtalim.* The words *hodon thalassēs* are missing in Septuagint B, but they appear in Septuagint Aleph, c, a, A, Q and were found in Aquila and Theodotion. The evangelist is probably using a textual tradition which was either different from that of the Septuagint or was an early form of the Septuagintal tradition which contained these words. However, whether that tradition was in written form or not cannot be established with great certainty. The phrase *peran to Iordanou* also appears in the Septuagint, as does the phrase *Galilaia tōn ethnōn.* Where the evangelist has *ho laos ho kathēmenos en skotei,* Septuagint B has *poreuomenos* (those driven into darkness) following the Hebrew. But Septuagint A has *kathemenos* (those sitting). The word *eiden* in the gospel also appears in Septuagint B as *idete.* Other Septuagintal variants are *eidete* and *eide.* Where the evangelist has *kai tois kathemenois* (and those who are sitting), the Septuagint has *hoi katoikountes* (those who live). Where the evangelist has *en kōrą kai skią thanatou* the Septuagint has the same, although Septuagint B omits *kai.* Where the evangelist has *fōs aneteilen (*light has risen), the Septuagint has *fōs lampsei* (light will shine).

These textual differences, between the text in the gospel and that of the Septuagintal traditions on the one hand, and the textual and syntactic differences between the text of the Hebrew original on the other hand, reveal that the evangelist developed the fulfilment quotation he employs more or less independently of these traditions. It will later be shown that the changes that the evangelist makes in the established textual traditions do serve his theological purposes.

The Historical Context of Isa 9:1-2 (Hebrew. 8:23 – 9:1)
The poetic text in the background to the quoted portion presents a picture of doom and darkness. It portrays a people (Hebrew *hā'am*) who are probably Jews, but they could as well be Israelites (Ephraimites) or even foreigners, passing through the country hopelessly and distressed. In their plight, they curse both king and God from whom they cannot get any help. They are completely surrounded with impenetrable gloom (Isa 8:21-22). This is probably a reminiscence of the terrible destruction caused by the Assyrian invasion led by Tiglath-Pilesser in 734 and 733-32 BC (II Kgs 15:29; Isa 8:4). At that time, the Assyrians invaded the Northern Kingdom and, under the leadership of Tiglath-Pilesser III, converted the traditional districts of Zebulun and Naphtali into three separate Assyrian provinces.[4] But the prophet sees a glorious future for the people of God who are currently enslaved by the Assyrians. In the oracle, the prophet sees a Davidic child-king who, in contrast with the faithless Ahaz, will faithfully exercise his task of government. In the meantime, the child-king will live in a time of great suffering. Before he is old enough, the Assyrians will match through the land. Devastated, the land will turn into a wilderness (Isa 7:16-17; 8:8). Despite this, however, the presence of the Immanuel – child will, for those with eyes to see, be a sign, an assurance, that God is with his people, taking them through the fire of divine judgment to the dawn of a new day, the day of salvation. Meanwhile, the Immanuel child himself shares in the people's sufferings. But his very presence is a surety for the promised glorious future. Once the Assyrian rule is removed, the child Immanuel will ascend his Davidic throne and rule over the people as God's agent.[5]

The darkness which fell upon the people of Galilee cannot be limited, however, to this particular Assyrian invasion. For centuries the region of

---

[4] In 734 BC the coastal districts of the kingdom of Israel were converted into the Assyrian province of Du'ru, named after its capital, Dor. In 732 BC, in a second invasion, the north and the eastern areas that formed the plain of Jezreel and Galilee were turned into a province called Magidu, with Megiddo as its capital. The area across the Jordan became the province of Gal'azu. See Otto Kaiser, *Isaiah 1-12, A Commentary*, OTL, London: SCM, 1972, p.126. Also R.E. Clements, *Isaiah 1-39*, NCBC, Grand Rapids: Wm. B. Eerdmans and London: Marshall, Morgan and Scott, 1980, p. 104.

[5] Anderson, *The Living World of the Old Testament*, pp. 333 – 334.

Galilee had been exposed to external military and political aggression more often than the Judean territory of southern Palestine. In addition, the Galilean region was more exposed to destructive moral and religious influences of a pagan environment. While a significant set of these elements was introduced through military campaigns,[6] probably they were mainly introduced through peaceful means across the centuries. Through Galilee ran the international trade route, "the way of the sea". It ran from Damascus in Syria through Galilee down to the Mediterranean Sea at Acre. This brought the residents of Galilee into close contact with foreigners who travelled up and down that road for social-economic reasons.[7]

This prophetic oracle, like many other famous messianic oracles has become a subject for much scholarly debate. It has been argued that the Hebrew text in vv. 19-23 (English: vv. 19- 9:1) was not originally a single piece, and that it is ambiguous with more than one corruption in its present form.[8] Verses 21-22 are said to begin "in the middle of a distich."[9] It has also been claimed that vv. 21-22 were added by a redactor.[10] These verses provide a background picture to the oracle proper in 8:23 – 9:6 (9:1-7). They portray a people who, faced with the coalition of Syria and Ephraim, become hopeless and resort to consulting the spirits of the dead in a desperate search for an interpretation of the future. This indicates lack of faith in Yahweh and his prophetic word. For this reason, their distress will become greater and greater in accordance with Yahweh's word given through Isaiah's prophecies. Overtaken by hunger and suffering, they cursed their king and their God. They have no hope for redemption and will finally be dragged into slavery in a foreign land. Within this portion, the opening phrase in v.21, which is translated as "And they will pass through it..." in AKJV is problematic. First, where there is "they" in the English translation, the Hebrew has an indefinite

---

[6] The worst and most extensive of these campaigns was the deportation of over 27000 Israelites into Persia and subsequent repopulation of Israel by colonialists brought in from Babylonia, Elam and Syria. See Anderson, *The Living World of the Old Testament*, p. 316. For a thorough discussion, see James B. Pritchard (ed.), *Ancient Near Eastern Texts, Relating to the Old Testament*, Third Edition, Princeton: Princeton University Press, 1969, pp. 284-87, but especially p. 284.

[7] Hendriksen, *Matthew*, p. 243.

[8] George Buchanan Gray, *The Book of Isaiah, A Critical and Exegetical Commentary*, ICC, Vol. Edinburgh: T & T Clark, 1912, reprint 1975, p. 161.

[9] *Ibid.*

[10] Clements, *Isaiah 1-39*, p.102.

"one" (Heb *we'ābar)*. This provides a picture of one man in distress and suffering, not many. Secondly, the "it" of that phrase *(bāh)* is left indeterminate. Clements, understanding this "it" as reference to Jerusalem rather than the land in general, suggests that the picture here is a reminiscence of the events of 587 BC that led to the Babylonian exile. Taking the verses 21-22 as a second redactor's addition, he sees no reason for searching for an antecedent in the preceding text.[11] Most scholars, however, regard the "it" of that phrase as a reference to the land in general rather than to Jerusalem, and associate the events referred to in this context as those related to the Assyrian invasion of the Northern Kingdom and its subsequent annexation of the northern areas of the Israelite Kingdom.[12] The indefinite "one" of the Hebrew text may be satisfactorily accounted for as a poetic or prophetic reference to the suffering people of the Northern Kingdom.

Much scholarly contention has centered on 8:23 (9:1). Most scholars have treated this verse as a secondary explanatory note intended to provide a historical background for the hope that follows upon those who have experienced distress and suffering.[13] Within this broader view of the redactionary nature of this verse, there are those who hold that the verse was added by Isaiah himself later, looking back to the events of 734 BC as he linked together the two oracles.[14] There are also those who hold that while the verse might have been inserted at an early stage to illuminate 9:1-6 (9:2-7), it was not part of the original oracle. It is viewed as a Josianic rather than an Isaianic redaction.[15] Others, however, see 8:23 (9:1) as forming a unity with 9:1-6 (9:2-7) which forms the oracle proper.[16]

---

[11]   *Ibid.*, pp. 102, 103.

[12]   For instance, see Christopher R. Seitz, *Isaiah 1-39, A Bible Commentary for Teaching*, Louisville: John Knox, 1993, pp. 82, 83; Kaiser, *Isaiah 1-12*, p. 122; Gray, *The Book of Isaiah*, p.161.

[13]   For instance, see Gray, *The Book of Isaiah*, p. 161; Clements, *Isaiah 1-39*, p.105; Seitz, *Isaiah 1-39*, pp. 84, 85.

[14]   For instance, Gray, *The Book of Isaiah*, p. 161 has the following comment: "If both (i.e. 8:21f and 9:1-6) are (the work of Isaiah), this note (i.e. 8:23/9:1) may have been added by him when he combined two poems of different periods."

[15]   Clements, *Isaiah 1-39*, p. 105 shares this view.

[16]   Kaiser, *Isaiah 1-12*, p. 125, shares this view and gives credit to Alt for it: "Albrecht Alt is responsible for having demonstrated ... the fact, assumed by Matt 4:15f, that 9:1-7 forms a unity."

One difficulty in the understanding of this verse relates to how we should translate the Hebrew word *hikbîd*, rendered as "he will make glorious" (RSV). Throughout this oracle, including its background text, the tenses that are employed are perfects and imperfects with *waw* consecutive. These tenses are naturally used in a historical narrative. Verses. 4 and 6 are the only exception from this practice. The Hebrew original for the phrase "he will make glorious" has a perfect tense which naturally implies a past action. The manner in which we understand this phrase determine the objects of the contrast implied in the text. Clements has attempted to understand this phrase as a reference to a past action. For him, the contrast is between the fate of Israel under Assyria, as a consequence of disunity between Ephraim and Judah, and the salvation which could come if the two were united under a single ruler:

> Quite evidently the intention is to contrast the disastrous fate of Israel at the hands of Assyria, which came as a consequence of disunity between Ephraim and Judah (and) the salvation which could come if they were reunited under a single Davidic ruler.[17]

Thus Clements and those who share his view hold that both temporal references ("In the former time in the latter time") refer to Assyrian supremacy. Accordingly, the phrase *wehā'aharôn hikkîd derek hayyām*, (" in the latter time he will make glorious the way of the sea") is by them rendered "in the latter time he treated harshly the way of the sea". The AKJV and the NKJV have followed this rendering. Seitz observes that Clements' reading would be favoured by the clear sense of the imminent judgment that was to be visited upon the Northern Kingdom through the Assyrians (7:8b, 15; 8:4). Judah too was to be punished as a consequence of Ahaz's disbelief (8:21-22).[18]

However, most scholars hold that the contrast is between the former and the latter periods and that the annexed territories are the referent in both cases. In this view, the contrast is thus not between the actual disastrous fate of divided Israel under the hand of Assyria and the conditional salvation that would have obtained for a united Israel, both of which were past as Clements suggests, but with yet another visitation of wrath looming in the imminent future. Rather, the verse speaks of an end to gloom and suffering for the one in anguish. God thoroughly judged the Northern Kingdom and handed it over to Israel's enemies. Not only is

---

[17]   Clements, *Isaiah 1-39*, pp. 104, 105.
[18]   Seitz, *Isaiah 1-39*, p. 85.

their land and freedom taken, but also the people themselves are marched into captivity. Darkness usually implies captivity, whether within Israel in the sense of foreign oppression or outside Israel in an exilic context. But this is not all that God will do. For the sake of his own glory in the sight of nations, he will fulfil the promises and bring into reality a kingdom in which all Israel would be united and enjoy a lasting peace under a Davidic ruler. Hence, the first verse promises that God would reverse the fate of the separated districts of the Northern Kingdom[19] and that this salvation will extend to Judah and beyond.

This interpretation of the temporal references is held by many. Gray comments that "the northern and north-eastern territory of Israel... will be compensated for its former distress by a corresponding glory."[20] Kaiser also speaks in terms of future glory for the once oppressed people, "The anger of God is not the end of all he has to do, but a transition to a new act of grace. For the sake of his glorification in the sight of the nations he will not abandon his people of the twelve tribes in the future. He will bring a new prosperity and freedom to the land which is oppressed at his command."[21] Kaiser then continues to speak about the annexed territory of the Northern Kingdom, converted into Assyrian provinces at the time.[22] The translators of the NIV and the RSV have also followed this future understanding of a clause in a perfect tense. It is important to note that even the evangelist understood the temporal references in a similar way. In line with this view, S. Mowinckel has made the observation that "Hebrew 'tenses' do not, like ours, express distinctions in time. Both the 'perfect' and the 'imperfect' in Hebrew can indicate events in the past, present, or future according to context."[23]

Although some have placed the oracle in the post-exilic period, it is generally accepted that the oracle has features which make pre-exilic dating more appropriate, although historical precision is almost unattainable.[24] Therefore, we can safely assume that the oracle is pre-

---

[19]   Kaiser, *Isaiah 1-12*, p. 125.

[20]   Gray, *The Book of Israel, A Critical and Exegetical Commentary*, p. 161.

[21]   Kaiser, *Isaiah 1-12*, p. 126.

[22]   *Ibid.*

[23]   S. Mowinckel, *He that Cometh*, New York and Nashville: Abingdon, 1959, p. 108.

[24]   Seitz, *Isaiah 1-39*, p. 4. Clements, *Isaiah 1-39*, p. 104, has also argued for the dismissal of the post – exilic dating. He argues that there is no hint in this prophecy to show that it concerned the restoration of Davidic monarchy, and that the language of royal birth and great international power that is to be achieved through the Davidic king does not accord with the

exilic along with many other scholars. The difficulty, however, is whether this oracle should be understood as historic referring to some particular birth (or accession) or whether it should be seen as prophetic and thus without any specific historical reference. Or indeed, whether it must be seen as part-prophetic and part-historical. It is possible to hold the last stated view since the tenses used in the oracle are suggestive of a historical event. At the same time the situation in vv. 1-3, 5, which does not appear to reflect any actual person, is suggestive of a prophetic character of the oracle. Gray has correctly noted the difficulty that would arise from this view:

> If this were actually so, the question would arise, how much is prophetic, how much historical? Has the great deliverance from foreign oppression actually taken place? Has some birth awaked the poet's hopes, but the actual present not yet fulfilled then by bringing the child born to the throne of David?[25]

In my opinion, the part-historical and part-prophetic nature of the oracle remains a great probability, especially when it is remembered that some prophetic oracles followed certain prophetic-symbolic actions that were historically actualized.[26] However, scholars have usually subscribed either to the historical view or to the prophetic view. Among those who have adopted the historical position are S. Mowinckel who has seen in v. 6 the proclamation of the birth of a Davidic prince but thinks it is impossible to identify him.[27] J. Lindblom has also regarded v. 6 as the prophetic announcement of the physical birth of a royal child, Immanuel himself, whom he identifies with Hezekiah.[28] Albrecht Alt also holds the

---

hopes and expectations concerning the restoration of a Davidic kingship in the sixth and fifth century BC. Albrecht Alt dates the oracle between 732-722 and holds that it was intended as a prophecy of the expulsion of Assyrian forces and the restoration of a United Kingdom under a Davidic prince. Quoted in Anderson, *The Living World of the Old Testament*, p. 334, note. 19.

[25] Gray, *The Book of Isaiah, A Critical and Exegetical Commentary*, p. 165.

[26] A good illustration of this practice are the actual births of Isaiah's sons and the subsequent prophetic names that were given to them. Jeremiah's symbolic actions of buying the field from Hinamel and his visit to the potter's house illustrate the same principle. See also H.H. Rowley, *Rediscovering the Old Testament*, London: Clark, 1947, p.106, for how the personal experience or events in the life of the prophet contributed to prophecy; J. Muilenburg, "Old Testament prophecy" in M. Black and H.H. Rowley (eds.), *Peake's Commentary on the Bible*, London: Routledge, 1962, reprint 1987, p. 481 for a brief discussion on prophetic – symbolic actions.

[27] For a thorough discussion, see S. Mowinckel, *He that Cometh*, pp. 102-110, especially p. 109.

[28] J. Lindbom, *Prophecy in Ancient Israel*, Oxford: Basil Blackwell, 1962, p. 247.

view that the prophet was prophesying an imminent liberation for the annexed territories of the Northern Kingdom and an imminent accession of a Davidic son who would fulfil the hope of the people.[29] Gerhard von Rad also holds the view that the prophecy of the people's liberation and the accession of a Davidic ruler would be imminently fulfilled:

> We must not think that the prophets looked for the coming of an anointed sometime in a vague future. Isaiah clearly envisaged the enthronement in the immediate future, that is to say within the context of the Assyria crisis and its defeat.[30]

More recently, Seitz has seen in this verse a proclamation for the birth of a royal, child Immanuel. He, however, identifies the child with Josiah rather than Hezekiah:

> It is for these reasons of mundane historical accuracy (i.e. the fact that the accession of Hezekiah does not historically coincide with the defeat of Assyria and that the latter was neither affected nor threatened by Hezekiah's accession) that Josiah has been put forward as a candidate who better fits the scenario of a possible Assyrian defeat .... If a link has been established intentionally between the "birth" of 9:6 and the promise of Immanuel at 7:14-16, then the effect is to focus the royal oracle on the birth rather than on the accession of Immanuel. The birth then portents great things.[31]

But the occurrence of such a provocative event should not necessarily mean that the prophecy finds its fulfilment in that event as these scholars appear to suggest. While the sign could be given in the present, its fulfilment would still lie in the distant future. And this appears to be the case here.

Among those who hold the view that the oracle must be seen as prophetic throughout are Gray who makes the following observation:

> It is more probable that the poem is prophetic throughout in all its direct statements, the light has not yet actually shone, the people have not yet actually rejoiced, the child has not yet actually been born; all these things are past, not in reality, but only in the hopeful vision of the poet.[32]

In a similar vein, Kaiser observes that:

[29]   Quoted in Otto Kaiser, *Isaiah 1-12, A Commentary*, Second Edition,. London: SCM, 1983, p. 204. For Kaiser's critic of this view, see pp. 204-206.

[30]   Gerhard von Rad, *Old Testament Theology*, Vol. 2, London: SCM, 1975, p. 171.

[31]   Seitz, *Isaiah 1-39*, p. 86.

[32]   Gray, *The Book of Isaiah, A Critical and Exegetical Commentary*, p. 165.

The prophetic character as a whole is explicitly emphasized by the conclusion. Consequently, it is pointless to relate this prophecy to the birth of a prince or the enthronement of a Davidic king during Isaiah's lifetime . For Isaiah, at his encounter with Ahaz, the ruling line of the royal house of Judah lay under judgment.[33]

As I indicated earlier, to attempt to understand this oracle as strictly historical or strictly prophetic is probably to miss the point. It is quite probable that a particular event, either a birth or an accession to the throne acted as a springboard for the oracle so grand in its hopes and expectations as not to fit the description of any known king in the history of the Israelite monarchy.[34]

Seitz has correctly observed that while the references to birth and the language of "child" "son" generally refers to the coronation of a new king in the spirit of Ps 2, the larger context of 7:1-9:7 to which this oracle belongs indicates an interest in the birth of the Immanuel child rather than his accession:

At 7:14-16 we hear of a similar provision of a name (Immanuel) and promises associated with it. The name reaches at 8:8 and 8:10 in visions of the future. But we hear nothing about the birth as such, as a concrete fulfilment of the word spoken to the prophet, which was to be a sign for the house of David. The royal oracle at 9:1-7 provides that concrete fulfilment: 'For a child has been born for us'. With us, for us (9:6), is Mighty God... The promise of the son is fulfilled. The promises related to his maturation await their fulfilment, even as the oracle closes with a vision of his reign.[35]

Of a particular interest to us in this oracle is v 5 (6), especially the names that are given to the royal child. The titles Wonderful Counsellor, Mighty God, Everlasting Father and Prince of Peace[36] are given to the royal child once he is raised to the status of "Son" by the Father. The titles set out the programme of his reign. With the coming of this king, the history of mankind hitherto characterised by unrest, strife, suffering and devastation approaches its conclusion. His righteous reign will bring to the world an all-embracing and never-ending salvation. Each name

---

[33]   Kaiser, *Isaiah 1-12*, p. 126.

[34]   Seitz, *Isaiah 1-39*, pp. 85; Clements, *Isaiah 1-39*, p. 105.

[35]   Seitz, *Isaiah 1-39*, pp. 86, 87.

[36]   For the view that the imagery and ideology is Egyptian in its ultimate origin but that at this time it had already become an integral part of the royal ideology in Judah, see Clements, *Isaiah 1-39*, pp. 107, 108. Also Kaiser, *Isaiah 1-12*, pp. 128, 129.

defines an aspect of his mission or reign. The name Wonderful Counsellor refers to the totality of wisdom within the person of the king so that he will not need any advice from outside himself. It also means that his plans, which reach out to the whole world, will ultimately, attain their intended goal because his thoughts are under the guidance of the Spirit of God.[37] The name Mighty God stresses the fullness of his power. As the Son of God, this name describes the king as the legitimate representative of God on earth. The name of Everlasting Father focuses on the enduring, fatherly, beneficent and righteous rule that this king will establish. And the name Prince of Peace points to the fullness of salvation that he will bring about. For the Israelites, peace meant total harmony and not the mere absence of war, or the continuation of war in more subtle forms. Peace referred to that perfect condition in which all creatures recognize God and willingly submit to his reign.[38]

The Theological Significance of the Fulfilment Quotation

Other scholars have not seen any relationship between the evangelist's application of this fulfilment quotation to the establishment of Christ's earthly mission in Galilee and the Old Testament historical context of this quotation. For instance, Beare holds the view that the reference to the tribal areas was "of no more than antiquarian interest."[39]

> In the time of Isaiah, the tribes were still to be found in the areas of their ancient settlement, and the oracle which he delivers looks back to the recent Assyrian conquest; but this historical reference is entirely lost from view in Matt.[40]

Meier thinks that the evangelist merely "plays loose with geography". According to him, the evangelist has sandwiched the information concerning Jesus' move to Capernaum between Mark 1:14a and 1:14b – 15. He further suggests that the evangelist has created this information out of the Old Testament text turning "a minor point of geography" into "a

---

[37] The Hebrew word for "counsel", (y's) includes both the decision and the power to carry that decision through. Thus, this king will not only make wise decisions but will also put them into operation and ensure that they remain effective.

[38] For a thorough discussion of the concept of peace in the biblical period, see Gerhard von Rad, "peace" and Forster, "*Eirene*" in Kittel Gerhard and Friedrich Gerhard (eds.), *Theology Dictionary of the New Testament*, Vol. 2, Grand Rapids: Wm. B. Eerdmans, 1964, reprint 1993, pp. 400-21, especially 400-406.

[39] Beare, *The Gospel According to Matthew, a Commentary*, p.115.

[40] *Ibid.*

major theological statement" in an attempt to assimilate the narrative to the citation.[41]

But this decided neglect of the Old Testament context is more apparent than real, intended to serve certain presuppositions. Even Beare rejects the relevance of the Old Testament context on one page[42] only to confess the evangelist's awareness of it on the next page:

> It may well be that Matthew *has in mind the rest of the oracle*, which sees the hope of deliverance in an heir to the throne, who has just been born, or (more likely) in a king who has just ascended the throne[43]

Then he quotes the verse: "For to us a child is born, to us a son is given; and the government will be upon his shoulder, and he will be called 'Wonderful in counsel, divine in might a father forever, a beneficent prince'" (Isa 9:6). It is significant here to note that this verse is five verses down from the verse (Isa 9:1) that the evangelist has actually quoted.

While unanimity of opinion on the exact meaning of this oracle may not be expected,[44] a closer study of the Old Testament context and the manner in which the evangelist applies this fulfilment quotation reveals that he was not only aware of that context, but also that he used that context as a basis for his theological reflection on the significance of Jesus' move to Galilee.

One way in which the evangelist's independent reflection on the Old Testament context relates to Jesus' move to Galilee is brought out through the mixed text-form of this quotation. The evangelist has significantly changed the syntactic form of the original Hebrew *parallelismus membrorum*. In the Hebrew original the first two items, "the land of Zebulun, and the land of Naphtali" are objects of the verb "brought into contempt". The last three "by the way of the sea, beyond Jordan, Galilee of the Gentiles" are objects of the verb "made glorious", or literally "made heavy". However, the evangelist has made all of these items nominatives in opposition with "the people sitting in darkness". The

---

[41] John P. Meier, *Matthew, New Testament Message, vol. 3*, A Biblical- Theological Commentary, Dublin: Veritas and Wilmington: Michael Glazier, 1980, p.32.

[42] Beare, *Matthew*, p.115.

[43] *Ibid*, p.116. Emphasis mine.

[44] R.B.Y. Scott, *"The Book of Isaiah Chap 1-39*, Introduction and Exegesis", George A. Buttrick (ed.), *The Interpreters Bible*, Vol. V, Nashville: Abingdon, 1980, p. 230, observes that "The exegesis of the passage has been the occasion of a long debate, and there is even now no unanimity".

predicate for all this is "have seen a great light". Thus, in the Hebrew original, the focus is on Yahweh. It is Yahweh who brought divine judgment over Zebulun and Naphtali, and it is Yahweh who thereafter brought redemption on the regions "by the way of the sea, beyond the Jordan, Galilee of the nations." It can be noted here that the object of divine judgment is a smaller area. But Yahweh's redemption will include regions that are outside Zebulun and Naphtali. It is usually understood that the region "by the way of the sea" was west of the land of Zebulun and the land of Naphtali and that it extended from north to south along the Mediterranean Sea. The region "beyond the Jordan" indicates the territory east of Jordan. It included the region of the Ten Cities (*Decapolis*). Perea in the New Testament times was part of this region. "Galilee of the Nations" was the northern-most part of what was traditionally called Naphtali, but became the Assyrian province of Megiddo in 732 BC. The glorification of the humiliated people shall be greater and far much wider than the divine judgment they initially experienced.

In the quotation as cited by the evangelist, the focus is no longer on Yahweh himself. The focus falls on the light itself and on those who experience it. The light is the Christ-event and the whole mission of redemption it ushered. Thus Christ, as Son of God, replaces and represents Yahweh. He is the agent of salvation. By his mission, he establishes the kingdom of God. Thus, by restructuring the parallelism of the original text, the evangelist is able to make a great Christological statement, namely that Jesus is the Messiah, the true representative of Yahweh who comes into the world to establish the kingdom of God on his behalf. The Kingdom of God begins to be realized in the ministry of Jesus. It can also be observed that by making all the places referred to in the quotation nominatives in apposition with "the people sitting in darkness", and then provide all of them with the predicate "have seen a great light", the evangelist points to the universality of the consequences of sin as well as to the universality of the kingdom of God that was to be established through the mission of the Messiah.

Some of the textual changes he brought into the fulfilment quotation also suggest certain lines of theological thought. Where the Septuagint B has *poreuomenos* (go, driven to) after the Heb. *mnudah* (driven, walk), the evangelist has *kathēmenos.* (sat). The Hebrew and the Septuagint texts portray a picture of a people moving into trouble. The suffering is just beginning. There was still room for repentance and the suffering would be averted. This fits well with the Isaianic text where this situation obtain. If Ahaz had repented, Assyria might not have come at the time she did. The evangelist replaces this word (walk to, driven) with another word that suggests a state of being settled, being complacent. He sees the Jews of his time not only moving toward a life of sin but also sees them quite settled and at home in sinful life. They are sitting in darkness. This suggests that they have reached a point at which a return to God on their own initiative is almost impossible. It is only God's direct intervention into the lives of men that would save the situation. Thus, the people that the evangelist sees are in a worse state than their Old Testament predecessors as portrayed by the original Old Testament texts. Another significant textual change involves the predicate to the word "light". Where the Hebrew has "has shone" ('ōr nāgah) and the Septuagint "will shine" (lampsei), the evangelist has 'has risen, is rising or dawning" (aneteilen). In the Hebrew, the light is not yet *shining*. It is eschatological, although the sign of its coming, e.g., a prophetic action or some historical event, may have already been given. The shining of the light is only present in the prophetic vision. Its effect still remains a future prospect.[45] Accordingly, the Septuagint translation, or better interpretation, of this perfect verb takes a future tense: "will shine". Thus the Jews of the Diaspora also understand this prophetic word in the Hebrew original as actually referring to an eschatological act of redemption. The evangelist, however, in line with his Christological understanding of the Old Testament prophecy sees this divine act of redemption summed up in Christ and his mission. He sees the light of salvation not as a future prospect but as a present reality. Now is the day of salvation. With the coming of Christ and the inauguration of his mission in Galilee, the eschatological day of salvation is dawning. The sun of righteousness which is the presence of God in Jesus and his mission has risen or is rising. The work of establishing the kingdom of God is beginning, and all are invited to join. Thus behind the slight change in the wording and the tense lie a Christological reflection of the quoted prophetic text. It is difficult to see how the evangelist would make these syntactic and textual modifications in his biblical texts without a

---

[45] Gray, *The Book of Isaiah, A Critical and Exegetical Commentary*, p.165; Kaiser, *Isaiah 1-12*, p. 125; Seitz, *Isaiah 1-39*, p. 85.

careful study of the Old Testament context of the quotation he draws and a thoughtful reflection of Christ and his mission.

Another way in which the evangelist's reflection on the Old Testament context relates to Galilee is indicated by his typological use of certain ideas or events. In light of the Old Testament context of Isa 8:23 (9:1), which the evangelist specifically quotes, the evangelist sees a typological relationship[46] between the promise of the birth of the Messiah which is the subject of his oracle (8:19-9:7) and the coming of Jesus and his mission.[47] One of the theological concepts that the evangelist sees in Jesus is the fulfilment of the Immanuel principle. In the person of Jesus, God has come down to live among his people. This is the doctrine of incarnation. In the move of Jesus to Capernaum in Galilee, the evangelist sees the divine movement of God himself. Accordingly, he sees the establishment of Jesus' mission in Galilee as the establishment of God's kingdom according to scripture. But the presence of God, like

---

[46] For a discussion of typological use of the Old Testament by New Testament writers, see Gerhard von Rad, "Typological Interpretation of the Old Testament", in Claus Westermann (ed.), *Essays on the Old Testament Hermeneutics*, Richmond: John Knox, 1963, pp. 18-39; Henning Graf Reventlow, *Problems of Biblical Theology in the Twentieth Century*, London: SCM, 1986, pp. 14-37, especially p.18 where he quotes a classical definition of typology found in C.T. Fritsch, *Bibliotheca Sacra*, 1947, p. 214. "A type is an institution, historical event or person, ordained by God, which effectively prefigures some truth connected with Christianity." R.T. France, *Jesus and the Old Testament, His Application of Old Testament Passages to Himself and His Mission*, London: The Tyndale Press, 1971, p. 40 defines it as "The recognition of a correspondence between New and Old Testament events (persons, institutions, experiences) based on conviction of unchanging character of the principles of God's working and a consequent understanding and description of the New Testament model", also pp. 38-80 for a detailed discussion. Walther Eichrodt, "Is Typological Exegesis an Appropriate method?" in Claus Westermann (ed.), *Essays on the Old Testament Hermenentics*, p. 225, who defines *tupoi* as "persons, institutions and events of the Old Testament which are regarded as divinely established models or prerepresentations of corresponding realities in New Testament salvation history." Also Gerhard Friedrich (ed.), *Theological Dictionary of the New Testament*, Vol. VIII, Grand Rapids: Wm B. Eerdmans, 1972, p. 252.

[47] For the view that the Immanuel prophecy at Isa 7:14 and the promise of the birth of a royal child at Isa. 9:6 refers to the same royal birth, see Seitz, *Matthew*, pp. 84, 86, 87. Both prophecies belong to the same complex of tradition that is closely knit. This tradition is placed at 7:1-9:7. Mowinckel, *He that Cometh*, pp. 183 – 184 observes that: "The disciples of Isaiah... had already taken the Immanuel prophecy to apply to the wonderful king of the future. By placing the promise about the royal child of David's line immediately after Isaiah's sayings in this period, they intended to bring out a connection between the two prophecies: in the birth of the royal child they saw the fulfilment of the Immanuel prophecy. Thus Immanuel is no longer merely a sign; and the emphasis is no longer on his birth, where Isaiah had laid it. He becomes the future king, who one day will come and reign in the restored kingdom". For the opposing view that the oracle of the royal birth has nothing to do with the birth of the Immanuel child of Isa 7:14, see Clements, *Isaiah 1-39*, p. 107.

true light, dispels all darkness. The presence of Jesus and his mission in all its shapes and forms are the means through which God will restore hope to his people. Thus, at the very outset of the mission narrative, the evangelist defines Jesus' mission in terms of an Old Testament quotation, which in its ideology, encompasses the whole range of Jesus' mission.[48] The idea of light is all – embracing. It will later be shown that the fulfilment quotations that follow define various spectra of this light all of which together contribute to the brightness that this light gives. In other words, the fulfilment quotations that will follow are employed to define aspects of Jesus' mission.

In the mission of Jesus, the evangelist sees the realization of the kingdom of God. As hinted earlier, the subject of the oracle from which the present fulfilment quotation is drawn is the birth of a royal child who was to establish a righteous, everlasting kingdom. In the Old Testament context, the reference is to the restoration of a united kingdom of Israel under a Davidic ruler. Yahweh would himself defeat the enemies of Israel. At the time these were the Assyrians who were oppressing the people. Once the enemies are defeated,[49] Yahweh would set upon the throne of David a ruler who would establish once more a united kingdom and lead it to prosperity through the administration of justice and righteousness in accordance with the Law.[50] The evangelist, again, sees in the mission of Jesus an ultimate fulfilment of the Davidic covenant.[51]

---

[48] Albright and Mann, *Matthew*, p. LXV, "This short section (i.e. Matt 4:12-25) provides occasion for an OT statement of the meaning of the *ministry*, and is characterized by a quotation from a 'Messianic' context in Isaiah (9:1-2)" [emphasis mine].

[49] O. Palmer Robertson has noted that "a situation of rest from oppressing enemies anticipates appropriately the eschatological kingdom of peace." See his *The Christ of the Covenants*, Phillipsburg: Presbyterian and Reformed, 1980, p. 231.

[50] Scott, "The Book of Isaiah, Chapters 1-39, Introduction and Exegesis", in Buttrick (ed), *The Interpreter's Bible*, Vol. V., pp. 232, 233 has rightly described the Jewish expectation of the Messiah: "At every coronation festival it stirred again in royal hearts. Is this he, the God – anointed one? Is this he, the Messiah? And though no prince of the house of David ever fulfilled the hope, and king after king brutally disillusioned the believing people, yet they went on hoping, praying, trusting; he will come; if not today, then some other day... It is true that if the Jews had cherished anything but a high spiritual ideal of the divine monarch, they might have hailed many a Messiah, for they had great and good kings. But in the very purity of their ideal they doomed themselves to disappointment, until in the fullness of time a king came, not with panoply and splendor but 'lowly, and riding upon an ass'."

[51] Robertson, *The Christ of the Covenants*, p. 229 regards this covenant as climactic within the Old Testament history of redemption: "In the Davidic covenant God's purposes to redeem a people to himself reach their climatic stage of realization so far as the Old Testament is concerned under David the kingdom arrives. God formally establishes the manner by which he

The establishment of Jesus' ministry in Galilee has yet another significance. It points to the universal character of his mission and his great concern for the lost. Robertson[52] has described Galilee as "the territory of the vast hordes of various nationalities representing all the peoples of the world." Galilee in general and Capernaum in particular[53] provided a strategic link between Jesus' ministry and the international communities of armies, merchants, administrators who frequented this area as they passed through "the way of the sea", an international highway that passed through Galilee and across Capernaum connecting the centres of ancient civilization particularly, the civilizations of the Near East like Assyria, Babylonia, Persia, Egypt and the western Greek and Roman civilizations. The word "Galilee" itself means "a circle". Galilee of the nations means a circle of the nations.

Thus the Gentile presence in Galilee is one of its most significant characteristics. "Jesus opened his public ministry by deliberately situating himself at Capernaum so he could reach out to touch all nations with his Gospel."[54] Capernaum was also strategic in the sense that from it most towns and villages of Galilee and the surrounding regions were accessible either by land or by the Sea of Galilee. It has been rightly argued that the future mission to the Gentiles is at this point merely hinted at since Jesus' ministry is restricted to Israel and that the reference to Gentiles is only negative, emphasizing the lowly religious state of this region. The issue at hand is not the salvation of the Gentiles but the salvation of Jews living in this spiritually darkened land. It is upon these Jews that the light of salvation has now dawned.[55]

But even if the view that the salvation mentioned is that of the Jews is accepted, the fact that the Gentiles have a place in that salvation cannot be categorically rejected. The Galilean ministry foreshadows the great Gentile mission that is to come. The residents of Galilee, whether Jew or

---

shall rule among his people... not only has the kingdom come. The king has come". For a thorough discussion of Jesus as fulfiller of the new covenant from the perspective of covenant theology, see *Ibid.*, pp. 271-300.

[52]   O. Palmer Robertson, *Understanding the Land of the Bible, A Biblical – Theological Guide, Phillipsburg*; Presbyterian and Reformed, 1996, p.33.

[53]   *Ibid* pp. 35-36 observes that "Capernaum is more significant as a point of passage for countless peoples travelling between the continents".

[54]   *Ibid.*, p. 36.

[55]   Meier, *Matthew*, p. 33 holds this position. He generally does not attribute great theological significance to this geographical factor. He complains that the evangelist has made a great theological statement out of "a minor point of geography". See *Ibid* p. 32.

non – Jew, were significantly influenced by Galilean subculture. This culture was characterized by its mixed form (it had Jewish and Gentile elements) and a loose religious life. There was great laxity in Galilee concerning the observance of the Law. From the days of the Assyrian occupation to the days of the New Testament, Galilee remained a humiliated and despised region within the Holy Land because of these factors.

The fact that this humiliated region is the object of the salvation prophesied by Isaiah and that Jesus moves into that region to fulfil that prophecy, reflects Jesus' interest to save not only the Jews but also the Gentiles who formed a significant portion of Galilean population. It is difficult, if not incomprehensible, to see why Jesus should start his mission in Galilee if his intention was to save Jews only. Even the prophetic oracle itself recognizes the presence of the Gentiles in this region and includes them among the beneficiaries of Yahweh's salvation. And there is sufficient evidence to suggest that Gentiles were included in the salvation that was realized in the mission of Jesus. For instance, in the post-resurrection period, Jesus gives a clear command to his disciples to convert Gentiles (Matt 28:19). There is nothing in the Gospel to show that this command expresses an exclusively post-resurrection interest. Indeed, some of the Gentiles were saved during his earthly ministry. By its very character, Galilee well symbolizes those who are spiritually weak or even lost. And the Gentiles are part of those who are lost in Galilee, and thus fall directly under the searching light of salvation that Jesus and his mission bear. Thus Galilee with all its experiences of suffering under various oppressive foreign reigns and spiritual weakness represents the Gentile world. Its choice as an object of redemption clearly demonstrates divine interest in saving the world through the redemptive mission that Jesus inaugurates there.[56] All this indicates the universal character of Jesus' mission.[57]

---

[56] Robertson, *Understanding the Land of the Bible*, p. 36: "At this locale he could preach to all the peoples of the world – not simply to the Jews – about the world wide 'kingdom of heaven' that was near."

[57] Most scholars accept the significance of Galilee in relation to the universality of Jesus' mission. Here I can only mention Hendriksen, *Matthew*, p. 242; Harrington, *Matthew*, p. 71; Wolfgang Trilling, *The Gospel according to St Matthew for Spiritual Reading*, London: Sheed and Ward, 1969, pp.49, 50; Beare, *Matthew*, p. 49; Robertson, *Understanding the Land of the Bible*, p. 36.

To sum up the discussion on this fulfilment quotation, two theological functions that it has served in the context of the Gospel of Matthew need to be emphasized. First, the fulfilment quotation has defined the meaning of the mission of Jesus. The mission establishes the kingdom of God. Secondly, by drawing attention to Galilee, the character of that mission or kingdom is further defined. It restores peace to the broken-hearted and extends that peace to all humanity. The kingdom that is established through Jesus' mission is not only righteous and just but also universal. This latter aspect necessitates that the kingdom must grow by drawing into itself members from humanity. In this sense the significance of Galilee is in its foreshadowing the church as Robertson observes:

> The gospel writer makes the point that Jesus deliberately launched his ministry by 'the way to the sea' in 'Galilee of the Gentiles' for the purpose of fulfilling prophecy. Throughout the ages, it had been God's plan to reach all the nations of the world with the saving Gospel of his son. This intent found fulfilment throughout Jesus ministry... After his resurrection, he delivered his Great Commission to his disciples in the region of Galilee of the Gentiles... From that point until today his Gospel has spread among all the nations of the world. In this sense, Galilee continues to have significance as a symbolic representation of the ongoing purposes of the Lord to minister his saving grace to all the peoples of the world.[58]

In order to establish this kingdom of God, Jesus embarks on a ministry of teaching, preaching and healing which includes the forgiveness of sins. The evangelist employs the next three fulfilment quotations to show that even these strategic means for the vindication of the presence of the kingdom of God are divinely ordained and prophetically revealed as Messianic tools for the work of establishing the kingdom of God. In this way, the evangelist sees all the activities of Jesus as he carries out his ministry in fulfilment of the prophetic word. Jesus, as he carries out his mission does not do anything that is outside the revealed will of God.

It is doubtful that the evangelist could carefully apply the Old Testament quotation he draws from the prophetic section of the Torah without first giving an equally careful consideration of the Old Testament context which provide background to a proper understanding of the cited quotation.

---

[58]   Robertson, *Understanding the Land of the Bible*, p. 36.

The Fulfilment Quotations in Matt 8:17

Verse 16. When evening came, they brought to him many that were possessed with devils, and he cast out the spirits with his word, and healed all that were sick v17. That it might be fulfilled which was spoken by Isaiah the prophet, saying, 'himself took our infirmities, and bare our sicknesses'.

Textual Observation

It is generally agreed that the evangelist has probably employed an independent translation of the Hebrew.[59] The Septuagint is, however, so different that the evangelist's rendering of the text can not be said to be based on it.[60] The Septuagint has "He bears our sins and was suffered on our account' (*Houtos tas hamartias hēmōn ferei kai peri hēmōn odunatai*). The Hebrew has "Surely, he has borne our sicknesses, and has carried our pains" ('*ākēn halāyēnû hû' nāsā' ûmake'obēnû sebālām*). The evangelist has "he took away our sicknesses [weaknesses] and carried our diseases" (*Autos tas astheneias hēmōn elaben kai tas nosous ebastasen*). Thus, where the Septuagint has "He bears our sins", the Hebrew original has "He has borne our sicknesses." The Septuagint text is probably a theological interpretation of the Hebrew, while the evangelist's version is a more literal rendering of the Hebrew. Hence, the central ideas in both the Hebrew and the evangelist's texts are the concepts of weaknesses and diseases. However, the evangelist has chosen the "colourless Greek verbs". *Lambanein (*to take away*)* and *bastadzein (*to carry*)* to represent the Hebrew original *nasa*' (has borne) and *sebālām (*carried*)* respectively. The use of these verbs by the evangelist gives us no hint whether the idea in his mind is that Christ took away and carried away diseases from those he healed or that he took upon himself and carried those diseases in his own person.[61]

This difficulty has led some scholars to conclude that the concept of vicarious suffering is missing in the gospel text. For instance, Meier

---

[59]   See Hendriksen, *Matthew*, p. 400; Allen, *Matthew*, p. 80; Meier, *Matthew*, p. 85; Beare, *Matthew*, p. 210.

[60] In a brief but penetrating article, Hilary B.P. Mijoga, "Some Notes on the Septuagint Translation of Isaiah 53," *ATJ*, Vol.19 no. 1, (1990), pp 85-90, observes that the LXX translation of Isaiah 53 is so coloured by theological considerations that the picture of the Servant it paints is substantially different from that of the MT. Among other things, he observes that the translator is persistently seeking to relieve God of the responsibility for the Servant's suffering. See especially, pp. 88-89.

[61]   Allen, *Matthew*, p. 80.

thinks that "Matthew shifts the meaning from vicarious, sacrificial death ('he took our infirmities on himself and suffered them') to miraculous cure ('he took away our infirmities')."[62] Beare comments that: "In Matthew's application, there is no trace of this thought of vicarious suffering; Jesus does not 'take' or 'bear' the diseases of the people whom he cures by suffering from them in his own person – he takes them away, or bears them off, by his word of power."[63] A closer examination of the gospel text, however, reveals that the concept of vicarious suffering is not lacking. Although Jesus delivers by the power of his word, this is done in the context of his mission as a Suffering Servant, who, according to the quoted Isaiah text, suffered on behalf of his people. It is because Jesus identifies himself with those who suffer through his great sympathy and compassion and through his suffering from the consequences of the sins of humanity throughout his ministry, passion and death that he delivers people from their burdens.[64]

That the evangelist thought in terms of vicarious suffering becomes even clearer when one becomes aware that even the healing ministry itself was an integral part of Jesus' overall mission as the suffering Servant of God characterized by suffering, self – denial, and death. The use of a fulfilment quotation which recalls the mission of the Suffering Servant within the gospel context that presents the healing power of Jesus' word at this point serves a significant function. It ties Jesus' healing ministry to his passion and death. His healing miracles anticipate his passion.[65]

The Historical Context of Isa 53:4
There are few other texts in the Old Testament which have caused great difficulties in the history of textual criticism as the fourth Servant Song in 52:13-53:12 has done. John Goldingay observes that "The chapter as a whole is a deep and mysterious one. It is one of the most difficult passages in the Old Testament to translate into English ... Many of the Hebrew words it uses are uncommon ones, the way the words fit together is often unclear."[66] Christopher R. North observes that "no

---

[62]   Meier, *Matthew*, p. 85.

[63]   Beare, *Matthew*, p. 212.

[64]   Hendriksen, *Matthew*, p. 400; Trilling, *Matthew*, p. 151.

[65]   Harrington, *Matthew*, pp. 115, 117; Hendriksen, *Matthew*, p. 400; Allen, *Matthew*, p. 80.

[66]   John Goldingay, *God's Prophet, God's Servant, A Study in Jeremiah and Isaiah 40-55*, Exeter: Paternoster, 1984, p.139.

passage in the OT, certainly none of comparable importance, presents more problems than this".[67] And U.E. Simon notes that "the history of its exegesis is one of great and lasting controversy."[68] Despite this difficulty, however, it is clear that the passage speaks of a Servant of Yahweh *par-excellence*. He would bring Israel back to Yahweh and he would also be a light to nations. Other nations would know Yahweh through him. It is the redemptive task of this Servant that is described in Isa 52:1-13 – 53:12. The historical context of the oracle is the latter period of the Babylonian exile, along with the so-called Second Isaiah, i.e., Isaiah 40-55. The whole of Second Isaiah reflects a historical setting in which Assyrian advance is no longer on the scene. Instead, Babylonia is the world power. The cities of Judah and the Jerusalem Temple lie in desolation and the people are already in Babylonian exile.[69] While the major theme of Second Isaiah is restoration[70] of Israel to Yahweh, the major focus falls on "the revelation (Second Isaiah) makes of the nature and purpose of God in his immanence in Israel as the Servant of the Universe."[71]

The oracle in 52:13-53:12, from which the evangelist draws a fulfilment quotation, portrays the Servant of Yahweh who through suffering and death atones for Yahweh's people Israel and the nations.[72]

---

[67] Christopher R. North, *The Second Isaiah, introduction, Translation and Commentary to Chapters XL – LV*, Oxford: Clarendon, 1964, p. 226.

[68] U.E. Simon, *A Theology of Salvation: A Commentary on Isaiah 40 – 55*, London: SPCK, 1953, p.198.

[69] George A.F. Knight, *Servant Theology, A Commentary on The Book of Isaiah 40-55, International Theological Commentary*, Edinburgh: Handsel and Grand Rapids: Eerdmans, 1984, p. 1. For a more detailed discussion of the historical background to Second Isaiah, see Anderson, *The Living World of the Old Testament*, pp. 468-474.

[70] Goldingay, *God's Prophet, God's Servant*, p. 75; Douglas R. Jones, "Isaiah II and III" in M. Black and H.H. Rowley (eds.), *Peake's Bible Commentary on the Bible*, London: Routledge, 1962, reprint 1987, p. 517.

[71] Knight, *Servant Theology*, p. 5.

[72] For a more detailed discussion of the textual problems involved in this section, see North, *The Second Isaiah*, pp. 226-46. For the fluidity in Jewish interpretation of this oracle in an attempt to belittle its Messianic import, see Simon, *A Theology of Salvation*, pp. 198, 199: "Jewish interpretation has changed as much as Christian; in the Targum of Jonathan it is the Servant Messiah who prospers, in the Talmud of Jerusalem Rabbi Aquiba takes the place of the suffering hero. In the Babylonian Talmud Moses, and in the Zohar the Shekinah, are mysteriously introduced for purposes of identification... Later Yephet Ben Ali believes that blood of many nations will be shed to bring victory. Ibn Ezra is content to state that whatever else may be said of the extremely difficult passage it must not be allowed to support 'our opponents' who claim that it refers to their god."

Structurally, the oracle consists of a report by a group of people (53:1-11a) set within the framework of divine proclamation (52:13-15 and 53:-11b-12). Both the report and the proclamation tell of the Servant's humiliation and exaltation. In the first part of the proclamation, God proclaims the success of the Servant in his redemptive mission: "Behold, my Servant shall prosper, He shall be exalted, lifted up, and very high" (52:13). This is a reference to the exaltation of the Servant. Thus the Servant will receive "a share in the dignity of Yahweh himself."[73] The Servant is in this verse described in divine terms. The language of "shall be exalted", "lifted up" is normally used of Yahweh himself in the Book of Isaiah and the Psalms. Note the use of "high and lifted up" in Isaiah 6:1; 57:15.[74] The Servant will be successful both in the execution of his mission and in the resultant effect of that mission. This is the force of the Hebrew word *yaskîl* which in English is generally rendered "shall deal prudently."[75] In the same part of the proclamation, v. 14 adds that the way to exaltation is through humiliation. The servant shall experience severe suffering which will disfigure his appearance, cutting him off from fellow human beings.[76]

Verse 15 describes the effect of the exaltation of the humiliated Servant. Many nations and kings will be so astonished at this turn of affairs that they will startle[77] and be speechless. They will "shut their

---

[73]   Jones, "Isaiah II and III," p. 527.

[74]   For a similar view, see Knight, *Servant Theology*, p. 166; North, *The Second Isaiah*, pp. 243-35; Goldingay, *God's Prophet, God's Servant*, p. 151.

[75]   The Hebrew word *yaskîl* denotes both the action and its result. A prudent action results in prosperity. See Claus Westermann, *Isaiah 40-66, A Commentary*, London: SCM, 1969, p. 258. Also North, *The Second Isaiah*, p. 234.

[76]   In the world of the Old Testament, the sense of community was very strong. Man could only exist when a positive relationship with society was maintained. To be denied participation in communal life was quite unbearable for anyone. Knight, *Servant Theology*, p.170, observes that "For OT man, even more than us, communal life was a *sine qua non*. No man at any period can develop to be truly human unless he lives in society; in fact a man goes mad if he is completely shunned by his kind. (Second Isaiah) therefore puts his finger on the point of the greatest sacrifice of all which the perfect Servant has to make. He is to be utterly lonely."

[77] The Hebrew word *yazzeh* was formerly rendered "sprinkle" in English. But this rendering is now generally abandoned in favour of "startle", i.e. "to leap in joyful surprise." To understand the verb *yazzeh* as meaning "sprinkle" does not suit the present context. The word "sprinkle" is a cultic word and therefore inappropriate at this point. See Westermann, *Isaiah 40-66*, p. 259; Knight, *Servant Theology*, p. 166. For objections to this rendering, see North, *The Second Isaiah*, p. 228 where three are listed: that it imports into the Hebrew a new element and gives it an emotional content that is lacking in the Arabic original; that it makes "many nations" an object of the verb instead of a subject; and that it gives no progression of thought.

mouth" in great astonishment.[78] This is because the Servant's exaltation is "something unheard of." It is something unprecedented. It never was that a man so disfigured and despised in God's and men's eyes could be given such a divine approval and exaltation. The thing reported was absolutely unique. God had traditionally revealed his power and glory through the mighty acts of his word. But now for the first time in the history of redemption, God reveals his power and glory in the suffering and weakness of his Servant,[79] a principle later observed by Paul in II Cor 12:19. Thus God's work which consists in the exaltation of the Servant is to be stupendous that people in far distant places (nations) and in high circles (kings) will hear it with great astonishment. Westermann,[80] here thinks that the Prophet Isaiah has in mind the widespread publicity given to the work but not of Gentile spheres outside Israel. But the language of the song suggests some measure of universalism as North correctly observes:

> We expect the efficacy of the Servant's work to be confessed by all who were included within the scope of his mission, i.e. the Gentiles (xlii. 1-4, xlix. 1-6), otherwise they are left at the end as mere spectators, with nothing to say. The shutting of the kings' mouths need not mean the dropping of the curtain for them. Their dumb astonishment - if that is what the words are meant to convey – might be temporary, to be followed by voluble speech. If it is argued that the heathen could not possibly give expression to thoughts so deep that they have no parallel in the OT, the same is equally true of the Jews. The interpretation of the Servant's sufferings must be the Prophet's, moved by the Holy Spirit. As such it is, in the universal setting of the passage, as appropriately voiced by Gentiles as by Jews.[81]

The report which runs from 53:1-11a develops the themes of humiliation and exaltation of the Servant of Yahweh. The first part of the report is found in 53:1-9. 53:1 is the beginning of a report by a group of people. For the group, the Servant event is something they have heard and have to pass on to others. In this introduction to the report proper, the element

---

[78]   Knight, *Servant Theology*, p. 166 observes that "When Easterners 'shut their mouth' under the influence of a powerful emotion, they show by their compressed lips and by drawing back the corners of their mouth that they are reacting with astonishment to a situation that has taken them unawares."

[79]   Mowinckel, *He that Cometh*, pp. 201-203. Also Westermann, *Isaiah 40-66*, p. 260.

[80]   Westermann, *Isaiah 40-66*, p. 259.

[81]   North, *The Second Isaiah*, p. 236.

of the unheard of and unbelievable event is carried on, and the verse sets the keynote for the whole passage, the note of astonishment. The report proper begins at 53:2. The first part of the report which runs from v. 2 to v. 9 tells of the humiliation of the Servant. The Servant leads a life of suffering right from his birth to his death, or more properly, to his grave. The prophet describes the suffering of the Servant in the language of the Psalms of lament. He grows up like a root or a shoot "out of dry ground", i.e. without strength, and has "no form or comeliness." And there was "no beauty" in him (vv 2-3). Thus weak and feeble as he is, the Servant seemed insignificant in the eyes of people. They consequently pay no regard to him. The Hebrew word to'ar which is rendered "form" or "beauty" is in the Old Testament associated with blessings (e.g. Joseph, Gen 39:6; David, I Sam 16:18). The Servant was without blessing as far as other people saw.

Beauty in the Old Testament is also something that comes and is experienced along with what happens to him. Not only was the Servant without beauty, i.e. blessings, but he was also humiliated by sickness or pain. The result was that he was despised. In the language of the Psalms of lamentation in the Book of Psalms, sickness or pain is always associated with being despised and rejected. This means that the language used here is traditional and refers to suffering in general terms. This makes it unnecessary to think of specific forms of suffering, for instance, leprosy as many have suggested.[82] Verse 3 emphasizes that the Servant's suffering isolated him in the community and that he was held in loathing and was despised.

Verses. 4-5 consists of a confession which interrupts the report. This is a confession of men who have changed their mind with regard to the suffering of the Servant. Verse 4b provides an explanation for the contempt and rejection that the Servant experienced. The Servant was smitten by God. It should be remembered here that this attitude was just as devote and orthodox in the ancient world. However, the men who are making the confession now view his suffering from a different perspective. The Suffering Servant bears the sin of others and the punishment that would result from them. The passive form of the verbs, "he was wounded" and "he was bruised" would, on the surface, appear to

---

[82] Westermann, *Isaiah 40-66*, p.261; Knight, *Servant Theology*, p. 171; Jones, 'Isaiah II and III," p. 527; North, *The Second Isaiah*, p. 238.

suggest that the role of the Servant in his suffering is a passive one. The Servant appears to be a helpless receiver of the affliction imposed upon him. However the emphatic use[83] of the Hebrew pronoun "*hû'*" i.e. "he", in this oracle points to the fact that the Servant is not passively accepting his suffering. Rather, the Servant is actually and voluntarily accepting the suffering that is brought upon him. It is this voluntary aspect which makes his suffering vicarious[84], intended to effect God's will that all men should possess the full covenant life and have all their diseases healed.

Although the idea of substitution in its various forms was already present in ancient Israel and the surrounding regions, the new thing in the present case was that the power to be a substitution and to atone was found in an ordinary and weak person, disfigured by suffering and held in contempt and abhorrence. It was those who make the confession who had strayed in sin, whereas the Suffering Servant took upon himself those sins and their punishment in order to procure healing and peace for them.

The report interrupted by the confession, now continues in verse 7. This verse begins the second part of the report and continues the idea of humiliation by describing the nature of the suffering that the Servant goes through. Verse 2 has already suggested that the suffering of the Servant is a life-long experience through the phrase "He grew up ... like a root out of dry ground".[85] Verse 4 has spoken of his suffering in terms of an illness, although the Hebrew word *holî* in v. 3 would refer to suffering in general.[86] But here in v. 7, the reference is to suffering at the hands of others. The Hebrew word *nagas* refers to physical violence, a meaning also reflected in Jer 11:19 and Ps 38:14. The metaphors used in v. 7b suggests the context of the court of law. Although the meaning of the first two parts of v. 8 is uncertain, it is clear that they refer to a violent action by others against the Servant in a similar context. Thus the

---

[83]   Knight, *Servant Theology*, pp. 171-72, Also Goldingay, *God's Prophet, God's Servant*, p. 145; North, *The Second Isaiah*, p. 238.

[84] Mijoga, "Some Notes on the Septuagint Translation of Isaiah 53," p. 88, observes that the vicarious suffering of the Servant is opposed to the popular principle outlined in Prov 17:15. Probably this explains why vicarious suffering was not a popular Messianic concept in New Testament times.

[85] Westermann, *Isaiah 40-66*, p. 261.

[86]   For the view that while *holî* denotes sickness or disease, it could also refer to a sickness caused by violence, see North, *The Second Isaiah*, pp. 242.

suffering of the Servant is described in traditional terms of disease and persecution as it is the case with the Psalms of lament.

The suffering of the Servant extends to the manner of his death. Although the text in vv. 8-9 is not clear whether the Servant died of a disgraceful illness or by physical violence or formal condemnation and execution, both aspects of suffering appear as found in the Psalms of lament. It is illness. And at the same time, it is persecution. These basic traditional modes of suffering indicate that the prophet portrays the Suffering Servant as a typical Sufferer.[87]

The speedy death of the Servant forms a logical end to a life of perpetual suffering.[88] Such a speedy and violent death is anticipated right from the beginning of the Servant's life. In this respect, the suffering and the death of the servant constitute one single thing. Just as his suffering is vicarious, his death is also vicarious. He suffers a death, not because of his own guilt, as earlier supposed by those who confess, but because of the sins of those who now report that death.

Verse 9 reveals that the Servant's suffering did not end with his death. It extended to his burial. The servant is even denied proper burial. He is buried along with rebellious people.[89]

Knight commenting on the phrase "his grace" observes that:

> Whatever the individual words mean, however, the main idea of the phrase is apparent. The Servant now accepts violence – and this word pictures rude excess and vicious spleen – so that he is brought down both to death and then to burial thereafter.[90]

In his burial, the status of the Servant as a social outcast was reinforced and deepened. He was denied the honour of being buried with his

---

[87]   For some discussion of the textual problems involved in these verses, see North, *The Second Isaiah*, pp. 230, 231.

[88]   The suffering of the Servant differs from the traditional forms of suffering in that it covers the entire span of his life. In the psalms of lament, suffering is a mere incident in a life of an otherwise healthy man. See Westermann, *Isaiah 40-66*, p. 261.

[89]   The terms "wicked" and "rich" may refer to the same category of people. North, *The Second Isaiah*, p. 231 quotes Nyberg as insisting that the terms are synonymous. North further observes that the Targum, in referring to the rich mentions the "rich in possessions they have obtained by violence." Knight, *Servant Theology*, p. 175, observes that: "In ancient times, however, it could be taken for granted that if a man unaccountably grew rich, then he must be wicked, that is to say he gained his wealth by bribery and corruption. Such an idea may be suggested here in that the Hebrew word for 'rich' is merely 'wicked' written backwards." Simon, *A Theology of Salvation*, p. 217, thinks that "rich" is the original word which was later changed to "evil-doer" and that the reverse is impossible.

[90] Knight, *Servant Theology*, pp. 175, 176.

ancestors, instead, he was buried in a common grave. Goldingay observes that:

> For an Old Testament Jew, to die was to join your ancestors. He joined them physically in the family tomb. To be deprived of that last privilege is the final indignity, the final sadness and loss... So what one actually saw in this man was a rather pathetic, underprivileged, unimpressive person; one who was disfigured by suffering and pain in such a way that he was shunned by men in general; one who was then assumed to be a marked transgressor and was treated as such, so that eventually he paid the ultimate penalty and was denied even family burial.[91]

Simon has correctly observed the implication of the disgraceful burial that was accorded to the Servant:

> At first the murderers dispose of the corpse secretly by hurling it into a common grave; then they light upon the fiendish idea of burying him with the 'rich', in the tomb of some hated and pros-perous family, implying thereby that the 'Eved was never a friend of the people but a traitor to the common folk.[92]

From v 10, the report develops the aspect of the exaltation of the servant. The verse begins with a *waw* adversative which frequently marks a turning point in the Psalms of lament: "Yet Yahweh took pleasure in him." Westermann has noted two things that are indicated here. First, this turning point reveals that in spite of all appearance that the Servant assumed, God sided all along with him. Secondly, it shows that after the Servant's death God gave his siding with him a practical effect. He revived and healed his Servant.[93]

Some scholars have seen a reference to the resurrection of the Servant. Mowinckel has suggested that the restoration of the Servant here, is a reference to his resurrection from death.[94] Knight also associates the idea of the Servant's exaltation with the idea of resurrection: "But at once we find this word (i.e. *yitselah*, from *tsalah,* to prosper) whose meaning we are examining is linked with the idea of the resurrection mentioned at Dan 12:2... 'Those who are wise' shall inherit the resurrection because... they shall 'turn many to righteousness.'"[95]

---

[91] Goldingay, *God's Prophet, God's Servant*, pp. 143, 144.

[92] Simon, *A Theology of Salvation*, p. 217, note 2.

[93] Westermann, *Isaiah 40-66*, pp. 266, 267.

[94] Mowinckel, *He that Cometh*, pp. 204-205. Also Westermann, *Isaiah 40-66*, p. 267.

[95] Knight, *Servant Theology*, p. 165.

However, it is important to bear in mind that the text makes no attempt to make this precise. The conceptual language that is used here in vv. 10b-11a, to indicate the consequences of God's act of restoring the Servant, is traditional and would not suit the new thing here. Rather, the text understands the Servant as having full life in the Old Testament sense. He will have a long life and see his descendants. He will enjoy full happiness and total satisfaction.[96]

Verses 11b-12 consists of a conclusion of the divine proclamation in continuation to 52:13-15. In the introductory proclamation of 52:13-15, the song proclaimed the astonishment of many at the fact that after humiliation the Servant would be exalted. Here, the proclamation expresses God's vindication of the Servant previously condemned in shame. God declares him righteous, rehabilitates him and restores his honour. Verse 12 sets out the meaning of the Servant's work. "He bore the sins of many." The verse takes the Servant's suffering and his death together and views them as a single act or process and attaches to it a single meaning, namely, that his work is in its totality vicarious:

> The really miraculous thing about the Servant's path in life, his suffering and his death is this. The suffering which overtakes an ordinary man without priestly status, a man buffeted and despised, makes it possible for him to take the sins of others upon himself, and so to avert from them the consequences of these, punishment.[97]

The same concept of expiatory or substitutionary sacrifice is in the same verse expressed under the concept of representation or intercession.[98]

The specific identification of the Servant within the Old Testament context remains an unresolved difficulty. Reference has already been made to Jewish attempts at the identification of the Servant.[99] In

---

[96]   Westermann, *Isaiah 40-66*, p. 267, Also Simon, *A Theology of Salvation*, pp. 219-220; North, *The Second Isaiah*, p.242.

[97]   Westermann, *Isaiah 40-66*, p. 269.

[98]   The term "intercession" in v. 12 does not imply that the Servant prays for others. It simply means that with his life, suffering and death the Servant took their place and underwent punishment on their behalf. See *Ibid.* Also Knight, *Servant Theology*, p.180 who says the expression merely means that the Servant became "the asham for the sins of the world", i.e., a guilt offering as substitute for the individuals presenting it. Similarly Simon, *A Theology of Salvation* pp. 220, 221 observes that "His intercession consists not of formal prayers but of active mediation."

[99]   See note 72 in this chapter.

Christian circles, some have suggested that the Servant is Israel.[100] Others have suggested that the Servant is an individual. But the picture of the Servant as portrayed in all of the Servant songs (Isa 42:1-4; 49:1-6; 50:4-9; 52:13-53:12) is such that it cannot squarely fit into either the mode of Israel as a community or the mode of an individual. It is not an either-or case. Anderson has made a worthy observation:

> We are confronted with a singular problem: On the one hand, in many cases the similarities between Israel and the Servant are so close as to indicate that they are the same; and, on the other, the differences seem to be so sharp as to indicate that Israel is not the Servant.[101]

Anderson then suggests that the problem is with the mode of our thinking:

> A great deal of light is thrown on the first question (i.e. whether Second Isaiah understood the Servant in a corporate or in an individual sense) by considering how the relationship between the individual and the community is understood in the scriptures of Israel. Again and again we have seen that an individual may incarnate the whole community of Israel or vice versa, the community may be addressed as an individual who stands in direct, personal relation to God. According to our way of thinking, the alternative is either collectivism or individualism, but in Israel's covenant faith the issue is not an either-or.[102]

He then concludes that the choice between the two alternatives is unnecessary as both are true to Israelite thinking:

> So it is unnecessary to choose between an individual and corporate interpretation of the Servant of Yahweh, for both are true to the Israelite sense of community. The conception oscillates between the servant Israel and the personal servant who would perfectly fulfil Israel's mission.[103]

However, Anderson tends to lean toward the view that the Servant is a person: "In his prophecy (i.e. Second Isaiah's) the Servant is a person, although no single person, past or contemporary, corresponds

---

[100]   George A.F. Knight is one of the strong proponents of this view in our time as his *Servant Theology* indicates.

[101]   Anderson, *The Living World of the Old Testament*, p. 491.

[102]   *Ibid.*, p. 493.

[103]   *Ibid.* p. 494.

completely to the type. For the person also includes and represents Israel, the community that is explicitly designed as Yahweh's servant."[104]

With regard to the genre of the literary style used in this oracle, some scholars have suggested that it is an individual psalm of thanksgiving.[105] However, there has been little agreement about this among form-critics. For instance, there is no consensus on whether the "we" verses should be understood as a penitential psalm or as a psalm of thanksgiving.[106] In line with conclusions drawn from form-critical study,[107] some scholars have held that "the passage has no obvious connection with either its preceding or following context."[108] Modern critical scholarship has, however, not only seen a relationship between this text and its context but has also emphasized that the passage fit well into that context despite the complexity of its literary form. Jones has observed that "There is solitariness about this passage, but that is because familiar themes and problems for a moment have a new dimension in depth, not because it is alien to its context."[109] Simon comments that "the form of the poem is striking but not incomprehensible, unless we remove it from its context and leave it hanging in the air."[110] Similarly, Anderson observes that:

> Some scholars... believe that the Servant poems had an independent origin. They argue that these poems stand by themselves as originally independent pieces and that they display a conception of the Servant not to be found elsewhere in the writings of Second Isaiah. Hence, they allege that the poems have been introduced into Second Isaiah's writings either by the prophet himself later in his career, or by prophetic editors. These arguments are not conclusive, however. The

---

[104]   *Ibid.* For a more detailed discussion of the problem, see pp. 488-94. For a thorough discussion on the problem of the identity of the Servant and the various interpretations that have been put forward, see Christopher R. North, *The Suffering Servant in Deutro-Isaiah,* Second Edition, New York: Oxford, 1956. Also H.H. Rowley, *The Servant of the Lord and Other Essays on the Old Testament* Second Edition, Oxford: Blackwell, 1965, pp. 3-60; North, *The Second Isaiah*, pp. 106-113; 185-190; 201-206; 226-46.

[105]   Westermann, *Isaiah 40-66*, p. 257.

[106]   North, *The Second Isaiah*, p. 234.

[107]   Knight, *Servant Theology*, p. 2. observes that "After the beginning of this century (i.e. the Twentieth Century), many scholars became so concerned to place the separate paragraphs of chapters in their various *Gattungen*, or types, that they lost all sense of the unity of the book as a whole."

[108]   North, *The Second Isaiah*, p. 234.

[109]   Jones, "Isaiah II and III," p. 527.

[110]   Simon, *A Theology of Salvation*, p. 199.

Servant poems are written in the style that is typical of Isaiah's poetry, and they fit well into their context.[111]

---

[111] Anderson, *The Living World of the Old Testament*, pp. 448, 489.

In the same vein Knight observes that Second Isaiah:

> Conceived his work in terms of a literary and theological whole... while he made use of a number of ancient forms of artistic writing for the sake of variety, he has threaded these units together to form one closely knit argument and developing thesis... The so-called 'Servant' passages... are to be understood best, when we read them as in the setting in which (Second Isaiah) actually placed them, for they each in turn advance the total argument just where they stand.[112]

This is the portrait of the Servant given by the prophet from which the evangelist draws his fulfilment quotation. In the next section, it will be shown that the many typological relationships between this portrait of the Servant and the life and mission of Jesus indicates that the evangelist was aware of this Old Testament picture and its context and that he applied it to Christ's event in that light. The specific quotation from Isa 53:4 provides further evidence in support of this argument.

The Theological Significance of the Fulfilment Quotation
Although the evangelist limits his fulfilment quotation to Isa 53:4, there are several typological lines of thought which he draws from the total picture of the Servant as presented by Prophet Isaiah. To see how these theological concepts from Isaiah are applied to the Christ-event one needs to have the picture of the whole gospel in mind. It has already been noted that the immediate context within which the fulfilment quotation appears portrays Jesus as a mighty man who conducts miracles simply by the use of his word of power. By the power of his word Jesus is able to heal, where other miracle-workers would necessarily resort to prayer, incantation or other material objects.[113] At

---

[112] Knight, *Servant Theology*, pp. 2, 3. One example of the manner in which an argument is advanced by a successive unit is the way the present Servant song develops the first Servant song in Isa 42:1-4. While Isa 42:1-4 tells us of the designation and origin of the work of the Servant, Isa 52:13-53:12 discusses its culmination, its success. See, Westermann, *Isaiah 40-66*, p. 258.

[113] Magic was a very influential art in the 1st Century AD, a means of affecting healing for diseases that a physician could not cure. R.M.L. Wilson, "Pagan Religion at the Coming of Christianity", in M. Black and H.H. Rowley (eds.), *Peake's Commentary on the Bible*, p. 714, observes that "Disease was attributed to the activity of demons, and we read of spells and charms and amulets to ward off all kind of ills." Helmut Koester, *Introduction to the New Testament, Vol. One, History, Culture and Religion of the Hellenistic Age*, New York and Berlin: Walter de Gruyter, 1987, p. 381: "Several attempts were made during 1 BCE to expel the 'Chaldeans' and sorcerers from Rome. But they returned and could be found everywhere advertising their craft...It apparently was not very difficult for any body to seek out a wizard

the very point at which the healing power of Jesus is first celebrated in this gospel, the evangelist draws the attention of the reader to the suffering and self-denial of the Servant of Yahweh. The healing activity is really the Servant's assumption of the sickness and diseases of others. And this is part of his suffering. In this way the evangelist, through the use of the fulfilment quotation at this point, places Jesus' healing ministry in the context of his passion.[114] Meier observes that the evangelist has extended the image of the servant hood to include powerful acts as well as a humble service through suffering and death:

> Matthew certainly knows the concept of Jesus as the suffering Servant who redeems us by his death. But he extends the image of servantn hood to include the powerful acts as well as the humble death of the Servant. Jesus the Servant makes us whole... the healings thus become part of Jesus' saving of his people... part of the eschatological event prophesied in the Old Testament.[115]

However, it is probably correct to say that the evangelist sees the image of the servant hood as it is portrayed in the Old Testament rather than saying that he "extends" it as Meier suggests. The themes of both humiliation and exaltation are simultaneously developed in all the major sections of the Servant Song. Both themes are mentioned in the introductory divine proclamation (52:13-15), in the report (including the confession) (53:1-11a) and in the concluding divine proclamation (53:11b-12). In other words, the element of exaltation which Meier calls "powerful acts" is not a Matthean *addendum* as he suggests. It is an integral part of servant hood as portrayed by the fourth Servant Song.[116] The suffering aspect in the healing ministry of Jesus becomes even clearer when we see it, with Albright, as a fight or struggle on the part of Jesus against "all disorders and chaos in God's creation (which) is inimical to the divine purpose and must be overcome,"[117] a fight which is

---

'philosopher', the priestess of a backstreet cult, or a useful magical book. How else could one manage to have an admired sweetheart yield to one's desires, get rid of a political opponent, be healed from a difficult disease no physician could cure, or make an important business trip despite ill omens! Magicians were badly needed, if people were unwilling to give up in the face of a menacing fate. Magic quickly conquered all classes of society."

[114] Harrington, *Matthew*, p. 115.
[115] Meier, *Matthew*, pp .85, 86.
[116] See my discussion in the previous section on the historical context of Isa 53:4.
[117] Albright and Mann, *Matthew*, p. LXV.

to bring Jesus "to final trial of strength at the passion."[118] Thus the very powerful healing ministry of Jesus already anticipates his passion and death.

The consequence of such an intimate connection between Jesus' miracles in general and his healing ministry in particular, and his passion including his death is that the evangelist sees both items (i.e. the miracles which demonstrate his power and the passion he goes through) as one act or process. For him to perform a miracle was not an act of glory but an act of suffering and humiliation, as such miracles only pointed to the inner struggle as he engaged into a conflict with the forces of Satan. This perspective of looking at Jesus' suffering, here represented by the healing miracles, and Jesus' passion and death (i.e. the "official" passion which begins from the moment Peter confesses him as the Messiah at Caesarea Philippi and continues through the cross to the grave) as a single act of humiliation is also not a Matthean creation. It is already present in the fourth Servant Song itself. Westermann observes that: "The Servant's death is to be regarded as the end appropriate to his suffering, for a speedy end had been in prospect from the beginning: The suffering and the death constitute one single thing."[119]

This perspective has a further theological consequence. Since the suffering, which includes the rest of Jesus' earthly ministry, and the death of the Servant are seen as a single act of humiliation both by the Prophet and the evangelist, it follows that both of them must have a single meaning. Indeed the purpose of this suffering in both contexts is vicarious. The Servant in Isaiah, just as Jesus in the gospel, suffers in order to bear the sins of others and the punishment for sin that would naturally fall upon them. This is primarily the point that the evangelist makes in his fulfilment quotation.

While the main purpose for the suffering of the Servant is atonement for sin and the forgiveness that follows upon it, Goldingay observes correctly that it was not the awareness of sin that brought people to the Servant. Rather, it was the diseases they suffered and the pain that resulted from them which compelled them to seek the Servant for physical healing.[120] It is from this reason that both the Hebrew of Isa 53:4

---

[118]   *Ibid.*

[119]   Westermann, *Isaiah 40-66*, p. 266.

[120]   Goldingay, *God's Prophets, God's Servant*, p. 155.

and the evangelist's version of it in Matt 8:17 emphasize diseases and weaknesses rather than sin in contrast to the Septuagint version.

But the connection between disease and sin is an intimate one. Hendriksen observes that "our physical afflictions must never be separated from that without which they never would have occurred, namely our sins."[121] This intimate relationship between disease and sin is reflected in the way the two are related in the Isa 53:4, 5 context: v. 4 has: "Surely, he has borne our sickness..." This is immediately followed by: "He was wounded for our transgressions (i.e. rebellions), he was bruised for our iniquities." Thus just as the physical suffering of the Servant has the spiritual value of atoning for the sins of many, the physical healings that many experience point to their spiritual gift of forgiveness for their sins. And this is the gift of salvation. Hence the healing ministry of Jesus cannot be divorced from its overall spiritual purpose, namely that of effecting atonement for many.

The nature of the suffering of the Servant in Isaiah also shares a typological relationship with the manner in which Jesus suffers. It has been observed that the way the Servant suffers is quite distinctive. In the traditional Psalms of lament, and the Old Testament in general, suffering is merely an isolated incident in a life of a healthy man or people. However, in the case of the Servant, suffering, like a blanket, covers his entire life span. Such phrases as "he grew up", "out of a dry ground", "he was buried" etc. point to this situation.[122] The Servant suffers both physical illness and violent persecution according to traditional modes of suffering. He is despised and rejected by the very people he comes to serve. His own community cuts him off and he is left lonely with no one paying any regard to him. This is the experience throughout his life. The use of the fulfilment quotation at Matt 2:18, discussed in the preceding chapter reflects among other things, the rejection and hatred that Jesus met right from his birth. It has been shown here that his miracles were an integral part of his overall mission as a Suffering Servant. It can also be shown that even his teaching and preaching ministries were also an integral part of his vicarious suffering. For Jesus, preaching the Gospel meant bringing light into the world. Light in scriptural language implies genuine learning or true knowledge of God which is life (Ps 36:9); a life

---

[121] Hendriksen, *Matthew*, p. 401.
[122] Westermann, *Isaiah 40-66*, p. 261.

to the glory of God (Eph 5:8,14); a life of joy and gladness (Ps 97:11). This means that for Jesus, teaching or preaching meant bringing salvation into the world. Obviously, this means fighting against darkness, i.e., the Devil and his wickedness which cause blindness of heart and mind (II Cor 4:4, 6; Eph 4:18); depravity (Acts 26:18); despondency and hopelessness (Isa 9:2-3).

Thus, Jesus' teaching and preaching, in so far as they constitute part of his struggle against the powers of darkness, are, like his healing ministry, an integral part of his mission of vicarious suffering. Hence, like the Servant of Isaiah, Jesus suffers throughout his life, from birth through ministry to death. Jesus is the object of Herod's persecution in his infancy and of hatred and rejection from the Jewish leaders in his ministry. The latter become instruments for bringing a sudden end to his life through cruel and violent death at the cross.

Another typological line of thought concerns the "new thing" in the drama of salvation. It has already been noted that the new thing in the mission of the Servant was that the power to atone was found residing in an ordinary man, without even a priestly status in the community, and despised and rejected by all. This new thing is also fulfilled in Jesus. Traditionally, God's power had been demonstrated through his mighty acts, i.e., his violent action against his enemies in human history. In the present case, however, God saves his people through the suffering, self-denial and shame of his own Servant.[123] It is in fact the incomprehensibility of the new thing in the history of redemption that led to his rejection for no one recognized him as coming from God. His suffering was thus mistaken for God's punishment for his own sin. Only those who repented would confess his lordship and the vicarious function of his suffering. This is true to both the Servant and Jesus.

The voluntary acceptance of vicarious suffering is yet another typological line of thought. The emphatic use of the pronoun *hû* in the Isaianic passage to stress the active role of the Servant in accepting suffering has already been noted. Jesus, like the Servant, also accepts suffering voluntarily. In the Matthean immediate context, Jesus' active role as a Suffering Servant is seen in the healing of Peter's mother in-law. Jesus heals her on his own initiative. None has requested him to do this, and no confession of faith is demanded on her side (Matt 8:14-15).

---

[123] Goldingay, *God's Prophet, God's Servant*, p 149.

This voluntary acceptance of suffering on the part of the Servant or Jesus is significant. It is this aspect which renders the suffering of the Servant or Jesus vicarious as Hendriksen observes:

> Isaiah had been lifted to the very top of the mountain of the prophetic vision, and uttered things which transcended his own understanding. He stood as it were, on Calvary, and pictured the substitutionary suffering of Christ as if it had already occurred. It was voluntary suffering. Apart from this voluntary character it would have had no atoning value.[124]

In a similar vein, Simon says:

> In the immolation of the victim, the priest does not commit murder but liberates the cleansing life, the flesh, the blood, the bones, and the fat so as to operate in the sphere of divine power. The remarkable thing, however, in this sacrifice is that the victim has taken the initiative altogether; He has identified himself with those who take his life.[125]

There is also a typological line of thought related to the universal effect of the vicarious suffering of the Servant. Simon here observes that:

> Isaiah includes Israel and probably the Gentiles too in this "we" of a universal penitent humanity; they detect the origin, purpose, and meaning of their own great tragic rejection and presently their recognition of the facts assumes the validity accorded to divine revelation. A spontaneous human realisation outlines the beginning of a dogma of atonement.[126]

Similarly, the mission of Jesus has universal effects. In the Matthean immediate context of the fulfilment quotation, this is reflected in the way the evangelist describes the people who were healed by Jesus. In v. 16, the evangelist says "many" sick people were brought to Jesus and "all" of them were healed. In the Marcan parallel (1:32, 33) that evangelist reverses the adjectives saying "all" the sick were brought to Jesus and "many" (i.e. not all) were healed. A similar phenomenon is found in Matt 12:15 (cf. Mark 3:7,10). Allen has described this feature as "a

---

[124] Hendriksen, *Matthew*, p. 400. Also Meier, *Matthew*, p. 85.

[125] Simon, *A Theology of Salvation*, p. 212. Also R.B. Kuiper, *The Bible Tells Us So*, Edinburgh: The Banner of Truth Trust, 1968, p. 75 who observes that: "In his suffering Christ was decidedly active."

[126] Simon, *A Theology of Salvation*, p. 211. Knight, *Servant Theology*, p. 170 also understands the "we" of those who confess as a universal reference: "We, that is to say, humanity at large, had imagined that this servant was suffering from a natural illness, so that his suffering was something that God had sent him as a punishment for his sins." Also North, *The Second Isaiah*, p.236.

heightening in the universal scope of Christ's healings"[127] by the evangelist Matthew.

The universal aspect of Jesus' mission is also reflected in the kind of people who experience healing in the first three healing miracles recorded in the gospel. They are a lowly people who in religious terms are classified with the Gentiles. They belong to the categories of people "who were excluded or enjoyed diminished rights within the Israelite community: a leper, a Gentile soldier and a woman."[128] This indicates that from the beginning, Jesus' mission was not limited to the Israelites. Rather, it was open to all who had faith in his redemptive work. Thus, just as the mission of the Servant in the Isaianic context included Gentiles, the mission of Jesus also extends to all including the outcasts in Israelite society as well as Gentiles.

This brings us yet to another redemptive principle which forms the basis for the inclusion into the kingdom of God. The principle of faith. In the Isaianic context, it is only those who repented that made the confession of faith in the vicarious suffering of the Servant. In the same way, only those with faith in Jesus were able to recognize the salvific role of his mission in the history of redemption.

A final typological line of thought to be mentioned here is the exaltation of the Servant. Like the theme of humiliation or suffering, this theme is developed in all the major sections of the Servant Song. Scholars have noted that the language of 'high" and "lifted up" in 52:13, in the introductory proclamation, is a reference to the divinity of the Suffering Servant since the same language is used in reference to God (cf. Isa 6:1; 57:15).[129] In 53:10,11, the report also refers to his exaltation when it speaks of the Servant's deliverance and the reward he would receive. Although the language that describes the reward is traditional, some scholars have held that the exaltation consists in the resurrection of the Servant and the blessings that would follow thereupon. That the exaltation lies outside the life-span of the Servant is clear. Thus, although the description of the blessings is couched in traditional language, i.e., in terms of enjoying a long life graced by the sight of many

---

[127]   Allen, *Matthew*, p. xxxii. Meier, *Matthew*, p. 85 sees in this feature an emphasis on the omnipotence of Jesus.

[128]   Meier, *Matthew*, p. 80.

[129]   Knight, *Servant Theology*, p. 166; Goldingay, *God's Prophet, God's Servant*, p. 151; North, *The Second Isaiah*, pp. 234-35.

children and full satisfaction, the idea of resurrection is already implied in that all these blessings lie outside the span of his life from birth, death to burial. And the concluding proclamation refers to the exaltation of the Servant by promising him restoration of his honour and glory (53:12). The New Testament writers have, in general, understood the reference to the exaltation of the Servant in this Isaianic passage as fulfilled in the resurrection of Jesus Messiah.[130] In Acts 3:13, Jesus is called "his servant Jesus" (Greek *Pais*). In v. 26 he is called "his servant". In Acts 2:33, he is "exalted" (Gr. *hypsōtheis*) at God's right hand. Certainly, this reference to exaltation is reminiscent of the Isaianic passage. The Septuagint uses this word (*hypsōthēsetai*) with reference to the Servant at 52:13. A more allusive New Testament reference to the exaltation of the Servant in the Isaianic passage with conviction that Jesus fulfills the vision of the Suffering Servant is seen in Paul's letter to the Philippians (Phil 2:7-9):

> But made himself of no reputation and took upon the form of a servant and was made in likeness of men

> And being found in fashion as a man he humbled himself, and became obedient unto death, even the death of the cross

> Wherefore God also hath highly exalted him and given him a name which is above every name.

The evangelist Matthew, like other New Testament evangelists,[131] has the full picture of the Suffering Servant as portrayed by Isaiah in this text in his mind when he draws a fulfilment quotation from it. The present discussion on the fulfilment quotation at 8:17 has revealed that the evangelist had a comprehensive understanding of the fourth Servant Song and that the specific fulfilment quotation is drawn simply because it best serves his theological interest at this point. The theological interest here is to show that Jesus Messiah's healing mission is an integral part

---

[130]   A. McGrath, *Affirming your Faith, Exploring the Apostles Creed*, Leicester: Inter-Varsity, 1991, p.82.

[131]   The picture of the Suffering Servant as portrayed in Isa 52:13-53-12 is reflected by other New Testament evangelists elsewhere. For instance, the sinlessness of the Servant described in 53:9 is alluded to by the writer of 1 Peter in 2:22. John 12:37-38 which speaks of the disbelief that Jesus meets in his mission is an allusion to 53:4. Paul in reference to Israel's rejection of the Gospel at Rom 10:16 alludes to 53:1. Acts: 3:32-33, in allusion to 53:7-8 speaks of Jesus' acceptance of oppression without any protest. Luke 22:37 portrays Jesus as allowing himself to be treated as a criminal in direct fulfilment of 53:12. The writer of 1 Peter in 2:24-25 also applies to Jesus the atoning value of the suffering and death of the Servant described in 53:5-6.

of his role as a Suffering Servant portrayed in the Isaianic prophecy. Thus, the quotation here is a mere pointer to a portion of his Servant theology. The fulfilment quotation well summarizes the purpose and meaning of the suffering and death of the Servant. He suffers in order to atone for the sins of others and bears the punishment that would be theirs.

The purpose, hence, of the evangelist in telling these healing miracles is not simply to emphasize the superior status of Jesus as a wonder-worker, a *thaumaturge,* as Dibelius and Bultmann who find their origin in the common Hellenistic miracle stories hold.[132] Rather, he sees in these miracles a fulfilment of the role of the Suffering Messiah, who bears the sins of many through his suffering, and thus bring *shalom* to the people of God, i.e., the very kingdom of God.

In conclusion, it can be said that this fulfilment quotation is intended to define the nature and purpose of redemptive mission of Jesus Messiah. It is a humble mission characterized by the Servant's suffering and self-denial. It is a mission intended to atone for the sins of many.[133] Even the exercise of his divine power, through the word or deed, was essentially an integral part of his suffering mission. As it has already been indicated, this fulfilment quotation places the whole healing ministry of Jesus into the context of his passion, i.e., His suffering and death. For the evangelist, the Christ-event can only be understood in light of Old Testament prophecy. Hence, a proper understanding of this fulfilment quotation can only be achieved when it is set within the context of both the gospel and Isaianic text.

The Fulfilment Quotation in Matt 12:17-21

The Hebrew original of Isaiah 42:1-4 may be transliterated as follows:
Behold, my Servant (*Hēn 'abdî*) whom I uphold,
My chosen, in whom my soul (*napshî*) delights
I have given my spirit on him

---

[132]   Quoted in Albright and Mann, *Matthew,* p. CXXV. Also see note 26 in chapter three above.

[133]   While the atoning value of the Servant's mission has a universal application, it does not mean that everyone would benefit from it. Christ died for those given to him by the Father, not all, as A.W. Pink, *The Sovereignty of God,* London: Banner of Truth Trust, 1961, pp. 57, 58 observes: "Christ did not die to make possible the salvation of all mankind, but to make certain the salvation of all that the Father had given to him... Before the foundation of the world the Father predestined a people to be conformed to the image of His Son, and the death and resurrection of the Lord Jesus was in order to the carrying out of the Divine purpose."

He shall bring forth justice (*mishpāt*) to the nations (*laggôyim*).
He shall not cry nor lift up his voice (*welo' yashmîaʹ*)
Nor cause it to be heard in the street (*bahûts*)
A bruised reed he shall not break
And a wick growing dim he shall not quench;
In truth (*le'emet*) he shall bring forth justice (*mishpāt*)
He shall not grow dim and not be crushed
Until he has established justice on earth
And the coastlands (*'iyyîm*) shall wait for his law.

The Isaianic text as quoted by the evangelist may be translated as follows:

Behold my servant (*Idou ho pais mou*) whom I have chosen (*hon hēretisa*).
My beloved one in whom my soul (*hē psychē mou*) is well pleased (*eudokēn*).
I will put my spirit upon him
And he will announce judgment to the Gentiles (*kai krisin tois ethnesin apaggelei*)
He will not wrangle, or cry aloud (*ouk erisei oude kraugasei*)
Nor will anyone hear his voice in the street.
He will not break a bruised reed (*kalamon syntetrimmenon ou kateaksei*)
or quench a smouldering wick (*kai linon tyfomenon ou sbesei*)
Until he brings justice to victory (*Heōs an ekbalē eis nikos ten krisin*)
And in his name the Gentiles will hope (*kai tō onomati autou ethnē elpiousin*)

Textual Observations

The rendation of the evangelist follows neither the Hebrew original of Isa 42:1-4 nor the Septuagint, nor indeed any other known Aramaic targum on the prophetic text. The only place where the evangelist shows some trace of the Septuagint over against the Hebrew original is in the last line where the Hebrew has "and for his law" (Heb. *Ûletôrātô*). Both the evangelist and the Septuagint have "and his name" (*kai tō onomati autou* and *kai epi tō onomati autou* respectively) at this point. Generally, however, the evangelist's quotation is closer to the Hebrew original. Allen thinks that the evangelist is more likely using an existing Greek version.[134] It is, however, highly probable that the evangelist is directly translating from the Hebrew original.

The opening words of the fulfilment quotation also support the view that the evangelist is closer to the Hebrew original than he is to the Septuagint. The Septuagint clearly identifies the Servant: "Jacob my Servant, I support you; Israel my chosen one whom my soul (Gr. *hē psychē mou*) accepts favorably." The Septuagint probably offers an interpretation based on Isa 41:41.[135] In the Hebrew original, the Servant is not identified. Similarly, the evangelist's quotation does not identify the Servant, although the context makes it clear that the concept is directly applied to Jesus Messiah.

The evangelist rendering of the Hebrew "my servant" (*'abidî*) has some significance. The expression could as well be rendered as *ho doulos mou*. The evangelist, at this point, follows the Septuagint in rendering it as *ho pais mou*. This, however, introduces an ambiguity into the Matthean fulfilment quotation. The term *pais* could also be rendered as "Son". The idea of "Son" in the term *pais* used here is further indicated by the themes of choice or election and love which are reminiscent of the divine language uttered both at Jesus' baptism (Matt 3:17 = *houtos estin huios mou ho agapētos, en hō eudokēsa* = This is my beloved Son in whom I am well pleased) and at his transfiguration (Matt 17:5 = *houtos estin ho huios mou ho agapētos en hō eudokēsa*) where the word "Son" (*ho huios*) is especially used. This suggests that the term *pais* here may also mean "Son" in the Matthean context. The evangelist deliberately exploits the ambiguity to refer to Jesus as both the Servant and the Son of God.[136]

The use of the aorist in *hon hēretisa* and *eudokēsen* is probably an imitation of the Hebrew terms. However, the evangelist appears to refer to an eternal pre-temporal act of God in the election of the Messiah. The good pleasure of God in the Messiah is shown in his election (cf Eph. 1:4-6). The Messiah is to proclaim (Gr. *apaggelei*; Heb. *yôtsî'* = bring

---

[134]   Allen, *Matthew*, p. 130. According to him, the Greek version is presupposed in Mark 1:11 where it is assumed that the original Greek form used the word *pais*. However, *huios* later was substituted for *pais* since it is more applicable to the Messiah. Thus, Allen claims that the use of *pais* in the present quotation is either a return to the original form of the quotation in Greek or it is a reminiscence of the LXX.

[135]   North, *The Second Isaiah*, p. 106.

[136]   Also Meier, *Matthew*, p. 1323; Harrington, *Matthew*, pp. 180, 181; Hendriksen, *Matthew*, p.120.

forth; LXX *kekraksetai* = call out or cry out) judgment or justice (Gr. k*risis*; Heb. *mishpāt*). The servant will not strive, fight or quarrel (Gr. *ouk erisei; Heb lo' yits`aq* = he shall not cry out). Matthew Black observes that *erisei* here has its origin in a Syriac Old Testament of Isa 42:2:

> The variant *erisei* in Matthew corresponds to nothing in a Greek or Hebrew source, but bears a curious resemblance to the Syriac *naribh*...The Syriac *naribh* comes from a Syriac Old Testament version of Isa. xlii. 2 .and has nothing to do with Heb. *ribh*; 'to strive'... G.S. Margoliouth (*Expository Times*, xxxviii, p. 278) regarded the Syriac as the original of Matthew's *erisei;* the translator was more familiar with the meaning of the Hebrew *ribh* than with the Syriac *rubh*, and has given the Hebrew meaning. In that case we must assume that Matthew's quotations go back at points to a Syriac Old Testament.[137]

The expression "My servant whom I uphold" of Isa 42:1a was not literally produced by the evangelist in v. 18a. However, Isaiah's full expression "My servant whom I uphold, my chosen in whom my soul delights" (Heb. *'abdî 'etmāk – bô behîrî rotstâ napshî*) offers the evangelist every right to translate the whole expression by saying "my beloved in whom my soul is well pleased" or "my beloved in whom I delight" (Gr. *idou hon pais mou hōn hēretisa*).

The expression "Nor cause it to be heard in the street" (*Heb. welo' yashmîa' bahûts*) in Isa 42:2b is not essentially different from the evangelist's "Nor shall anyone hear his voice in the street" (Gr. *oude akousei tis en tais plateiais tēn fōnēn autou*) in v 19b.

The expression "He will not break a bruised reed" of v. 20 (Gr. *kalamon syntetrimmenon ou kateaksei*) is not the same as the Septuagint's *kalamon tethlasmenon ou syntripsei* and can easily be recognized as a direct translation from Heb. *qāneh rātsûts lo' yishbôr*.

The last phrase of v. 20 "until he brings justice to victory" (Gr. *heōs an ekbalę eis nikos tēn krisin*), cannot readily be derived from the Heb of Isa 42:3, "He shall bring forth justice to truth" or "He will faithfully bring forth justice" (Heb. *le'emet yôtsî' mishpāt*). Neither can it be readily derived from the Septuagint's "until he lays justice on earth." (*heōs an thę epi tēs gēs krisin*). But a theological reflection of the prophetic text "he shall bring forth justice in truth " (Heb. *le'emet yôtsî' mishpāt*) in 42:3b and "until he has set in the earth justice" (Heb. *'ad-yāsîm bā'ārets mishpāt*)

---

[137] Matthew Black, *An Aramaic Approach to the Gospels and Acts*, Third Edition, Oxford: Oxford University Press, 1967, p. 257.

enables the evangelist to say "Until he leads justice on to victory" here in v 20 b.

After the word *krisin* in v 20, the evangelist omits Isa 42:4a (*lo' yikheh welo' yārûts 'ad-yāsîm bā'ārets mishpāt* = "He shall not grow dim and not be crushed until he has set in the earth justice"). His attention passes from *mishpāt* to the second occurrence of the same word. The omitted text, however, influenced his translation as I have just indicated in the preceding paragraph.

With regard to the lasting establishment of justice, it has been suggested that there is some influence from Habakkuk 1:4 here.[138] In suggesting that in "his name the Gentiles will hope" (Gr. *kai tō onomati autou ethnē elpiousin*), the evangelist agrees with the Septuagint (*kai epi tō onomati ethnē elpiousin*). The Hebrew has "and the coastlands wait for his law" (*ûletôrātû 'iyyîm yeyahêlû*). Here, the song includes the idea of Gentile participation in the mission of God's meek and gentile Servant. The "coastlands" (*'iyyîm*) of Isa 42:4b refers to the farthest regions. It represents the nations outside Israel. The evangelist is hence correct in v. 21 in rendering this phrase as "the Gentiles" or "the nations". It is also important to note that the "waiting" of the Hebrew text is a waiting with confident anticipation, a hoping. This is a reference to an eschatological and universal salvation that will come with the advent of the Servant of Yahweh, the Messiah.

This discussion on the textual character of the fulfilment quotation has revealed that the evangelist is not engaged in a word-for-word translation of the Hebrew original or copying of the Septuagint. The evangelist is rather engaged in a theological reflection of both the Hebrew and the Septuagint texts of the prophetic oracle, and that much of this is based on the Hebrew original. In this way the Old Testament text, as quoted by the evangelist, is itself a Christological interpretation of the original prophetic text by the evangelist himself.

The Historical Context of Isa 42:1-4

It has been suggested by some scholars that the Servant Songs of Isaiah belong to a special strand of traditional material in Second Isaiah. For this reason, it has been maintained by some that they did not come into existence at the same time as the tradition in their current context.[139]

---

[138] Harrington, *Matthew*, p. 180.
[139] E.g. Claus Westermann, *Isaiah 40-66*, p. 92.

In contrast, most scholars have seen a meaningful relationship between the songs including this song, and their contexts. It is, however, generally understood that they owe their origin to Second Isaiah.[140]

The song of Isa 42:1-4 is set in the context of Yahweh's disputation with the nations. This confrontation is sometimes called "The Trial of the nations." James Muilenburg has argued that this song forms the climax of the whole poem recorded in Isa 41:1-42:4, a passage he understands as "The Trial of the nations."[141]

The figure of the Servant first appears in this disputation. The nations are summoned before Yahweh, the Creator and Lord of history for a judicial inquiry. They are asked to interpret the rise of Cyrus, the conqueror who is greeted with victory wherever he goes (41:1-4). When the nations give no answer except encouraging one another in their idolatrous activities (vv. 5-7), Yahweh turns to Israel and tells her not to fear for he has chosen her to be his Servant. Accordingly, he will strengthen her (vv.8-10). In a later section of the poem, the nations are summoned once more to present their case before Yahweh. They are challenged to provide evidence to support their claims that gods have been able to foretell the new, eschatological age initiated by Cyrus. It is then asserted that only Yahweh is God. It is only Yahweh who knows the meaning of the past events and determines the course of future history. It is Yahweh who stirred up Cyrus who is to act as an agent for the salvation of his people (vv. 21-29).

Again, however, there is no answer from the nations. So, Yahweh turns a second time to the Servant (this time not explicitly identified with Israel). The Servant is not only "chosen" and "upheld". The Servant is also Yahweh's agent, endowed with the Spirit of God, who will quietly and gently bring justice to the nations (Isa 42:1-4).

In Isa 42:10-17, the whole creation is summoned to sing praises to Yahweh who is coming triumphantly to judge the world and lead his people to freedom. In Isa 43:8-13, the judicial scene is again presented.

---

[140]   *Ibid.*

[141]   James Muilenburg, "The Book of Isaiah Chap. 40-66", in George Arthur Buttrick (ed.), *The Interpreter's Bible*, Vol. V, Nashville: Abingdon, 1965, reprint 1980, pp. 406-14, 447-66, especially p. 447. The idea of a court trial in the poem as a whole has been questioned by Roy F. Melugin, *The Formation of Isaiah 40-55*, Berlin: Walter de Gruyter, 1976, pp. 8-10, 53-63 who regards it as a non-forensic disputation intended "to convince doubters that Yahweh is God." Most scholars, however, understand the poem as reflecting a judicial process, e.g. North, *The Second Isaiah*, p. 92; Knight, *Servant Theology*, p. 27; Simon, *A Theology of Salvation*, p. 68.

Yahweh orders his people to be brought into the general assembly of nations as witnesses to the fact that there is no God except Yahweh. The nations are again challenged to provide evidence if any god ever foretold the future. The Lordship of Yahweh in history and in eternity is once again vindicated through the witness of Israel.

Thus it is clear that the context of Second Isaiah shows that Isa 42:1-4 is a strand of tradition within the "trial of nations" tradition complex. The same could be said of the other servant songs in 49:1-6; 50:4-9 and 52:13-53:12. In the context of divine judgment upon the nations Israel, only presupposed in the present song, is called to be Yahweh's instrument for bringing salvation to the world. Each song focuses on some aspect of the extraordinary way in which Yahweh's Servant is to bring salvation to the nations. In the following discussion of Isa 42:1-4, it will be particularly shown that its main thrust falls on the meekness and gentility of the Servant in the execution of his divine mission.

Scholarly attempts to identify the Servant, the nature of his task and the context in which his designation within the Old Testament takes place have proven to be quite difficult. Westerman observes that:

> Clear and concise though the song is, its interpretation is very difficult. On three matters we are left in the dark. Who is the Servant here designated by God for a task? What is the nature of the task? In what context is the designation made? ... The cryptic veiled language used is deliberate. This is true of every one of the servant songs alike. From the very outset there must be no idea that exegesis can clear up all their problems. The veiled manner of speaking is intentional, and to our knowledge much in them was meant to remain hidden even from their original hearers. [142]

Similarly, Goldingay comments that "the Servant's job is to make that possible. He brings God's judgment, God's covenant, God's light. Precisely how he does that is not here explained." [143] He further suggests that "one way that Israel will bring light to the world is by letting God's light flood through her own life." [144] But as he correctly points out, this suggestion is based on a different passage, precisely, Isa 2:5, not on the present Servant song. This idea is probably missing in Isa 42:1-4, and clearly it is not its main thrust.

---

[142] Westermann, *Isaiah 40-66*, p. 93.
[143] Goldingay, *God's Prophet, God's Servant*, p. 95.
[144] *Ibid.*

The first verse of the song announces the designation of the Servant. Yahweh publicly proclaims the election of his Servant. The Servant is introduced as if already present while his mission and its fulfilment still lie in the future. Some have seen in this designation the main thrust of the song's message.[145] The Servant receives a royal designation as indicated not only by the divine proclamation but also his acclamation by the witnessing audience implied in the cry "Behold my Servant." Royal designation is further suggested by the endowment of the Spirit upon him.[146] Although the word used here to denote the coming of the Spirit upon the Servant is *nātan* which need not imply permanent endowment of the Spirit, it can hardly be doubted that the Spirit is given to the Servant in no less measure than it is given to the Messianic prince as an abiding gift. In Isa 11:2 the Spirit rests (Heb. *ruah*) upon the prince as a permanent endowment.[147] The first verse also summarizes the task of the Servant: "He shall bring forth justice (*mishpāt*) to the nations (*lagoyyîm*) literally "He shall cause *mishpāt* to go out."[148] The word *mishpāt* is one of those terms in the Old Testament that are difficult to define. It has many connotations. Broadly speaking, it can be defined as a way of life that is shaped by the revealed will of God. Probably, *The Shorter Oxford English Dictionary's* definition as quoted by North is still one of the best attempts at defining the term: "The body of command-ments which express the will of God with regard to the conduct of His intelligent creatures."[149] Thus *mishpā*t refers to the quality of life in which the revelatory will of God is lived out. The word has a forensic origin.[150]

---

[145] For instance, Knight, *Servant Theology*, pp. 43-47 has devoted much space to vv. 1 and 4. He dismisses vv. 2 and 3 with a single short paragraph. Similarly, Westerman, *Isaiah 40-66*, p. 92, sees a "keynote" to understanding the song in the first two words "Behold, my Servant."

[146] Westerman, *Isaiah 40-66*, pp. 93-95.

[147] For a discussion on other verbs used to denote the giving of the spirit upon individual persons, see North, *The Second Isaiah*, p. 107.

[148] North, *The Second Isaiah*, p.107, finds a keynote to the passage in these words: "These words must be the key to the understanding of the passage, since they recur in v3, and in v4 the Servant is to 'establish' *mishpāt* in the world."

[149] North, *The Second Isaiah*, p. 108.

[150] For a thorough discussion of the term *mishpāt*, see Simon, *A Theology of Salvation*, pp. 83, 84; Westermann, Isa .40-66, p. 95; North, *The Second Isaiah*, pp. 107, 108; Knight, *Servant Theology*, pp. 44, 45. Hilary B.P. Mijoga, *The Pauline Notion of the Deeds of the Law*, San Francisco – London -Bethesda: International Scholars Publications, 1999, pp. 64-67 renders the term as "regulation(s)" and observes that it is often used in parallel to such terms as statute, torah and commandment. This suggests its revelatory character. For a convenient list of other

The declarations of v. 1 have a background in earlier Isaianic passages. The words used to designate the Servant, "My Servant ...my chosen" are also used of Israel in 41:8. The expression, "I support" is again used in reference to Israel in Isa 41:10. It carries the sense of grasping by or with the hand. Isa 11:1-10 speaks of a Davidic prince upon whom the spirit rests (*ruah*) as a permanent endowment (v. 2). The idea of the Servant bringing in *mishpāt* is reflected in vv. 3, 4 where it is said that the prince will not judge according to what is in sight but in accordance with righteousness: *welo'-lemar' ēt 'ênāyu yishpôt... weshāpat betsedeq dallîm*, literally "But not by seeing of his eyes he shall judge... but he shall judge in righteousness the poor." Thus derivatives of the word *mishpāt* are already used here in Isa 11:3, 4.

It has already been noted above that some have seen a keynote to the song in either the designation of the Servant or his task of bringing *mishpāt* to the world. It has also been observed that some only see a veiled hint on the way in which the Servant will bring this *mishpāt* in vv. 2-3. A closer study of the song, however, reveals that the main thrust of the song is in vv. 2-3 where the manner in which the Servant will carry out his mission is indicated. The method through which the Servant will bring *mishpāt* is quite extraordinary. The Servant will carry out his mission quietly, gently and persistently until he establishes *mishpāt* in the whole world.

In order to emphasize on the significance of the Servant's quiet and gentle method, the prophet uses a figure of speech known as litotes "by means of which a positive truth is conveyed by the negation of its opposite."[151] The real significance of the seven negative expressions: "not cry", "not lift up (his voice)", "not caused to be heard", "not break", "not quench", "not grow dim", "not be crushed" is that actually the Servant will treat the weak and broken-hearted with profound sympathy and tender concern. He will actually impart strength to the weak and to all who while wasting away will turn to him in faith. The Servant will not seek public fame and will not use his power to oppress and to condemn

---

nuances of this term, see Georg Fohrer (ed.), *Hebrew and Aramaic Dictionary of the Old Testament*, London:: SCM, 1973, p. 166.
[151] Hendriksen, *Matthew*, p. 522. North, *The Second Isaiah*, pp. 108, 109. Also A.S. Hornby, *Oxford Advanced Learners Dictionary of Current English,* Fourth Edition, Oxford: Oxford University Press, 1989, p. 728.

the weak and the oppressed. His saving power will reach out even to the most abandoned outcast.

In this way, the seven negatives serve to define and emphasize the contrast in the use of royal power between the Servant and those who might compete for the title like the early prophets, the denunciatory prophets (like Amos) or Cyrus.[152] The *mishpāt* (i.e. Justice or judgment) that the Servant will bring to the whole earth is really a proclamation of salvation, an invitation to the nations to enter into a covenant relationship with Yahweh and to live out a life guided by the revealed word of God that the Servant declares. The primary purpose of the judgment that the Servant brings is not punishment and destruction. It is aimed at bringing salvation to the weak and broken-hearted, and establishing the kingdom of God in which people shall live in accordance with the revealed will of God.

The other songs focus on different aspects of the Servant's mission. The song in Isa 49:1-6 focuses on the victorious nature of his mission at the appointed time. The one in Isa 50:4-9 emphasizes the closer relationship the Servant has to God which enables him to bear affliction submissively. While the one in Isa 52:13-53:12 stresses the suffering aspect of his mission. Similarly, the present song in Isa 42:1-4 focuses on the quiet and gentle character in the Servant's approach to his mission. The information about his royal designation and the statement on his task of bringing *mishpāt* to the whole earth in v. 1 is only included at this point to put the discussion of his extraordinary approach to his mission into a proper perspective.[153] The universal dimension of the judgment he brings is described in v. 4. The term "coastlands" is a reference, as I have indicated earlier, to Gentile nations in general who await the Servant's judgment with confident anticipation.

The Theological Significance of the Fulfilment Quotation
Like the other fulfilment quotations, the present one in 12:17-21 reveals that the evangelist used such quotations theologically in the light of their Old Testament contexts. It offers further support to the present argument that the evangelist theologically reflected not only on the specifically quoted verses, but also on the wider context to which the specific quotation belongs. The choice of the text quoted, within the portion under

---

[152] North, *The Second Isaiah*, p. 108.
[153] Anderson, *The Living World of the Old Testament*, pp. 495, 496.

theological reflection, depends on the theological emphasis that the evangelist wants to make in its application to the Christ event. The quotation does not appear to be a mere patch from an isolated independent source forced upon a gospel tradition, drawn from a Marcan source or the other postulated sources for the gospel tradition, as some would suppose. Rather, the manner in which the present fulfilment quotation is used fits the theological context of both the Old and the New Testaments.[154]

The Old Testament context has already been discussed. The discussion has revealed that Isa 42:1-4 falls within the context in which Yahweh summons the nations for judgment and commissions his Servant to bring that judgment into effect. The quoted text of Isa 42:1-4 then defines not only the royal designation and the divine task of this servant but also the extraordinary character of the way in which the Servant will bring this judgment to the nations. The unusual character of the way in which the Servant employs his royal powers in bringing this judgment into the world is indeed, the focus of this text in both Isaiah and the gospel. We observe with Harrington that "The emphasis of the servant song in Isa 42:1-4 is the meekness and gentleness of the Servant so too is the thrust of its application in Matt 12:18-21."[155]

Within the Matthean context, the evangelist sees in Jesus' mission the fulfilment of Isaianic prophecy. The immediate context of the fulfilment quotation centres on the rejection of Jesus by the Pharisees. Jesus is accused for allowing his disciples to do "work" on the Sabbath (Matt 12:1-8) and for having himself conducted the "work" of healing on the Sabbath during a Sabbath worship (Matt 12:9-12). He is also accused of casting out demons by the power of Beelzebub, the prince of the devils (Matt 12:22-30). Opposition to him gets so intense that the Pharisees and the Herodians discuss plans on how to get him killed (Matt 12:14).

The manner in which Jesus responded to the controversy with the Pharisees and the deadly hatred that they developed against him is seen by the evangelist as fulfilling the role of the Servant of Isaianic prophecy. The evangelist sees Jesus as the royal Servant of God. In the Old Testament context, royal designation was marked by divine election, public acclamation by Israel and the endowment of the Spirit of God.

---

[154] Similarly, Albright and Mann, *Matthew*, p. LXVIII observes that "the fulfilment texts must be seen in total context, both of the OT passages in question and also of the gospel."
[155] Harrington, *Matthew*, p. 180.

Divine election and public acclamation are, for instance, presupposed in the divine exclamation: "Here is the man" in connection with Saul (I Samuel 9:15-17). The royal designation of David adds the endowment of the Spirit (I Sam 16). The expression "Here is the man" or "Behold, the man!" (*Hinne ha 'ish*) is parallel to the expression in Isa 42:1, "Behold, my Servant!" (Heb. *Hēn 'abdî*).

Within the Matthean context, the evangelist sees the royal designation of Jesus as a Servant of prophetic expectation at his baptism in the Jordan. Not only does the Spirit of God rest upon him, but also the voice from heaven (i.e. God's) declare "This is my beloved Son, in whom I am well pleased" (Matt 3:17). In this expression, the evangelist has conflated two quotations: "You are my Son" (Ps 2:7) "in whom my soul delights" (Isa 42:1). By associating the two passages, the evangelist indicates that he sees something more in Jesus. He is not only the Servant of Yahweh. He is indeed the Son of God. The qualifications Jesus has as a royal representative also qualify him to be the mediator between God and man. He combines the roles of both priest and prophet. As a priest, he administers divine justice, and as a prophet he proclaims it to the world.

In the immediate context, the fulfilment quotation is drawn to explain theologically two themes, namely, his withdrawal from the Pharisaic circles in the district and his continued healing ministry, in the face of mounting opposition. In Jesus' withdrawal and sustained healing ministry the evangelist sees a sharp contrast between the meek, gentle and compassionate Jesus and the selfish, cruel and ostentatious Pharisees. While the Pharisees have plotted to kill him and are looking for some legal ground for arresting him, Jesus does not respond with a counter-attack against the religious leaders, for instance, by forming an underground force to frustrate their plans. His response conforms to Isaianic prophecy:

> He shall not cry nor lift up his voice
>
> Nor cause it to be heard in the street
>
> A bruised reed he shall not break
>
> And a wick growing dim he shall not quench
>
> In truth he shall bring forth justice (Isa 42:2-3)

As already indicated, this is the main thrust of the Servant Song in the Isaianic passage. It is the unusual character of the method that the Royal Servant follows in bringing the judgment of God to the world that is of particular interest in this prophetic text. Royal princes would normally establish justice in their realm through an effective use of the military means at their disposal. Such victory would come, usually, after much bloodshed and destruction of cities, villages, fields and other social infrastructures. Once victory was achieved and order established, the new king would re-enact the laws of the land and have them proclaimed again throughout the realm. The same could be done whenever a new king succeeded to the throne in the ancient Near East.[156] The justice and peace so established, however, was neither perfect nor lasting. This could be said of Cyrus as a Servant of Yahweh.

But the Servant's achievement of victory, as described in this poem, is in sharp contrast with the methods of a military conqueror like Cyrus. The Servant of Yahweh of this poem sets a totally new approach to the use of power. He does not follow tradition and cry aloud in public. Rather, he executes justice quietly, gently and persistently. He is unostentatious and refrains from public notice. He comes not to oppress the poor and the broken-hearted but to give them hope and meaning in life.

The extraordinary character of the Servant's approach to mission as outlined in vv. 2-3 of the Isaianic prophecy is also the main thrust of the fulfilment quotation within the Matthean context. The evangelist sees Jesus' approach to his divine mission as an exact parallel to the prophetic passage. We have just noted above that despite Jesus' awareness of the plot to kill him masterminded by the religious leaders of his nation, he does not form any resistant movement to counter-attack the murder plot. He does not even engage in a public confrontation with them in order to expose and then disfuse that plot. Instead, Jesus withdraws from the religious leaders, but continues to proclaim divine judgment, i.e., the Gospel, and healing the sick wherever he goes.

In accordance with his humble approach to the mission, he orders all who are healed not to publicize his healing activity. Just as the Servant of Isaianic prophecy does not break a bruised reed and quench a wick growing dim, Jesus does not contribute to the suffering of the weak, the sick and the broken-hearted. Instead, he actively deals with them with

---

[156]   Westermann, *Isaiah 40-66*, p. 96.

great sympathy and loving concern so that they become strong, healthy and hopeful. He imparts strength to the morally and spiritually weak that come to him for help. He heals the physically sick (4:23-25; 9:35; 11:5; 12:15). He seeks and saves sinners (9:9, 10), gives comfort to mourners (5:4), courage to the fearful (14:10-12), reassurance to those who doubt (11:2-6), food to the hungry (14:13-21) and forgiveness to those who repent of their sins (9:2). Along with his healing ministry, Jesus maintains his teaching and preaching ministries always declaring the will of God, even in the face of mounting opposition to his mission.

Jesus persistently carries out his mission against all odds as "he brings forth justice in truth" (Heb.), i.e., "until he leads justice on to victory" (Gr.), in the death-resurrection[157] when he is finally declared "to be the Son of God with power" (Rom 1:4). In this eschatological event, the time comes when the command not to make Jesus known (12:16) ceases, and Jesus the Saviour of Israel, becomes "the Saviour of the world'" (John 4:42; 1 John 4:14). Once his mission is completed and he is vindicated by the resurrection, Gentiles can look to his name, i.e., to Christ as revealed to the world, for salvation (12:21). The period of secrecy and withdrawal (12:15, 16) is then replaced by that of wide publicity as the Church, the new eschatological community, fulfills its mission around the world (28:18-20; Acts 22:21; Eph 2:11-22).

The mission of the Servant of Isaianic prophecy which Israel failed to accomplish is fulfilled in Jesus' humble and gentle ministry, and is later carried on by the Church in its mission to "all nations." The *mishpāt* of the Isaianic prophecy, fulfilled in the mission of Jesus Messiah of the gospel text continues to be proclaimed to the world "even unto the end of the world" (28:20) when all things get to the final consummation. Then all those who are saved both from Israel and the nations shall receive the crown of salvation to the glory of the Servant-Son, and God the Father (Rev 7:4, 9-17).

The typological relationship between the definition of the Servant's extraordinary mission and the actualization of Jesus' redemptive mission reveals a meticulous grasp of the prophetic word and a careful theological reflection on the part of the evangelist. It is hardly conceivable that the evangelist could come up with such a systematic

---

[157] Meier, *Matthew*, p. 132; Bruce J. Malina and Richard L. Rohrbaugh, *Social-Science Commentary on the Synoptic Gospels*, Minneapolis: Fortress, 1992, p. 96.

theological analysis of prophecy without himself having a meaningful access to the Old Testament context of the text he quotes.

The Fulfilment Quotation in Matt 13:35

34. All these things Jesus spoke to the multitude in parables; he did not speak to them without a parable.

35. That it might be fulfilled which was spoken by the prophet, saying:

"I will open my mouth in parables,

I will utter things which have been kept secret from the foundation of the world."

Textual Observation

This fulfilment quotation comes from Ps 78:2 (LXX 77:2). The first line of the quotation, "I will open my mouth in parables (Gr. *parabolais*) is reminiscent of the LXX. It corresponds to the LXX text word for word. However, the Greek of the first line also fully translates the Hebrew original, except that the evangelist follows the LXX in using the plural "parables." The Hebrew has the singular "with a parable" (*bemāshāl*). If, however, the Hebrew singular is representative, which is most likely, then either of the rendering would be appropriate. The "one" of the Hebrew original would really stand for the "many" of both the LXX and the gospel texts. For the evangelist, the plural is more appropriate since Jesus used many parables.

The second line reflects an independent translation of the Hebrew. The verb *ereuksomai* basically means "I will pour out/give out/throw out something into something else", "I will disgorge."[158] Here it is used in the sense of declaring, telling. This translates well the Hebrew *'abbî'â* (I will speak). In the Hebrew original the words *māshāl* (parable) and *hîdôt* (secret things or mysteries) are set in poetic parallelism. The literary construction suggests that the psalmist views *māshāl* as a "mystery". *Kekrymmena* is a perfect passive participle of *kryptō* (= "I hide, conceal"). It can, therefore, be rendered: "hidden things." This shows that both the psalmist and the evangelist had in mind the truth that only became known through revelation, the truth that would otherwise remain unknown. The expression *apo kataboles* (= "from the beginning/foundation/creation") translates well the Hebrew *minnî-qedem*.

---

[158] Hendriksen, *Matthew*, p. 556.

The word *kosmou* that ends the quotation in the Matthean text has a weak textual support here[159], although the expression *apo katabolēs kosmou* (= "from the foundation of the world") occurs several times in other books within the New Testament. The expression occurs, for instance, at Matt 25:34; Luke 11:50; John 17:24; Eph 1:4; Heb 4:3; 9:26; 1 Pet 1:20. Such a widespread occurrence of the expression in the New Testament writings suggests that it entered the tradition at a very early date, and this would argue for its authenticity as a Matthean expression.

If the expression *kosmou* is authentic it would mean that Jesus declares mysteries from eternity. While it is true that Jesus deals with eternal truth (Eph 1:4,11), the idea is not necessarily hinted on in Ps 78:2, nor is this suggested anywhere in the Psalter. The Psalmist broadly speaks on the history of ancient Israel. He neither speaks about eternity nor does he tell us anything about creation. The LXX has totally a different set of expressions in the second line. The only common word between the LXX and the evangelist is *apo* (LXX: *phthegsomai problēmata ap' archēs*). Although the LXX text here may offer a satisfactorily alternative rendering of the Hebrew, the fact that the set of words is almost totally different from the one used by the evangelist sufficiently argues against the evangelist's dependency on that tradition.

The Historical Context of Psalms 78:2 (LXX 77:2)

Psalm 78:2 is generally taken as a didactic psalm,[160] applying the lessons from the ancient history of Israel. The psalm has generally been dated as far back as the period between the break-up of the Davidic united monarchy (922 BC) and the fall of the Northern Kingdom to the Assyrians in 721 BC. It is argued that even the linguistic features of the psalm support an early dating.[161] It is also generally accepted that the probable *Sitz im Leben* of the psalm is the ritual of covenant-making[162]

---

[159]   See the Textual Apparatus on the text in the Greek New Testament.

[160]   Charles A Briggs and Emilie G Briggs, *A Critical and Exegetical Commentary on the Book of Psalms* Vol II ICC, Edinburgh: T&T Clark, 1907, p. 178; Mitchell Dahood, *Psalm II 51-100*, Anchor Bible, New York: Doubleday, 1968, p. 78; G.W. Anderson "The Psalms" in M.Black and H.H.Rowley (eds.) *Peake's Commentary on the Bible*, p. 429; Arnold B. Rhodes, *The Book of Psalms*, Vol. 9, The Layman's Bible Commentary, Richmond: John Knox, 1960, p 113.

[161]   Dahood, *Psalms II*, p. 238. Anderson, "The Psalms", p. 429 argues that the psalms reflects Deuteronomic exaltation of Zion and suggests that it comes from the post-exilic period. He finds it unlikely that vv. 59-72 could be used in the undivided kingdom.

[162]   B.K. Rattey, *The Gospel According to Saint Matthew*, Oxford: Clarendon, 1938, reprint 1969, p. 136 suggests that the psalms was sung during the Feast of Tabernacles.

when the people would be challenged to avoid the sins of their fathers, commit themselves faithfully to God, and praise him for the marvellous works he performed for the redemption of his people[163]. In terms of a genre, the Psalm is couched in a style of wisdom writings[164] and presented in a parabolic form. It has been observed that "the most famous form used by Jesus in his teaching is the parable... (It) is the most characteristic element of his teaching, for not less than thirty-five percent of his teaching in the synoptic gospels is found in parabolic form."[165] However, it is not only the extent of parabolic material in the gospels that has attracted scholarly attention. The parables are reflective of both Jesus' mission and his unique approach to it. Jeremias finds that "they reflect with peculiar clarity the character of his good news, the intensity of his summons to repentance, and his conflict with Pharisaism."[166] He further observes that:

> Jesus' parables are something entirely new. In all the rabbinic literature, not one single parable has come down to us from the period of Jesus (except for only two similes from R. Hillel, c20 BC). The uniqueness of Jesus' parables comes out clearly when they are compared with analogous productions from the same period and cultural context, such as the Pauline similitudes or the rabbinic parables. Its among the saying of Rabbai Jochanan ben Zakai (d.c. AD 80) that we first meet with a parable. Comparison reveals a definite personal style, a singular clarity and simplicity, a matchless mastery of construction.[167]

But what is a parable? The word derives from the Greek *parabolē* which basically means "to put side by side," "a comparison." In Greek, the word could be used of any comparison. The idea of analogy is basic in

---

[163] Rhodes, *The Book of Psalms*, p. 113. Briggs, *A Critical and Exegetical Commentary on the Book of Psalms*, p. 178 thinks that vv 40-48, 51, 53 describing the Egyptian plagues are an insertion by the editor from an ancient poem and that the chapter has legalistic (vv 4b-7a, 10-11, 56b) and expansive glosses (vv. 15, 21-22, 25, 28-30a, 36-37, 49-50, 58-59, 62, 65-66, 69, 71c-72).

[164] Derek Kidner, *Psalms 73-150, A Commentary on Books II-V of the Psalms*, Leicester +Downers Grove: Inter-Varsity, 1975, p. 281.

[165] Robert, H. Stein, *The Method and Message of Jesus' Teaching*, Philadelphia: Westminster, 1978, p. 34.

[166] Joachim Jeremias, *The Parables of Jesus*, London: SCM, 1972, p. 11.

[167] *Ibid.*, p. 12.

classical Greek.[168] But the word in the New Testament has a Semitic background. It translates the Hebrew word *māshāl* which in the Semitic context has many nuances. It represents a variety of figures of speech. In the Old Testament it could refer to a proverb (I Sam 24:13); a satire or taunt (I Kings 9:7; Deut 28:37; Ps 69:11); a riddle (Ezek 17:2; Ps 49:4; Hab 2:6) or a story parable or allegory (Ezek 17:2-10; 20:49-21:5; 24:2-5;). Similarly, the word *māshāl* in the New Testament refers to a variety of different figures of speech including a metaphor (Mark 7:14-16; Luke 5:36-39); a proverb (Luke 4:23; Mark 3:23-24); a similitude or expanded simile (Mark 4:26-29, 30-32; Matt 13:33; 18:22-34; Luke 11:11-13; 15:8-10; 17:7-10); a story parable (Matt 8:2-8; 21:28-31; Luke 8:2-8; 15:11-32; 16:1-9) example parable (Matt 18:23-35; Luke 10:29-37; Luke 12:16-21; 14:7-14; 16:19-31; 18:9-14); and an allegory (Mark 4:3-9; 13-20; 12:12; Matt 13:24-30; 22:2-14; 36:43)[169]

The most important element in these Semitic nuances of the word *parabolē* or *māshāl* is the enigmatic quality that is basic to them all. It is not a simple comparison.

There is always something hidden, something mysterious with regard to its meaning so that the meaning of the *māshāl,* whatever form it takes, is not immediately apparent to the simple minded or the uninitiated. Gibson compares the parable to a nut which has both a shell and a kernel of meaning. He compares the shell to the simple meaning of a parabolic story and the kernel to its deeper meaning which is not always apparent, lying hidden inside the shell.[170] It is this capacity to both reveal and conceal the truth that makes the parabolic form especially suitable for religious teaching.

The whole of Ps 78 (LXX 77) is itself a *parabolē*, a *māshāl* in which God's grace and love for his people are the underlying principles to both the mighty acts he performs for them and the terrible judgment he metes out to them for their characteristically sinful and rebellious nature. Throughout its history, the Servant Israel remained disobedient and rebellious. Yet – and this is the hidden truth - God had chosen Israel as

---

[168] Douglass, R A Hare, *Matthew A Bible Commentary for Teaching and Preaching,* Lousville: John Knox, 1993, p. 146. Also Stein, *The Method and Message of Jesus' Teaching,* p. 35.

[169] For a thorough discussion of these various connotations of the word *māshāl* = parable, see Stein, *The Method and Message of Jesus' Teaching,* pp. 35-39.

[170] John Monro Gibson, *The Gospel of St. Matthew,* The Expositors Bible, New York: A.C. Armstrong, 1905, pp.176, 177.

his Servant through whom his mighty acts might be revealed not only to her but also to the whole world, in an ultimate redemptive plan designed to draw the Gentiles through the Servant's witness to both his power and his loving-kindness.

The parable of Psalm 78 is intended to reveal the glorious power and the gracious love of God as manifested in ancient history of Israel. This revelation is intended to help present and future generations of Israel learn the mighty acts of God, be faithful to his will, and avoid walking in the sinful and rebellious way of their forefathers (vv. 6-8).

God performed miracles in Egypt which led to their release. At the Red Sea he held out the waters so that Israel crossed on dry ground. He guided them with a cloud during the day and a pillar of fire at night, and provided them with streams of water from the rock (vv. 12-16).

Despite these mighty acts the people rebelled against God and tempted him by asking for food (vv. 17-20), which he provided (vv. 23-24, 26-27). But this provision was immediately followed by divine judgment (vv. 30-31). The effect of this judgment upon them caused them to remember their God (vv. 32-35) who immediately responded with compassion and forgiveness (v. 38). He considered their human weakness and failure to respond in faith to the many miracles he had performed for their redemption in Egypt and during the Exodus (vv. 39-42). Even the administration of his divine judgment upon Egyptians did not cause any genuine repentance (vv. 43-51). In light of his compassionate understanding of this human failure, he forgave them and led them as a flock through the wilderness (v 52). He guided them safely to the Holy Land and gave it to them for an inheritance (vv. 54-55).

But Israel's history was not better in the Promised Land. They rebelled against him and involved themselves in a flirtation with Canaanite deities (vv. 56-57). In anger, God rejected Shilo (v. 60), gave up his "power" and "glory" (i.e. his ark) along with his people and handed them over into captivity (v 61). Consequently, all classes of people perished (vv. 63-64). However, for the sake of his glorious power and gracious love, he chose Judah and Mount Zion to replace Ephraim (vv. 9, 67, 68) and David to be a shepherd for his people (vv. 70-71), and through David, he guided his people with a tender concern. The Psalm ends on a climactic and triumphant note, indicating how God chose David to be Israel's shepherd. This implies the establishment of the

Davidic covenant[171] which forms the background to Messianic prophecy consequently fulfilled in Jesus Messiah.

Clearly, the Psalm narrates the history of ancient Israel "in which some deeper meaning lies, to be gleaned by means of the hidden comparison."[172] The human story is set side by side with the divine proclamation of God's glorious power and gracious love. In a historical context dominated by Israel's rebellion and divine judgment, God still manifests his saving power.

The Theological Significance of the Fulfilment Quotation
Matthew 13 falls within the context of the rejection of Jesus and divine judgment that this rejection brings, already observed in our previous discussion of the fulfilment quotation at 12:17-21. Jesus is rejected. He is denied his true identity as the Servant/Son of God who carries out the mighty works of his father, particularly in the form of miraculous healings. Even the meekness and gentility that characterize his mission does not help the Jewish leaders acknowledge him for what he really is. Thus, Israel, represented by its leadership, in the time of Jesus is as disobedient and rebellious to God as their forefathers were.

It is in response to this rebellion that Jesus declares the judgment of God primarily through the parabolic teaching. The parables provide an explanation for the unresponsiveness of contemporary Israel to his authoritative teaching of God's word and his manifestation of God's power through the healing miracles he performed.[173] We have already noted in our discussion of the textual character of this fulfilment quotation that a parable in the Semitic sense of a *māshāl* denotes some hidden truth which must be revealed in order to be comprehended. We also noted in the same section that both the psalmist (or the prophet as the evangelist calls him, cf. II Chron 29:30) and the evangelist hold that the truth, though old and already in existence, can only be known through revelation. This is why the Psalmist calls that truth the "dark things of old" (*hîdôt minnî-qedem*) and the evangelist calls it *kekrymmena* (hidden things). Jesus finds the parabolic form an appropriate method for teaching God's truth, God's judgment to the rebellious generation of God's people, Israel.

---

[171]   For a thorough discussion of this covenant, see Robertson, *The Christ of the Covenants*, pp. 229-269.

[172]   Dahood, *Psalm II 51-100*, p. 239.

[173]   Hare, *Matthew*, p. 147.

The parabolic form of teaching God's truth or judgment has a unique advantage in that it suits better the divine purposes of bringing judgment, but at the same time showing God's gracious love and forgiving mercies. As exemplified in the parabolic Psalm 78 from which the evangelist draws the present fulfilment quotation, this method serves a dual purpose. It conceals the truth to the hard hearted but reveals it to the repentant. Psalm 78 (LXX 77) communicates God's saving power and unfailing love to those who repented, though temporarily. At the same time, it communicates the wrath of God to those who refuse to acknowledge the manifestation of his glorious power in the miracles he performs and his gracious love in the tender care and guidance he provides. Thus, through the parabolic form, God communicates simultaneously both his wrath and his grace.

In a similar fashion, Jesus proclaims the judgment of God to the rebellious generation of the Israel of his day in order to both conceal and reveal the truth. In the face of the proclamation of the judgment of God, the Messianic Community of Israel gets divided. While others reject the truth, others receive it with faith. The structure of Matthew 13 reflects this intended purpose.[174] In the first half of the chapter, vv. 1-33, the evangelist reports parables that Jesus delivered to the crowds who simply did not understand them (v. 11). The crowd in this section well represents those who are not committed to a personal companionship with Jesus. In the last half, vv. 36-52, the evangelist presents the disciples of Jesus as having understood the parables, and only in exceptional cases do they ask for more details as in the present case regarding the meaning of the "parable of the tares of the field" (v. 36).

But this divine concealment of the truth to some does not mean that the object of the parables is to teach "predestination in its hardest sense, dooming the poor misguided soul to hopelessness forever."[175] There is always an intention to reveal even behind the apparent concealment of the truth carried through the parabolic dress. The simple – common -life story form of the parable makes it memorable and easy to be remembered and reflected upon. This offers the listeners the gracious advantage of having to reflect on the parable repeatedly until their hearts are ready to accept the truth hidden in that parable when it crosses their

---

[174] Edward Schweizer, *The Good News According to Matthew*, London: SPCK, 1976, p. 308.
[175] Gibson, *Matthew*, p. 179.

mind. This is not the case with the truth that is presented directly like the "Sermon on the Mount" in Matthew 5-7. Such direct truth has to be either accepted or rejected immediately. The form in which it is presented does not guarantee further opportunities for reflection. Once accepted or rejected, the matter is settled. Gibson has made a similar observation:

> It is true that the object of a parable was to veil as well as to reveal and the effect, which was also the intended effect, was to veil it from the unprepared heart and reveal it to the heart prepared; but in as much as the heart which is unprepared today may be prepared tomorrow, or next month, or next year, the parable may serve, and is intended to serve the double purpose of veiling it and revealing it to the same person.[176]

Commenting on the love of God and his will to save, even the hard-hearted, that underlies the parabolic form of presenting the truth, Gibson makes the following important observation:

> Thus while this method of instruction was of the nature of judgment on the hard-hearted for the moment, it was really in the deepest sense a device of love, to prolong the time of their opportunity, to give them repeated chances instead of only one. It was judgment for the moment with a view to mercy in the time to come. So we find, as always, that even when our Saviour seems to deal harshly with men, His deepest thoughts are thoughts of love.[177]

All the parables in this chapter are "Kingdom parables", primarily concerned with God's action or judgment in the present and people's response to it. Since people's reaction to Jesus' message divides them sharply into the receptive and the non-receptive, the kingdom parables do speak of separation and judgment. It is noteworthy that the evangelist concludes this chapter with the motif of refusal and rebellion (13:53-8) in the face of divine judgment.[178]

Thus the themes of God's judgment, God's gracious and persistent love, Israel's rebellion, God's manifestation of his power through miraculous deeds and God's forgiveness that form the context of Psalms 78 are all present in the context of Matthew 13 in which the evangelist draws a fulfilment quotation from that text. In both the Old and the New Testaments, the truth of God's saving power and gracious love that lies

---

[176]   *Ibid.* p. 178.
[177]   *Ibid.*
[178]   Hare, *Matthew*, pp. 147, 148; Albright and Mann, *Matthew*, p. LXIX.

beneath the apparent divine wrath and judgment is reflected in the parabolic method of communicating divine truth.

The evangelist sees in this method as adopted and applied by Jesus Messiah the fulfilment of divine prophecy. Jesus enters into the role of the unknown Psalmist Prophet of the Old Testament. It is Jesus, in this capacity as the Messiah, who declares the mysteries of the kingdom of God to the Messianic Community of Israel and the Church.[179] Just as it is in the context of the Psalm, the *māshāl* that Jesus declares are the glorious deeds and the saving activities of God. The only distinctive factor between the two settings is that while in the Old Testament God reveals himself directly through his glorious power and gracious love, in the gospel setting, God reveals his power and love through his Servant/Son. Jesus himself, as the Messiah, embodies the mysteries of God in his person. He is himself the revealed truth of God.

Through this fulfilment quotation, the evangelist defines a specific method of Jesus' teaching as he carries out his mission. The role of the parabolic method in reflecting the nature of Jesus' mission, and the uniqueness of his parables has already been noted.

It is again very unlikely that the evangelist could apply the present fulfilment quotation to Jesus and his mission in the manner he has done without a thorough reflection of its Old Testament background. His application reflect diligent study and thoughtful reflection of Psalm 78 in its Old Testament Context.

Exegetical: Theological Analysis of the Fulfilment Quotations in the Passion Narrative

With Jesus' entry into Jerusalem, the period of his formal passion has come. It has been already shown in the preceding fulfilment quotations that largely define his Galilean mission that the element of suffering, hence, passion, was always present in his ministry. Even when, *prima facie*, his authoritative word of preaching, teaching or healing were the focus, his passion always underlined the purpose of his ministry. The totality of his earlier ministry in a sense anticipated his final passion in Jerusalem leading to his death on the cross. The final passion thus long awaited begins here with his physical entry into the city of Jerusalem. It is, indeed, the events of the passion week that form the central message of the Gospel, namely, his death on the cross and his resurrection. This

---

[179]   Hans-Joachim Kraus, *Theology of the Psalms*, Minneapolis: Fortress, 1992, p. 197.

section focuses on those fulfilment quotations that are found in the passion narrative of the gospel. These are Matt 21:4-5 and Matt 27:9-10.

The Fulfilment Quotation in Matt 21:4-5
    Say to Daughter of Zion
    Behold your king is coming to you
    Gentle and mounted on a donkey
    Even upon a colt, the foal of a luggage animal.

Textual Observation
The fulfilment quotation here combines two different prophetic texts. The first line, "Say to Daughter of Zion" (*Eipate tē thygatri Siōn*) is reminiscent of the LXX of Isa 62:11 which it follows at this point word for word. Both the LXX and the evangelist here offers a natural rendering of the Hebrew (*'imrû lebat – Tsiyôn*). In Hebrew, v.11 begins with "Behold, the Lord has proclaimed (*hishmîa'*)." The word *hishmîa'* is a technical term for the proclamation of the message of salvation.

Lines two and three of the evangelist largely agree with LXX text of Zech 9:9, almost word for word. Line two has "Behold, your King is coming to you" (*Idou, ho Basileus sou erchetai soi*). At this point, the evangelist omits two important adjectives found in both the LXX and the Hebrew of Zech 9:9 (LXX: *dikaios kai sōdzōn autos* = "He is righteous and victorious (lit. brings salvation)." Hebrew original: *tsadîq wenôsha' hû'* = "righteous and victorious (saving) is he"). The word *nôshā'* here is in a passive form.[180] The word occurs in the active form in Zeph 3:17.[181]

Despite the omission, however, the idea of riding to victory is not missing (cf. Ps 45:4; Rev 6:2; 17:14).

Line three corresponds to the LXX, except for the final word *hypodzygion* (luggage animal).[182] The evangelist has *onon* at this point instead of the LXX *hypodzygion*. Here the evangelist is closer to the Hebrew in describing the animal as "a donkey" (i.e. *onon*). The LXX describes it as "a luggage animal" (i.e. *hypodzygion*).

The evangelist's final line: *epi onon kai epi pōlon huion hypodzygiou* looks like a translation of the Hebrew *'al-hamôr we'al – 'ayir ben – 'atonôt* (i.e. on an ass even on a colt, the son of a she-ass), with adaptation of

---

[180]   J. Weingreen, *A Practical Grammar for Classical Hebrew*, Oxford: Clarendon, 1939, reprint 1955, p.311.
[181]   Scholars have found that the theological concepts in Zech 9:9 have their background in earlier prophecy. See Carroll Stuhlmueller, *Rebuilding with Hope, A Commentary on the Books of Haggai and Zechariah*, International Theological Commentary, Grand Rapids: Wm B. Eerdmans + Edinburgh: Handsel, 1988, pp. 123-25.
[182]   Stephen W. Paine, *Beginning Greek, A Functional Approach*, New York: Oxford University Press, 1961, p. 321.

the words of the LXX. In this line, the evangelist, like the Hebrew but unlike the LXX describes the animal as "a colt, the foal of a luggage – animal." The LXX here has *epi hypodzygion* i.e. "on a luggage-animal."

Most scholars have generally accepted the view that the evangelist has presented Jesus as sitting on two animals at the same time in the evangelist's attempt to see a literal fulfilment of Zech 9:9. On this account, some have charged the evangelist with twisting the scriptures. It is often argued that the evangelist deliberately altered the gospel narrative in order to serve his interests in literal fulfilment of Scripture.[183] The difficulty is caused by the lexical prefix *we* in the clause *we'al – 'ayir* translated in the LXX and the New Testament Greek by the conjunction *kai*. In the English versions, it is often rendered by the coordinate conjunction "and". The force of this conjunction has led most scholars to see two animals in the Zechariah text on which the king mounts, and to see the evangelist as portraying the same picture with Jesus riding on both animals simultaneously.

It is, however, not often recognized that the prefix *we* can also be legitimately rendered as "even" instead of "and". Since the animals in Zech 9:9 are named in a context of Hebrew parallelism, the real meaning may as well be that the humble king comes riding a young donkey, probably not used for a similar purpose before. It is hard to see the humble king riding on both of the named animals here. The evangelist also employs a parallelism here. He does not see Jesus riding on the two animals as it is often suggested. Rather, he employs a parallelism here to emphasize that Jesus mounts on a young donkey, probably not used for a similar purpose before. This meaning comes out clearly when the *we* prefix and the *kai* conjunction are understood in the sense of "even" not "and".

Further the word *autōn* (i.e. "them") appears twice in Matt 21:7. The first is a reference to the animals. The clothes are put on "them", i.e., the two animals. But the second "them" does not refer to the animals. Its closet antecedent is not *tēn onon kai ton pōlon* ("the ass and the colt"). Rather it is *ta himatia* ("the garments"). The meaning is that Jesus sat not on the two animals but on the garments. Obviously, he could only physically sit on the garments put on one of the two animals. Both the prophet and the evangelist suggest that the humble king sat on the

---

[183] For this position, see S.V.M. McCasland, "Matthew Twists the Scriptures," *Journal of Biblical Studies Literature* (June 1961), p.145.

young animal. The evangelist speaks of bringing two animals to Jesus, over against Mark (11:2) and Luke (19:30). But whatever he says about them through his parallelism, he does not say that Jesus sat on both animals.[184]

From the textual character of this fulfilment quotation, it would appear that the evangelist is responsible for its formation. While translating from the Hebrew, he feels free to adopt the LXX rendering where that serves his purpose. For instance, he follows the LXX in rendering the Hebrew *rokēb* ('riding") with *epibebēkōs* ("mounted"), but renders the Hebrew *hamor* ("an ass") as *onon* ("donkey") instead of the more general term, *hypodzygion* ("a pack-animal") which the LXX uses. This shows that the evangelist was not simply copying from or following the translation of a particular tradition. Rather, he was working out his own text based on the older traditions, especially the Hebrew text.

The Historical Context of Isa 62:11 and Zech 9:9
It is generally agreed that the final eleven chapters of the Book of Isaiah were written by a disciple of the so-called Second Isaiah, the writer of chapters 40-55 of the same book. Consequently, these chapters are usually referred to as Third Isaiah.[185] The historical situation presupposed in this book of Isaiah is that of the post exilic period. The people have returned from Babylonian exile and are in Jerusalem where they face the difficulties of the restoration. The social-economic conditions that obtain are clearly reflected in the Book of Haggai. Only the well-to-do among the returnees are able to build good houses and live comfortably in Jerusalem (Hag 1:4). However, the majority who are relatively poor face great hardships. After staying idle for almost half a century, the land becomes unproductive and renders farming futile. Frequent droughts and famine aggravate the situation (1:10, 11). Those who are employed in various sectors of business receive very low wages (1:16). These social and economic difficulties probably account for the

---

[184]   For a similar view, see Hendriksen, *Matthew*, p. 764. Also R.G.V. Tasker, *The Gospel According to St. Matthew*, Grand Rapids: W. B. Eerdmans, 1961, p. 198.

[185]   For a recent discussion on the problem of the unity of Isaiah, see Walter Brueggemann, "Unity and Dynamic in the Isaiah tradition," *Journal for the Study of the Old Testament* 29 (1984), pp. 89-107; Ronald E. Clements, "The Unity of The Book of Isaiah", *Interpretation* 36 (1982), pp. 117-29. Also Ronald E. Clements, "Beyond Tradition-History: Deutero-Isaianic Development of First Isaiah's Themes", *Journal for the Study of the Old Testament* 31 (1985), pp. 95-113. For a canonical approach to the problem, see Brevard Childs, *Introduction to the Old Testament as Scripture*, Philadelphia: Fortress, 1979, pp. 325-38.

failure to embark on a Temple building project as soon as possible following the return. In addition, there are political factors which include the problem of Samaritan hostility.[186]

Thus the social, economic, political and religious life looks so bleak that the people begin to question the reality of the promises of God as especially prophesied by Second Isaiah. The promises of salvation do not appear to be fulfilled in the hard reality of post-exilic life. To many, it seemed that the judgment of God or at least its effects are still upon them. Indeed, prophet Haggai attributes these difficulties to the failure of the restored community to build the Temple. This puts Isa 62:11 in a context of divine judgment.

Isaiah 60-62 is a single prophetic complex uttered in response to community lament. Isaiah 60 is a response to the communal lament because of their enemies. The prophetic response was that these nations would be subdued and would come to Zion to worship Yahweh. Isaiah 61 is a response to a communal lament for the shame that the restored community was put in through their difficulties. The prophetic response was that Yahweh would restore Zion to her former glory. Isaiah 62 is a prophetic response to the charge that God has forsaken his people. To this the prophetic response was that God will turn afresh to Zion and fulfil all the promises he made to her.[187]

Isa 62:11, from which the evangelist draws the first line of his fulfilment quotation, is a final promise which Yahweh introduces with summons to go forth to all nations. The message that is to be proclaimed is that of salvation: "Say to the daughter of Zion" states the summons. And what is declared to Zion is "Behold, your salvation comes." Set against the background of an epiphany (cf. v. 1b and 60:1b), the word "salvation" in v. 11 must refer to God himself.

Westermann observes that: "This is one of the numerous passages in Trito-Isaiah where he speaks of the coming of salvation in words which properly refer to God's coming."[188] Thus the coming of salvation means the coming of God himself to Zion. The LXX has accordingly personified

[186] Anderson, *The Living World of the Old Testament*, pp. 510-20; P.R. Ackroyd, "Haggai", in Black and Rowley (eds), *Peake's Commentary on the Bible*, pp. 643, 644.

[187] Westermann, *Isaiah 40-66, pp.* 373, 374.

[188] *Ibid.*, p. 375. Also George A.F. Knight, *The New Israel, A Commentary on the Book of Isaiah 56-66*, International Theological Commentary, Edinburgh: Handsel + Grand Rapids: Wm B Eerdmans, 1985, p. 69.

the Hebrew *yish'ēk* (your salvation) and renders it as *sōtēr* (Saviour or Redeemer) instead of simply *sōteria* or *sōterias* (salvation).

Thus, in the context of communal lament, because of the difficult life that the post-exilic community experiences, Third Isaiah sees prophetic intercession for redemption as his central calling "to put God in remembrance" of his promised salvation.[189] This intercession will not cease, hence, giving Yahweh no rest until the prophecies that relate to Zion are ultimately fulfilled. In the meantime, the community still feels the sad effects of divine judgment upon them, the judgment that led their forefathers into exile.

The evangelist moves on in his fulfilment quotation to the prophecy of Zech 9:9. Here, in reference to the coming of the same salvation to Zion, the text specifically personifies the word "salvation" in the Hebrew original, replacing it with "king": "Behold, your king is coming" (Heb. *Malkēk*).

Although there is no great difference between the Isaianic text and that of Zechariah, the evangelist prefers the Zechariah text because it clearly sees the embodiment of salvation in the person of the Redeemer. The evangelist continues to quote Zech 9:9 because it further serves his theological purpose. It defines the character of the king and the manner of his arrival in Zion. Isa 62:11 stops at defining the gift of salvation that Yahweh brings. It does not proceed to define his character. The theological interest is simply on God's turning to his people.

The wider context of Zech 9:9 also presents a picture of divine judgment. The overall theme of Zechariah 9 is to show the manner in which God's kingdom is to be created.[190] Zech 9:1-8 focuses on the international extent of Yahweh's sovereignty. It is an oracle of judgment and promise.[191] Judgment is proclaimed against the cities and states of northern Israel (vv. 1-7), and a promise of salvation is given to Judah (v. 8). The oracle is delivered in an indicative mood and forms the basis for the assurance of salvation for Judah.

---

[189] Douglas R. Jones, "Isaiah II and III," in Black and Rowley (eds), *Peake's Commentary on the Bible*, p. 533.

[190] David, L. Petersen, *Zechariah 9-14 and Malachi, A Commentary,* Old Testament Library, London: SCM, 1995, p. 56.

[191] P.R. Ackroyd, "Zechariah", in Black and Rowley (eds), in *Peake's Commentary on the Bible*, p. 652.

The oracle in 9:9-12 to which v. 9 belongs, is given in the imperative mood. Now that the redemption of Zion has been assured, Zion is herself challenged to repentance. Yahweh's immediate presence among his people provides ultimate ground for the imperative call to repentance at vv. 9, 12.

Yahweh is committed to peace and he himself takes the initiative in bringing salvation to Zion. His redemptive actions are based on the covenant relationship he established with Israel: "As for you also, by the blood of your covenant (*bedam berîtēk*) I have sent forth your prisoners out of the pit" (v. 11). This is a reference to the blood rite which ratified the covenant between Yahweh and Israel at Sinai (Exod 24:8). The language of "their God" (*`Elohēhem*); "his people" *('amô)* in v. 16 is further indication of this covenant relationship. Zion must return to her God (v. 12). The language of "return" in this verse is a reference to repentance unlike Isa 52:11; Zech 2:6-7 where the reference is to a physical return to Jerusalem.[192]

Verses 12-16 focus on what Yahweh will do for his people in the course of bringing their salvation without the participation of any earthly king. Yahweh himself "will appear", "will trumpet" (v. 4), "will protect", "will save" (v. 15). The salvation of Zion will be an act of God's grace alone.

Verse 13 identifies the object of divine judgment. It is *Yāwān* (i.e. Greeks). While the historical background to this reference may be real conflict between the Greeks and the Persians[193], the prophet sees in this the eschatological Day of the Lord in which Yahweh engages himself in a cosmic conflict with the enemies of his people, here identified as *Yāwān* (v. 14). In that cosmic context, Yahweh acts as a military hero who fights for his people with great determination for victory (v. 15). In vv. 16-17, the imagery shifts from that of a military hero to that of a shepherd of Israel. By leading his people as a flock, God, like a shepherd, saves them.

In the last four verses, i.e., 14-17, the poem focuses on Yahweh's redemptive actions for his people. It should be noted, however, that the

---

[192]   Petersen, *Zech 9-14 and Malachi*, p. 61.

[193]   Petersen suggests that the historical background to the reference to the Greeks as an object of divine judgment could be the Greek-Persian wars of 490, 480-79, 460 BC. These could have affected Syria-Palestine through the general Persian militarization of the region. Since Jewish interests sometimes favoured the health of the Persian empire, Greek hostility against Persia was likely to be viewed as a hostility against Syria-Palestine itself. See *Ibid.*, p.63.

emphasis is on Yahweh himself as the sole actor. The role of the king mentioned in v. 9 is not preeminent. Yahweh himself takes up his role as a military hero and as a shepherd of Israel. This appears to suggest that the tradition here does not suggest an expectation for a reappearance of the monarchy. The role of the king falls into the background.[194] It is Yahweh himself who saves his people.

It is within this context that Zech 9:9 quoted by the evangelist falls. It is a context of divine judgment and promise. Yahweh himself brings judgment upon the enemies of his people, firstly identified as the cities and states of northern Israel (vv. 1-8), and secondly identified as Yāwān (v.13). Yahweh also promises salvation to his people on the basis of the covenant he established with Israel. The judgment and the promise become operational in a context of a cosmic struggle in which Yahweh himself acts as a military hero and a shepherd for his people.

In this context, v 9 appears to stand alone in offering an extraordinary definition of the manner in which Yahweh will bring this judgment and salvation to Zion. We have already noted that it defines the character of the king, the Redeemer, and the manner of his arrival in Zion. It has been suggested that the verse has its background in earlier prophecy with Zeph 3:14 and Zech 2:10, 13 as critically important textual forerunners.[195] It is clear that the reference to "king" in Zeph 3:14 and the surrounding context relates to Yahweh himself and not the Messiah.[196] The reference in Zech 2:10-13 is probably also to Yahweh's immediate presence.

However, it is generally agreed that Zech 9:9 is a reference to a human king, the Messiah. Some have suggested that the original reference was to Zerubbabel, a Persian governor in Judah but also a member of the Davidic royal house.[197] The argument that this verse is a description of a human king, the Messiah, is a weighty one.[198] This is

---

[194]   *Ibid.*, p. 57.

[195]   *Ibid.*, p. 57.

[196]   *Ibid.*, Also J.P. Hyatt, "Zephaniah" in Black and Rowley (eds), *Peake's Commentary on the Bible*, p. 642 who sees in this reference "the presence of Yahweh" and compares vv. 14-15 to the "Psalms of Yahweh's enthronement," eg. Pss 47, 48, 95-9.

[197]   Michael Fallon, *The Winston Commentary on the Gospels*, Sydney: Winston, 1980, p. 316.

[198]   Among those who argue for this position, Petersen, *Zechariah 9-14 and Malachi*, p. 57, note 45 mentions Saebo, *Sacharja 9-14*; Mason, *The Use Earlier Biblical Material in Zechariah IX-XIV*, p. 88; Baldwin, *Haggai, Zechariah, Malachi*, p. 165; Rudolph, *Sacharja 9-14*; Hanson, *The Dawn of Apocalyptic*, p. 320.

evidently the way in which the evangelist also understands the passage. The Messiah is here, in Zech 9:9, defined as "triumphant", "victorious" and "humble." The word rendered "triumphant" (Heb. *Tsaddîq* or Gr. *dikaios*) actually means "righteous one" or the "just one" or "the one declared right or acquitted." It refers to Yahweh's justice toward himself and to his word by fulfilling all the divine promises in every respect.[199] The word rendered "victorious" is the Hebrew. *Nôshā'* i.e. "to save". It is here in the passive form. Customarily, the word has received an active rendering in the Greek and other translations. According to the Hebrew, the Messianic king who brings salvation to Zion experiences Yahweh's saving activity in himself. The king is himself the servant and follower of God. As he leads others, he is himself led along the way of righteousness and obedience filled with wisdom and the Spirit of God. He receives in himself the salvation he imparts to others.[200]

Thus, in the very process of saving others the Messianic king is himself saved. This means that the Messianic king identifies himself with both God and man through this attribute. Like Yahweh he brings salvation embodied in his own person[201]. Like man, he himself experiences the salvation he brings to others, and is himself led and guided by the Spirit of God.

The king is also described as 'humble" (Heb '*ānî*). Although it may be difficult in the present context to press for a meaning of suffering and humiliation,[202] it is clear that this character is an exception to the royal imagery painted by the preceding qualities. It is however, generally taken that the word can mean "stricken", "afflicted" and that it is also used in the general sense of humility. In this connection, the word is often used in the corporate sense. This is actually the way in which the word is used in prophetic texts that form a background to Zechariah's use at this point.

---

[199]   B. Davidson, *The Analytical Hebrew and Chaldee Lexicon*, London: Samuel Bagster + New York: Harper, 1950, p. DCXL. Also Stuhlmueller, *Rebuilding with Hope*, p. 124; Ackroyd, "Zechariah", in Black and Rowley (eds), *Peake's Commentary on the Bible*, p. 652.

[200]   Stuhlmueller, *Rebuilding with Hope*, p. 124.

[201]   Petersen, *Zechariah 9-14 and Malachi*, pp. 57, 58 also observes that the king shares the two qualities of being "righteous" and "victorious" (i.e. "saving") with God. He further observes that: "by connotation through allusion the author indicated that the arrival of this king should be celebrated in much the same way that Yahweh's presence as king deserved accolade."

[202]   In the ancient Near East, donkeys or asses were a normal mount for royal princess who proceeded in a friendly and peaceful way through their territories. In this sense, mounting a donkey would not in itself connote any sense of suffering or humiliation, see Stuhlmueller, *Rebuilding with Hope*, p. 25.

For instance, Zeph 3:12 employed the word "humble" to describe a group of an oppressed and lowly people: "I will also live in the midst of thee an afflicted (i.e. humble) and poor people." This is a corporate reference to the oppressed and lowly people of Zion. The corporate usage of the word in reference to a suffering and humiliated people also appears in Isa 49:13; 51:21, 53:4, 54:11.

With such a prophetic background usage of the word "humble", it is almost certain that the prophet Zechariah at 9:9 sees in the king's act of riding a donkey as he entered Zion a self-imposed element of suffering and humiliation. The donkey was not the animal to mount if the glorious power and majesty of a king were an object of ostentation. This is further supported by the fact that in the wider context of Zech 9:9 where Yahweh is himself the bringer of salvation, he is always portrayed not as a humble Saviour but as a Mighty Redeemer of his people. Since the Messianic king is coming with salvation to Zion, as Yahweh would, it must be an act of suffering and humiliation for him to adopt a quiet, peaceful and humble stance as he claims Zion for himself. In fact, as I have already indicated, it is only this quality of humility which the king does not share with the deity.[203]

By defining the Messianic king as "humble," a term whose general prophetic background connects it with the suffering and lowly people of Zion, the prophet identifies the king with the people he comes to save. The king will himself experience suffering and humility and by so doing identify himself with the people he comes to serve.

Thus, though quite brief, Zech 9:9 gives a powerful theological definition of the Messianic king and his mission. The Messianic king will establish Yahweh's kingdom not by victorious campaigns but through a ministry of peace and loving concern for the lowly and the oppressed. Thus the divine approach to the establishment of the kingdom of God is very extraordinary. The king brings God's judgment and divine salvation not by mere ostentation of his glorious powers but through a humble mission which takes him through suffering and humiliation.

---

[203]   Petersen, *Zechariah 9-14 and Malachi*, p. 58 similarly observes that: "The sole exception to this pervasively royal imagery (i.e. relate to Yahweh as king) is the term 'humble', which is used here to redefine the character of the divine king."

The Theological Significance of the Fulfilment Quotation

Some have not seen any theological significance in the event in its relation to the original Jerusalem community. Beare makes the following comment on the event:

> The Zechariah oracle is not cited in Mark (or by Luke), but it certainly underlines the Marcan story and may even have led to its composition. John adds the comment that the disciples did not at the time attach any great significance to the manner of Jesus entry into the city, and that it was only 'when Jesus was glorified' that they recognised its Messianic character. It was not at all uncommon for anyone to ride into the city on an ass and the event may well have been quiet unspectacular in its actual occurrence. There is no reason to think that Jesus deliberately stage-managed his entry into the city with the intention of presenting himself in the guise of the lowly king of the oracle. For that matter, the procurement of an ass cannot be taken to show that Jesus had a friend in Bethany and knew that he always kept an ass...tethered at the door. In Matthew's own story, Jesus had never been near Jerusalem before. He had the supernatural knowledge of a prophet. The same feature is seen in the story of Saul and Samuel, when the prophet is able to tell the future king all about what will happen to him after he leaves... (I Sam 10:2-6) ... The story of the entry is composed with the same freedom of fancy.[204]

Beare here seems to suggest that the actual occurrence of the entry does not fit the picture that the evangelist presents. The event was itself unspectacular and passed unnoticed by both the disciples and the rest of the people. It was only after the resurrection that any theological significance was led into it. Then the evangelist composed the fanciful narrative that we now have before us. Thus Beare, here, claims that the narrative as it stands is an imaginative creation of the evangelist designed to "fulfill" the Zechariah prophecy. Clearly, Beare's view presupposes the theory of the Messianic Secret and takes certain form-critical assumptions relating to the origins of the gospels for granted. However, in modern critical scholarship the theory of the Messianic Secret is largely abandoned[205] and certain form-critical assumptions previously taken for granted are critically questioned. Consequently, the entry, as presented by the evangelist, has become once more an issue

---

[204]   Beare, *Matthew*, p. 414.

[205]   For a critical discussion of this theory, see Hendriksen, *Matthew*, pp. 60, 61.

worth of rigorous theological investigation. The present study proceeds from this perspective.

It has been noted earlier that the wider contexts of both Isa 62:11 and Zech 9:9 concern divine judgment to the world and a promise of salvation to Zion. Yahweh was to bring both of these in person. Zech 9:9 puts this eschatological event into a Messianic perspective. The judgment and the promised salvation are to be realized through the person of the Messianic king. The day of the Lord becomes the eschatological day of the Messiah.

Similarly, the evangelist employs a fulfilment quotation in a Matthean context characterized by the atmosphere of divine judgment and promise. Jesus' extraordinary entry into Jerusalem is seen by the evangelist as a final challenge to the people of Zion.[206] They are for the last time offered the gracious privilege of being invited to repentance. According to Zecharian prophecy, the promise of salvation to Zion was an act of divine grace based on the covenant relationship which Israel enjoyed. The Messianic king was expected to bring this promise into practical effect. However, the Messiah finds that the covenant is not honoured by Israel. Consequently, Israel is condemned for her unproductiveness. The fig tree in Matt 21:19 offers this lesson. Judgment is further noted in Jesus' condemnation of the Temple activities. The Temple was to be vindicated by the Messiah (Zech 6:13), but now it has become an object of his judgment (Matt 21:12). In overturning the tables in the Temple court, Jesus proclaims judgment over the Temple system. Instead of holding the light of true religion and worship to the world, the system has become an instrument for furthering nationalistic interest. Instead of being used as a tool for the proclamation of the will of God, and the declaration of his loving presence to the nations, Israel keeps these blessings to herself.[207]

While Jesus enters as a royal king and as an eschatological Davidic Messiah, the residents of Jerusalem fail to recognize him for what he is. The Messiah then brings salvation to those who recognize his Messiahship. To the city of Jerusalem and its leaders, however, Jesus is simply a "prophet" (v. 11, chapters 23, 24) of its eschatological judgment.[208] The city expresses final rejection of its eschatological king

---

[206] Albright and Mann, *Matthew*, p. 253.
[207] Fallon, *The Winston Commentary on the Gospels*, p. 318.
[208] Trilling, *Matthew*, p. 376.

through the crucifixion. The crucifixion of the Messiah is an ultimate expression of rejection which consequently vindicates divine judgment upon Zion itself.[209]

But the manner of the Messiah's entry into Jerusalem was primarily intended to bring salvation to Zion. It was a supreme expression of God's covenant love for his people. In the Isaianic and Zecharian contexts, the single act of Yahweh's visitation, through the Messianic king, was intended to work out judgment and condemnation to the enemies of Israel, but salvation to Israel herself. It was only after Israel's failure to maintain its covenant relationship with God that the judgment intended for her enemies actually fell upon her. This is also the case with Jesus Messiah. The good news he brings to Zion only becomes a message of her condemnation after it is rejected. Initially, Jesus enters the city as a Redeemer of God's people. He brings God's salvation in his own person. Accordingly, he enters the city not as a militant Messiah of the popular expectations but as a peaceful and gentle king of the prophetic word. It is this peaceful and humble approach to the work of establishing the kingdom of God that primarily concerns the evangelist's application of the fulfilment quotation at this point. Through this quotation, the evangelist defines the peaceful and gentle character of Jesus' Messianic mission.

That he who brings salvation to Zion is the meek and gentle Jesus is significantly shown by what the evangelist does not say. In the discussion on the textual character of the fulfilment quotation, it has been noted that the evangelist omits from the Zecharian prophecy the clause "triumph and victorious is he." It has been argued earlier that the two adjectives contained in the clause do have a great theological significance. By omitting these two adjectives, the evangelist reveals his primary concern with the humility and the meekness of the peaceful king.[210] That the evangelist knew the theological significance of these two adjectives is indicated in Matt 1:21 where one of them is used to describe Jesus' mission on earth. Jesus came to "save" his people. The word "save" is the same as the word "victorious" in the omitted phrase.

We also noted that the word "triumphant" in the phrase actually means 'the just one." God is the "just one" in the sense that he is faithful

---

[209] *Ibid.*, p. 373.

[210] Also Hendriksen, *Matthew*, p. 764; Harrington, *Matthew*, pp. 293, 295; Meier, *Matthew*, p. 233.

to his own will and that he brings that will faithfully into operation, and thus ensuring successful actualization of his works – hence the word "triumphant." This again applies favorably to Jesus who successfully carries out God's will through an ultimate act of obedience to God, an obedience which inevitably led him to the cross. The LXX makes the meaning of the two omitted adjectives very clear. It refers to the king as "just and saving" as well as "humble."

The evangelist, however, skips these important words and rests his eyes on the third quality of the Messianic king, namely, that the Messianic king is humble. He finds this Messianic humility in Jesus who deliberately prepares a public proclamation of his Messiahship in deliberate fulfilment of the Isaianic and Zecharian prophecy (*contra* Beare).[211] Jesus enters Zion mounting an ass as a Messianic king who brings salvation to Zion in accordance with the prophetic word of Zech 9:9. The fulfilment quotation here forms the linchpin to the discussion of the whole chapter.[212] Although there are many other ordinary quotations that are fulfilled at various points in the narrative, they all serve to support the theme of humility and gentleness of the peaceful king.

In the ancient world, the triumphant kings on a conquest campaign normally rode high-spirited war steeds or prancing stallions as a symbol of their glorious and royal power. They pranced into a foreign capital as they publicly declared their possession of it along with the nation it represented. But Jesus enters Jerusalem, not as a glorious and powerful conqueror but as a meek, gentle, peaceful and gracious king. In this way he claims possession of the city, its Temple and its people in the manner predicted of the Messianic king. He comes to save, not to destroy; to strengthen the weak, not to oppress the poor; to heal the sick, not to condemn them as outcasts; to serve and not to be served. He comes not as a violent and terrorizing foreign conqueror, but as Jerusalem's own loving and gracious king in whom the Messianic prophecies are fulfilled. He comes as the eschatological Son of David with a mission to establish the eschatological kingdom of God. He embodies the salvation of Zion in

---

[211]   Trilling, *Matthew*, p. 373.

[212]   Meier, *Matthew*, p. 232 similarly observes that "the whole story must... be read from its theological centre, the fulfilment quotation in vv. 4-5."

his own person. This is the major focus of the evangelist as we noted earlier.[213]

The eschatological procession gives Jesus a red carpet treatment (v. 18). Branches of trees and people's garments are laid along the road so that the donkey carrying the eschatological king would walk over them. The use of palm branches is usually associated with the joyful celebrations of the Feast of the Tabernacles and the Hanukkah (Lev 23:39-43; II Macc 10:7). But in I Macc 13:51, the palm branches are associated with a celebration for victory over the defeat of Israel's enemy. The throwing down of garments is associated with the proclamation of Jehu as king in II Kgs 9:13. Thus through the red carpet offer, Jesus is proclaimed as the eschatological king who conquers the enemies of Israel, and in that way save his people.

As the eschatological procession matches on into Jerusalem, Jesus is greeted by the Hosanna acclamation (v. 9) (Ps 118:25, 26), a customary way of greeting the Passover pilgrims as they arrived in Jerusalem. In the context, the greeting functions as a greeting of homage rather than a cry for help. Each pilgrim came in the name of Lord, "but this 'pilgrim' riding in is blessed beyond others. No one but the Son of David was to be welcomed with such hopes and expectations since no one else came in the name of the Lord as he did." (*contra* Beare).[214]

As the crowds shout "Hosanna" to Jesus, the divine summons: "Tell the daughter of Zion" (Isa 62:11), "that your salvation comes"(Zech 9:9) unwittingly gets fulfilled. At the sight of the excited procession, the residents of Jerusalem become perplexed and ask who it is that enters the city in that manner. The evangelist tells us that "all the city was moved" (v. 10). The verb used here is *eseisthē*. It is a strong word which is also used to describe the effects of an earthquake (25:51). The evangelist emphasizes the eschatological effect of Jesus' entry. The residents of Jerusalem are told that it is "Jesus the prophet of Nazareth in Galilee" (v. 11). The mention of "prophet" certainly recalls in their minds the Prophet like Moses (Deut 18:15, 18) who has now made his appearance in the form of a humble Messianic king. On the one hand,

---

[213] Malina and Rohrbaugh, *Social-Science Commentary on the Synoptic Gospels*, p. 128; Fallon, *The Winston Commentary on the Gospels*, p. 317; Trilling, *Matthew*, pp. 372-75; Meier, *Matthew*, p. 232; Harrington, *Matthew*, p. 294; Hendrikson, *Matthew*, p. 760; Albright and Mann, *Matthew*, p. 253.

[214] Trilling, *Matthew*, p. 374.

while being the eschatological Davidic Messiah, Jesus also fulfills the prophecy of Deuteronomy concerning the Prophet like Moses. On the other hand, the identification of Jesus as a prophet may only serve to conceal his true identity as the Davidic Messianic king to the Jerusalem residents because of their lack of faith in him.

According to the evangelist, the climax of the eschatological event is the cleansing of the Temple (21:12-17). The eschatological work of cleansing the Temple follows immediately upon the entry into the city, according to the evangelist, placing it at a climactic position within his entry narrative. For Mark, the cleansing event takes place on the following day (Mark 11:11-15). According to the evangelist, however, the Messianic king immediately moves on to the Temple area and passes judgment upon it. The whole system is condemned.

The religious leadership is condemned (v. 13) into a "den of robbers" (Jer 7:11). "To call the Temple a den of robbers is to judge it to be an institution seeking gain and gain is always construed as extortion and greed."[215] While in the Temple area, Jesus heals the "blind and the lame" (v. 14) who, under the current religious regulations were not expected to enter the area (II Sam 5:8). Jesus' healing of these people add to the Messianic excitement that has already began with the entry (Isa 35:5-6). Jesus heals them in his capacity as the eschatological Son of David (v. 15).

But the shouts of praise addressed to Jesus as the Son of David in response to the Temple healings attract the attention of the Temple leadership. They accuse Jesus for what they see as irrelevant and irresponsible noise-making in the sacred place. Jesus defends the people by challenging the religious leaders that the people were only singing praises to the Son of David for the salvation he brings in fulfilment of Ps 8:2. The rest of the chapter in vv. 18-42 continues the theme of divine judgment that the Messianic king brings upon the Jewish leadership.[216]

It is noteworthy to observe the double effect that the proclamation of salvation to Zion by the Messianic king has. For those who believe the Day of the Lord becomes the day of their salvation. However, for those

---

[215] Malina and Rohrbaugh, *Social Science Commentary on the Synoptic Gospels*, p. 128.

[216] For a discussion on how these other quotations relate to their Old Testament setting, and the relevance of that setting to the gospel context, see Albright and Mann, *Matthew*, p. LXXI; Harrington, *Matthew*, pp. 294-96; Fallon, *The Winston Commentary on the Gospels*, pp. 318-19.

who harden their hearts, the Day of the Lord turns out to be a day of divine judgment upon them. Lack of faith in him leads to a complete breach of the covenant relationship with Yahweh, a relationship that forms the basis for the grace of salvation. In the absence of a functional relationship, unrepentant Zion is then treated like one of the Gentile nations and receives the divine judgment it deserves. This is the fate that Jewish religious leadership faces, and through them, all Israel. But those who receive the grace of salvation form the basis for the establishment of the kingdom of God.

It was noted earlier that the Hebrew word *nôshā'* in Zech 9:9 is passive but that it is often rendered as active in Greek and other translations. The Hebrew suggests "to be saved", while the other renderings take it to mean "to save". But the evangelist, acquainted with the Hebrew as the fulfilment quotations suggest, sees in Jesus a Messianic king who brings salvation to others. But in the process of saving others, he is also saved. Jesus himself receives the salvation that he imparts upon others. This accords well with the evangelist's picture of a humble, Messianic king who "is both great and humble, exalted and lowly. He is the One who in this very act is riding … to his death, and thus to victory, a victory not only for himself but also for his true people, those who believe in him."[217] This victory is ultimately experienced in the resurrection. As one who needs salvation, he experiences suffering and death on the cross. In that state he needed the Spirit of God to restore him to life, although that Spirit was already embodied in his person. As one who saves, Jesus is vindicated by the power of the resurrection and is raised to glory at the right hand of God. In that glorified state Jesus receives cosmic powers to bring ultimate judgment and salvation to the world (28:18-20).

The manner in which the evangelist formulates the fulfilment quotation in 21:4-5 from Isa 62:11 and Zech 9:9 and his decision to quote more of the latter prophetic text, not only reflects a careful study of these quotations in their Old Testament setting, but also reveals an inspired reflection on the Christ-event. The claim that the evangelist simply follows the Marcan account and only appends fulfilment quotations to that text coupled with a few redactional changes falls far short from explaining the theological implications that the fulfilment quotations have.

---

[217] Hendriksen, *Matthew*, p. 765.

The way in which the present fulfilment quotation is used by the evangelist further supports the argument that he applies them to the Christ-event in full light of their Old Testament context.

The fulfilment Quotation in Matt 27:9-10

9. And they took the thirty pieces of silver,
the price of the one that was valued,
whom they from the sons of Israel did price and
10. gave them for the field of the potter as the Lord directed me.

Textual Observations

This is the last fulfilment quotation in the gospel. It shares all the characteristic features of this special group of quotations in this gospel. The first problem one faces is that the evangelist says he is quoting from Jeremiah. But the text quoted is not found anywhere in that prophetic book. Nowhere in Jeremiah is there a mention of "the thirty pieces of silver, the price of the one that was valued." It is actually a quotation from Zech 11:13, probably with allusions to the "field" and "potter" passages in Jeremiah (i.e. Jer 18:1-12; 19:1-13; 32:6-9).[218] In Zech 11:12:13 we read:

And I said to them, 'If (it is) good in your eyes, give me my wages; but if not, let it go.' So they weighed for my wages thirty shekels of silver. Then the Lord said to me, 'Throw it to the potter' the splendid price at which I was valued by them. And I took the thirty (pieces of) silver and threw it to the potter in the house of the Lord.

The text as quoted by the evangelist is significantly different from the LXX. A comparative study of the Hebrew original suggests that the evangelist has the Hebrew text in mind but quotes from memory. The clause "the price of the one that was valued, whom they from the sons of Israel did price" appears to be a loose translation of "the splendid price at which I was valued by them" in the Hebrew. The clause "And gave them for the field of the potter" is a loose translation of "and threw it... to the potter." The idea of "field" here is a contribution from the evangelist. The last clause in the evangelist's quotation, "as the Lord directed me" is a loose translation of the first clause in the Hebrew text, "and the Lord said to me."

In the evangelist's text, the reading *edōkan* (2nd aorist, third person plural of *didomai* = to give) does not fit the context well. The first person

---

[218] For a critical discussion of some theories on the problem, see *Ibid.*, pp. 947, 948 especially note 870.

of the original Hebrew and the first person in the clause "as the Lord directed me (*moi*) suggest that *edōka* (2nd aorist, first person singular) would be a better reading.

But a major hermeneutical problem surrounds the variants *'ôtsar* ("treasury") and *yôtsēr* ("potter"). The Hebrew of Zech 11:13 has "potter." Since the time of C.C. Torrey, who argued for the existence of furnaces for burning offerings and smelting coins at the temples of the ancient world, most scholars have in the past, favored the variant "potter"[219] of the Hebrew original. This view is, however, losing ground in current scholarship. Most scholars suspect interpolation or wordplay in the Hebrew original (MT) and have adopted the Syriac reading which has "treasury".[220]

The latter view is probably to be favoured. The word "treasury" is directly concerned with money and was, obviously, an integral part of the Temple. In the context of Zechariah, the thirty pieces of silver could not be returned to the treasury for it had been used as payment for a despised labour of a prophet. It is, indeed, an equivalent of the price of a slave. But the "potter" rendering would be free of this connotation. The evangelist would also find the "potter" rendering more appropriate. He is already thinking of the potter's field which was bought by the Sanhedrin using the money that Judas returned. Again this money could traditionally not be put back into the treasury. It was "blood money."[221] However, the way in which the evangelist alludes to both words in the context (vv. 6, 7) seems to suggest that the evangelist was aware of the background to the Syriac tradition.[222]

It is not possible to identify the particular text or texts from Jeremiah which the evangelist alludes to. But the mention of the buying of the field of a potter suggests an allusion to the "field" (Jer 32:1-15) and "potter" (Jer 18:12; 19:1-13) passages in that prophetic book.[223]

---

[219] C.C. Torrey, "The foundry of the Second Temple at Jerusalem," *Journal of Biblical Literature* 55 (1936), pp. 247-60 for a discussion of this theory.

[220] Harrington, *Matthew*, p 368; Beare, *Matthew*, p. 525; Albright and Mann, *Matthew*, p. 340; Stuhlmueller, *Rebuilding with Hope*, p. 140; Petersen, *Zechariah 9-14 and Malachi*, p. 87.

[221] For a similar view, see Allen, *Matthew*, p. 288.

[222] Beare, *Matthew*, p. 525; Allen, *Matthew*, p. 288.

[223] Hendriksen, *Matthew*, p. 948, thinks that Jeremiah 19 is the only source for the evangelist's allusive reflection. Many, however, see in addition to Jeremiah 19 elements of Jeremiah 18 and 32 in the evangelist's quotation. See Harrington, *Matthew*, p. 386; Meier, *Matthew*, p. 339. Beare, *Matthew*, p. 525, on the other hand, finds that the whole question of

Probably the most significant observation that can be made here is the fact that the fulfilment quotation in both the Zecharian and gospel contexts focuses on the treacherous rejection of the prophet (and the Messiah in the gospel) reflected in the low value that is placed on him.[224] The focus is not on the death of Judas nor is it on the potter's field his money buys. The focus is Messianic or Christological. It emphasizes the leaders' responsibility for Jesus' death. The shepherd of Israel receives as wages from the rulers of the people a paltry some of money. This symbolizes ultimate rejection of the prophet or Messiah by his own people.

This understanding, of course, depends on our assessment of the "thirty pieces of silver." Some have argued that the "thirty pieces of silver" was just an appropriate payment. It was "no mean sum."[225]

The Biblical texts mostly used in this discussion are Exod. 21:32 and Neh 5:15. It is important to note that in both of these texts the noun *shekel* is used. However, in Zech 11:12, the word takes the form of a verb and simply means "to weigh out", "to measure." This means that Zech 11:12 leaves the denomination of payment indeterminate.

It is, however, generally accepted that the phrase refers to an insignificant amount: "In sum the expression 'thirty pieces of silver' should be understood as an insultingly low wage."[226] Fallon observes that the Jewish leaders "insulted God by offering his prophet the price of a slave... for wages."[227] Petersen reports Erica Reiner's observation that in the Sumerian poem of "Gilgamesh and the Huluppu tree" the phrase "thirty shekels" expresses a trifling or minimal amount. Petersen also reports a similar finding made by Lipinski who studied the Akkadian texts from Tell el Amarna.[228] From these observations, it may be concluded that the expression in the ancient Near East meant an insignificant sum

allusions to the Book of Jeremiah (18:2; 32:9) "is completely irrelevant in this Matthean context." Beare's view is critically discussed later in this study.

[224] Hendriksen, *Matthew*, p.948 sees the focus of the quotation on the suicide of the traitor and the purchase of the field with his money. Harrington, *Matthew*, p.387, sees it in the fulfilment of scripture in Judas' death and the shameful behaviour of the chief priests.

[225] Joyce G. Baldwin, *Haggai, Zechariah, Malachi, An Introduction and Commentary*, London: Tyndale, 1972, p. 184 holds this view.

[226] Petersen, *Zechariah 9-14 and Malachi*, pp. 96, 97.

[227] Fallon, *The Winston Commentary on the Gospels*, p. 415. Malina and Rohrbaugh, *Social-Science Commentary on the Synoptic Gospels*, p. 160 sees the incident as part of the process of "a public ritual of humiliation" for Jesus.

[228] Petersen, *Zechariah 9-14 and Malachi*, pp. 96, 97.

of money. It is the latter understanding of this phrase that is adopted in this study.

This textual study of the fulfilment quotation has shown that this quotation, like the other fulfilment quotations discussed in this study, is the evangelist's own loose translation of the Hebrew, possibly, quoted from memory. It has also shown that the evangelist alludes to certain passages in the Book of Jeremiah in addition to his loose quotation of Zech 11:13. It has also shown that the focus of the fulfilment quotation here is not Judas and the use to which the money that was paid to him was put. Rather, it focuses on the humiliation and rejection of the Prophet-Shepherd of Israel at the hands of his own people which is partly expressed through the insulting wage or price they set for his betrayal.

The Historical Context of Zech 11:13 and Jeremiah 18, 19, 32

We have already noted in our discussion of the previous fulfilment quotation partly drawn from Zech 9:9 that Zechariah was a contemporary of Haggai. Both prophesied during the post-exilic period. The process of restoration was beset with many difficulties. Only the well-to-do could live comfortably. The majority poor experienced severe difficulties. The land had become unproductive. Wages were very low and life was generally difficult. Judah was still under the Persian control although it was given freedom to run its own affairs under a Persian governor.

Zecharian prophecy falls within this historical context.[229] Zechariah is generally difficult to interpret. His oracles are quite enigmatic. Zechariah 11 is not an exception from this. Despite this, however, the general message of the prophet is reasonably clear. In the context of Zechariah 9-14, chapter 11 reflects human failure set in a larger context in which divine action ushers in the eschatological age. The prophet sees the

---

[229] Many have seen *Zechariah 9-14* as a separate book from *Zechariah 1-8*. Linguistic and stylistic features have been used to support this view, for instance, Hinckley G. Mitchell et al., *A Critical and Exegetical Commentary on Haggai, Zechariah, Malachi, and Jonah*, ICC, Edinburgh: T&T Clark, 1912, pp. 232-259. But these are capable of a satisfactory explanation, and there are points of contact between the two sections. We may note, here, with Ackroyd, "Zechariah", in *Peake's Commentary*, p. 651 that "the divine protection of 9:8 resembles that of 2:5; the wording of the commands to the prophet in 11:4, 13, 15 is not unlike that of visions in 1-6, and perhaps more particularly of 6:9-14. More evidently, too, the whole emphasis on divine deliverance and the age of salvation provides close contacts, though the distinction must be observed between the immediacy of the promises of the new age in 1-8 (especially 7-8), linked to the rebuilding of the Temple, and the apocalyptic tone of 9-14." It appears that there is no compelling reason to question the unity of the book.

collapse of world powers before the humble and peaceful king. Yahweh leads his people through the darkness of depression and apostasy to the day of salvation (9:1-11:3). Human failures and sorrows even among God's people give way to eschatological victory on the Day of the Lord (chap 14).

Whatever might be the vernal practices associated with the religious leaders (10:1-2; 11:5-6), the prophecy closes at a joyous note with the glorious celebration of a universal Feast of the Tabernacles. Thus, although chap. 11 ends with the rejection of the prophet (v. 17), the prophecy as a whole concludes with an optimistic note. Yahweh leads history forward so that on the day of the Lord (11:11) history is brought to its final consummation before his victorious presence.[230]

When chapter 11 is taken by itself, the ideas of failure and rejection run through the whole of it like a thread. The rejection of the Messianic Shepherd-King is emphasized. The Lord commissions his Prophet-Shepherd-King to "feed the flock" (v. 4). The Prophet-Shepherd-King prepares for his task and adopts a covenantal approach. He selects two staffs (Heb. *Maqlôt*) and labels them "Grace" (Heb. *No'am*) and "Union" (Heb. *hoblîm*) (v. 7). He then engages with other shepherds and dismisses some of them, a move which earns him much disdain from them (v. 8). The Shepherd-King decides not to function as a shepherd to the flock. "In so doing he continues to act out Yahweh's command. This statement is not a rejection of the deity's mandate. Instead, it is a further working out of the Shepherd's task, which has already included the removal of several shepherds from their position."[231]

The Prophet-Shepherd in a further symbolical act breaks one of his tools for effective shepherding, the staff "Grace." This symbolic act is a reference to "Israel's 'nullification' of the old covenant. making null and void the promises of blessing associated with the covenant relationship."[232]

---

[230] Also see Stuhlmuller, *Rebuilding with Hope*, pp. 133-35.

[231] Petersen, *Zechariah 9-14 and Malachi*, p. 95.

[232] Robertson, *The Christ of the Covenant*, pp. 284, 285 and note 15. Scholars have attempted to specify the covenant relationship that is referred to here. Suggestions include Israel's covenant (Otzen), universal eschatological judgment (Elliger), Abrahamic covenant (Mason) and the Noahic covenant between Yahweh and humanity (Petersen). But the cryptic nature of Zecharian prophecy makes this task extremely difficult and any certainty on this is probably unattainable although the reference to divine covenant is quite clear. See Petersen, *Zechariah 9-14 and Malachi*, p. 95.

While the purposes of God are reflected in names of the staffs: "grace" and "union", the disobedience of the people frustrates those purposes. Consequently, God does not pity them. Zechariah here sees a collapse of what Ezekiel had enunciated about the Good Shepherd. Yahweh himself would save (Ezek 34:9-16), and anoint one shepherd to feed them. He would establish a covenant of peace (v. 25) and bless them (vv. 26-31). In contrast, here in Zechariah 11 the Lord scatters (v. 6), and raises a shepherd who opposes them (v. 16). The covenant is nullified and doom and destruction show their ugly faces.

With this revision or termination of the divine promises regarding the protection of humanity, the Lord turns his sovereignty to those shepherds in charge of various nations (v.10).[233] This act of covenantal abrogation receives an eschatological dimension in v. 11 where the shepherds who now receive ultimate political authority witness it for themselves and take it as an emphasis on their ultimate control.[234]

With his task at an end, the Prophet-Shepherd-King seeks payment for the work of shepherding he has undertaken. The demand for payment includes a quality judgment: "If it is good in your eyes give me my wages but if not, let it go" (v. 12). It is in response to this demand for his wages that the Prophet-Shepherd receives the "insulting low wage" of "thirty pieces of silver" discussed earlier.

In giving "thirty pieces of silver", an equivalent of the sum that would be given to an owner of a gored slave (Exod 21:32) for a price, the other shepherds express their rejection of the divinely commissioned Prophet-Shepherd-King. In responding to this insult, the Lord orders his Prophet-King to throw the insulting wage toward the temple treasury. Immediately, the prophet breaks the remaining staff "Union" (v.14). Petersen understands this staff as a symbolic reference to the Davidic covenant, a covenant which unifies all of God's people and in that way concern the very existence of God's people.[235] This further abrogates the promises of blessing associated with Israel's covenant relationship with the Lord. What Gerhard von Rad observes about Jeremiah's view of Israel might also be said of Zechariah at this point: "... the old covenant is broken, and in Jeremiah's view Israel is altogether without one."[236]

[233]   Petersen, *Zechariah 9-14 and Malachi*, p.96.
[234]   *Ibid.*
[235]   *Ibid.*, p. 98.
[236]   Gerhard von Rad, *Old Testament Theology*, vol. .II, London: SCM, 1965, p. 212.

Zechariah sees Israel's covenant with the Lord as totally terminated at this point.

But the consequences for their rejection of the anointed king are dire. The Lord has given over control of human affairs to shepherds and sheep-dealers who have rejected his anointed. They fail in their performance. The flock is doomed (vv. 4,5,7). To this failure, humanity responds with a curse in response to their plight (v.17) against the worthless shepherd(s). At this point, the situation is ripe for divine judgment.[237]

Similarly, the Jeremiah passages alluded in this fulfilment quotation appear in a context of divine judgment offering both the message of divine condemnation and divine promise.

There are three passages which form a possible background to certain elements in this fulfilment quotation as earlier indicated. These are Jer 18:1-12;19:1-13; 32:1-15. The first reference concerns a potter's wheel, the second a potter's flask and the last a purchase of a field. In Jer 19:1-13 the prophet is commanded to buy a potter's (i.e. earthen) flask and go down, along with some priests and elders of the people, to the valley of Ben Hinnom near the entrance to the Potsherd Gate. There he is to break the vessel in a symbolic act and announce that the Lord will destroy the people and the city in the same manner. Following the symbolic act, the prophet repeats the proclamation of doom and destruction in the Temple court (v. 14, 15). The significance of such a symbolic act is well expressed by Bright who observes that it was no mere dramatic illustration of a point. It was rather viewed "as the actual setting in motion of Yahweh's destroying word."[238] There is a wide scholarly consensus over the interpretation of this symbolic act. The irrevocability of divine judgment and destruction over the Temple, the city and its people, indeed over Judah as a whole, is the essence of the action.[239] The sins of Judah have reached untold proportions.

---

[237]   Petersen, *Zechariah 9-14 and Malachi*, p. 101. For a thorough discussion of Zechariah 11, see *Ibid.*, pp. 89-101. Stuhlmueller, *Rebuilding with Hope*, pp. 133-41. For a brief but helpful discussion, see Ackroyd, "Zechariah" in Black and Rowley (eds) in *Peake's Commentary on the Bible*, p. 653.

[238]   John Bright, *Jeremiah*, The Anchor Bible, New York: Doubleday, 1965, p. 133.

[239]   For instance, H. Cunliffe-Jones, *The Book of Jeremiah, Introduction and Commentary*, London: SCM, 1960, p. 141, observes that "the breaking of the earthenware flask, a highly expensive water decanter which could not be repaired, symbolizes and helps to bring about the destruction of Jerusalem and Judah." Robert P. Caroll, *Jeremiah, A Commentary*, London:

Of the three passages, Jer 19:1-15 has much in common with the evangelist's context in Matt 27:1-10. Just as Judas in the gospel, Jerusalem in the prophetic text shades innocent blood (Jer 19:4; Matt 27:4). In both, the chief priests and the elders are preeminent (Jer 19:1; Matt 27:3, 6, 7). A potter is also mentioned (Jer 19:1, 11; Matt 27:7, 10). Traditionally, the Potter's field is located in Tophet, i.e., the Valley of Hinnom. In the prophetic text, the name of the valley is changed to "the Valley of Slaughter." This is almost identical with the "Field of Blood" known to both the evangelist and Luke (Jer 19:6; Matt 27:8; Acts 1:19). The Valley or the Field becomes a famous burial ground (Jer 19:11; Matt 27:7). Clearly, there is much in the evangelist's account that reflects this particular prophetic text.

In both texts, the theme of rejection stands out clearly. Just as the word of God and the prophet behind it are rejected, so is the gospel and the Messiah behind it. For the first time[240] in his ministry, the prophet is physically persecuted and exposed to public shame by religious leaders. He is beaten and then put in stocks and placed at the Temple gate. The prophet resents this and correctly sees it as an affront to the majesty of God whose words he proclaims (Jer 20:1-6). In the gospel setting, Jesus the Messiah is also rejected by the religious leaders and no effort is spared in order to get him executed by the Roman officials (Matt 27:22, 27, 35).

But Jeremiah 19 does not settle the whole problem. It does not state anywhere that Jeremiah actually bought a potters' field (Matt 27:10). Neither is this stated anywhere in the Old Testament. In search for further possible background texts to the fulfilment quotation, Jeremiah 18 and 32 have often been cited.

The preceding context to Jeremiah 18 reveal that the sin of Judah is so firmly rooted that it has reached indelible proportions. Consequently, divine judgment is now irrevocable: "The sin of Judah is written with a pen of iron, and with the point of a diamond" (17:1). This method of writing was used to inscribe the most vital and permanent record (Job

SCM, 1986, pp. 386, 387, also notes that "the breaking of the ceramic object is the destruction of the city and its people... The broken flask remains broken because the fired clay cannot be remoulded, so the action represents and anticipates the permanent destruction of the city... Hope is no longer on the agenda."

[240] John Paterson, "Jeremiah", in Black and Rowley (eds), *Peake's Commentary on the Bible,* London: Routledge, 1962, reprint 1987, p. 549.

19:24). The sins of Judah are inscribed in this way to be remembered by God, not to be atoned for (Lev 16:18). Yahweh will therefore send them into exile (17:2-4). Judah has served foreign gods, and to a foreign land, to the land of those gods, she must go (vv 10-13).

Jer 18:1-12 presents the prophet's visit to the potter's house. The Lord commands the prophet to visit this place and observe how the potter works with his clay. The prophet notices that the potter is ultimately free to make or remake the kind of vessel he wants. Then the Lord declares that he has ultimate freedom and sovereignty to deal with Judah the way he wills just as the potter has over the clay.

Some have found a great difficulty in the seemingly contradictory views of the deity toward the nations. In vv. 7-10, national changes bring about changes in the deity. The future of any nation is presented not as predestined by the sovereignty of the deity but as determined by its (the nation's) readiness to change. Here the flexibility of the divine attitude to nations and call for repentance are emphasized. Carrol puts it in this way:

> A rather different understanding of the piece (i.e. vv 1-12) is provided by the inclusion of vv 7-10... These verses set out a general point about divine attitudes, using some Deuteronomistic terminology which removes the image of the potter's activity as a positive one and focuses on the clay as a substance with its own capacity for choosing what will happen to it... The theoretical nature of vv 7-10 with their image of a predictable deity contracting with nations and kingdoms a reciprocal agreement of corresponding and alternating plans for the future is idyllic and unreal... It is partly composed by the redactional variations on the motifs "pluck up", "break down", "destroy", "build" and "plant" which run through the construction of the book... In the latter stages of the employment of these motifs they are applied to nations and 18:7-10 belongs to this state (by this stage of the tradition Jeremiah has been transformed into a prophet to the nations, hence his message to them here).[241]

Thus the difficulty here is that the flexibility of the divine attitude to the nations in vv. 7-10 contradicts the traditions which view divine judgment for Israel as irrevocable since turning for Israel is no longer a possibility. On the ground of this seeming contradiction, vv. 7-10 are taken by some as a late Deuteronomistic insertion into the text. When these verses are

---

[241]   Carrol, Jeremiah, pp. 372, 373.

removed from the text as redactional, the emphasis moves back from the clay to the potter and hence, divine capacity becomes once more the focus. This carries with it hope for the future: "The potter's activity provides a metaphor of divine capacity. As such the piece is a positive, optimistic metaphor of hope for the future."[242]

But this view has been rejected by others. Paterson, in response to Cornill who would remove vv. 5-12 as a later insertion, argues that: "It may have been worked over by a Deuteronomist but it bears the genuine Jeremianic ring. Moreover, these verses convey a clear logical thought and the meaning is clear. History depends on the response men make to the will of God... His omnipotence is not arbitrary."[243] Similarly, Bright rejects the proposed insertion theory and stresses that the central message of Jeremiah 18 is not hope but divine judgment:

> The point is not, as some think, that Yahweh will continue to work patiently with his people, and inspite of the fact that they may temporarily thwart him, will in the end make them the 'vessel' that he had intended them to be... The point... is precisely that the clay *can* frustrate the potter's intention and cause him to change it: as the quality of the clay determines what the potter can do with it so the quality of the people determines what God can do with them... This point is developed in vv 7-10, which are not to be deleted as a mistake expansion as those who give the passage an optimistic interpretation are obliged to do. This, too, is the point that Jeremiah is told (v11) to proclaim to the people: God's present intention is to judge them, but if they repent, they have still a chance. But this (v12) they refuse to do.[244]

Brueggemann also dismisses the insertion theory and observes that:

> Yahweh's responsive sovereignty and Judah's determinative obedience are both constitutive of Judah's life... resistance to God practised so long eventually nullifies the capacity to chose life... Jerusalem's judgment is sealed because Judah has been too stubborn. Judah rejects God's plan which is for covenantal obedience... Such refusal ends in death ... As the potter shapes clay (v4) so Yahweh shapes evil for Judah (v11)... The potter is not endlessly committed to working with this clay, if the

---

[242] *Ibid.*, p. 372.

[243] Paterson, "Jeremiah", in Black and Rowley (eds), *Peake's Commentary on the Bible*, p. 549.

[244] Bright, *Jeremiah*, pp. 125, 126.

clay is finally recalcitrant. The potter will finally quit which means that the clay has no future.[245]

It is thus clear that the main thrust of the message in this oracle is on the impending judgment. For the moment this is settled for Israel has refused to repent (vv. 12, 17). While the oracle brings forth the significance of God's sovereign power over his people, it is important to note that God is sovereign in both judgment and salvation. In the present oracle, it is his sovereignty in judgment that finds clear expression. Brueggemann correctly observes that the potter-clay metaphor in Jeremiah has a "deathly use".[246] There is a pervasive sense of judgment throughout this chapter. This makes it an appropriate background to a fulfilment quotation used by the evangelist in a context of divine judgment upon Israel as its leaders reject and crucify their own Messiah.

Jeremiah 32 is also set within the context of judgment. However, the symbolic prophetic act in that chapter has an optimistic interpretation in contrast to the two Jeremianic passages just discussed.

In Jeremiah 32 the prophet is directed by the Lord to buy a field from Hanamel his cousin in Anathoth (vv. 7-8). The formalities involving the transaction are meticulously followed. The price of the field which is seventeen shekels of silver, is carefully weighed in the presence of witnesses. Legal documents for the transaction are also carefully prepared. Two copies of the deed are made, a sealed copy to guarantee safe-keeping and avoid tampering with it; and an open copy to facilitate easy reference. The deed is then given to Baruch his secretary and trusted friend for safe-keeping in the presence of witnesses. The discovery of the Dead Sea scrolls preserved in earthen jars has revealed that such jars were used for the safekeeping of essential documents. Baruch possibly used a similar jar for this purpose.

Then, the symbolic act receives its divine interpretation. "For thus says the Lord of hosts, the God of Israel; Houses and fields and vineyards shall be possessed again in this land" (v. 15). Under God's constraint, the prophet buys the field from his cousin as a sign of confidence in the future of his nation. By the time this is taking place, the siege of Jerusalem is already underway (39:1-2). The incidents of chapter 37 have already taken place. Jeremiah has already been in

---

[245] Walter Brueggemann, *To pluck up, to Tear Down, Jeremiah 1-25*, ITC, Grand Rapids: Wm. B. Eerdmans & Edinburgh: Handsel, 1988, pp. 161, 162.
[246] *Ibid.*, p 162, note 63.

prison (37:5). Following his request to the king, Jeremiah is allowed the easier conditions of the court of the guards (37:21) where people can visit him and freely conduct the transaction.

It is generally taken that the story of the purchase in chap 32 has received an inaccurate setting.[247] Verses 1-2 are seen as putting the incident within its historical context. The siege of Jerusalem by the Babylonian army started in 588 BC, the ninth year of King Zedekiah, and continued till his eleventh year, 586 BC (39:12). The incident narrated here took place in the midst of this long siege in 587 BC during a temporary withdrawal of the Babylonian forces so that they would face the troops of Pharaoh Hophra (37:11).[248]

Verse 3 attributes the imprisonment of Jeremiah to King Zedekiah. This is seen as an editorial inaccuracy since it was actually the princes who imprisoned him (37:15) on the charge of high treason (37:13). Verses 4-5 are also considered as an insertion. Although this prophecy against Zedekiah comes from the prophet (34:2-5), it is felt to be out of place here.[249] Verses 6-15 which give an account of the deed are generally attributed to Jeremiah himself, while the rest of the chapter, i.e., vv. 16-44 is by some considered as a latter expansion. This section consists mainly of a prayer by Jeremiah and an answer from God. On this so-called later expansion, Cunliffe-Jones makes the following comment:

> But some later thought that the obvious needed elucidation and that it could be done by means of a prayer and an answer from God. Most of both are irrelevant to Jeremiah's situation, and where relevant they tell us nothing that we do not know from vv 6-15. Jeremiah could not have been so lacking in perception.[250]

But it does not seem to be quiet necessary to attribute vv. 16-44 to a latter editor. The section does not seem to be as "irrelevant to Jeremiah's situation" as Cunliffe-Jones, among others, claim. We observe with Bright that: "Jeremiah's action in this regard was intended symbolically as an earnest of Yahweh's promise that normal life would one day be resumed in the land. This theme, which is made specific in v 15, is

---

[247] Cunliffe-Jones, *The Book of Jeremiah*, p. 204.

[248] Anderson, *The Living World of the Old Testament*, p. 417.

[249] Cunliffe-Jones, *The Book of Jeremiah*, p 205.

[250] *Ibid.*, p. 207.

developed through the remainder of the chapter."[251] When verses 16-44 are taken as genuine, Jeremiah's prayer in vv. 16-25 seems to indicate that the prophet was unable to grasp the full meaning of the word that has come to him (v.15). This perfectly suits the situation of the prophet. With Judah facing an imminent invasion, destruction and possible exile from a super power, and with the historical demise of the lost Ten Tribes of Israel through an Assyrian exile more than a century earlier in 722 BC, neither history nor current situation would support any hope for a return. It was human enough for the prophet in these circumstances to doubt the reality of a future hope for Judah.

Further, the fourfold answer from the Lord in vv. 26-44 are in line with Jeremiah's other teachings.[252] It makes it clear that Yahweh, not the Babylonians, is Lord of history (v. 27). It also makes it clear that divine judgment for Judah is certain and irrevocable and that it will fall upon sinners (vv. 28-35). The impending divine judgment is, however, not to be an annihilation. It will be followed by a restoration in which normal life shall return (v.43). The destruction that preceded the restoration is, in fact, its guarantee (v.42). The reference to an everlasting covenant in v. 40 recalls the New Covenant of 31:31-34.[253] Here the future hope for Judah based on her covenantal relationship finds a clear expression.

It may be concluded, therefore, that the whole of chap. 32 is a unit and that vv. 16-44 must be seen as its integral part. Its central message is that Judah will shortly go into exile in Babylon where there is only suffering, horror and death. But God will later restore her to the Promised Land, and all covenantal blessings will be renewed. The prophet's purchase of land, seen from this perspective, is an eschatological event in which that restoration is divinely assured (15). Yahweh has a future for the land of Judah.

Jeremiah 32 is set in a wider context which consists of prophecies of judgment and hope for redemption, namely, Jeremiah 26-35. Within that wider context chap 32 takes its place in a more immediate setting of 30:1-33:26, generally known as "The Little Book of Comfort."[254] This

---

[251] Bright, *Jeremiah*, p. 297.

[252] Paterson, "Jeremiah", in Black and Rowley (eds), *Peake's Commentary on the Bible*, p. 557.

[253] For a thorough discussion of the New Covenant in Jer 32:31-34, see Robertson, *The Christ of the Covenant*, pp. 271-300.

[254] Anderson, *The Living World of the Old Testament*, p. 393.

section portrays the ultimate restoration of both Israel and Judah. It is the longest sustained passage in that prophetic book dealing with the future hope of the people of God. Chapter 32 contributes to this glorious picture of the future for the people of God.

Beare has strongly objected to the view that the evangelist makes a meaningful allusion to the Jeremiah passages in his fulfilment quotation:

> It contains only two stray phrases from Jeremiah, viz,18:2, 'go down to the potter's house' and 32:9 'I bought the field at Ana-thoth from Hanamel my cousin, and weighed out the money to him, seventeen shekels of silver' (39:9, LXX). This is completely irrelevant in the Matthean context; there is nothing but the mention of a potter in the one passage, and of a field that is purchased with pieces of silver (shekels) in the other.[255]

It is significant here to note that Beare does not account for the many allusions that the evangelist in Matt 27:1-10 has to Jeremiah 19. Beare has limited himself to Jeremiah 18 and Jeremiah 32. But even in that case the ideas of "potter" in Jeremiah 18 and "field" in Jeremiah 32 are thematic in those chapters so that it is not surprising for them to live a deep impression on the mind of the evangelist. Further tradition appears to have connected the two ideas long before. Hendriksen has suggested that the term "potter's field" probably indicates a field from which potters (or a potter) used to get their (his) clay, but which had become depleted. Since it could no longer serve as a source for further supplies, it was offered for sale. The religious leaders then planned to turn this piece of land into a burial place.[256]

We have already noted in our discussion of Jeremiah 19 that tradition identifies the potter's field with the Valley of Hinnom. The existence of a parallel tradition in Acts 1:18-19 where it is Judas who purchases the field and later dies on it, further supports the traditional connection between the two ideas. Although Acts 1:18-19 does not say that the field which Judas bought was formerly a potter's field, the possibility cannot be ruled out. The relationship between the ideas of "potter" and "field" in the evangelist's tradition appears to have deeper roots than can possibly be unraveled.

In this light, Beare's contention that Jeremiah 18 and 32 are "completely irrelevant in the Matthean context" loses its force. Even if

---

[255] Beare, *Matthew*, p. 525.
[256] Hendriksen, *Matthew*, p. 945.

there were no traditional linkages between the two ideas of 'field" and "potter", the mere mention of them in these chapters, as Beare himself acknowledges, would be sufficient ground for the evangelist's allusion to them.

Thus our discussion here of Zech 9:9 and the Jeremiah passages indicates that all of them, in their varying degrees, made a theological contribution to the evangelist's formulation of the fulfilment quotation. This presupposes a meticulous study and much theological reflection of the Old Testament context of the passages quoted or alluded to.

The Theological Significance of the Fulfilment Quotation

It is quite difficult to reconcile Luke's version of the betrayal found in Acts 1:18-19 with the one our evangelist records at 27:3-10. In Luke's tradition, it is Judas who buys the field and later dies violently on it. The field is later called "Field of Blood" because of Judas' blood shed there. In our evangelist's tradition, it is the Sanhedrin which buys the field, presumably, after Judas' suicide. The field is called the "Field of Blood" because it was bought with blood money, that is the money given in exchange for the shedding of Jesus' innocent blood.

However, in the evangelist's account, at least three facts relating to the gospel tradition on which the application of prophecy depends can be singled out. First, Judas had thrown thirty pieces of silver into the Temple. Secondly, the Sanhedrin refused to put this money back into the treasury. And, thirdly, the money he rejected was used for the purchase of a potter's field.[257]

There are several typological lines of thought between the prophetic contexts of the texts quoted or alluded to and the gospel situation on which the evangelist comments. We have noted that all the Old Testament contexts of the passages applied to the Christ- event speak of both divine judgment and promise of salvation. Zechariah 11 speaks of the treachery of those who were supposed to be the shepherds of the people. Not only do they betray their leadership roles, turning it into a personal career geared towards their own personal gain,[258] but also rejected the only person, the humble Prophet-Shepherd-King, commissioned to save them.[259] The prophetic mission of the Shepherd-

---

[257]   Allen, *Matthew*, p. 945.

[258]   Stuhlmueller, *Rebuilding with Hope*, p. 135.

[259]   Petersen, *Zechariah 9-14 and Malachi*, pp. 96-97.

King is insultingly valued by the leaders of the people at thirty silver pieces, essentially a mere price of a slave gored to death (Exod 21:32). This is symbolic of the ultimate rejection and betrayal of the divinely commissioned Shepherd-King. At the Lord's command, the Prophet-King throws the thirty pieces of silver in the Temple.

The evangelist sees the outworking of this prophetic symbolic act in the passion of Jesus, the humble Prophet-Shepherd-King of the eschatological age. Jesus is also ultimately rejected by those who should have been the shepherds of Israel, i.e., the religious leaders of the people. His redemptive mission is also insultingly valued at thirty pieces of silver by the false shepherds of the people. The prophet's casting of the silver pieces at the Temple is seen by the evangelist as prophetic of the Sanhedrin's rejection of the proffered wages of Judas, and the giving of them for the potter's field. The throwing of the silver pieces back to the Temple in both the Old Testament and the gospel contexts emphasizes the responsibility of the leaders for the rejection and betrayal of the divinely commissioned Shepherd-King. It also anticipates divine judgment upon these leaders.[260]

Thus by referring to the prophetic symbolic act in Zecharian prophecy, the evangelist condemns the religious leaders for repeating the horrible sin of their predecessors, namely, their rejection and betrayal of the humble Shepherd-King, the Messiah. In the immediately preceding context (27:1-3), the Sanhedrin has just made a decision to get Jesus executed, and to effect that decision they have referred him to Pontius Pilate on charges of high treason. Stendahl, commenting on vv. 3-10, observes that: "By placing the account of the death of Judas at this point...Mt. indicates that he understands the decision of the Sanhedrin as the crucial one."[261]

The natural consequence of the Sanhedrin's decision to reject and betray their divinely commissioned Shepherd-King, the Messiah, was to have Jesus pass through a series of "status degradation rituals"[262] which

[260] Hendriksen, *Matthew*, pp. 946, 947; Albright and Mann, *Matthew*, pp. LXXII, 340; Allen, *Matthew*, p.287.

[261] Krister Stendahl, "Matthew", in Black and Rowley (eds), *Peake's Commentary on the Bible*, p.796.

[262] Malina and Rohrbaugh, *Social-Science Commentary on the Synoptic Gospels*, p. 159 define "social degradation ritual" as "a process of public recasting, relabeling, humiliating, and thus recategorizing a person as a social deviant. Such rituals express the moral indignation of

inevitably led to his crucifixion. The dreadful chorus of the religious leaders and their people as they cried out, "Let him be crucified" (27:22, 23) is an ultimate expression of their rejection of the Messiah.

The physical agony and mental torture as well as the public shame that accompanied crucifixion as a method of punishment in the ancient world has been well documented by Hengel.[263] Crucifixion in itself was "the most wretched of deaths."[264] To speak of the crucifixion of Jesus as the crucifixion of the Messiah and Son of God was not only insultingly offensive to the cultured man but also totally incomprehensible even to the man of limited intelligence:

> A crucified messiah, son of God or God must have seemed a contradiction in terms to anyone, Jew, Greek, Roman or barbarian, asked to believe such a claim, and it will certainly have been thought offensive and foolish.[265]

The problem of the crucifixion of the Son of God has posed one of the greatest difficulties of the Christian faith not only to primitive Christianity[266] but also to contemporary Christian faith. Hengel observes that "the theological reasoning of our time shows very clearly that the particular form of the death of Jesus, the man and the Messiah, represents a scandal which people would like to blunt, remove or domesticate in any way possible."[267] The humility and shameful cross of

---

the denouncers and often mock or denounce a person's former identity in such a way as to destroy it totally."

[263] Martin Hengel, *Crucifixion in the Ancient World*, Philadelphia: Fortress, 1977.

[264] *Ibid.*, p. 8, quoting Josephus.

[265] *Ibid.*, p. 10.

[266] Paul the Apostle observes that the message of the cross is a "stumbling block to Jews and foolishness to Gentiles" (1 Cor 1:23). Several voices in antiquity support the apostle's observation: Justin says: "They say that our madness consists in the fact that we put a crucified man in second place after the unchangeable and eternal God, the creator of the world" (*Apology* I, 13.4). Minucius Felix adds: "To say that their ceremonies centre on a man put to death for his crime and on the fatal wood of the cross... is to assign to these abandoned wretches sanctuaries which are appropriate to them... and the kind of worship they deserve" (*Octavius* 9:4). An oracle of Apollo given in response to a man's inquiry on what to do to dissuade his wife from the Christian faith recorded by Porphyry and preserved by Augustine says: "Let her continue as she pleases, persisting in her vain delusions, and lamenting in song a god who died in delusion, who was condemned by judges whose verdict was just, and executed in the prime of life by the worst of deaths, a death bound with iron" (*Civitas Dei* 19:23)- Quoted in Hengel, *Crucifixion*, pp. 1, 3, 4. Hengel then concludes that the evidence "makes it clear that the death of Jesus on the cross was inevitably folly and scandal even for the early Christians... pagan opponents quite unjustly assert that Christians worship 'a criminal and his cross'... No criminal, indeed no earthly being whatsoever deserves to be regarded as a god," *Ibid.*, p.3.

[267] *Ibid.*, p.90.

Jesus Messiah has left an indelible mark on the face of the Christian faith, a constant reminder of his suffering and rejection by his own covenant people. Left unenlightened by the prophetic word, the cross remains a strange constituent element of the Gospel itself.

In light of what we have seen so far relating to the evangelist's approach to the use of Scriptures, namely, his meticulous study of passages he quotes and his studious attention to their wider context, it would not be a far-fetched idea to suggest that he may have seen the crucifixion of Jesus foretold in Zech 13:7:

> Awake, O sword, against my shepherd and against the man that is my fellow, says the LORD of hosts: Smite the shepherd, and the sheep shall be scattered: and I will turn my hand upon the little ones [268].

In this context of rejection, betrayal and divine judgment, Judas must be seen as one with the false shepherds. The whole scene "throws into high relief the infamy of one who had been called to shepherd the new Messianic community and had failed his calling."[269] Further, the name "Field of Blood" given to the piece of land bought with the thirty pieces of silver bears "a continuing testimony against Judas, the priests and all who had agreed with them."[270] In a mysterious way Judas becomes an uncalled - for instrument in the process of prophetic fulfilment: "In the suicide of the traitor and the purchase of a field with his blood money prophecy is again being fulfilled, and God's plan is being carried out."[271]

But the wider context of Zech 11:13 and the Jeremiah passages alluded to do not only speak about rejection, treachery and divine judgment. They point forward to a new age marked by Yahweh's dramatic victory through his humble Messianic Shepherd-King over all his enemies and an establishment of the kingdom of God in which all covenantal blessings shall be renewed. While the context of the "potter" passages in Jeremiah 18 and 19 speak of imminent and inevitable divine

---

[268] Many scholars have associated this utterance with the shepherd imagery of Zech 11:4-17, placing it immediately after the latter. Although we cannot be sure that the shepherd of Zech 13:7 is identical with that of Zechariah 11, it is probably inappropriate to conclude that the evangelist would not see them as identical. Some have preferred to treat as a separate shepherd imagery linked not to 11:4-17 but to 12:1-13. See Ackroyd, "Zechariah", in Black and Rowley (eds) *Peake's Commentary*, p. 654.

[269] Albright and Mann, *Matthew*, p. LXXII.

[270] Hendriksen, *Matthew*, p. 946.

[271] *Ibid.*, p. 948. Also Harrington, *Matthew*, p. 378.

judgment upon the people of God, the "field" passage in Jeremiah 32 is an assurance of salvation. In the midst of contemporary rejection, treachery and divine destruction in which the whole life and ministry of Jeremiah is set,[272] the prophet rises above the troubled waters of the contemporary situation and proclaims salvation. On the prophetic horizon beyond the contemporary clouds of suffering, Jeremiah sees a ray of hope. For the people of God who are to be scattered abroad imminently, especially in Babylon, will later be gathered back to the Promised Land to form a new eschatological community. Life will come back to normal and people will once again enjoy the fruits of a renewed covenant relationship with their God. This is the message of the "field" passage in Jeremiah 30-33, the so-called "The Little Book of Comfort." Israel and Judah will be ultimately restored to the joy of the covenant people and to the glory of Yahweh their God.

The same is the case with Zecharian prophecy. In Zechariah 11, there is no hope on the prophetic horizon. The chapter ends with the rejection of the prophet (v. 17). The emphasis lies on the rejection of the Prophet-Shepherd-King (vv. 12-13) and the lowly condition of the people or flock (vv.7, 11). In vv. 7, 11, the LXX has "Canaanites." The original meaning of the term "Canaanites" was "merchants' or 'traffickers" (Job 41:6; Prov 31:24; Zech 14:21). The translations that have "merchants" or "traffickers", like the RSV, are based on the LXX and a slight emendation of the Hebrew.[273] The Hebrew, however, has 'aniyê hatso'n, literally "the poor of the flock." Following the Hebrew, the AKJV has "the poor", and the NIV has "the oppressed."

The wider context of Zechariah 11, however, has an overall momentum toward a victorious and happy conclusion. In Zechariah 11 the prophet presents the rejection, apparent failure and divine judgment as a prelude to Yahweh's final eschatological victory. Present rejection, suffering and divine judgment are a guarantee for future redemption (cf. Jer 32:42).

In Zech 12:1-14:21, the prophet portrays the eschatological siege of Jerusalem. The Messiah returns to inflict a crushing defeat on the enemies of Israel and to establish his kingdom. As the siege of

---

[272] For discussion of Jeremiah's rejection as a prophet by his contemporaries including his relatives as well as leaders, see Paterson, "Jeremiah', in Black and Rowley (eds), *Peake's Commentary on the Bible*, pp. 537-539.
[273] Stuhlmueller, *Rebuilding with Hope*, p 141.

Jerusalem takes its course (12:1-3; 14:1-2), Judah's enemies gain an initial and temporary victory (14:2). But the Lord sets up a defence for Jerusalem (14:3-4) and brings judgment upon nations (12:9; 14:3). Topographical changes take place in Judah, setting the conflict in an eschatological context (14:4-5). In the end, the Lord wins ultimate victory (14:9) and restores Jerusalem (14:11). Then, the new eschatological community which includes people from other nations celebrates the glorious Feast of Tabernacles (14:16-19). The Lord establishes ultimate holiness for Jerusalem and her people (14:20-21). Thus, God transforms victoriously the once devastated area with new life.

The evangelist, similarly, sees a typological relationship between this overall message of redemption and the Christ-event. Although the focus of his fulfilment quotation is the rejection, betrayal and suffering of Jesus Messiah,[274] the evangelist, in drawing upon prophecy in an account of Jesus' suffering and death already anticipates Jesus' ultimate victory in the resurrection. For Jesus, the humiliation, sorrow, suffering and death which he experiences only guarantee a new life in a new age. They lead to a full and glorious life in eternity. For Jesus, the passion only guarantees a glorious victory in the resurrection and his session at the Father's right hand.

As a victorious Messiah or Shepherd King, Jesus ultimately fulfills the role of Israel as a Servant-Shepherd-King rendering Yahweh's throne of grace accessible to all who through him enter into the new covenant. God finally vindicates his Servant-Shepherd-King by declaring him Son of God by his resurrection from the dead (Matt 28:6-7; Rom 1:4).

In and through the resurrected Son of God, the Kingdom of God has truly and finally come. To be with the Son (Matt 28:20) is to enter into the very presence of God, and this is what the kingdom of God is. The eschatological kingdom of God is now here with us.

It is, again, extremely difficult to imagine that the evangelist did not have a meaningful access to the wider prophetic context of Zech 11:13 and the Jeremiah passages he alludes to. Like the preceding fulfilment

---

[274] Donald Senior, *The Passion of Jesus in the Gospel of Matthew*, Collegeville: Liturgical Press, 1990, pp. 112-122, especially 120, 122, also observes that the rejection of Jesus by Israel had a double effect. It was judgment upon Israel in the sense that the gospel would turn away from her to Gentiles who would be more responsive. In this way, Israel would lose her exclusive claim to be God's people. Israel's rejection was also a blessing, "a paradoxical moment of grace" because from Israel's failure would come the Christian mission to Gentiles, leading to the establishment of a new eschatological community, the catholic Church.

quotations, the present one reveals that the evangelist undertook meticulous study of the Old Testament background to his fulfilment quotations. It also reveals that he engaged himself in an intense theological reflection of the gospel tradition. His theological use of the fulfilment quotation at this point is then a fruit of much labour on his part. The theological richness of the fulfilment quotations as shown by closer examination of their Old Testament contexts and the manner in which the evangelist applies them to the Christ-event cannot be satisfactorily accounted for by a mere literary dependence on sources, with Marcan gospel prominent among them, as many would suppose.

Conclusion

This chapter reveals that the evangelist is responsible for the formulation of the mixed text-form of the fulfilment quotations in both ministry and passion narratives of the evangelist's gospel. Exegetical analysis of these quotations has consistently pointed to an independent construction by the evangelist with, especially, the Hebrew bible (our Old Testament) in the background, and some allusions to the LXX where that tradition would better serve his purpose.

The chapter also reveals that the redemptive mission of the Messiah essentially takes the form of suffering, rejection, humiliation and death which eventually lead to his glorification in the resurrection. It also shows that the Old Testament context of the fulfilment quotations used in the ministry-passion narrative section of the gospel provide the conceptual framework for the evangelist's understanding of these elements in the redemptive mission of the Messiah.

In this regard, crucial to the evangelist's understanding of the Christ-event are the imageries of the Suffering Servant of the Lord of Isaianic prophecy (Isa 42:1-4; 53:4) and the divinely commissioned but rejected Shepherd-King of Zecharian prophecy (Zech 9:9; 11:3). According to these Messianic categories, the Messiah suffers rejection, humiliation and death before he is restored or raised to ultimate glory through divine vindication of his seemingly lowly and humble service. Through this humble service of the Servant-Shepherd-King, the eschatological kingdom of God finds its ultimate establishment in the world and begins to draw people from all nations around the world. Although in reality the Christ-event transcends[275] these traditional categories of Messianic

---

[275] In this sense, the Christ-event does not only fulfil prophecy but also critics it.

conception, they are instrumental for the evangelist's understanding of this essentially new and unparalleled event.

This chapter also shows that the thorough grasp of these categories and their theological application to the Christ-event presuppose a thorough understanding of their Old Testament context by the evangelist. This further presupposes meticulous study and intense theological reflection of those prophetic sections in preparation for their theological application to the Christ-event within the context of his gospel.[276]

---

[276] Kennedy, *New Testament Interpretation through Rhetorical Criticism*, p. 42 rightly observes that "a doctrinaire insistence on source criticism tends to underestimate Matthew's abilities as a writer and the perceptual sensitivity of his intended audiences."

Chapter 5

Conclusions

The study leads to quite stimulating, if not provocative conclusions. Here, these can only be treated in a summary fashion. The study has revealed that biblical quotations were used theologically in ancient Judaism and early Christianity and that these provide a literary background to the evangelist's use of fulfilment quotations. The practice continued right into the early centuries of the Christian church. The evangelist, thus, falls within such a literary environment (chap 2).

The results have also shown that the evangelist formulated the fulfilment quotations himself for theological purposes, although it remains unclear whether he draws the variants from other textual traditions or whether they are his own textual contribution. The results also show that he applied them to the Christ-event not only in full awareness of their Old Testament contexts, but also taking into full account those prophetic contexts in his theological application (chaps. 3, 4). Hence, the overall results support the thesis of the present study. The fulfilment quotations in this gospel are applied theologically to the Christ-event by the evangelist, in light of their Old Testament contexts. This theological role is reflected in the way these Old Testament quotations are formulated, and in the manner in which they are used by the evangelist.

The study has also shown that the fulfilment quotations in the infancy narrative define the Person of Jesus as the Messiah who is both human and divine. Jesus is both Son of David and Son of God. It has also shown that the fulfilment quotations in the ministry and passion narratives define the redemptive work in terms of suffering, rejection, humiliation and death which, eventually lead to final victory and glory in the resurrection. It has also shown that the aspect of suffering characterized the whole of his life and ministry. Jesus as the Messiah takes the roles of the Servant of the Lord of Isaianic prophecy and the Shepherd-King of Zecharian prophecy. Thus, in general, the results reveal that the Old Testament prophetic contexts of the fulfilment quotations provide a conceptual framework for the evangelist's understanding of the nature of the Person of Jesus and the form of his redemptive mission. This in turn reflects a thorough grasp of the Old Testament prophetic contexts in which the Messianic categories he applies to Jesus originally appear (chaps. 3, 4).

These results from the research do have significant implications on the Matthean authorship and the Synoptic Problem in general. The evangelist's independence in the formulation of the fulfilment quotations and his distinctive theological application of these quotations to the Christ-event point to the evangelist's freedom and independence as a writer as he brings to bear upon his theological reconstruction the raw materials of gospel tradition (oral or written) and prophecy. Thus, the results portray the evangelist as an independent theologian engaged in a theological discussion of the Person and work of Jesus as the Messiah in light of the prophetic word.

This sharply contradicts the popular scholarly opinion that the evangelist was primarily concerned with the needs of his community over against the Christ-event itself and with the construction of a Marcan-based theology over against an independent theological reconstruction using the gospel traditions and prophecy at his disposal. In this way the research puts the theory of Marcan priority[1] and the creation of the so-

---

[1] The Two-Source hypothesis and its corollary of Marcan priority, taken for granted by most critical scholars for many years can no longer be accepted uncritically in our time. After an extensive study of the nature and development of the Marcan hypothesis in his *History and Criticism of the Marcan Hypothesis*, Macon: Mercer University & Edinburgh: T&T Clark, 1980, Hans-Herbert Stoldt concludes that: "The Marcan Hypothesis for more than a hundred years almost universally regarded as the solution of the Synoptic Problem, is untenable (p.xv... We can state that the second Gospel does not possess priority over Matthew and Luke and was not their source. Therefore the result of our critical examination is that the Marcan hypothesis is false – false in its conception, execution and conclusion" (p. 221). In an introduction to Stoldt's book, William R Farmer observes that "There is little evidence for Marcan priority... Every attempt to resolve the issue of priority in open discussion... by appealing to redactional considerations, has thus far failed to produce critical consensus ... the Marcan hypothesis, in light of Stoldt's research, appears increasingly problematic" (p. xvii). Similarly, Albright and Mann, *Matthew*, observe that "The more critically the material in the three synoptic gospels is examined, the harder it is to determine precisely what – if any dependence there was of Matthew and Luke on Mark, or in what way – if at all Matthew or Luke were dependent on each other (p. XL1)... Mark and Matthew may represent two quite separate collections of tradition; it is only a failure to take tradition itself seriously that has driven many to assume the existence of almost a multitude of copies of written gospels on which the evangelist could exercise scissors and paste" (p. XLViii). In an unpublished article, "Christology", 2000, p. 39, note 65, Ulf Strohbehn observes that "Newer research gives credible evidence that the gospel of Matthew was written very early-around 60 AD. This would add a lot of credibility to Matthew's record, since many eyewitnesses would have still been alive and were able to confirm his gospel".

called Matthean community, based on it and the Two-Source hypothesis, into serious question. The results point to an early date for the Matthean authorship and a parallel development[2] of the gospel tradition reflected in the synoptic gospels, woven together like a piece of a string. In this view the differences in the synoptic tradition would be better accounted for by such factors as geographical, theological and literary differences, rather than by positing a very long time-lag between the writing of the gospels as the trend is in much of contemporary Matthean scholarship. The pre-Christian character of the Dead Sea Scrolls with which the evangelist shares in the theological use of quotations and other literary aspects further supports the early date for the evangelist's gospel. Even if the evangelist had access to the Marcan gospel, it does not follow that his gospel depended on it. Access and dependency are quite different issues. Scholars in all ages have had access to each other's material but that has never meant dependency on those other works in the manner the evangelist's gospel is said to depend on its Marcan counterpart.

The results further provide a new perspective to the role of prophecy in gospel tradition with particular reference to the Matthean gospel. The results bring the Old Testament into a central position as a source which played a significant role in the evangelist's theology. This further

---

Strohbehn bases this observation on the findings of Carsten P. Theide in his *Der Jesus Papyrus*, German edition, Luchterhand, 1996. In a personal communication to me, Strohbehn further noted that Thiede's finding is all the more significant since Thiede was not a confessing Christian at the time he published his study of this ancient Matthean Papyrus. His finding, therefore, cannot be said to have been coloured by any apologetic considerations. Thus his early dating of this Papyrus cannot be accounted for by any such considerations. See also Richard N. Ostling, "A Step Closer to Jesus?" *Time Magazine* (Amsterdam, 1995), p. 59. Ben F. Meyer, *The Aims of Jesus*, (London: SCM, 1979) p. 71, opts for a qualified Marcan priority. He accepts Marcan priority provided that, that does not systematically guarantee relative antiquity of Marcan traditions over against those in Matthew, Luke and John; that it does not provide grounds for wholesale deductions as is often the case in critical scholarship; and that even when priority is established this does not in itself establish a superior claim to historicity: "To confuse relative antiquity vis-à-vis other traditions with superiority in the claim to historicity is to deny a *priori* that a tradition arising to correct or clarify an earlier tradition might do so in historically valid fashion." That there is a growing dissatisfaction with the Marcan hypothesis in modern critical scholarship is clear from these observations.

[2] The view that the synoptic gospel tradition had a parallel development is shared by E.P. Sanders in his *The Tendencies of the Synoptic Tradition*, Cambridge: University Press, 1969 and John A.T. *Robinson in his Redating the New Testament*, London: SCM, 1976 pp. 93-117. For a convenient summary of alternative views, see France, *Matthew*, pp. 335-37. John Wenham holds the view that there was "a large measure of independence as well as an important measure of interdependence". See his *Redating Matthew, Mark and Luke, A Fresh Assault on the Synoptic Problem*, London & Sydney: Hodder & Stoughton, 1991, p. 10.

suggests that it is inappropriate to disregard the Old Testament as source in favour of such sources as Mark, Q, M, Testimonia, if such sources really existed as *sources* for the evangelist.

As I have indicated earlier, the research does not intend, nor claim, to present systematically a coherent synoptic theory of parallel development of the synoptic tradition. Rather, it only points this out as a possible solution to this difficult problem, in view of the main results of the inquiry, as a logical consequence of those results.

It is hoped that the insights presented in this study provide a unique contribution to New Testament study in general and Matthean scholarship in particular.

Select *Bibliography*

"Haggai". In M. Black and H.H. Rowley. Eds. *Peake's Commentary on the Bible.* London: Routledge, 1990. pp 643-45

Ackroyd, P.R. "Zechariah". In M. Black and H.H. Rowley. Eds. *Peake's Commentary on the Bible.* London: Routledge, 1990.

Aland, Kurt, et al. *Nestle – Aland Novum Testamentum Graece.* Stuttgart: Deutsche Bibelgesellschaft, 1898, 1979.

Albright, W.F. and Mann, C.S. *Matthew.* AB New York: Doubleday, 1971.

Allegro, J.M. *The Dead Sea Scrolls*, Harmondsworth: Penguin,1959.

Allen, W.C. *A Critical and Exegetical Commentary on the Gospel According to Matthew.* ICC. Edinburgh: T&T Clark, 1912.

Anderson, B.W. *The Living World of the Old Testament.* Harlow: Longman, 1967.

Anderson, G.W. "Psalms" in M. Black and H.H. Rowley. Eds. *Peake's Commentary on the Bible.* London: Routledge, 1990. pp 409-43

Argyle, A.W. *The Gospel According to Matthew, A Commentary.* Oxford: Basil Blackwell, 1981.

Attridge, Harold, W. *The Epistle to the Hebrews, A Critical and Historical Commentary on the Bible.* Hermeneia, Philadelphia: Fortress, 1989.

Baker, David, W. *Nahum, Habakkuk and Zephaniah, An Introduction and Commentary.* Leicester: Inter-Varsity, 1988.

Baldwin, Joyce, G. *1&2 Samuel, An Introduction and Commentary.* TOTC. Leicester: Inter-Varsity, 1988.

Baldwin, Joyce, G. *Haggai, Zechariah, Malachi, An Introduction and Commentary.* London: Tyndale, 1972.

Beare, Francis, W. *The Gospel According to Matthew, Commentary.* Oxford: Basil Blackwell, 1981.

Bettenson, Henry, Ed. + Transl *The Early Christian Fathers, A Selection from the writings of the Fathers from St Clement of Rome to St Athanasius.* London: Oxford University Press, 1969.

Betz, Otto and Riesner, Rainer. *Jesus, Qumran and the Vatican.* London: SCM, 1994.

Black, M. Ed. *Theological Collection II: The Scrolls and Christianity, History and Theological Significance.* London: SPCK, 1969.

Black, M. "The Theological appropriation of the Old Testament by the New Testament." *SJT.* Vol. 39, no. 1. 1986. pp. 3, 10-12.

Black, M. and Rowley, H.H. Eds. *Peake's Commentary on the Bible.* London: Routledge, 1990.

Black, M. *An Aramaic Approach to the Gospels and Acts.* Oxford: Clarendon, 1954.

Bornkamm, G. *Jesus of Nazareth.* London: Hodder and Stoughton, 1973.

Botterweck, G. Johannes and Ringgren, Helmer. *Theological Dictionary of the Old Testament.* (ET John T. Wills) 6 vols Grand Rapids: Wm. B. Eerdmans, 1977.

Briggs, C.A. and Briggs, E.G. *The Book of Psalms.* 2 vols. ICC Edinburgh: T&T Clark, 1906.

Bright, John. *Jeremiah.* AB. New York: Doubleday, 1993.

Brown, R.E. *The Birth of the Messiah.* AB. New York: Doubleday, 1993.

Bruce, F.F. *Biblical Exegesis in the Qumran Texts.* London: Tyndale, 1960.

Brueggemann, Walter. "Unity and Dynamic in the Isaiah Tradition". *JSOT* 29 1984. pp. 89-107.

Brueggemann, Walter *To Pluck Up, To Tear Down, Jeremiah 1-25.* ITC Grand Rapids: Wm. B. Eerdmans and Edinburgh: Handsel, 1988.

Bultmann, R. *The History of the Synoptic Tradition.* Oxford: Basil Blackwell, 1972.

Burrows, M. *More Light on the Dead Sea Scrolls and New Interpretations with Translations of Important Recent Discoveries.* London: Secker and Warburg, 1958.

Burrows, M. *The Dead Sea Scrolls with Translation by the Author.* New York: Viking, 1955.

Carrol, Robert, P. *Jeremiah, A Commentary.* London: SCM, 1986.

Charles, R.H. Ed. *The Apocrypha and Pseudepigrapha of the Old Testament* 2 vols. Oxford: Clarendon, 1913, 1969.

Childs, Brevard, S. *Introduction to the Old Testament as Scripture.* Philadelphia: Fortress, 1979.

Childs, Brevard, S. *The New Testament as Canon, An Introduction.* London: SCM, 1984.

Clements, Ronald, E. "Beyond Tradition History: Deutero-Isaianic Development of First Isaiah's Themes". *JSOT* 31, 1985. Pp. 95-113.

Clements, Ronald, E. "The Unity of the Book of Isaiah." *Interpretation* 36. 1982. Pp. 117-129.

Clements, Ronald, E. *Isaiah 1-39* NCBC Grand Rapids: W. B. Eerdmans and London: Marshall Morgan and Scott, 1988.

Cohen, A. *Everyman's Talmud.* London: J.M. Dent and Sons and New York: E.P. Dutton, 1949.

Conn, Harvie, M. Ed. *Inerrancy and Hermeneutic, A Tradition, a Challenge, a Debate.* Grand Rapids: Baker, 1988.

Cornfeld, Gaalyah. *Archaeology of the Bible.* London: Adams and Charles Black, 1977.

Cross, F.M. *The Ancient Library of Qumran and Modern Biblical Studies.* Grand Rapids: Baker, 1980.

Cunliffe-Jones, H. *The Book of Jeremiah, Introduction and Commentary.* London: SCM, 1960.

Dahood, Mitchell. *Psalms II 51-100.* AB. New York: Doubleday, 1968.

Danby, Herbert *The Mishnah.* London: Oxford University Press, 1933.

Davidson, B. *The Analytical Hebrew and Chaldee Lexicon.* London: Samuel Bagster and New York: Harper, 1950

Davies, A. Powell. *The Meaning of the Dead Sea Scrolls.* New York: The American Library, 1956.

Davies, W.D. *The Setting of the Sermon on the Mount.* Cambridge: Cambridge University Press, 1963.

Dibelius, Martin. *From Tradition to Gospel.* London and Cambridge: James Clarke, 1971.

Dodd, C.H. "The Framework of the Gospel Narrative". *Expository Times* 43. 1932. Pp. 396-400.

Dodd, C.H. *The Apostolic Preaching and Its Development.* London: Hodder & Stoughton, 1936.

Dodd, C.H. *The Authority of the Bible.* London: Nisbet, 1928, reprint 1947.

Dodd, C.H. *According to Scriptures.* London: Nisbet, 1952 and Collins Fontana, 1965.

Driver, G.R. *The Judean Scrolls The Problem and a Solution.* Oxford: Basil Blackwell, 1965.

Dunn, James, D.G. *Unity and Diversity in the New Testament, An Inquiry into the Character of Earliest Christianity.* Second ed. London: SCM and Philadelphia: Trinity, 1990.

Elliger, K. and Rudolph, W. Eds. *Biblia Hebraica Stuttgartensia.* Stuttgart: Deutsche Bibelgesellschaft, 1967, 1977.

Ellingworth, Paul. *The Epistles to the Hebrews, A Commentary on the Greek Text.* NIGTC. Grand Rapids: Wm. B. Eerdmans & Carlisle: Paternoster, 1993.

Ellis, E.E. *Paul's Use of the Old Testament.* London: Oliver Boyd, 1957.

Fallon, Michael. *The Winston Commentary on the Gospels.* Sydney: Winston, 1980.

Fiedler, Klaus. *The Story of Faith Missions.* Oxford: Regnum and Lynx, 1994.

Filson, Floyd, V.*A. Commentary on the Gospel According to Matthew.* London: Adams and Charles Black, 1971.

Finegan, Jack. *The Archaeology of the New Testament, The life of Jesus and the Beginning of the Early Church.* Princeton: University Press, 1969.

Fohrer, Georg. Ed. *Hebrew and Aramaic Dictionary of the Old Testament.* London: SCM, 1973.

France, R.T. *Jesus and the Old Testament.* London : SCM, 1971.

France, R.T. *The Gospel According to Matthew, An Introduction and Commentary.* Leicester: Inter-Varsity and Grand Rapids: Wm. B. Eerdmans, 1988.

Gailey, Jnr., James, H. *Micah, Nahum, Habakkuk, Zephaniah, Haggai, Zechariah, Malachi.* Vol. 15. LBC. Richmond: John Knox, 1962.

George, Timothy. *Theology of the Reformers.* Nashville: Broadman, 1988.

Gerhard, Friedrich and Gerhard, Kittel. Eds. *Theology Dictionary of the New Testament.* 10 Vols. Grand Rapids: Wm. B. Eerdmans, 1964-1976.

Gerhardson, B. *The Origins of the Gospel Tradition.* London :SCM, 1977.

Gibson, J.M. *The Gospel of St Matthew,* The Expositors Bible. New York: A.C. Armstrong, 1905.

Goldingay, John. *Approaches to Old Testament Interpretation* Leicester: Apollos, 1990.

Goldingay, John. *God's Prophet, God's Servant, A Study in Jeremiah and Isaiah 40-55.* Exeter: Paternoster, 1984.

Goulder, M.D. *Midrash and Lection in Matthew.* London: SPCK, 1974.

Gray, George, Buchanan *The Book of Isaiah, A Critical and Exegetical Commentary.* Vol. 1. ICC. Edinburgh: T&T Clark, 1912, reprint 1975.

Gundry, Robert, H. *Matthew, A Commentary on his Literary and Theological Art.* Grand Rapids: Eerdmans, 1982.

Gundry, Robert, H. *The Use of the Old Testament in St Matthew's Gospel.* Leiden: Brill, 1967.

Guthrie, Donald *New Testament Introduction.* London: Tyndale, 1970.

Hare, Douglas, R.A. *Matthew, A Bible Commentary for Teachimg and Preaching.* Interpretation, Lousville: John Knox, 1993.

Harrington, Daniel, J. *The Gospel of Matthew.* Vol. 1. Sacra Pagina Series, Collegeville: The Liturgical Press, 1991.

Harris, J. Rendel. *The Testimonies.* 2 vols. Cambridge: Cambridge University Press, 1916, 1920.

Hastings, James. *Dictionary of the Bible.* Revised by Frederick C. Grant and H.H. Rowley. Second Edition. Edinburgh: T&T Clark, 1963.

Hendriksen, William. *An Exposition of the Gospel According to Matthew.* Grand Rapids: Baker, 1973.

Hengel, Martin. *Crucifixion in the Ancient World.* Philadelphia: Fortress, 1977.

Hengel, Martin. *Studies in the Gospel of Mark.* London: SCM 1985.

Hengel, Martin. *The Son of God, The Origin of Christology and the History of Jewish Hellenistic Religion.* London: SCM, 1976.

Hennecke, E. *New Testament Apocrypha.* 2 vols. London: SCM, 1965.

Hinson, David, F. *Theology of the Old Testament, Old Testament Introduction 3.* London: SPCK, 1976.

Hong, In Gyu. *The Law in Galatians.* JSNT 81. Sheffield: Sheffield Academic Press, 1993.

Hornby, A.S. *Oxford Advanced Learner's Dictionary of Current English.* Fourth Edition. Oxford: Oxford University Press, 1989.

Jeremias, J. *The Parables of Jesus.* Revised Edition. London: SCM, 1972.

Jones, Douglas, R. "Isaiah II and III." In M. Black and H.H. Rowley. Eds. *Peake's Commentary on the Bible.* London : Routledge, 1962, reprint 1987.

Kaiser, Otto. *Isaiah 1-12, A Commentary.* OTL. London: SCM, 1972.

Kaiser, Otto. *Isaiah 1-12, A Commentary.* Second Edition. OTL. London: SCM, 1983.

Kaiser Jr., Walter C. *Toward An Exegetical Theology, Biblical Exegesis for Preaching and Teaching.*
Grand Rapids: Baker, 1981

Keegan, Terence, J. *Interpreting the Bible, A Popular Introduction to Biblical Hermeneutics.* New York: Paulist, 1985.

Kennedy, George A. *New Testament Interpretation through Rhetorical Criticism.* Chapel Hill and London: University of North Carolina Press, 1984.

Kidner, Derek. *Psalms 73-150, A Commentary on Books III-V of the Psalms.* Leicester and Downers Grove: Inter-Varsity, 1975.

Knight, George, A.F. *The New Israel, A Commentary on the Book of Isaiah 56-66.* ITC. Edinburgh: Handsel and Grand Rapids: Wm. B. Eerdmans, 1985.

Knight, George, A.F. *Servant Theology, A Commentary on the Book of Isaiah 40-55* ITC Edinburgh: Handsel and Grand Rapids: Eerdmans, 1984.

Koester, Helmut. *Introduction to the New Testament, History, Culture and Religion of the Hellenistic Age.* 2 vols. New York and Berlin: Walter de Gruyter, 1987.

Kuiper, R.B. *The Bible Tells Us So.* Edinburgh: The Banner of Truth Trust, 1968.

Leaney, A.R.C. *et al.* Eds. *A Guide to the Scrolls, Nottingham Studies on the Qumran Discoveries.* London: SCM, 1958.

Lindars, B. *New Testament Apologetic.* London : SCM, 1961.

Lindblom, J. *Prophecy in Ancient Israel.* Oxford: Basil Blackwell, 1962.

Luz, Ulrich. *Matthew 1-7, A Continental Commentary.* Minneapolis: Fortress, 1985.

Luz, Ulrich. *The Theology of the Gospel of Matthew.* Cambridge: Cambridge University Press, 1995.

Malina, J. and Rohrbaugh, Richard, L. *Social Science Commentary on the Synoptic Gospels.* Minneapolis: Fortress, 1992.

Manson, T.W. *The Sayings of Jesus.* London: SCM, 1949.

Marshall, I.H. Ed. *New Testament Interpretation.* Carlisle: Paternoster, 1985.

Marshall, I.H. *Luke, Historian and Theologian.* Exeter: Paternoster, 1970.

McCasland, S.V. "Matthew Twists the Scriptures". *JBL* (June 1961). P145.

McGrath, A. *Affirming your Faith, Exploring the Apostles' Creed.* Leicester: Inter-Varsity, 1991.

McKenzie, John, L. *Second Isaiah.* AB. New York: Doubleday, 1968.

McKnight, Edgar, V. *What is Form Criticism?* Philadelphia: Fortress, 1969.

McKnight, Scot. *Interpreting the Synoptic Gospels.* Grand Rapids: Baker, 1988.

Meier, John, P. *Matthew, New Testament Message, A Biblical – Theological Commentary.* Vol. 3. Dublin: Veritas and Wilmington: Michael Glazier, 1980.

Melugin, Roy, F. *The Formation of Isaiah 40-55.* Berlin: Walter de Gruyter, 1976.

Metcalfe, John. *The Messiah, The Apostolic Foundations of the Christian Church.* Vol. 3. Penn: John Metcalfe, 1978.

Meye, R.P. *Jesus and the Twelve, Discipleship and Revelation in Mark's Gospel.* Grand Rapids: Eerdmans, 1968.

Meyer, B.F. *The Aims of Jesus.* London: SCM, 1979.

Mijoga, Hilary, B.P. "Some notes on the Septuagint Translation of Isaiah 53." Vol. 19, no.1. 1990. Pp 85-90.

Mijoga, Hilary, B.P. *Separate But Same Gospel, Preaching in African Instituted Churches in Southern Malawi.* Blantyre: CLAIM, 2000.

Mijoga, Hilary, B.P. "Some notes on the Septuagint Translation of Isaiah 53" *ATJ* Vol 19, no. 1, 1990, pp. 85-90.

Mijoga, Hilary, B.P. *The Pauline Notion of Deeds of the Law.* San Francisco – London – Bethsda: International Scholars Publications, 1999.

Mitchell, Hinckley, G. *et al. A Critical and Exegetical Commentary on Haggai, Zechariah, Malachi and Jonah.* ICC. Edinburgh, T&T Clark, 1912.

Mondin, Battista. *Philosophical Anthropology, Man: An Impossible Project?* Rome: Urbaniana University Press, 1985.

Moore, George, F. *Judaism in the First Centuries of the Christian Era.* Vol. 1 New York: Schocken, 1971.

Morris, L. *Luke, An Introduction and Commentary.* Leicester; Inter-Varsity, 1988.

Moule, C.D.F. *The Birth of the New Testament.* London: Black, 1962.

Mowinckel, S. *He That Cometh.* New York and Nashville: Abingdon, 1954.

Muilenburg, James "Old Testament Prophecy". In M. Black and H.H. Rowley. Eds. *Peake's Commentary on the Bible.* London: Routledge, 1962, reprint 1987. pp. 475-83

Muilenburg, James. "The Book of Isaiah chaps 40-66". In George Arthur Buttrick. Ed. *The Interpreter's Bible.* Vol. V. Nashville: Abingdon, 1956, reprint 1980. pp. 381-773

Myers, Jacob, M. *Hosea, Joel, Amos, Obadiah, Jonah.* Vol. 14 LBC Richmond: John Knox, 1959.

Newman, Jr., Barclay, M. *A Concise Greek – English Dictionary of the New Testament.* Stuttgart: German Bible Society, 1993.

Nielsen, E. *Oral Tradition.* SBT. No. 11, London: SCM, 1954.

Nkhoma, J.S. "The Significance of the Dead Sea Scrolls (Qumran Literature) for the study of the New Testament". Unpublished MA Module 2. University of Malawi, 1999.

Nkhoma, J.S. "The New Testament Use of the Old Testament". Unpublished MA Module 3. University of Malawi, 1999.

North, Christopher, R. *The Second Isaiah, Introduction, Translation and Commentary to chapters XL – LV.* Oxford: Clarendon, 1964.

North, Christopher, R. *The Suffering Servant in Deutero – Isaiah.* Second Edition. New York: Oxford, 1956.

O' Collins, Gerald. *Interpreting Jesus.* London: Casell, 1983.

Ostling, R.N. "A Step Closer to Jesus". *Time Magazine.* Amsterdam, 1995. p.59

Paine, Stephen, W. *Beginning Greek, A Functional Approach.* New York: Oxford University Press, 1961.

Paterson, J. "Jeremiah." In M. Black and H.H. Rowley Eds. *Peake's Commentary on the Bible.* London: Routledge, 1990. Pp.537-62

Perrin, N. *What is Redaction Criticism?* London: SPCK, 1970.

Pesch, R. "Der Gottessohn im Matthaischen, Evangelien prolog (Mt 1-2) Beobachtungen, zu den Zitationsformeln de Reflexionszitate". *Biblica.* Vol 48. 1967 Pp. 397-400.

Petersen, David, L. *Zechariah 9-14 and Malachi, A Commentary.* OTL. London: SCM, 1995.

Pink, A.W. *The Sovereignty of God.* London: Banner of Truth Trust, 1961.

Plattel, Martin, G. *Social Philosophy.* DSPS 18. Pittsburgh: Duquesne University Press, 1965.

Pritchard, James B. *Ancient Near Eastern Texts relating to the Old Testament with Supplement.* Third Edition. Princeton: Princeton University Press, 1969.

Rad, Gerhard von. *Old Testament Theology.* Vol. 2. London: SCM, 1975.

Rad, Gerhard von. *The Message of the Prophets.* London: SCM, 1968.

Rahlfs, Alfred. *Septuaginta, Id est Vetus Testamentum Graece.* Stuttgart: Deutsche Bibelgesellschaft, 1935, 1979.

Rattey, B.K. *The Gospel According to Saint Matthew, with Introduction and Commentary.* Oxford: Clarendon, 1938, reprint 1969.

Reventlow, Henning, Graf. *Problems of Biblical Theology in the Twentieth Century.* London: SCM, 1986.

Rhodes, Arnold, B. *The Book of Psalms.* Vol. 9. LBC. Richmond: John Knox, 1960.

Ringgren, Helmer. *The Messiah in the Old Testament.* Vol.18. *SBT.* Chicago: Allenson, 1956.

Robertson, O. Palmer. *Joel, The Day of the Spirit's Restoration of all Things.* 1994 (Then unpublished).

Robertson, O. Palmer *The Book of Nahum, Habakkuk and Zephaniah* NICOT Grand Rapids: Eerdmans, 1985.

Robertson, O. Palmer. *The Christ of the Covenants.* Phillipsburg: Presbyterian and Reformed, 1980.

Robertson, O. Palmer. *Understanding the Land of the Bible, A Biblical-Theological Guide.* Phillipsburg: Presbyterian and Reformed, 1996.

Robinson, H. Wheeler. *Inspiration and Revelation in the Old Testament.* Oxford: Clarendon, 1962.

Robinson, James, M. *A New Quest of the Historical Jesus.* London: SCM, 1959.

Robinson, John, A.T. *Redating the New Testament.* London: SCM, 1976.

Rowdon, Harold, H. Ed. *Christ the Lord, Studies in Christology presented to Donald Guthrie.* Leicester: Inter-Varsity, 1982.

Rowley, H.H. *Rediscovering the Old Testament.* London: James Clarke, 1947.

Rowley, H.H. *The Servant of the Lord and other Essays on the Old Testament.* Second Edition. Oxford: Blackwell, 1965.

Sanders, E.P. *The Tendencies of the Synoptic Tradition.* Cambridge: Cambridge University Press, 1969.

Sawyer, John, F.A. *The Fifth Gospel, Isaiah in the History of Christianity.* Cambridge: Cambridge University Press, 1996.

Schechter, Solomon. *Aspects of Rabbinic Theology.* New York: Schocken, 1961.

Schubert, Kurt. *The Dead Sea Community, Its Origins and Teachings.* Westport: Greenwood, 1959.

Schweitzer, A. *The Quest of the Historical Jesus.* London: A&C Black, 1910.

Schweitzer, Eduard. *The Good News According to Matthew.* London SPCK, 1976.

Scott, R.B.Y. "The Book of Isaiah chap 1-39, Introduction and Exegesis". In George A. Buttrick. Ed. *The Interpreter's Bible.* Vol. V. Nashville: Abingdon, 1980. Pp. 149-381

Seitz, Christopher, R. *Isaiah 1-39 A Commentary for Teaching and Preaching.* Interpretation, Lousville: John Knox, 1993.

Senior, Donald. *The Passion of Jesus in the Gospel of Matthew.* Collegeville: Liturgical Press, 1990.

Simon, U.E. *A Theology of Salvation, A Commentary on Isaiah 40-55.* London: SPCK, 1953.

Smith, John, Merlin, Powis *et al. A Critical and Exegetical Commentary on Micah, Zephaniah, Nahum, Habakkuk, Obadiah and Joel.* ICC. Edinburgh: T&T Clark, 1911.

Stanton, Graham, N. *A Gospel for a New People, Studies in Matthew.* Edinburgh: T&T Clark, 1992.

Stein, Robert, H. *The Method and Message of Jesus' Teaching.* Philadelphia: Westminster, 1978.

Stein, Robert, H. *The Synoptic Problem, An Introduction.* Grand Rapids: Eerdmans, 1987.

Stendahl, Krister. Ed. *The Scrolls and the New Testament.* Westport: Greenwood, 1975.

Stendahl, Krister. *The School of St Matthew and Its Use of the Old Testament.* Second Edition. Lund: Gleerup and Philadelphia: Fortress, 1968.

Stoldt, Hans-Herbert. *History and Criticism of the Marcan Hypothesis.* Macon: Mercer University Press and Edinburgh: T&T Clark, 1980.

Strecker,G. *Der weg der Gerechtigkeit, Forschungen zur Religion und Literatur des alten und Neuen Testaments 82.* Second Edition. Gottingen: Vandenhoeck, 1966.

Streeter, B.H. *The Four Gospels.* London: Macmillan, 1924.

Strobehn, Ulf. "Christology". Blantyre, 2000. An unpublished manuscript.

Stuhlmueller, Carroll. *Psalms 2: Psalms 73-150.* Wilmington Delaware: Michael Glazier, 1983.

Stuhlmueller, Carroll. *Rebuilding with Hope, A Commentary on the Books of Haggai and Zechariah.* ITC Grand Rapids: Wm. B. Eerdmans and Edinburgh: Handsel, 1988.

Szeles, Maria, E. *Wrath and Mercy, A Commentary on the Books of Haggai and Zechariah.* ITC. Grand Rapids: Wm. B. Eerdmans and Edinburgh: Handsel, 1987.

Tasker, R.G.V. *The Gospel According to St Matthew.* Grand Rapids: Wm. B. Eerdmans, 1961.

Taylor, V. *The Formation of the Gospel Tradition.* London: Macmillan, 1935.

Thiede, C.P. *Der Jesus Papyrus.* German Edition. Luchterhand, 1996.

Torrey, C.C. "The Foundry of the Second Temple at Jerusalem". *JBL.* Vol 55. 1936. Pp. 247-260.

Trilling, Wolfgang. *The Gospel According to St. Matthew for Spiritual Reading.* London: Sheed and Ward, 1969.

Tucker, G.M. *Form Criticism of the Old Testament.* Philadelphia: Fortress, 1971.

VanderKam, James C. *The Dead Sea Scrolls Today.* Grand Rapids: Wm B Eerdmans, 1994.

Vermes, G. *The Dead Sea Scrolls in English.* Third Edition. London: Penguin, 1987.

Virkler, Henry, A. *Hermeneutics, Principles and Processes of Biblical Interpretation.* Grand Rapids: Baker, 1981.

Waltke, Bruce, K. "Micah, An Introduction and Commentary". In David W. Baker *et al. Obadiah, Jonah and Micah.* TOTC. Leicester: Inter-Varsity, 1988 Pp. 134-207.

Warfield, Benjamin, B. *Christology and Criticism.* New York: Oxford University Press, 1929.

Warfield, Benjamin, B. *The Inspiration and Authority of the Bible.* Philadelphia: Presbyterian and Reformed, 1948.

Weingreen, J. *A Practical Grammar for Classical Hebrew.* Oxford: Clarendon, 1939, reprint 1955.

Wenham, J.W. *Christ and the Bible.* London: Tyndale, 1927.

Westermann, Claus. Ed. *Essays on Old Testament Hermeneutics.* Richmond: John Knox, 1963.

Westermann, Claus. *Isaiah 40-66, A Commentary* London: SCM, 1969.

Wise, Michael, O. *et al.* Eds. *Methods of Investigation of the Dead Sea Scrolls and the Khirbet Qumran Site.* New York: New York Academy of Sciences, 1994.

Wright, N.T. *Who was Jesus?* London: SPCK, 1992.

Index of modern authors

Index of Subjects

Printed in the United States
58266LVS00005B/169-177